P9-AFU-772

STOCKS *for the* LONG RUN

Siegel, Jeremy J.,
Stocks for the long run : the
definitive guide to financial
[2023]
33305254297165
ca   11/15/22

STOCKS *for the* LONG RUN

SIXTH EDITION

THE DEFINITIVE GUIDE TO FINANCIAL MARKET RETURNS AND LONG-TERM INVESTMENT STRATEGIES

JEREMY J. SIEGEL

with Jeremy Schwartz

Mc
Graw
Hill

New York Chicago San Francisco Athens London Madrid
Mexico City Milan New Delhi Singapore Sydney Toronto

Copyright © 2023, 2014, 2008, 2002, 1998, 1994 by Jeremy J. Siegel. All rights reserved. Printed in the United States of America. Except as permitted under the United States Copyright Act of 1976, no part of this publication may be reproduced or distributed in any form or by any means, or stored in a database or retrieval system, without the prior written permission of the publisher.

1 2 3 4 5 6 7 8 9   LCR   27 26 25 24 23 22

ISBN   978-1-264-26980-8
MHID   1-264-26980-3

e-ISBN   978-1-264-26981-5
e-MHID   1-264-26981-1

This publication is designed to provide accurate and authoritative information in regard to the subject matter covered. It is sold with the understanding that neither the author nor the publisher is engaged in rendering legal, accounting, securities trading, or other professional services. If legal advice or other expert assistance is required, the services of a competent professional person should be sought.

—*From a Declaration of Principles Jointly Adopted by a Committee of the American Bar Association and a Committee of Publishers and Associations*

Library of Congress Cataloging-in-Publication Data

Names: Siegel, Jeremy J., author.
Title: Stocks for the long run : the definitive guide to financial market returns
    & long-term investment strategies / Jeremy Siegel.
Description: 6th edition. | New York, NY : McGraw Hill, [2023] | Includes
    bibliographical references and index.
Identifiers: LCCN 2022017730 (print) | LCCN 2022017731 (ebook) |
    ISBN 9781264269808 (hardcover) | ISBN 9781264269815 (ebook)
Subjects: LCSH: Stocks. | Stocks—History. | Rate of return.
Classification: LCC HG4661 .S53 2023 (print) | LCC HG4661 (ebook) |
    DDC 332.63/22—dc23
LC record available at https://lccn.loc.gov/2022017730
LC ebook record available at https://lccn.loc.gov/2022017731

McGraw Hill books are available at special quantity discounts to use as premiums and sales promotions or for use in corporate training programs. To contact a representative, please visit the Contact Us pages at www.mhprofessional.com.

McGraw Hill is committed to making our products accessible to all learners. To learn more about the available support and accommodations we offer, please contact us at accessibility@mheducation.com. We also participate in the Access Text Network (www.accesstext.org), and ATN members may submit requests through ATN.

Contents

Chapter 3

Risk, Return, and Portfolio Allocation:
Why Stocks Are Less Risky Than Bonds in the Long Run   41

Chapter 4

Global Investing: Disappointment and Promise   59

PART II

STOCK RETURNS: MEASUREMENT AND VALUATION

Chapter 5

Stock Indexes: Proxies for the Market   75

Chapter 6

The S&P 500 Index: More Than One-Half Century of US Corporate History   89

Chapter 7

Sources of Shareholder Value: Earnings and Dividends   101

Chapter 8

Interest Rates and Stock Prices   115

PART IV

STYLES, TRENDS, AND THE CALENDAR

Chapter 15

ESG Investing   211

Chapter 16

Technical Analysis and Investing with the Trend   221

Chapter 17

Calendar Anomalies   235

Foreword

In July 1997 I called Peter Bernstein and said I was going to be in New York and would love to lunch with him. I had an ulterior motive. I greatly enjoyed his book *Capital Ideas: The Improbable Origins of Modern Wall Street* and the *Journal of Portfolio Management*, which he founded and edited. I hoped there might be a slim chance he would consent to write the preface to the second edition of *Stocks for the Long Run*.

His secretary set up a date at one of his favorite restaurants, Circus on the Upper East Side. He arrived with his wife, Barbara, and a copy of the first edition of my book tucked under his arm. As he approached, he asked if I would sign it. I said, "Of course" and responded that I would be honored if he wrote a foreword to the second edition. He smiled; "Of course!" he exclaimed. The next hour was filled with a most fascinating conversation about publishing, academic and professional trends in finance, and even what we liked best about Philly and New York.

I thought back to our lunch when I learned, in June 2009, that he had passed away at the age of 90. In the 12 years since our first meeting, Peter had been more productive than ever, writing three more books, including his most popular, *The Remarkable Story of Risk*. Despite the incredible pace he maintained, he always found time to update the preface of my book through the next two editions. As I read through his words in the fourth edition, I found that his insights into the frustrations and rewards of being a long-term investor are as relevant today as they were when he first penned them nearly two decades ago. I can think of no better way to honor Peter than to repeat his wisdom here:

> Some people find the process of assembling data to be a deadly bore. Others view it as a challenge. Jeremy Siegel has turned it into an art form. You can only admire the scope, lucidity, and sheer delight with which Professor Siegel serves up the evidence to support his case for investing in stocks for the long run.
>
> But this book is far more than its title suggests. You will learn a lot of economic theory along the way, garnished with a fascinating history of both the capital markets and the U.S. economy. By using history to

maximum effect, Professor Siegel gives the numbers a life and meaning they would never enjoy in a less compelling setting. Moreover, he boldly does battle with all historical episodes that could contradict his thesis and emerges victorious—and this includes the crazy years of the 1990s.

With this fourth edition, Jeremy Siegel has continued on his merry and remarkable way in producing works of great value about how best to invest in the stock market. His additions on behavioral finance, globalization, and exchange-traded funds have enriched the original material with fresh insights into important issues. Revisions throughout the book have added valuable factual material and powerful new arguments to make his case for stocks for the long run. Whether you are a beginner at investing or an old pro, you will learn a lot from reading this book.

Jeremy Siegel is never shy, and his arguments in this new edition demonstrate he is as bold as ever. The most interesting feature of the whole book is his twin conclusions of good news and bad news. First, today's globalized world warrants higher average price/earnings ratios than in the past. But higher P/Es are a mixed blessing, for they would mean average returns in the future are going to be lower than they were in the past.

I am not going to take issue with the forecast embodied in this viewpoint. But similar cases could have been made in other environments of the past, tragic environments as well as happy ones. One of the great lessons of history proclaims that no economic environment survives the long run. We have no sense at all of what kinds of problems or victories lie in the distant future, say, 20 years or more from now, and what influence those forces will have on appropriate price/earnings ratios.

That's all right. Professor Siegel's most important observation about the future goes beyond his controversial forecast of higher average P/Es and lower realized returns. "Although these returns may be diminished from the past," he writes, "there is overwhelming reason to believe stocks will remain the best investment for all those seeking steady, long-term gains."

"[O]verwhelming reason" is an understatement. The risk premium earned by equities over the long run must remain intact if the system is going to survive. In the capitalist system, bonds cannot and should not outperform equities over the long run. Bonds are contracts enforceable in courts of law. Equities promise their owners nothing—stocks are risky investments, involving a high degree of faith in the future. Thus, equities are not inherently "better" than bonds, but we demand a higher return from equities to compensate for their greater risk. If the long-run expected return on bonds were to be higher than the long-run expected return on stocks, assets would be priced so that risk would earn no reward. That is an unsustainable condition. Stocks must remain "the best investment for all those seeking steady, long-term gains" or our system will come to an end, and with a bang, not a whimper.

—Peter Bernstein

Preface to the Sixth Edition

I am honored by the tremendous reception that *Stocks for the Long Run* has received since the publication of the first edition nearly 30 years ago. This sixth edition is the most extensive revision to date, adding six full chapters that include factor or style investing; the efficient market hypothesis; the future of value investing; environmental, social, and governance (ESG) risks; the Covid pandemic; as well as an extensive discussion of the impact of inflation and interest rates on stock prices. Other chapters have also been greatly expanded, including for the first time an analysis of the returns on real estate, the optimal stock/bond allocation, the fate of companies that had become the most valuable in the world, the future of Bitcoin and cryptocurrencies, and an analysis of whether "hot-handed" money managers have continued beating the market. Almost all the data are updated through 2021.

The first edition of *Stocks for the Long Run* was published using financial data through 1992 so this edition includes nearly three decades more data than the first. Those 30 years have witnessed dramatic shocks: the Asian and Long-Term Capital Management crises, the stock market crash of 1987, the dot-com bubble, the Great Financial Crisis, and the Covid-19 pandemic. Yet despite this volatility, the superior returns to stocks have not only persisted, but in fact increased over these past 30 years.

But that does not mean there have been no financial surprises. One of the most unexpected developments is the steep and persistent decline in both nominal and especially real interest rates. Chapter 8 discusses the forces behind this development: the decline in growth in the developed countries, the aging of the population, and particularly the emergence of sovereign debt as the prime "hedge asset." A second unexpected development has been a sharp decline in the returns to *value investing*. I conclude that the fundamental dynamics of market pricing still strongly suggest paying close attention to financial fundamentals as the best investment strategy for long-term investors.

A final surprise has been the disappointing returns in foreign markets, including Europe and especially in the emerging economies. The reasons for the lag are legion: governmental interference with growth, particularly in China and Russia, and the relatively poor performance of *value stocks*, which are far more numerous outside the United States.

But the most important reason for the lag in value stocks has been the remarkable performance of technology firms in the United States. Apple, Microsoft, Google, Amazon.com, and Tesla are the five largest stocks in the United States and five of the six largest (with Saudi Aramco) in the world. Only Apple and Microsoft were trading when the first edition of *Stocks for the Long Run* was published, and they were selling for 30 cents and $2.50 per share, respectively. Tech giants NVIDIA and Meta (formerly Facebook) were nonexistent in 1994.

But just below these top five tech giants is Berkshire Hathaway, Warren Buffett's conglomerate that is the epitome of value investing. No investment style stays in favor forever and the great bull market in tech stocks may have peaked. Admittedly, for short-term traders, fundamentals may matter little and momentum rules the roost. But for those devoted to long-term investment, the reasons for broad diversification and value investing are still persuasive.

In 1937, John Maynard Keynes stated in *The General Theory of Employment, Interest and Money*, "investment based on the genuine long-term expectation is so difficult today as to be scarcely practicable." It is certainly no easier nearly a century later.

But those who have persisted with equities have always been rewarded. No one has made money in the long run betting against stocks. It is the hope that the latest edition will fortify those who will inevitably waver when pessimism once again grips investors. History demonstrates that stocks have been and will remain the best investment for all those seeking long-term growth.

CONCLUDING COMMENTS

My Princeton colleague Burton Malkiel emailed me recently asking if he could use my graph of 220 years of assets returns for the fiftieth anniversary edition of his classic *A Random Walk Down Wall Street*. I am in awe of his vigor as he will turn 90 next August. His advice to me was, "Stay active, Jeremy, stay active!"

And I most certainly will. But I am a realist. I retired as Emeritus Professor of Finance at the Wharton School of the University of Pennsylvania in July 2021 after teaching at that prestigious institution and the

University of Chicago for 49 years. It was deeply fulfilling to instruct over 10,000 students during that nearly one-half century, many of whom have become leaders in the investment, public, and nonprofit sectors.

No one knows how many years we have left. But after completing this edition, I feel free to pursue those activities that in the past came *after* my work: time with family and friends, hobbies, and sorting through years of memorabilia—photos, letters, and research that I have accumulated through my life. But at this moment I am proud to publish what I believe is the best and most inclusive edition of *Stocks for the Long Run* to a much wider audience than I could reach from any university.

Acknowledgments

It is never possible to list all the individuals and organizations that have contributed to *Stocks for the Long Run*. But one individual stands out: Jeremy Schwartz, my star student at Wharton who currently serves as Global Chief Investment Officer at WisdomTree Investments.

I offered Jeremy the job of principal research assistant for the fourth edition of this book in 2001, immediately after he took my Wharton honors class during his sophomore year. I was investigating some complicated risk-return analysis using varying time horizons. On Friday, I gave him the data and a brief outline of what I wanted to do and told him to come back Monday morning so we could discuss the methodology needed to solve the problem. When he arrived after the weekend, I asked him if he had a chance to look over the data. He responded, "Yes, in fact I have all the results that you asked for!" Indeed he did. I knew I had found someone very special.

At that time, I was also considering a second book, *The Future for Investors*. Although Jeremy had his heart set on spending his junior year abroad in Australia, he instead took the entire year off to help me do the research for that book. As I acknowledged in *The Future for Investors*, I could not have written that book without his analysis and encouragement. Many of the themes we developed were added to subsequent editions of *Stocks for the Long Run*. It is for these reasons that I have added Jeremy Schwartz's name to mine as one of the authors for this edition of *Stocks for the Long Run*.

Of course, there were others who contributed importantly to this edition. Joseph Attia, currently a sophomore at Wharton, was my second principal researcher. His diligence in collecting and processing the data, particularly for the new material, was invaluable. And his "eagle eye" in catching mistakes and improving the presentation as the manuscript passed through various proofs far exceed my already-high expectations of this young man.

Elroy Dimson of London Business School, whose *Triumph of the Optimists* (2000) did for international markets what I had done for US markets, was especially generous with his material and research. David

Bianco, the CIO of DWS Americas, has provided me with data on S&P profit margins, and we have enjoyed many discussions on this topic.

Erica DiCarlo provided me vital background information on my chapter on ESG investing, and Casey Clark, President and Chief Investment Officer at Rockefeller Asset Management provided data on ESG returns. Liqian Ren, Director of Modern Alpha at WisdomTree, completed the extensive Monte Carlo simulations that informed the analysis of the proper stock/bond allocation for a forward-looking portfolio, and Matt Wagner, Research Associate at WisdomTree, provided useful assistance in evaluating buybacks and international markets. I also want to thank Robert Ibbotson and Yakov Amihud for providing me with their data on liquidity stock returns.

But importantly, my Wharton colleague Robert Stambaugh has been an invaluable resource for all the chapters relating to factor investing and ESG, among other topics. Despite his busy schedule, he responded quickly and thoroughly to all my questions and unstintingly shared his material with me.

And I cannot ignore the contributions of Shaun Smith to *Stocks for the Long Run*. Although he did not contribute to this edition, he was my prime researcher for the very first edition. Most of the tables and charts that have been updated through the next five editions are built on his earlier efforts.

I also wish to thank Judith Newlin, who had been so patient with the time it took to develop my new chapters. I wanted the material to be as accurate as possible, and she provided invaluable suggestions to make this the best, most complete edition to date. Finally, I wish to thank the management of WisdomTree, and particularly the CEO, Jonathan Steinberg, for supporting the literally hundreds of talks and presentations I have given in these past nearly 20 years.

It was at 6:30 a.m., Thursday, March 17, when I sent my last chapter to my editor. I was on a family vacation in the British Virgin Islands and I wanted to work early (getting up each day at 5 a.m.) so I could have more time with my family. Authors know the burdens that writing places on those around you, and I am grateful that those closest to me, and especially my wife, Ellen, have given me time to indulge my passion. It is liberating that I can enjoy our next trip: a cruise through Belgium this April, ending with the Keukenhof Tulip Festival and the Floriade Expo 2022 in Amsterdam, knowing that the great bulk of my responsibilities for this book are behind me.

March 2022

STOCKS *for the* LONG RUN

I

VERDICT OF HISTORY

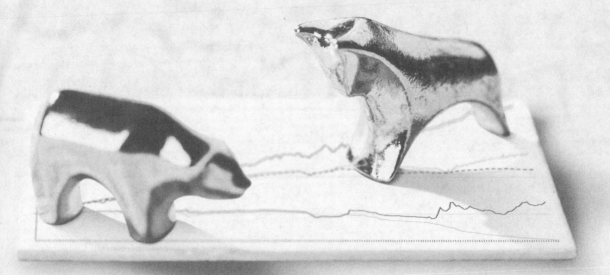

The Case for Equity

Historical Facts and Media Fiction

The "new-era" doctrine—that "good" stocks (or blue chips) were sound investments regardless of how high the price paid for them—was at the bottom only a means of rationalizing under the title of "investment" the well-nigh universal capitulation to the gambling fever.

—Benjamin Graham and David Dodd, 1934[1]

Investing in stocks has become a national hobby and a national obsession. To update Marx, it is the religion of the masses.

—Roger Lowenstein, 1996[2]

Stocks for the Long Run *by Siegel? Yeah, all it's good for now is a doorstop.*

—Comment from caller on CNBC, March 2009, at the bottom of the worst bear market in 80 years

"EVERYBODY OUGHT TO BE RICH"

In the summer of 1929, a journalist named Samuel Crowther interviewed John J. Raskob, a senior financial executive at General Motors, about how the typical individual could build wealth by investing in stocks. In August of that year, Crowther published Raskob's ideas in a *Ladies' Home Journal* article with the audacious title "Everybody Ought to Be Rich."

In the interview, Raskob claimed that America was on the verge of a tremendous industrial expansion. He maintained that by putting

3

just $15 per month into good common stocks, investors could expect their wealth to grow steadily to $80,000 over the next 20 years. Such a return—24 percent per year—was unprecedented, but the prospect of effortlessly amassing a great fortune seemed plausible in the atmosphere of the 1920s bull market. Stocks excited investors, and millions put their savings into the market seeking quick profit.

On September 3, 1929, a few days after Raskob's advice appeared, the Dow Jones Industrial Average hit a historic high of 381.17. Seven weeks later, stocks crashed. The next 34 months saw the most devastating decline in share values in US history.

On July 8, 1932, when the carnage was finally over, the Dow Industrials stood at 41.22. The market value of the world's greatest corporations had declined an incredible 89 percent. Millions of investors' life savings were wiped out, and thousands of investors who had borrowed money to buy stocks were forced into bankruptcy. America was mired in the deepest economic depression in its history.

Raskob's advice was ridiculed and denounced for years to come. It was said to represent the insanity of those who believed that the market could rise forever and the foolishness of those who ignored the tremendous risks in stocks. Senator Arthur Robinson of Indiana publicly held Raskob responsible for the stock crash by urging common people to buy stock at the market peak.[3] In 1992, 63 years later, *Forbes* magazine warned investors of the overvaluation of stocks in its issue headlined "Popular Delusions and the Madness of Crowds." In a review of the history of market cycles, *Forbes* fingered Raskob as the "worst offender" of those who viewed the stock market as a guaranteed engine of wealth.[4]

Conventional wisdom holds that Raskob's foolhardy advice epitomizes the mania that periodically overruns Wall Street. But is that verdict fair?

The answer is decidedly no. Investing over time in stocks has been a winning strategy whether one starts such an investment plan at a market top or not. If you calculate the value of the portfolio of an investor who followed Raskob's advice in 1929, patiently putting $15 a month into the market, you find that his accumulation exceeded that of someone who placed the same money in Treasury bills after less than four years! By 1949 his stock portfolio would have accumulated almost $9,000, a return of 7.86 percent, more than double the annual return in bonds. After 30 years the portfolio would have grown to over $60,000, with an annual return rising to 12.72 percent. Although these returns were not as high as Raskob had projected, the total return of the stock portfolio over 30 years was more than eight times the accumulation in bonds and more than nine times that in Treasury bills. Those who never bought stock, citing the Great Crash as the vindication of their caution, found their savings far lower than investors who had patiently accumulated equity.[5]

The story of John Raskob's much-ridiculed advice illustrates an important theme in the history of Wall Street. Bull markets and bear markets lead to sensational stories of incredible gains and devastating losses. Yet patient stock investors who can see past the scary headlines have always outperformed those who flee to bonds or other assets. Even such calamitous events as the Great 1929 Stock Crash, the financial crisis of 2008, or the Covid-19 pandemic have not negated the superiority of stocks as long-term investments.

ASSET RETURNS SINCE 1802

Figure 1.1 is the most important chart in this book. It traces year by year how real (after-inflation) wealth has accumulated for a hypothetical investor who put a dollar in (1) stocks, (2) long-term government bonds, (3) US Treasury bills, (4) gold, and (5) US currency over the past two centuries. These returns are called *total real returns* and include income (dividends and interest) distributed from the investment (if any) plus capital gains or losses, all measured in constant purchasing power. The compound annual real returns for these asset classes are also shown on Figure 1.1.

These returns are graphed on a *ratio*, or *logarithmic*, scale. Economists use this scale to depict long-term data, since a straight line represents a constant percentage change. The ability of stock returns to hug that trendline is striking.

Over the 220 years we have examined asset returns, the average compound annual real return on a broadly diversified portfolio of stocks has averaged 6.9 percent per year. That 6.9 percent per year means that a fully diversified stock portfolio, such as an index fund, has nearly doubled in purchasing power on average every 10 years over the past two centuries.

It is noteworthy that if we extend the stock returns through the bear market that occurred in the first half of 2022, the long term real return is reduced to 6.7% per year, exactly the same return I indicated in the first edition of Stocks for the Long Run, published almost 30 years ago.

The real return on fixed-income investments has averaged far less; on long-term government bonds, the average real return has been 3.6 percent per year, and on short-term fixed-income assets, such as Treasury bills, 2.5 percent per year.

FIGURE 1.1

Total real return indexes (1802–2021)

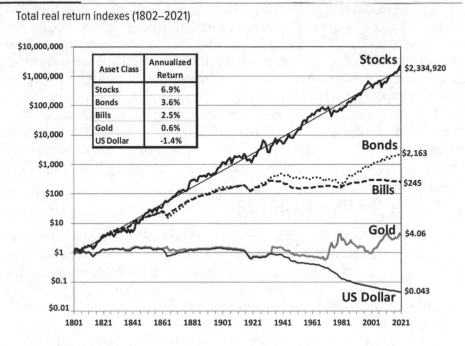

Asset Class	Annualized Return
Stocks	6.9%
Bonds	3.6%
Bills	2.5%
Gold	0.6%
US Dollar	-1.4%

The average annual real return on gold has been only 0.6 percent per year. In the long run, gold prices have risen just ahead of the inflation rate, but little more. The dollar has lost on average 1.4 percent per year of purchasing power since 1802, with most of the depreciation coming after World War II.

In the short run, stock returns are very volatile and are driven by changes in earnings, interest rates, risk, and uncertainty as well as psychological factors, such as optimism and pessimism. The downward blips of the stock return line in Figure 1.1 represent major bear markets, which frighten so many investors and keep them out of the market. Yet these blips fade into insignificance when compared to the broad upward thrust of stock returns.

We shall examine the returns of the major assets in detail in the next chapter. In the remainder of this chapter we shall look at how economists, investment professionals, and market pundits have viewed the investment value of stocks over the course of history and how the great bull and bear markets impact both the media and investors.

HISTORICAL PERSPECTIVES ON STOCKS AS INVESTMENTS

Throughout the nineteenth century, stocks were deemed the province of speculators and insiders but certainly not conservative investors. It was not until the early twentieth century that researchers came to realize that equities might be suitable investments for a broader group of investors under certain economic conditions.

In the 1920s, the great US economist Irving Fisher, a professor at Yale University and an extremely successful investor, believed that stocks were superior to bonds during inflationary times but that common shares would likely underperform bonds during periods of deflation, a view that became the conventional wisdom during the early twentieth century.[6]

Edgar Lawrence Smith, a financial analyst and investment manager of the 1920s, exploded this conventional wisdom. Through his historical research, Smith was the first to demonstrate that accumulations in a diversified portfolio of common stocks outperformed bonds not only when commodity prices were rising but also when prices were falling. Smith published his studies in 1925 in his book *Common Stocks as Long-Term Investments*. In the introduction he stated:

> These studies are a record of a failure—the failure of facts to sustain a preconceived theory, . . . [the theory being] that high-grade bonds had proved to be better investments during periods of [falling commodity prices].[7]

Smith maintained that stocks should be an essential part of an investor's portfolio. By examining stock returns back to the Civil War, Smith discovered that there was a very small chance that an investor would have to wait a long time (which he put at 6 and at most, 15 years) before being able to sell your stocks at a profit. Smith concluded:

> We have found that there is a force at work in our common stock holdings which tends ever toward increasing their principal value. . . . [U]nless we have had the extreme misfortune to invest at the very peak of a noteworthy rise, those periods in which the average market value of our holding remains less than the amount we paid for them are of comparatively short duration. Our hazard even in such extreme cases appears to be that of time alone.[8]

Smith's conclusion was right, not only historically but also prospectively. It took just over 15 years to recover the money invested at the 1929 peak, following a crash far worse than Smith had ever examined. And since World War II, the recovery period for stocks has been even better. The longest it has ever taken an investor to recover an original investment in the stock market (including reinvested dividends) was the five-year, eight-month period from August 2000 through April 2006.

The Influence of Smith's Work

Smith wrote his book in the 1920s, at the outset of one of the greatest bull markets in our history. Its conclusions caused a sensation in both academic and investing circles. The prestigious weekly the *Economist* stated in 1925, "Every intelligent investor and stockbroker should study Mr. Smith's most interesting little book and examine the tests individually and their very surprising results."[9]

Smith's ideas quickly crossed the Atlantic and were the subject of much discussion in Great Britain. John Maynard Keynes, the great British economist and originator of the business cycle theory that became the paradigm for future generations of economists, reviewed Smith's book with much excitement. Keynes stated:

> The results are striking. Mr. Smith finds in almost every case, not only when prices were rising, but also when they were falling, that common stocks have turned out best in the long-run, indeed, markedly so. . . . This actual experience in the United States over the past fifty years affords prima facie evidence that the prejudice of investors and investing institutions in favor of bonds as being "safe" and against common stocks as having, even the best of them, a "speculative" flavor, has led to a relative over-valuation of bonds and under-valuation of common stocks.[10]

Smith's writings gained academic credibility when they were published in such prestigious journals as the *Review of Economic Statistics* and the *Journal of the American Statistical Association.*[11] Smith acquired an international following when Siegfried Stern published an extensive study of returns in common stock in 13 European countries from the onset of World War I through 1928. Stern's study showed that the advantage of investing in common stocks over bonds and other financial investments extended far beyond America's financial markets.[12] Research demonstrating the superiority of stocks became known as the "common stock theory of investment."[13]

Smith's research also changed the mind of the renowned Yale economist Irving Fisher, who saw Smith's study as a confirmation of his own long-held belief that bonds were overrated as safe investments in a world with uncertain inflation. In 1925 Fisher summarized Smith's findings with these prescient observations of investors' behavior:

> It seems, then, that the market overrates the safety of "safe" securities and pays too much for them, that it overrates the risk of risky securities and pays too little for them, that it pays too much for immediate and too little for remote returns, and finally, that it mistakes the steadiness of money income from a bond for a steadiness of real income which it does not possess. In steadiness of real income, or purchasing power, a list of diversified common stocks surpasses bonds.[14]

Irving Fisher's "Permanently High Plateau"

Professor Fisher, cited by many as the greatest US economist and the father of capital theory, was no mere academic. He actively analyzed and forecasted financial market conditions, wrote dozens of newsletters on topics ranging from health to investments, and created a highly successful card-indexing firm based on one of his own patented inventions. Despite hailing from a modest background, his personal wealth in the summer of 1929 exceeded $10 million, which is over $150 million in 2021 dollars.[15]

Irving Fisher, as well as many other economists in the 1920s, believed that the establishment of the Federal Reserve System in 1913 was critical to reducing the severity of economic fluctuations. Indeed, the 1920s was a period of remarkably stable growth, as the variation in such economic variables as industrial production and producer prices was greatly reduced, a factor that boosted the prices of risky assets such as stocks. As discussed in Chapter 23, there was a remarkable similarity between the stability of the 1920s and the decade that preceded the 2008 financial crisis. In each period, not only had the business cycle moderated, but there was great confidence that the Federal Reserve would be able to mitigate, if not eliminate, the business cycle.

The 1920s bull market drew millions of Americans into stocks, and Fisher's own financial success and reputation as a market seer gained him a large following among investors and analysts. But in early October 1929, market turbulence greatly increased investors' interest in his forecasts. Market followers were not surprised that on the evening of October 14, 1929, when Irving Fisher arrived at the Builders' Exchange

Club in New York City to address the monthly meeting of the Purchasing Agents Association, a large number of people, including news
reporters, pressed into the meeting hall.

Investors' anxiety had been rising since early September when
Roger Babson, businessman and market seer, predicted a "terrific" crash
in stock prices.[16] Fisher had dismissed Babson's pessimism, noting that
he had been bearish for some time. But the public sought to be reassured
by the great man who had championed stocks for so long.

The audience was not disappointed. After a few introductory
remarks, Fisher uttered a sentence that, much to his regret, became one of
the most-quoted phrases in stock market history: "Stock prices," he proclaimed, "have reached what looks like a permanently high plateau."[17]

On October 29, two weeks to the day after Fisher's speech, stocks
crashed. His "high plateau" quickly dissolved into a bottomless pit.
The next three years witnessed the most devastating market collapse
in history. Despite all of Irving Fisher's many accomplishments, his
reputation—and the mantra that stocks were a sound way to accumulate wealth—was shattered.

A Radical Shift in Sentiment

The collapse of both the economy and the stock market in the 1930s left
an indelible mark on the psyches of investors. The common stock theory of investment, as Smith's research came to be known, was attacked
from all angles. Many summarily dismissed the idea that stocks were
fundamentally sound investments. Lawrence Chamberlain, an author
and well-known investment banker, stated, "Common stocks, as such,
are not superior to bonds as long-term investments, because primarily
they are not investments at all. They are speculations."[18]

In 1934, Benjamin Graham, an investment fund manager, and
David Dodd, a finance professor at Columbia University, wrote *Security
Analysis*, which became the bible of the value-oriented approach to analyzing stocks and bonds. Through its many editions, the book has had a
lasting impact on students and market professionals alike.

Graham and Dodd clearly blamed Smith's book for feeding the bull
market mania of the 1920s by proposing plausible-sounding but falla-
cious theories to justify the purchase of stocks. They wrote:

> The self-deception of the mass speculator must, however, have its
> element of justification. . . . In the new-era bull market, the "ratio-
> nal" basis was the record of long-term improvement shown by

diversified common-stock holdings. [There is] a small and rather sketchy volume from which the new-era theory may be said to have sprung. The book is entitled *Common Stocks as Long-Term Investments* by Edgar Lawrence Smith, published in 1924.[19]

The Postcrash View of Stock Returns

Following the Great Crash both the media and analysts trashed the stock market and those who advocated stocks as investments. Nevertheless, research on indexes of stock market returns received a big boost in the 1930s, when Alfred Cowles III, founder of the Cowles Commission for Economic Research, constructed capitalization-weighted stock indexes back to 1871 of all stocks traded on the New York Stock Exchange (NYSE). His total return indexes included reinvested dividends and are virtually identical to the methodology used today to compute stock returns. Cowles confirmed the findings that Smith reached before the stock crash and concluded that most of the time stocks were undervalued and enabled investors to reap superior returns by investing in equities.[20]

After World War II, two professors from the University of Michigan, Wilford J. Eiteman and Frank P. Smith, published a study of the investment returns of actively traded industrial companies and found that by regularly purchasing these 92 stocks without any regard to the stock market cycle (a strategy called dollar cost averaging), stock investors earned returns of 12.2 percent per year, far exceeding those in fixed-income investments. Twelve years later they repeated the study, using the same stocks they had used in their previous study. This time the returns were even higher despite the fact that they made no adjustment for any of the new firms or new industries that had surfaced in the interim. They wrote:

> If a portfolio of common stocks selected by such obviously foolish methods as were employed in this study will show an annual compound rate of return as high as 14.2 percent, then a small investor with limited knowledge of market conditions can place his savings in a diversified list of common stocks with some assurance that, given time, his holding will provide him with safety of principal and an adequate annual yield.[21]

Many dismissed the Eiteman and Smith study because the period studied did not include the Great Crash of 1929–1932. But in 1964, two professors from the University of Chicago, Lawrence Fisher and James H. Lorie, examined stock returns through the stock crash of 1929, the

Great Depression, and World War II.[22] Fisher and Lorie concluded that stocks offered significantly higher returns (which they reported at 9.0 percent per year) than any other investment vehicle during the entire 35-year period, 1926 through 1960. They even factored taxes and transaction costs into their return calculations and concluded:

> It will perhaps be surprising to many that the returns have consistently been so high. . . . The fact that many persons choose investments with a substantially lower average rate of return than that available on common stocks suggests the essentially conservative nature of those investors and the extent of their concern about the risk of loss inherent in common stocks.[23]

Ten years later, Roger Ibbotson and Rex Sinquefield published an even more extensive review of returns in their article "Stocks, Bonds, Bills, and Inflation: Year-by-Year Historical Returns (1926–74)."[24] They acknowledged their indebtedness to the Lorie and Fisher study and confirmed the superiority of stocks as long-term investments. Their summary statistics, which are published annually in yearbooks, are frequently quoted and have often served as the return benchmarks for the securities industry.[25]

THE GREAT BULL MARKET OF 1982–2000

The 1970s were not good years for either the economy or the stock market. Surging inflation and sharply higher oil prices produced negative real stock returns for the 15-year period from the end of 1966 through the summer of 1982. But as the Fed's tight money policy quashed inflation, interest rates fell sharply and the stock market entered its greatest bull market ever, a market that would eventually see stock prices appreciate by more than tenfold. From a low of 790 in August 1982, stocks rose sharply and the Dow Industrial Average surged past 1,000 to a new record by the end of 1982, finally surpassing its 1973 highs it had reached nearly a decade earlier.

Although many analysts expressed skepticism that the rise could continue, a few were very bullish. Robert Foman, president and chairman of E.F. Hutton, proclaimed in October 1983 that we are "in the dawning of a new age of equities" and boldly predicted the Dow Jones average could hit 2,000 or more by the end of the decade.

But even Foman was too pessimistic, as the Dow Industrials broke 2,000 in January 1987 and then surpassed 3,000. Certainly there were blips in the market. The Great Stock Crash of October 19, 1987, witnessed the greatest one-day decline in US stock market history. But this decline was quickly erased by the force of the ongoing bull market.

The 1990s were another fabulous decade for stocks. The world witnessed the collapse of communism and diminished threat of global conflict, while the United States, the sole remaining superpower, represented capitalism and entrepreneurialism.

Warnings of Overvaluation

Yet as stocks moved upward, many doubted the bull market would last. In late 1995, the persistent rise in stock prices caused many analysts to sound the alarm. Michael Metz of Oppenheimer, Charles Clough of Merrill Lynch, and Byron Wien of Morgan Stanley expressed strong doubts about the underpinnings of the rally. In September 1995, David Shulman, chief equity strategist for Salomon Brothers, wrote an article entitled "Fear and Greed," which compared the current market climate to that of similar stock market peaks in 1929 and 1961. Shulman claimed intellectual support was an important ingredient in sustaining bull markets, noting Edgar Smith and Irving Fisher's work in the 1920s, the Fisher and Lorie studies in the 1960s, and my *Stocks for the Long Run*, published in 1994.[26] But once again, these bears were wrong and stocks marched upward.

By 1996 price/earnings ratios on the S&P 500 Index reached 20, considerably above its average postwar level. More warnings were issued. Roger Lowenstein, a well-known author and financial writer, asserted in the *Wall Street Journal*:

> Investing in stocks has become a national hobby and a national obsession. People may denigrate their government, their schools, their spoiled sports stars. But belief in the market is almost universal. To update Marx, it is the religion of the masses.[27]

Floyd Norris, lead financial writer for the *New York Times*, echoed Lowenstein's comments by penning an article in January 1997 "In the Market We Trust."[28] Henry Kaufman, the Salomon Brothers guru whose pronouncements on the fixed-income market had frequently rocked bonds in the 1980s, declared that "the exaggerated financial euphoria is increasingly conspicuous," and he cited assurances offered by optimists to be equivalent to Irving Fisher's utterance that stocks had reached a permanently high plateau.[29]

Warnings of the end of the bull market did not just emanate from the media and Wall Street. Academicians were increasingly investigating this unprecedented rise in stock values. Robert Shiller of Yale University and John Campbell of Harvard wrote a scholarly paper showing that the market was significantly overvalued and presented this research to the board of governors of the Federal Reserve System in early December 1996.[30]

With the Dow surging past 6,400, Alan Greenspan, chairman of the Federal Reserve, issued a warning in a speech before the annual dinner for the American Enterprise Institute (AEI) in Washington on December 5, 1996. He asked, "How do we know when *irrational exuberance* has unduly escalated asset values, which then become subject to unexpected and prolonged contractions as they have in Japan over the past decade? And how do we factor that assessment into monetary policy?"

His words had an electrifying effect, and the phrase "irrational exuberance" became the most celebrated utterance of Greenspan's tenure as Fed chairman. Asian and European markets fell dramatically as his words were flashed across computer monitors and the next morning Wall Street opened dramatically lower. But investors quickly regained their optimism, and stocks closed in New York with only moderate losses.

Late Stage of Great Bull Market 1997–1999

From there it was onward and upward, with the Dow breaking 7,000 in February 1997 and 8,000 in July. Even *Newsweek*'s cautious cover story "Married to the Market," depicting a Wall Street wedding between America and a bull, did little to quell investor optimism.[31]

The market became an ever-increasing preoccupation of many Americans. Business books and magazines proliferated, and the all-business cable news stations, particularly CNBC, drew huge audiences. Television sets in bars, airports, and other public places were invariably tuned to an all-business network. Electronic tickers and all-business TV stations were broadcast in lunchrooms, bars, and even lounges of the major business schools throughout the country. Cruise ships and resorts in some of the world's most isolated locations were sure to carry all-financial stations. Flying 35,000 feet above the sea, air travelers could view up-to-the-minute Dow and Nasdaq averages as they were flashed from monitors anchored to the back of the seats facing the travelers.

Adding impetus to the already surging market was the explosion of communications technology. The internet allowed investors to stay in touch with markets and their portfolios from anywhere in the world. Whether it was from internet chat rooms, financial websites, or emailed newsletters, investors found access to a plethora of information at their fingertips. CNBC became so popular that major investment houses made sure all their brokers watched the station on television or their desktop computers so they could be one step ahead of clients calling in with breaking business news.

The bull market psychology appeared impervious to financial and economic shocks. The first wave of the Asian crisis, sent the market down a record 554 points on October 27, 1997, and stopped trading temporarily, but this did little to dent investors' enthusiasm for stocks. On March 29, 1999, the Dow Industrials closed above 10,000 for the first time and continued upward to a record close of 11,722.98 on January 14, 2000.

To the Top of the Technology Bubble

As has happened so many times, at the peak of a bull market the discredited bears retreat, while bulls, whose egos have been inflated by the continued upward movement of stock prices, become even bolder. In 1999, journalist James Glassman and economist Kevin Hassett published their book *Dow 36,000*. They claimed that the Dow Jones Industrial Average, despite its meteoric rise, was still grossly undervalued, and its true valuation was three times higher at 36,000. Much to my surprise, they asserted that the theoretical underpinning for their analysis came from my book *Stocks for the Long Run*! They claimed that since I showed that bonds were as risky as stocks over long horizons, therefore stock prices must rise substantially. I disavowed their conclusion, noting that real interest rates had risen above the expected return on stocks.[32]

Despite the upward march of the Dow Industrials, the real action in the market was in the technology stocks that were listed on the Nasdaq, including such firms as Cisco, Sun Microsystems, Oracle, JDS Uniphase, and other companies, as well as the rising group of internet stocks. From November 1997 to March 2000 the Dow Industrials rose 40 percent, but the Nasdaq index, filled with technology stocks, rose 185 percent, and the dot-com index of 24 online firms soared nearly tenfold from 142 to 1,350.

The Bubble Bursts

The date March 10, 2000, marked the peak not only of the Nasdaq but also of many internet and technology stock indexes. Even I, a longtime bull, wrote that the technology stocks were selling at ridiculous prices that presaged a collapse.[33]

When technology spending unexpectedly slowed, the bubble burst and a severe bear market began. Stock values plunged by a record $9 trillion and the S&P 500 Index declined by 49.15 percent, eclipsing the 48.2 percent decline in the 1972–1974 bear market and the worst since the Great Depression. Nasdaq fell 78 percent and the dot-com index by more than 95 percent.

Just as the bull market brought out the optimists, the collapsing stock prices brought out the bears in droves. In September 2002, with the Dow hovering around 8,500, and just a few weeks before the bear market low, Bill Gross, the legendary head of PIMCO, then-home of the world's largest mutual fund, came out with a piece entitled "Dow 5,000" in which he stated that despite the market's awful decline, stocks needed to fall more than 40 percent further to be as they should be on the basis of economic fundamentals. In the letter he said, "Forget about 'Stocks for the Long Run' until [stocks] slim down to the point from which even yours truly can admit that they will outperform the bond market, and that means Dow 5,000."[34] It was startling that within a period of two years, one well-regarded economist asserted the right value for the Dow was as high as 36,000, while another acclaimed analyst said the index should fall to 5,000!

Stocks never fell near 5,000, and a month after Gross's warning began an extraordinary bull market run. Nevertheless, the "Tech Wreck," as the bear market became known, squelched public interest in the market. As one bar owner colorfully put it, "People are licking their wounds and they don't want to talk about stocks anymore. It's back to sports, women, and who won the game."[35]

FROM TECH BUST TO FINANCIAL CRISIS

From the ashes of the technology bust of 2000–2002, economic growth propelled the stock market from its low of 7,286 on October 9, 2002, to its all-time high of 14,165 exactly five years later on October 9, 2007. In contrast to the peak of the technology boom, when the S&P 500 was selling for 30 times earnings, there was no general overvaluation at the 2007 market peak, as stocks were selling for a much more modest 16 times earnings.

But there were signs that all was not well. Real estate prices after having nearly tripled in the previous decade peaked in the summer of 2006 and were heading downward. All of a sudden, subprime mortgages experienced large delinquencies. The Great Financial Crisis, which I detail in Chapter 23, saw the Dow plunge 53.5 percent from its October 2007 high to its March 2009 low, a decline that eclipsed the tech bust and was the largest since the Great Depression.

The US recovery from the Great Financial Crisis was long and labored and the slowest since World War II. The economies in Europe fared even worse. In 2011, the European Union suffered a debt crisis that sent its GDP falling further than the financial crisis had two years earlier. But in the United States the economic recovery persisted, and by February 2013 the S&P 500 surpassed its precrisis high.

As the market continued upward, bears reappeared. Many based their skepticism on the high level of the CAPE ratio, or cyclically adjusted price-to-earnings ratio, developed by Professor Shiller of Yale University. The CAPE ratio computed a 10-year past average of earnings for calculating the P/E ratio, rather than a one-year backward or earning forward forecast. Because of the hole in earnings caused by the financial crisis, the CAPE ratio was very high and forecasted an extremely low 10-year return for the US equities market.

The learned *Economist* magazine, founded in 1843, was a particularly enthusiastic devotee of the CAPE ratio and persistently bearish during the bull market. As early as May 2011, in the article "In defense of the Shiller PE," they concluded, in a smugly dismissive rebuttal to the bulls, "In short, if you don't like what Shiller is telling you, it is because you're are a 'bull' who thinks 'this time is different.'"[36]

The bearishness of the CAPE ratio was echoed by another favorite indicator of Wall Street analysts, the Q ratio. The Q ratio is the level of stock prices relative to their book value, an indicator first developed by Professor James Tobin of Yale University. This indicator was enthusiastically supported by the well-known and well-respected British money managers Andrew Smithers and Steve Wright in their book *Valuing Wall Street*. The Q ratio, like the CAPE ratio, gave an extremely bearish outlook for equities. In fact, in early 2013, Smithers's prediction for 10 US equities returns was −3 percent.[37]

The CAPE ratio (and the Q ratio) was also championed by well-respected US money managers Cliff Asness of AQR Investments[38] and Robert Arnott[39] of Research Affiliates. But Jeremy Grantham of the money management firm GMO, lionized for his accurate warnings of the 2000 technology and the 2007 housing bubble, was perhaps the biggest bear throughout the entire stock market boom that followed the 2008 financial crisis.

At the end of 2010, Grantham predicted that seven-year annualized real returns in US stocks would be about zero; in fact, returns were a robust 12 percent.[40] When the Dow Jones Industrials broke 20,000 on January 25, 2017, he became very bearish, and in an early 2018 interview by the *Institutional Investor* market, he maintained that the market "feels like a full-fledged bubble" and that a huge decline of 50 percent would likely happen soon.[41]

But the bears were wrong again. The economic expansion accelerated and the pro-business Trump presidency, combined with corporate and personal tax cuts, drove the stock market ever higher. The Dow reached 29,400 in February 2020, but then a totally unexpected crisis hit: the Covid-19 pandemic.

Although the pandemic produced a sharp economic contraction and a severe bear market, which I detail in Chapter 22, a massive fiscal and monetary response sent stocks flying again, and in November the Dow surpassed its February high. Thus ended the shortest bear market—and shortest recession—in US history. By November 2021, the Dow crossed 36,000, Yet that bull market itself was cut short when over-speculation in the "hyper" growth stocks and cryptocurrencies came to a crashing halt in 2022 as the Fed tightened credit to curb the accelerating inflation.

OPTIMISM, PESSIMISM, AND PSYCHOLOGY

When I was planning the first edition of *Stocks for the Long Run* in the early 1990s, one publisher told me that pessimism outsells optimism three-to-one in book sales. Although I have not verified that contention, casual observation suggests indeed that the "doom-and-gloomers" control both the airwaves and the printed page. Optimists on the market are regarded as Panglossian, well-intentioned, but simple-minded prognosticators who push feel-good forecasts with no appreciation of the risks found in history nor the actions of malevolent governments, corporations, or other destructive institutions.

Since the natural disposition of most individuals is optimistic, those who present a pessimistic picture of the future are often assumed to possess special insights, which make them more believable. Seers who accurately predict market crashes are given special praise, even if virtually all their other forecasts are dead wrong.

Joe Granville was lauded for his 1982 bear market call but remained staunchly bearish during the tremendous bull markets that followed. Elaine Gazarelli warned of the 1987 stock market crash, but missed virtually every market move subsequently. Others praised Alan Greenspan's famous "irrational exuberance" call, in December 1996, although it occurred more than three years before the market peaked.

I find that many who boast of accurately predicting market crashes rarely tell the "back end" of their investment strategy: When or *if* they ever got back into the market? Late in February 2020, I went to a dinner party where a physician said that the coronavirus was going to cause a disastrous pandemic and sold 100 percent of his stock portfolio. In the next month, as the spreading virus forced most into isolation and stocks crashed, I admired his foresight. But a few months later, when the market climbed above the level stocks had been when he made his warning, I learned that he had not reentered the market. Once again, the buy-and-hold investor outperformed those who might accurately predict market downturns.

Even investors who recognize that bear markets are temporary find it most difficult, if not impossible, to take advantage of short-term fluctuations. One money manager I know added to his stock position from cash as the market fell during the coronavirus pandemic, correctly assessing that the sell-off far exceeded any rational response. Of course, this strategy caused the performance of his portfolio to trail the popular averages. At the bottom, his lead investor, exasperated by his large underperformance, bailed from the fund, forcing him to close. Despite the fast recovery that fully vindicated his strategy, irreparable damage was done.

In short, our inherent psychology militates against the buy-and-hold investor. As events shake the world markets, the strategy of "doing nothing" seems counterintuitive, if not downright irresponsible. Yet data have shown that attempting to "time" the market is a fool's errand, and the buy-and-hold approach is the best strategy. The following chapters show why stocks create such consistent long-term returns, explain the forces behind short-term fluctuations, and provide a guide for realizing the best return from equities.

Asset Returns Since 1802

I know of no way of judging the future but by the past.
—Patrick Henry, 1775[1]

FINANCIAL MARKET DATA FROM 1802 TO THE PRESENT

This chapter analyzes the returns on stocks, bonds, and other assets classes over the last two centuries. The data are divided into three subperiods. In the first subperiod, from 1802 through 1870, the United States made a transition from an agrarian to an industrialized economy, comparable to the changes that many "emerging markets" of Latin America and Asia have made over the past half century. In the second subperiod, from 1871 through 1925, the United States became the foremost political and economic power in the world. The third subperiod, from 1926 to the present, covers the Great Depression, the postwar expansion, the tech bubble, the financial crisis, and the 2020 Covid-19 pandemic.

These time periods are chosen not only because of their historical significance, but because they also mark breaks in the quality and comprehensiveness of the historical data on stock returns. The most difficult and controversial data comes from the early subperiod, particularly before 1834, and those data are described in the next section. From 1871 through 1925 the returns on stocks are calculated using a capitalization weighted index of all NYSE stocks (including reinvested dividends) and are taken from the well-regarded indexes compiled by the Cowles Foundation and reported by Shiller (1989).[2]

The data from the third period, from 1925 to the present, are the most thoroughly researched and are taken from the Center for Research in Security Prices (CRSP). These are a capitalization weighted index of all NYSE stocks, and starting in 1962, all American and Nasdaq stocks. The behavior of stock and bond returns since 1925 have also been researched by Roger Ibbotson, who has published yearbooks that have become benchmarks for US asset returns since 1972.[3] All the stock and bond returns reported in this volume, including those from the early nineteenth century, are free from survivorship bias, which arises from using the returns from firms that have survived and ignoring the lower returns from firms that have disappeared over time.

Very Early Stock Market Data

The most difficult stock returns to collect were those from 1802 through 1871, because little dividend data were available from that period. In prior editions of *Stocks for the Long Run*, I used a stock price index based on the research of Professor William Schwert.[4] But his research did not include dividends, so I estimated dividend yields using dividend data and macroeconomic information from the second subperiod. The dividend yields I derived for the first period were consistent with other historical information that had been published about early-period dividend yields.[5]

In 2006, two of the prominent researchers in the field of US stock returns, Bill Goetzmann and Roger Ibbotson of Yale University, published the most thoroughly documented research on stock returns before 1871.[6] Their research, which took more than a decade to complete, determined monthly price and dividend data on more than 600 individual securities from over more than a century of stock data. The 6.9 percent annual stock return that I use in this volume for the 1802–1871 period is based on this Goetzmann-Ibbotson research and is only 0.2 percent lower than my earlier estimates of early nineteenth-century stock returns.[7]

Recently Edward F. McQuarrie, an emeritus professor at Santa Clara University, has called some of the early stock market returns into question.[8] McQuarrie claims that these stock returns are too high because they exclude the extraordinarily poor returns of the First and Second Banks of the United States—in effect, our early Federal Reserve banks. Including these very large banks in a capitalization-weighted index does indeed lower the returns on stocks from 1802 through 1834, particularly when the Second Bank of the United States failed. For the whole period 1802–1871, real stock returns are reduced to 5.4 percent from 6.9 percent.

McQuarrie concluded that my returns are correct if we exclude these banks from the data, which he claims is "exactly what most prior accounts [such as Smith and Cole, Goetzmann, and others] have done."[9]

One can debate whether the average investor should have made these two banks the majority of their portfolio, since these two banks were so large that they totally dominated a capitalization-weighted indexed portfolio. Such a strategy would have provided investors virtually no diversification. Nevertheless, the stock market returns calculated after 1834 are not in dispute and are near 7 percent after inflation. If we include the McQuarrie adjustment, real stock returns from 1802 through 2021 are reduced from 6.9 percent per year to 6.4 percent over the 220-year period and do not affect any of the data over the last 187 years.

TOTAL ASSET RETURNS

The history of the returns to these asset classes is told in Figure 2.1. It depicts the total nominal (*not* inflation adjusted) return indexes for stocks, long- and short-term government bonds, gold, and commodities from 1802 through 2021. *Total return* includes changes in the capital value plus interest or dividends and assumes that all these cash flows are automatically reinvested in the asset over time.

FIGURE 2.1

Total nominal return indexes, 1802–2021

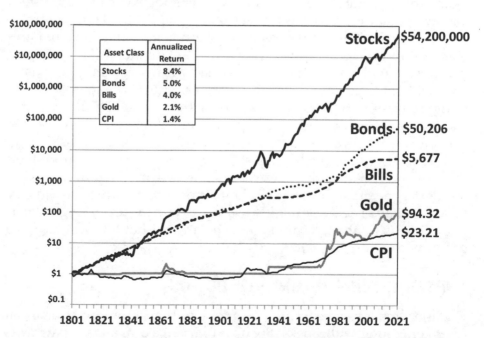

Asset Class	Annualized Return
Stocks	8.4%
Bonds	5.0%
Bills	4.0%
Gold	2.1%
CPI	1.4%

It can be easily seen that over the past two centuries the total return on equities dominates all other assets. One dollar invested in a capitalization-weighted portfolio in 1802 with reinvested dividends would have accumulated to over $54 million by the end of 2021. Even the cataclysmic stock crash of 1929, which caused an entire generation of investors to shun stocks, or the financial crisis of 2008 appears as a mere blip in the total stock return index. As noted earlier, bear markets, which so frighten investors, pale in the context of the upward thrust of total stock returns.

It is important to understand the total return on stocks depicted in Figure 2.1 does *not* represent the growth in the total value of the US stock market, which increases at a significantly slower rate that approximates the rate of growth of GDP. That is because investors as a group consume most of the dividends paid by stocks, and therefore, these dividends are not reinvested into the stock market and cannot be used by firms to create capital. Another way of understanding that the return in the US stock market is far greater than the growth rate of US capital is by noting this simple calculation. It would take only a mere $1 million invested in the stock market in 1802 to grow, with dividends reinvested, to $54 trillion at the end of 2021, more than the total value of US stocks at this time. Yet $1 million in 1802 is equivalent to only $22 million in today's purchasing power, a sum far less than the value of the US stock market at that time, which is estimated to be at least $100 million.[10]

Although financial theory (and government regulations) requires that total return be calculated with reinvested dividends (or other cash flows), it is rare for anyone to accumulate wealth for long periods of time without consuming part of his or her return. The longest period of time investors typically hold assets, without touching the principal and income, occurs when they are accumulating wealth in pension plans for their retirement or in insurance policies that are passed on to their heirs. Even those who bequeath fortunes untouched during their lifetimes must realize that these accumulations are often dissipated in the next generation or spent by the foundations to which the money is bequeathed. The stock market has the power to turn a single dollar into millions by the forbearance of generations—but few will have the patience to endure the wait.

THE LONG-TERM RETURNS OF BONDS

Fixed-income investments are the largest and most important financial asset competing with stocks. Bonds promise fixed monetary payments over time. In contrast to equity, the cash flows from bonds have a maximum monetary value set by the terms of the contract. Except in the case of default, bond returns do not vary with the profitability of the firm.

The bond series shown in Figure 2.2 are based on long- and short-term US Treasury bonds, when available; if they were not, as occurred in some of the early years of our sample, the highest-grade municipal bonds were chosen. Default premiums were estimated and removed from the interest rates of riskier securities in order to obtain a comparable high-grade sample over the entire period.[11]

The interest rates on long-term bonds and short-term bonds (called *bills*), over the 220-year period are displayed in Figure 2.2. Interest rate fluctuations during the nineteenth and early twentieth centuries remained within a narrow range. But from 1926 to the present, the behavior of both long- and short-term interest rates changed dramatically. The Great Depression of 1930 caused short-term rates to go to near zero, and inflation in the late 1970s caused rates to surge. But when inflation was brought under control, interest rates continued to fall, reaching record low levels during the Covid-19 pandemic. The fundamental determinants of interest rates are discussed in detail in Chapter 8.

FIGURE 2.2

US short- and long-term interest rates, 1800–2021

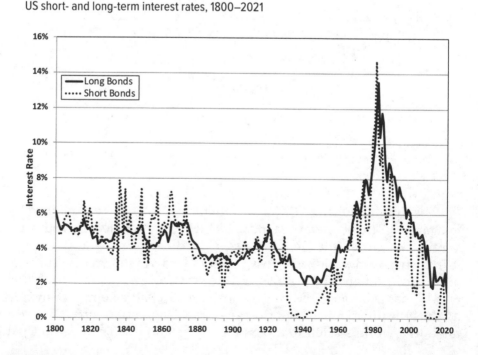

GOLD, THE DOLLAR, AND INFLATION

Consumer prices in the United States and the United Kingdom over the past 220 years are depicted in Figure 2.3. In each country, the price level at the beginning of World War II was essentially the same as it was 150 years earlier. But after World War II, the nature of inflation changed dramatically. The price level rose almost continuously after the war, often gradually, but sometimes at double-digit rates as in the 1970s. Excluding wartime, the 1970s witnessed the first rapid and sustained inflation ever experienced in US or British history.

FIGURE 2.3

US and UK consumer price indexes, 1800–2021

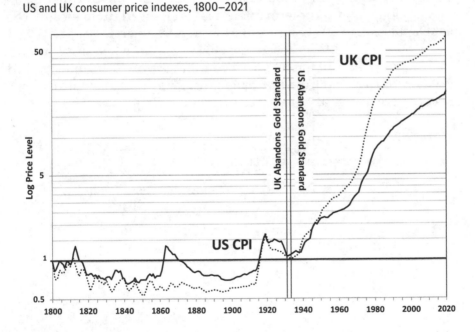

The dramatic changes in the inflationary trend can be explained by the change in the monetary standard. During the nineteenth and early twentieth centuries, the United States, United Kingdom, and the rest of the industrialized world were on a gold standard. As shown in Figure 2.3, the price of gold and the price level were very closely linked during this period. That is because the gold standard restricts the supply of money and thus the inflation rate. But from the Great Depression through World War II, the world shifted to a paper money standard. There is no legal constraint on the issuance of money under a paper money standard, so inflation is subject to political as well as economic forces. Price stability depends on the desire of central banks to limit the growth of the supply of money in order to counteract deficit spending and other inflationary forces that result from government spending and regulation.

The chronic inflation that the United States and other developed economies have experienced since World War II does not mean that the gold standard was superior to the current paper money standard. The gold standard was abandoned because of its inflexibility in the face of economic crises, particularly during the banking collapse of the 1930s. The paper money standard, if properly administered, can prevent runs on banks and severe depressions that plagued the gold standard while maintaining inflation at low to moderate levels.

But monetary policy was not run properly. Gold prices soared to $850 per ounce in January 1980, following the rapid inflation of the 1970s. By the end of 2021, the price of gold surpassed $1,800 and $1 of gold bullion purchased in 1802 was worth $98 at the end of 2021, while the price level itself increased by a factor of more than 21 times. Despite outpacing inflation, the yellow metal offers little additional returns. Whatever hedging property gold possesses, its long-term returns fall far behind stocks and will likely exert a considerable drag on the return of a long-term investor's portfolio.[12]

TOTAL REAL RETURNS

The focus of long-term investors should be the growth of purchasing power of their investment—that is, the creation of wealth adjusted for the effects of inflation. Figure 2.4 reproduces Figure 1.1 in Chapter 1 and is constructed by taking the dollar returns and correcting (or deflating) them by the changes in the price level. The annualized real returns for the various assets classes are found in the upper left corner of the graph.

The compound annual real return on stocks from 1802 through 2021 is 6.9 percent per year after inflation. This return is 0.2 percentage points higher than the 6.7 percent return that I reported in the first edition of *Stocks for the Long Run,* using data through 1992.[13]

Some have maintained that this return is not sustainable, since it is almost double the growth rate of real GDP.[14] This contention is incorrect. Even if the economy is not growing at all, capital will receive a positive return because it is a scarce resource, just as labor will be paid positive wages and land will be paid positive rents whether their quantity is growing or not. As noted earlier, the total real return on stocks assumes that all dividends and capital gains are reinvested into the market, and this sum grows far faster than total stock wealth or GDP itself.[15]

FIGURE 2.4

Total real return indexes, 1802–2021

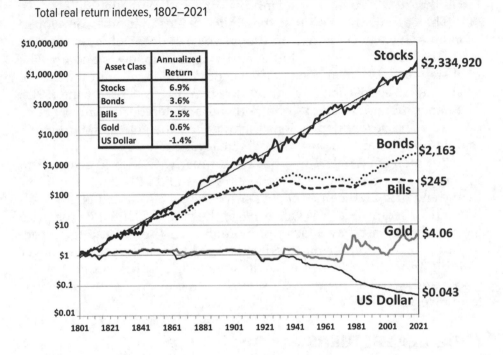

The annual returns on US stocks over various time periods are summarized in Table 2.1. Note the extraordinary stability of the real return on stocks over all major subperiods: 6.7% percent per year from 1802 through 1870, 6.6 percent from 1871 through 1925, and 7.1 percent per year from 1926 through 2021, a return which is brought down to 6.76% if we include the bear market in the first half of 2022.

The robust real return on stocks in the last period is significant. Virtually all the inflation that the United States has experienced over the past 220 years has occurred since the end of World War II. Yet this has not at all diminished the real return on equities. This is because stocks represent real assets, which in the long run appreciate at the same rate as inflation so that long-run real stock returns are not adversely affected by changes in the price level.

The long-term stability of stock returns has persisted despite the dramatic changes that have taken place in our society during the last two centuries. The United States evolved from an agricultural to an industrial economy and then to the postindustrial, service- and technology-oriented economy it is today. The world shifted from a gold-based to a paper-money-based standard, and is toying with adopting a digital currency. Information, which once took weeks to cross the country, can now be instantaneously transmitted and simultaneously broadcast around the world. Yet despite mammoth changes in the basic factors generating wealth for shareholders, equity returns have shown an astounding stability.

TABLE 2.1

Stock market returns

Return = compound annual return
Risk = standard deviation of arithmetic returns
All data in percent (%)

		Total Nominal Return		Nominal Capital Appreciation		Dividend Yield	Total Real Return %		Real Capital Appreciation		Real Gold Retn	Price Inflation
		Return	Risk	Return	Risk		Return	Risk	Return	Risk		
	1802-2021	8.4	17.5	3.3	17.1	4.9	6.9	17.8	1.9	17.8	0.6	1.4
	1871-2021	9.2	18.7	4.7	18.2	4.2	7.0	18.8	2.6	18.8	0.8	2.1
Major Sub-Periods	I 1802-1870	6.9	14.5	0.4	14.0	6.4	6.7	15.4	0.3	15.4	0.2	0.1
	II 1871-1925	7.3	16.5	1.9	15.9	5.3	6.6	17.4	1.3	17.4	-0.8	0.6
	III 1926-2021	10.2	19.7	6.4	19.2	3.6	7.1	19.6	3.4	19.6	1.8	2.9
Postwar Periods	1946-2021	11.3	17.0	7.7	16.5	3.3	7.3	17.3	3.9	17.3	1.6	3.7
	1946-1965	13.1	16.5	8.2	15.7	4.6	10.0	18.0	5.2	18.0	-2.7	2.8
	1966-1981	6.9	19.8	2.9	19.0	3.9	-0.1	19.0	-3.8	19.0	8.8	7.0
	1982-1999	17.5	12.7	14.1	12.6	3.0	13.8	12.8	10.5	12.8	-4.9	3.3
	2000-2021	7.8	18.2	5.9	17.8	1.8	5.2	17.6	3.5	17.6	6.3	2.3

But stability in the long-run returns on stocks in no way guarantees stability in the short run. From 1982 through 1999 during the greatest bull market in US history, stocks gave investors an extraordinary after-inflation return of 13.6 percent per year, approximately double the historical average. These superior returns followed the dreadful returns realized in stocks during the previous 15 years, from 1966 through 1981, when stock returns fell behind by inflation 0.4 percent per year. Nevertheless, this great bull market carried stocks too high, and the valuation of the market reached record levels at the top of the internet peak in 2000. Despite three subsequent bear markets, real stock returns from that market peak have averaged 5.2 percent per year, which has exceeded the real return on fixed income assets.

REAL RETURNS ON FIXED-INCOME ASSETS

As stable as the long-term real returns have been for equities, the same cannot be said of fixed-income assets. As Table 2.2 indicates, the real return on Treasury bills has dropped precipitously from 5.1 percent in the early part of the nineteenth century to a bare 0.4 percent since 1926, a return only slightly above inflation.

The real return on long-term bonds has shown a similar, but more moderate decline. Bond returns fell from a generous 4.8 percent in the first subperiod to 3.7 percent in the second, and then to only 2.6 percent in the third. The decline in real yield on government bonds over time is discussed in Chapter 8.

TABLE 2.2

Fixed income returns

Return = compound annual return
Risk = standard deviation of arithmetic returns
All data in percent (%)

		Long Term Governments					Short Term Governments			Price Inflation
		Coupon Rate	Nominal Return		Real Return		Nominal Rate	Real Return		
			Return	Risk	Return	Risk		Return	Risk	
	1802-2021	4.6	5.0	6.8	3.6	9.1	4.0	2.5	5.9	1.4
	1871-2021	4.5	5.1	8.0	3.0	9.4	3.4	1.4	4.4	2.1
Major Sub-Periods	I 1802-1870	4.9	4.9	2.8	4.8	8.3	5.2	5.1	7.7	0.1
	II 1871-1925	4.0	4.3	3.0	3.7	6.4	3.8	3.1	4.8	0.6
	III 1926-2021	4.9	5.6	9.8	2.6	10.8	3.3	0.4	3.8	2.9
Postwar Periods	1946-2021	5.4	5.8	10.7	2.0	11.4	3.9	0.2	3.1	3.7
	1946-1965	3.1	1.6	4.9	-1.2	7.1	2.0	-0.8	4.3	2.8
	1966-1981	7.2	2.5	7.1	-4.2	8.1	6.8	-0.2	2.1	7.0
	1982-1999	8.5	12.1	13.8	8.5	13.6	6.3	2.9	1.8	3.3
	2000-2021	3.6	7.0	11.4	4.6	11.5	1.5	-0.8	1.9	2.3

The short-run volatility of stock returns from decade to decade is not unexpected. What may surprise investors is that the volatility of the returns on government bonds is also quite large. For the 35-year period from 1946 through 1981, the real return on Treasury bonds was negative. In other words, the coupon on the bonds did not offset the decline in bond prices brought about by rising interest rates and inflation. As we shall see in the next chapter, there never has been even a 20-year period, not to mention 35-year period, where real stock returns were negative.

The decline in real returns on bonds since 1926 would have been much greater if it were not for the stellar bond returns of the past four decades. Since 1981, the decline in inflation and interest rates has pushed the price of bonds upward and greatly improved bondholder returns. Although bond returns fell well short of equities during the mega bull market in stocks from 1981 through 1999, bonds easily outpaced stocks in the following decade. In fact, for the entire four decades that followed the peak in bond yields in the early 1980s, bond returns virtually matched those of equities.

THE CONTINUING DECLINE IN FIXED-INCOME RETURNS

But those spectacular bond returns cannot continue. Prospective real returns for Treasury bonds became far easier to determine when, in January 1997, the US Treasury introduced Treasury Inflation-Protected Securities (TIPS). The coupons and principal from these bonds, backed by the full faith and credit of the US government, are linked to the US consumer price index so that the yield on these bonds is a *real*, inflation-adjusted yield shown in Figure 2.5.

The steady decline in the yields on these bonds is readily apparent, and the reasons will be explored in detail in the next chapter. When these bonds were first issued, their yield was just short of 3.5 percent. That is almost identical to the historical real return on government bonds that I had found in my research dating from 1802. After issuance, the yield on TIPS increased, reaching a high of 4.40 percent in January 2000, the month that also marked the peak of the tech and internet bubble.

From that date, the yield on TIPS began a relentless decline. From 2002 through 2007 the yield fell to 2 percent. As the financial crisis deepened, the yield continued to decline and sank below zero in August 2011, reaching nearly –1 percent by December 2012 and fell below this level during the pandemic. This negative real yield was similar to the expected real yields on the standard, nonindexed Treasury bonds. In recent years yield on the 10-year Treasury bond has fallen well below the ongoing and forecast rate of inflation turning their prospective real returns negative. The decline in real yields will be discussed in detail in Chapter 8.

THE EQUITY RISK PREMIUM

The return on stocks above the return on bonds is referred to as the *equity risk premium*, or ERP. From 1802 through 2021, the historical ERP (compound annual returns) has been 3.3 percent per year against

long-term bonds and 4.3 percent against short-term bonds. Looking forward from the end of 2021, the equity premium looks even larger. Even
if we assume that the forward-looking return on equities falls 2 percentage points from its historical level of 6.8 percent to 4.8 percent, the real
return on bonds has fallen much further. As noted earlier, the 10-year
Treasury inflation-protected security, which promises to compensate
bond-holders for inflation, yielded –1 percent at the end of 2021, which
suggested a forward-looking ERP of almost 6 percent, nearly double its
historical average. The expected equity risk premium against short-term
fixed income assets is even higher.

FIGURE 2.5

10-year TIPS yields, 1997–2021

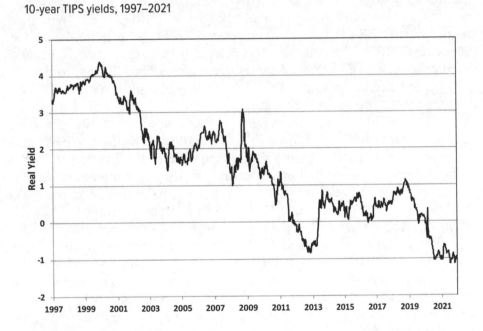

Of course, only time will reveal the future margin by which stocks
beat bonds. Nevertheless, economists have been wrestling with why the
ERP is so high, given the long-term real growth of output and stocks
prices.[16] This high premium of stocks over bonds has been termed *equity
premium puzzle*, and there have been hundreds of academic articles seeking an answer to this question. To be sure, economic recessions mark our
history, but they are nowhere near the magnitude to cause the fluctuations we see in the stock market. This has also led to the phenomenon

called the *excess volatility puzzle*, which was sparked by Professor Robert Shiller's landmark research in 1982, described in Chapter 10.[17]

WORLDWIDE EQUITY AND BOND RETURNS

When I published *Stocks for the Long Run* in 1994, some economists questioned whether my conclusions, drawn from US data, might overstate historical equity returns measured on a worldwide basis. They claimed that US stock returns exhibited *survivorship bias*, a bias caused by the fact that returns are collected from successful equity markets, such as the United States, but ignored in countries where stocks have faltered or disappeared outright, such as Russia or China.[18] This bias suggested that stock returns in the United States, a country that over the last 200 years has transformed from a small British colony into the world's greatest economic power, are unique, and historical equity returns in other countries would be lower.

Inspired by this question, three UK economists examined the historical stock and bond returns from 19 countries since 1900. Elroy Dimson and Paul Marsh, professors at the London Business School, and Mike Staunton, director of the London Share Price Database, published in 2002 their research in a book entitled *Triumph of the Optimists: 101 Years of Global Investment Returns*.[19] This book provides a rigorous yet readable account of worldwide financial market returns in 19 different countries.

Updated data from this study are shown in Figure 2.6. Despite the major disasters visited on many of these countries, such as war, hyperinflation, and depression, every one of these countries exhibited substantially positive after-inflation stock returns. In those countries, such as Italy, Belgium, France, and Germany, that had lower equity returns, the returns on fixed-income assets were much lower, so the equity premium was substantial in every country examined.

The average historical real stock, bond, and bill returns of the 21 countries analyzed from 1900 through 2020 are shown in Figure 2.7. Real equity returns ranged from a low of 0.9 percent in Austria to a high of 7.1 percent in South Africa. Stock returns in the United States, although quite good, were third highest. The real annualized return for the world is 5.3 percent, 1.3 percentage points below the United States. All countries had higher equity returns than fixed-income returns, and those countries that had lower stock returns also had lower fixed-income returns. Over the entire 121 years, the equity risk premium, or return on stocks over long-term bonds, was 4.4 percentage points in the United States, 3.7 percentage points when averaged over all markets and 3.2 percent for the world market.

FIGURE 2.6

Average annual real stock, bond bill returns, 1900–2020

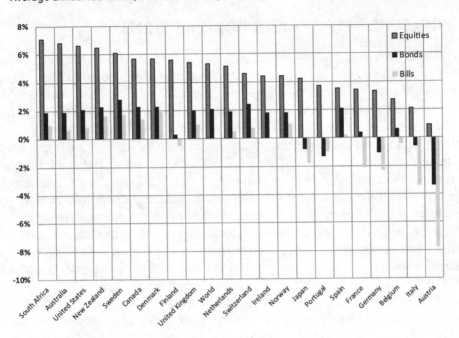

When all the information was analyzed, the authors concluded in the first edition of their book,

> that the US experience of equities outperforming bonds and bills has been mirrored in all sixteen countries examined . . . Every country achieved equity performance that was better than that of bonds. Over the 101 years as a whole, there were only two bond markets and just one bill market that provided a better return than our *worst* performing equity market.

Furthermore,

> While the US and the UK have indeed performed well, . . . there is no indication that they are hugely out of line with other countries . . . Concerns about success and survivorship bias, while legitimate, may therefore have been somewhat overstated [and] investors may have not been materially misled by a focus on the US.[20, 21]

This last statement is significant. More studies have been made of the US markets than the markets of any other country in the world. Dimson, Marsh, and Staunton are saying that the results found in the United States have relevance to all investors in all countries. The title of their book, *Triumph of the Optimists,* suggests their conclusion: It is the *optimists,* not the pessimists, who take positions in the equity market, and they have decidedly triumphed over more cautious investors over the last century. International studies have reinforced, not diminished, the case for equities.

REAL ESTATE RETURNS

In earlier editions of *Stocks for the Long Run,* I did not report on real estate as an asset class. It is not because I did not consider real estate important. Indeed, total real estate wealth falls just shy of stock wealth in the United States, and in many countries, especially emerging economies, real estate constitutes the largest asset class.[22]

The reason for excluding real estate is that in contrast to the other asset classes, it is extremely difficult to compute long-term returns on real estate. We do have long-term series of real estate *prices,* but virtually all of real estate's real return comes from its net rental income, and comprehensive data on net rental income are sparse and difficult to determine.

Robert Shiller has developed a series of owner-occupied housing prices from 1890 to the present, which shows a 1.9 percent real compound annual increase in *prices,* far short of total return.[23] Òscar Jordà, Katharina Knoll, Dmitry Kuvshinov, Moritz Schularick, and Alan Taylor in "The Rate of Return on Everything, 1880–2015" attempted to determine real estate returns in 16 advanced countries using measures of imputed rent. They claimed that the average annual return on real estate matches or exceeds the return on equity in most countries and displays far less volatility.[24] The similarity of returns on real estate with stocks has been supported in a recent study by Francis and Ibbotson, which imputed rent to owner-occupied housing and farmland.[25] They claim that from 1991 through 2018, the compound return to residential real estate amounted to 9.0 percent per year, virtually matching that of the market, and farmland performed even better.

But other researchers, such as David Chambers, Christophe Spaenjers, and Eva Steiner who analyzed actual portfolio returns of real long-term estate holders, have voiced serious objections to these high returns.[26] Chambers carefully analyzed the return to the large and diversified real estate holdings of the Oxford and Cambridge endowment in the United Kingdom from 1901 through 1983. He found that the compound net real return to the agricultural real estate was only 4.5 percent per year and only 2.3 percent for residential real estate. They claim that other researchers have underestimated maintenance and other transaction costs, as well as ignored the impact of vacancies. Furthermore, rental indexes ignore the continuous improvement in the quality of new rental housing and thus overstate the rental income to investors in older structures. Chamber's estimates that net real estate returns are far lower than those on equities in the United States and most other countries in the world.

Market-Determined Returns

The problems with rental imputations and cost estimates can be circumvented if we examine the returns of *real estate investment trusts*, or REITs, which are securities that represent real estate assets that are traded on organized exchanges.[27] The National Association of Real Estate Investment Trusts (NAREIT) has published an index of such returns since January 1971. As a result, we have a half century of market data on real estate returns, shown in Figure 2.7.

FIGURE 2.7

Total REIT, All Equity REIT, and S&P 500 returns, 1971–2021

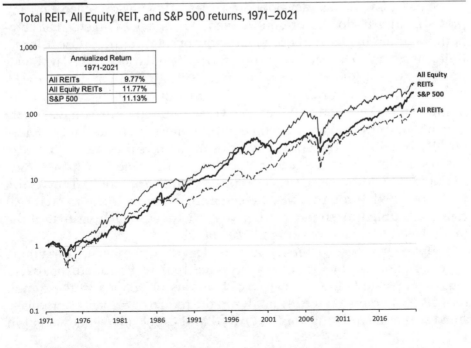

Annualized Return 1971-2021	
All REITs	9.77%
All Equity REITs	11.77%
S&P 500	11.13%

From 1971 through November 2020, the All REIT index returned 9.8 percent per year, trailing the 11.20 percent return for the S&P 500. But REIT returns from the All REIT index were significantly dragged down by the performance of mortgage REITs, financial entities that finance real estate, which realized returns of only 5.3 percent per year over that period. Equity REITs, which include entities that hold and manage real estate, have performed much better, returning about 11.7 percent. Equity REITs returns bested the 11.2 percent return on the S&P 500 Index by approximately 0.5 percentage points per year over that period.[28]

But can the returns on a historically constructed index be realized by investors? In 1996, Vanguard offered an Equity REIT fund (VGSIX) designed to mimic the returns on the REIT equity index. Since inception, the annual return on the Vanguard fund has been 9.90 percent, trailing the annual compound return of the REIT equity index by 0.5 percentage point. If one applies this differential to the 50-year return on the NAREIT index, this implies that the realized returns on REITs over the last half-century are virtually identical to large capitalization equities.

Volatility of Real Estate Returns

There is a common perception that the risk—measured as the standard deviation of annual price fluctuations—of real estate is lower than that of equities. If that is so, then real estate becomes an extremely attractive asset class, especially since its return approximates that of stocks. The lower volatility allows investors to leverage real estate holdings, and since the borrowing cost is lower than the expected return, amplify their return while still keeping their total risk at or below that of equities. However, the volatility of real estate returns derived from series of reported sales, such as the Case-Shiller or Federal Housing Finance Agency (FHFA) series of housing prices derived from monthly data on home price sales, greatly understates the true volatility of real estate returns.

This fact was reported nearly a century ago by John Maynard Keynes, who oversaw the Oxbridge endowment, which contained substantial real estate holding. In a memo to the Estates Committee at King's College, Keynes wrote:

> Some Bursars will buy without a tremor unquoted and unmarketable investments in real estate which, if they had a selling quotation for immediate cash available at each audit, would turn their hair grey. The fact that you do not know how much its ready money quotation fluctuates does not, as is commonly supposed, make an investment a safe one.[29]

Keynes's contention is confirmed by examining the actual data on the returns on REITs traded on organized exchanges. During the 2007–2009 financing crisis, the REIT index fell 74.5 percent versus only 57.7 percent for the S&P 500. During the bear market brought on by the Covid-19 pandemic, the REIT index fell by 43 percent versus 35.4 percent for the S&P 500. The same underperformance of REITs was observed during the 1973–1974 and 1990–1991 bear markets.

There was one market cycle where the returns on REITs and stocks have differed markedly; when stock prices rose in the late 1990s, REIT prices badly lagged. But when stock prices collapsed following the internet bubble in 2000, REIT prices rose. In that cycle, real estate served as an effective hedge against stock losses, although it did not do so in other bear markets.

Summary of Real Estate Returns

Very long-term real estate data are fraught with imprecise estimates of costs and net rental receipts, but analysis over the last half century show real estate returns approximating those on equity. Certainly, REITs are viable investment vehicles and their unique characteristics justify their designation as a separate asset class.[30]

The percentage of value represented by REITs in the S&P 500, which in 2021 stood just over 2 percent, far understates the value of real estate assets in the economy. According to the Federal Reserve's quarterly financial accounts, total housing equity comes close to the value of stocks held.

However, one must consider the value of one's home when planning overall asset allocation, so the percentage of real estate in one's *stock* portfolio should not be as high as the percentage of a nation's real estate wealth relative to total wealth. Nonetheless, REITs do allow stockholders to access nonresidential real estate, which allows investors to effectively diversify their asset holdings.

CONCLUSION: STOCKS FOR THE LONG RUN

Over the past 220 years, the compound annual real return on a diversified portfolio of common stock in the United States has been nearly 7 percent, and it has displayed a remarkable constancy over time. Certainly, the returns on stocks are dependent on the quantity and quality of capital, productivity, and the return to risk taking. But the ability to create value also springs from skillful management, a stable political system that respects property rights, and the capacity to provide value

to consumers in a competitive environment. Swings in investor sentiment resulting from political or economic crises can throw stocks off
their long-term path, but the fundamental forces producing economic
growth have always enabled equities to regain their long-term trend.
That is why stock returns have displayed such stability despite the radical political, economic, and social changes that have impacted the world
over the past two centuries.

Yet one must be aware of the political, institutional, and legal
framework in which these returns were generated. The superior performance of stocks over the past two centuries might be explained by
the growing dominance of nations committed to free-market economics. Few expected the triumph of market-oriented economies during the
dark days of the Great Depression and World War II. If history is any
guide, government bonds in our paper money economies may fare far
worse than stocks in any political or economic upheaval. As the next
chapter shows, even in stable political environments, the risks in government bonds often outweigh those in stocks for long-term investors.

Risk, Return, and Portfolio Allocation

Why Stocks Are Less Risky Than Bonds in the Long Run

As a matter of fact, what investment can we find which offers real fixity or certainty income? . . . As every reader of this book will clearly see, the man or woman who invests in bonds is speculating in the general level of prices, or the purchasing power of money.

—Irving Fisher, 1912[1]

MEASURING RISK AND RETURN

Risk and return are the building blocks of finance and portfolio management. Once the risk, expected return, and correlations between asset classes are specified, modern financial theory can help investors determine the best portfolios. But the risk and return on stocks and bonds are not physical constants like the speed of light or gravitational force, waiting to be discovered in the natural world. Investors cannot, as in the physical sciences, run repeated controlled experiments, holding all other factors constant and hone in on the "true" value of each variable.

This means that despite the overwhelming quantity of historical data, one can never be certain that the underlying factors that generate asset prices have remained unchanged. As Nobel Laureate Paul Samuelson was fond of saying, "We have but one sample of history."

Yet one must start by analyzing the past in order to plan for the future. The last chapter showed that not only have fixed-income returns lagged substantially behind those on equities, but because of the uncertainty of inflation, bonds can be quite risky for long-term investors. In this chapter, investors will see that their portfolio allocations depend crucially on investors' planning horizons.

RISK AND HOLDING PERIOD

For many investors, the most meaningful way to describe risk is by portraying a worst-case scenario. The best and worst after-inflation returns for stocks, bonds, and bills from 1802 over holding periods ranging from 1 to 30 years are displayed in Figure 3.1. Here stock returns are measured, as before, by dividends plus capital gains or losses on a broad-based capitalization-weighted index of US stocks, all reassured after inflation.

FIGURE 3.1

Maximum and minimum real holding period returns, 1802–2021

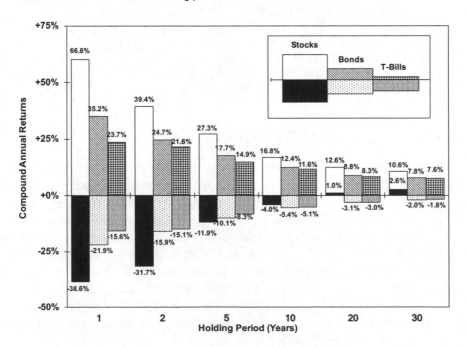

Note that the height of the bars, which measures the difference between best and worst returns, declines far more rapidly for equities than for fixed-income securities as the holding period increases.

Stocks are unquestionably riskier than bonds or Treasury bills over one- and two-year periods. However, in every five-year period since 1802, the worst performance in stocks, at –11.9 percent per year, has been only slightly worse than the worst performance in bonds or bills. And for 10-year holding periods, the worst stock performance has actually been *better* than that for bonds or bills.

For 20-year holding periods, stock returns have never fallen below inflation, but returns for bonds and bills fell more than 3 percent per year below the inflation rate from 1961–1981. During that inflationary episode, the real value of a portfolio of Treasury bonds, including all reinvested coupons, fell by nearly 50 percent. The worst 30-year return for stocks remained comfortably ahead of inflation by 2.6 percent per year (1902–1932), a return that is not far below the *average* performance of fixed-income assets.

It is very significant that in the more than two-century history of financial returns, stocks, in contrast to bonds or bills, have never delivered a negative real return over periods as short as 17 years. Although it might appear to be riskier to accumulate wealth in stocks rather than in bonds over long periods of time, for the preservation of purchasing power, precisely the opposite is true: the safest long-term investment has clearly been a diversified portfolio of equities.

Some investors question whether holding periods of 20 years, 30 years, or even longer are relevant to their planning horizon, but one of the greatest mistakes that investors make is to underestimate their holding period. This is because many investors think only about the holding periods of a particular stock, bond, or mutual fund. However, the holding period that is most relevant for portfolio allocation is the length of time the investors hold *any* stocks or bonds, no matter how many changes are made among the individual issues in their portfolio.

The percentage of times that stock returns outperform bond or bill returns over various holding periods is shown in Table 3.1. As the holding period increases, the probability that stocks will outperform fixed-income assets increases dramatically. But over one- and even two-year periods, stocks outperform bonds or bills only about three out of every five years. This means that nearly two out of every five years a stockholder's return will fall behind the return he or she would get on Treasury bills or bank certificates. The probability that bonds and savings accounts have frequently outperformed stocks in the short run is the primary reason why it is so difficult for many investors to stay in stocks.[2]

For 10-year horizons, stocks beat bonds and bills about 75 percent of the time; for 20-year horizons, about 85 percent of the time; over 30-year horizons, it is 91.6 percent of the time; and since 1871, 99.3 percent of the time.

TABLE 3.1

Holding period comparisons: percentage of periods when stocks outperform bonds and bills

Holding Period	Time Period	Stocks Outperform Bonds	Stocks Outperform T-Bills
1 Year	1802-2021	59.5	63.2
	1871-2021	62.3	68.2
2 Years	1802-2021	61.2	64.4
	1871-2021	64.9	72.2
3 Years	1802-2021	67.2	70.2
	1871-2021	68.7	73.3
5 Years	1802-2021	69.0	69.4
	1871-2021	70.9	75.5
10 Years	1802-2021	73.5	74.9
	1871-2021	79.5	85.4
20 Years	1802-2021	84.1	88.1
	1871-2021	95.4	99.3
30 Years	1802-2021	91.6	91.6
	1871-2021	99.3	100.0

In the first four editions of *Stocks for the Long Run*, I noted that the last 30-year period when the return on long-term bonds beat stocks ended in 1861, at the onset of the US Civil War. That is no longer true. Because of the precipitous large drop in government bond yields over the last several decades, the 11.03 percent annual return on long-term government bonds just passed the 10.98 percent on stocks for a single 30-year period from January 1, 1982, through the end of 2011. This striking event caused some researchers to conclude that stock returns can no longer be counted on to surpass bond returns.[3]

But a closer look at why bonds outperformed stocks during this period shows that it is almost impossible for bonds to repeat that feat in the coming decades. In 1981 the interest rate on 10-year US Treasury bonds surpassed 16 percent. As interest rates fell, bondholders benefited from both high coupons and capital gains on their bonds. Recall that the return on long-term bonds is calculated by selling a long-term bond *each* year, collecting your proceeds, and reinvesting them into a new long-term bond. This strategy resulted in a real return on bonds of 7.8 percent per year from 1981 to 2011, approximately the same real return as on stocks. A 7.8 percent real return is only about 1 percentage point above the stocks' 220-year average, but it is double the average historical real return on bonds and almost three times the real bond return since 1926.

As interest rates have fallen to historic lows, bondholders face a wholly different situation in 2021. At the end of that year, the yield on nominal bonds was about 1.5 percent and inflation-indexed bonds at near −1 percent. To garner returns anywhere near stocks, interest rates on nominal bonds would have to fall well below zero (far more than yields fell in Europe or Japan) and yields must become far more negative on inflation-protected bonds.

STANDARD MEASURES OF RISK

Random Walk Theory

In the 1960s, increasing evidence about the unpredictability of stock prices fostered a belief in the *random walk* theory of stock market returns. A *random walk* means that the next period's price change is completely independent of this period's change. Indeed, in 1965 Professor Paul Samuelson, the first American Nobel Prize–winning economist, published an influential paper, "Proof That Properly Anticipated Prices Fluctuate Randomly," which lent support to the random walk theory.[4] This was followed by prodigious work that tended to confirm that the statistical behavior of stock prices—at least in the short run—was indistinguishable from a random walk.[5]

If stock prices are random walks, then it does *not* follow that a portfolio built for a long-horizon investor should be more heavily invested in stocks than one for a short-horizon investor. Samuelson demonstrated that there is no "time diversification" in the market that displays a random walk. That is, in the long run the ups do not cancel the downs to leave an investor with a more stable return.[6] To be sure, the *percentage* of times stocks beat bonds will increase as the holding period increases, but when there is a loss, it could be devastating to your portfolio and well-being. In a random walk world, the percentage of one's portfolio in stocks does not depend on the holding period.

Mean **Reversion** *of Equity Returns*

The data demonstrate that the random walk hypothesis for stock return cannot be maintained for the long term. The risk—defined as the standard deviation of average real, after-inflation annual returns—for stocks, bonds, and bills based on the historical sample of 220 years is displayed in Figure 3.2.

FIGURE 3.2

Standard deviation of average real return over various holding periods, 1802–2021 (historical risk versus risk based on random walk hypothesis)

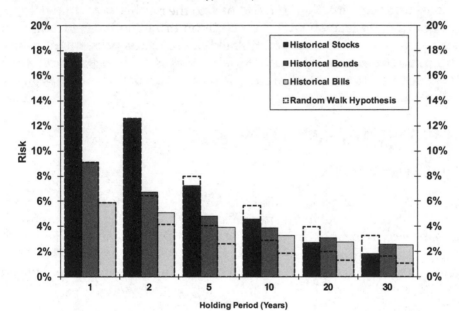

Although the standard deviation of stock returns is higher than for bond returns over short-term holding periods, once the holding period increases to between 15 and 20 years, stocks become less risky than bonds. Over 30-year periods, the standard deviation of the return on a portfolio of equities falls to less than three-fourths that of bonds or bills. As the holding period increases, the standard deviation of average returns falls nearly twice as fast for stocks as for fixed-income assets.

If asset returns follow a random walk, the standard deviation of each asset class will fall by the square root of the holding period. The dashed bars in Figure 3.2 show the decline in risk predicted under a random walk. Clearly, the random walk predictions do not hold.

When the standard deviation of average stock returns declines faster than predicted by the random walk hypothesis, this is called *mean reversion* of stock returns. Note that mean reversion does *not* claim that the *total* risk of a portfolio of stocks *falls* as we extend the time period. The standard deviation of *total* stock returns does indeed rise with time, but it does so at a diminishing rate.[7] It is the "per year" risk that falls as the time period becomes longer.

I was not the first to suggest that long-term stock returns followed a mean-reverting process. James Poterba and Lawrence Summers (1988) and Eugene Fama and Kenneth French (1988) showed that long-term stock returns did not appear to conform to the random walk hypothesis.[8] Yet even when I published the first edition of *Stocks for the Long Run* in 1994, the random walk theory still held sway and there was much skepticism about whether mean reversion actually existed in the stock data.

Paul Samuelson remained a skeptic. In 1992, as I published my long-term data, he cautioned:

> Since it takes a long time to duplicate statistical samples of long-term epochs, our confidence in the strength of [mean reversion] must be guarded. Moreover, the size of the alleged effect, particularly after we discount for the possible one-time nature of the 1920–1945 swings of the Great Depression and World War II, may not be great quantitatively. For these reasons, a certain caution toward the new results would seem prudent.[9]

He emphasized, "We have only one history of capitalism. Inferences based on a sample of one must never be accorded sure-thing interpretations. How did 1913 Tsarist executives fare in their retirement years on the Left Bank of Paris?"[10]

In the early 1990s, the profession was split on the existence of mean reversion of stock returns.[11] But the consensus was shifting; in 1999, John H. Cochrane wrote:

> The last 15 years have seen a revolution in the way financial economists understand the investment world. We once thought that stock and bond returns were essentially unpredictable. Now we recognize that stock and bond returns have a substantial predictable component at long horizons.[12]

More recently, he indicated to me that he believed that over 90 percent of financial economists would agree that equity returns display long-term mean reversion.[13]

Mean Aversion in Bonds

Although stock returns display mean reversion, the situation is exactly the opposite for bonds. As shown in Figure 3.2, the standard deviation of average returns for fixed-income assets does not fall as fast as the random walk theory predicts. This is a manifestation of *mean aversion* of bond returns. Mean aversion implies that once an asset's return deviates from its long-run average, there is an increased chance that it will deviate further, rather than return to more normal levels.

Mean aversion of bond returns is especially characteristic in hyperinflations, where prices rise at an accelerating pace, rendering paper assets worthless. But mean aversion is also present in the more moderate inflations that have impacted the United States and other developed economies. Once inflation begins to accelerate, the inflationary process becomes cumulative and bondholders have virtually no chance of making up losses to their purchasing power. In contrast, stockholders who hold claims on real assets rarely suffer a permanent loss due to inflation.

VOLATILITY MEASURED FROM HISTORICAL DATA

Some researchers have questioned whether stock returns really do display the longer-term stability that the data suggest. Professors Robert Stambaugh and Luboš Pástor have written an article, "Are Stock Really Less Volatile in the Long Run?"[14] They claim that the standard techniques that economists use to estimate long-term risk, such as computing standard deviations from historical data, underestimate long-term volatility because of a number of factors, including parameter uncertainty, the uncertainty of the model generating those returns, among other factors. They claim that this additional uncertainty offsets the mean reversion shown in historical stock return data and that stocks may well be riskier in the long run than economists have calculated. If this is the case, they claim that the recommendation that investors with longer horizons should have a greater share of their portfolio in stocks may not be warranted.

In their analysis they assume there is a certain, after-inflation (i.e., real) risk-free financial instrument that investors can buy to guarantee purchasing power for any date in the future. But TIPS (Treasury Inflation-Protected Securities), although the safest bonds to protect purchasing power, have a number of flaws. Because of the methodology used to create the consumer price index (CPI), this index often lags inflation and there is always the possibility that in the future the government will manipulate the construction of the index to understate the inflation for political purposes.

More seriously, the inflation adjustment that is applied to TIPS bonds is done so with a calculation of *past*, not current, inflation. If inflation accelerates, and certainly if inflation turns into hyperinflation, TIPS will provide very little protection.

Additionally, the same caution about the interpretation of historical risk that applies to stocks also applies to *every* asset. All assets are subject to extreme outcomes called *tail risks* or *black swan events*. Certainly, some stock markets have gone to zero, such as those in Russia and China in the mid-twentieth century, as Samuelson noted. But government bonds have become worthless with an even greater frequency. Furthermore, other forms of wealth, such as land, can be expropriated by governments hostile to private property, and even gold, one of the few assets that has possessed value throughout history, may be shunned in favor of digital currencies by future generations. Equities, legal claims on productive capital, are more likely to retain real value in a world based on fiat currency that constantly faces inflationary threats.

CORRELATION BETWEEN STOCK AND BOND RETURNS

Although the returns on bonds fall short of those on stocks, bonds may still serve to diversify a portfolio and lower overall risk of the portfolio, especially in the short run. This will be particularly true if bond and stock returns are *negatively correlated*, which would happen if bond and stock prices move in opposite directions.[15]

The diversifying strength of an asset is measured by the correlation coefficient. The *correlation coefficient* ranges between –1 and +1 and measures the comovement between an asset's return and the return of the rest of the portfolio. The lower the correlation coefficient, the better the asset serves as a portfolio diversifier. Assets with zero, or particularly negative, correlations with stocks are particularly good diversifiers. As the correlation coefficient between the asset and portfolio returns increases, the diversifying quality of the asset declines.

Figure 3.3 displays the correlation coefficient between annual stock and bond returns for three subperiods between 1926 and 2021. From 1926 through 1965 the correlation was only slightly positive, indicating that bonds were fairly good diversifiers for stocks. Bonds were good diversifiers in this period because it included the Great Depression, which was characterized by falling economic activity and consumer prices, a situation that was bad for stocks, but good for US government bonds.

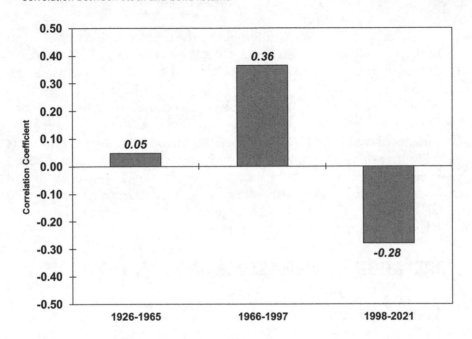

FIGURE 3.3

Correlation between stock and bond returns

However, from the 1960s through the mid-1990s, bad economic times were more likely to be associated with *inflation*, not deflation. This was true as the government attempted to offset economic downturns, particularly those caused by oil price hikes engineered by OPEC oil restrictions, with more expansionary monetary policy, adding fuel to the inflationary economy. Under these circumstances stock and bond prices tend to move together, reducing the diversifying qualities of government bonds.

This positive correlation has switched in recent decades. Since 1998, stock prices have become *negatively* correlated with government bond prices. The reason for this change is twofold. In the early part of that period, the world markets were roiled by economic and currency upheavals in Asia, the deflationary economy in Japan, and then the terrorist events of September 11, 2001. The 2008 financial crisis stoked fears of the 1930s, when deflation ruled and government bonds were the only appreciating asset. These events led the US government bond market to once again become a safe haven for those investors fearing more economic turmoil and lower stock prices. The same situation prevailed during the Covid-19 pandemic. Chapter 8 shows why this inverse correlation has been a major contributor to the decline of long-term interest rates over the past several decades.

It should be noted that these correlations are measured over one-year periods. Financial crises or pandemics caused investors to rush to safe assets, of which government bonds stand preeminent. But over longer-term periods, the risk to the bondholder is inflation. Whatever short-term comfort bondholders receive from offsetting short-term stock volatility is lost in the longer term, when inflation becomes a significant risk.

RISK-RETURN TRADE-OFFS

Modern portfolio theory describes how investors may alter the risk and return of a portfolio by changing the mix between assets. Figure 3.4 displays the risks and returns that result from varying the proportion of stocks and bonds in a portfolio over various holding periods ranging from 1 to 30 years based on the historical data from 1802 through 2021.

The open square at the bottom of each curve represents the risk and return of an all-bond portfolio, while the solid square at the top of the curve represents the risk and return of an all-stock portfolio. The circle on the curve indicates the minimum risk achievable by combining a varying proportion of stocks and bonds. The curve that connects these points represents the risk and return of all blends of portfolios from 100 percent bonds to 100 percent stocks. This curve, called the *efficient frontier*, is the heart of modern portfolio analysis and is the foundation of asset allocation models.

Note that the allocation that achieves the minimum risk is a function of the investor's holding period. Investors with a one-year horizon seeking to minimize their risk should hold almost their entire portfolio in bonds, and that is also true for those with the two-year horizon. At a 5-year horizon, the allocation of stock rises to 25 percent in the minimum risk portfolio, and it further increases to more than one-third when investors have a 10-year horizon. For 20-year horizons, the minimum risk portfolio is over 50 percent in stock, and for a 30-year horizon it is 68 percent. It should be noted that investors should hold a *greater* fraction in equities than the minimum risk allocations, since the gain in return from adding equities far outweighs the extra risk from doing so.[16]

Given these striking results, it might seem puzzling that the holding period had not been considered when modern portfolio theory was developed in the 1950s and 1960s. This is because, as noted earlier, at that time the vast majority of the academic profession believed in the random walk theory of security prices. When prices are a random walk, the risk over any holding period is a simple function of the risk over a single period, so the relative risk of different assets does not depend on the holding period. In that case the efficient frontier is invariant to the holding period, and asset allocation does not depend on the investment horizon of the investor. When security markets do not obey random walks, then the investment horizon must be considered in portfolio allocation.

FIGURE 3.4

Risk-return trade-offs for various holding periods based on historical data, 1802–2021

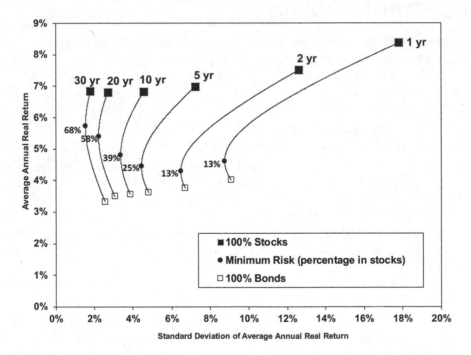

STOCK-BOND ALLOCATION

Fundamental Considerations

A number of factors must be considered when deciding what percentage of one's portfolio should be in equities and bonds. Naturally risk preferences are important. If one is interested in protection against short-term risks, bonds have a place in the investor's portfolios. For longer-term investors, where inflation uncertainty predominates, the percentage allocated to bonds should be much lower, and bonds that protect investors from inflation (TIPS) are much more important.

Another factor in determining portfolio allocation is age. Mean reversion of stock returns implies that the young should have a higher fraction in stocks than the old.[17] On reason for this is that younger investors have a higher percentage of their wealth in human capital not financial capital. This means that one can vary the amount of effort you undertake, what economists refer to as altering your labor-leisure choice. In particular, if one experiences a bad outcome in the stock market, one can work harder to rebuild financial wealth. This also implies the young should have a higher proportion of wealth in equities.

The 60/40 Retirement Portfolio

For many individuals approaching retirement, there are two main goals: first, to establish a retirement fund that will support a certain level of consumption during your retirement period, and second, to leave a legacy if the retirement fund survives your lifetime. Achieving these two goals is seen as a balancing act: since stocks have higher returns than bonds, raising stock allocations will certainly raise the expected legacy value of a retirement portfolio. However, stocks also have higher short-term volatility, so tilting a portfolio toward stocks will increase the probability of being unable to fund a steady withdrawal plan. What then is the best balance between stocks and bonds?

Historically, a popular stock/bond allocation, particularly for retirement portfolios, is the 60/40 portfolio, which specifies that 60 percent of your assets should be in stocks and 40 percent in bonds. The origin of this recommendation is generally attributed to William Bengen's 1994 article "Determining Withdrawal Rates Using Historical Data."[18] By using simulations of actual historical stock and bond returns from 1926, Bengen counseled that an optimal asset allocation would be between 50 and 75 percent in equities, based on the client's comfort zone. Many advisors settled on 60 percent in stocks, and the 60/40 stock-bond allocation became a common benchmark.

The 60/40 portfolio was considerably more aggressive than the *age in bonds* rule, which prevailed in the 1950s and 1960s and stipulated (without much theoretical or empirical basis) that the percentage of the portfolio that was allocated to bonds should equal the age of the investor.

Perhaps in recognition of the superior performance of stocks in recent decades and the increasing life expectancy of individuals, the age in bonds rule has transformed to an "age minus 20" percentage in bonds, which recommends someone aged 60 would adhere to the 60/40 stock-bond portfolio. Steven Dolvin and others have noted that many of the current target-date portfolios are roughly allocated along these lines.[19]

Figure 3.5 shows the probability of running out of money for a retiree with two different withdrawal rates: either 4 percent or 5 percent annually (all corrected for inflation) based on all historical real stock and bond returns from 1926 through 2021. During that period, the average real return has been 7.12 percent for stocks and 2.58 percent for bonds. The probabilities of running out of money are determined using a Monte Carlo procedure of randomizing historical annual returns and running thousands of simulations. These simulations include all the bear markets in both stocks and bonds that occurred this past century.

FIGURE 3.5

Probability of running out of money after 30 years. Historical 1926–2021: real stock return (7.12 percent) and real bond return (2.58 percent)

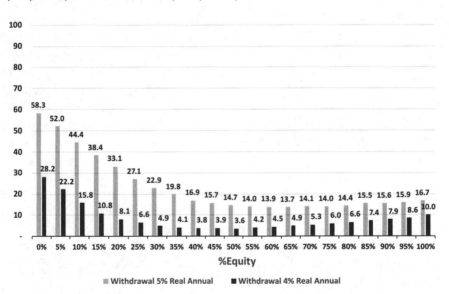

Figure 3.5 shows that using historical data, the probability of running out of money with a 4 percent withdrawal rate is very low and is minimized at 3.6 percent, with a 50/50 stock-bond portfolio. With an all-stock portfolio, the probability of running short rises to 10 percent, but

the expected legacy more than doubles in size. The optimal allocation would be between the 50/50 stock-bond portfolio and the all-stock port-folio, depending on how an investor weighs the probability of running out of money versus the size of the legacy.

At a 5 percent annual withdrawal rate, the minimum probability of a spending shortfall occurs at a higher stock allocation, specifically at 65 percent stocks and 35 percent bonds. At this allocation, the short-fall allocation is 13.6 percent and only rises 3 percentage points for an all-stock portfolio. The legacy rises by almost 40 percent going to an all-stock portfolio.

It might seem surprising that a 100 percent stock portfolio does not increase the risk of running out of money appreciably while significantly raising the legacy. In fact, the recommendation of a 100 percent stock portfolio for retirees has been suggested by other researchers. Javier Estrada studied 19 countries over the 110-year period between 1900 and 2009 and concluded that a retirement portfolio "fully invested in stocks is a strategy that should be seriously considered by retirees."[20]

Even Paul Samuelson, who, as noted, was skeptical of the mean reversion of stocks, toyed with the idea of a 100 percent stock retirement portfolio more than a half century ago. In a 1967 column for *Newsweek* magazine, he asked "Is 100 percent [in stocks] wise?" Surprisingly, "per-haps yes", but then Samuelson states that "an investor would probably sleep better if he only puts 60 percent to 80 percent of surplus savings (defined as liquid assets minus life insurance), into common stocks." He continued, "I know older trust officers will raise an eyebrow at this departure from 50/50. But remember, we live in an age of growth and inflation."[21] And more than five decades after he issued this warning, that threat of inflation is as relevant now as it was then.

Figure 3.5 used historical data. It is quite likely that future asset returns after 2021 may be lower, especially for bonds. In Chapter 8 we discuss the dramatic decline in the real yields on bonds over the past several decades. Real return for stocks may also be lower, due to factors discussed in Chapter 10.

Figure 3.6 does the same exercise at Figure 3.5, but assumes that the real return on stocks over the next 30 years falls to 4.5 percent per year, more than 2.5 percentage points below the historical average, and the forecast real return on bonds falls to −0.5 percent, the real yield on the 30-year TIPS at the end of 2021.[22]

The impact of lower returns on stocks and bonds on the optimal portfolio allocation is striking. Certainly, the probability of running out of money, for a given withdrawal rate, rises for any allocation. But this does not mean you should become more conservative; in fact, the reverse is true: an investor reduces the probability of running out of money by allocating *more* toward stocks when expected returns decline. For a 4 percent withdrawal rate, the minimum probability of running out of money occurs with an 80/20 stock-bond portfolio, and for a 5 percent withdrawal rate, the minimum is achieved between a 95 percent and 100 percent stock portfolio. In the simulation, we lowered the future bond returns by a bit more than stock returns, but even if we lower the forward-looking real stock return by the same amount as the bond return, the optimal portfolio shifts strongly to stocks.

FIGURE 3.6

Probability of running out of money after 30 years. Assumptions: real stock return (4.5%) and real bond return (−0.5%)

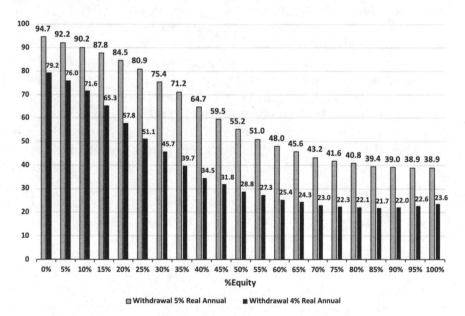

CONCLUSION

No one denies that in the short run stocks are riskier than fixed-income assets. But in the long run, history has shown that stocks are safer than bonds for long-term investors whose goal is to preserve the purchasing power of their wealth. The inflation uncertainty that is inherent in a paper money standard means that fixed income does not mean fixed purchasing power, just as Irving Fisher conjectured more than a century ago.

Despite the dramatic slowing in the rate of inflation over the past decade, there is much uncertainty about what a dollar will be worth in the future, especially given the huge deficits and accommodating monetary policy followed by the world's central banks. Historical data show that we can be more certain of the purchasing power of a diversified portfolio of common stocks 30 years hence than we can of the buying power of the principal on a 30-year US Treasury bond. The drop in the forward-looking returns on stocks, and especially bonds, argues for an even higher stock allocation for retirement portfolios.

4

Global Investing

Disappointment and Promise

> *Today let's talk about a growth industry. Because investing worldwide is a growth industry. The great growth industry is international portfolio investing.*
>
> —John Templeton, 1984[1]

> *It's been a long time since globally diversified investors could point to their foreign stock allocations with pride.*
>
> —Eric D. Nelson, 2021[2]

When John Templeton spoke to the Financial Analysts Federation in 1984, international investing was indeed a "great growth industry." In the 1950s and 1960s, the United States basically ruled the roost. By the mid-1960s, the US share of world GDP almost doubled from the level that prevailed before the war. US stocks comprised almost 75 percent of the world's total equity value. The productive capacity in Europe and Japan had been destroyed by World War II. Japan, along with many European countries, suffered economic turmoil, and many experienced hyperinflation as their governments tried to rebuild the economy.

In the 1970s, the world suffered stagflation, prompted by OPEC oil prices and excessive monetary accommodation. But as the 1980s dawned, there was hope in the air for stock investors. Ronald Reagan adopted an aggressively pro-capital stance in the United States, and Margaret Thatcher revived the capitalist spirit in the United Kingdom.

But it was Japan that became the first star of international investing. That country not only avoided the inflation that plagued most of the rest of the world in the late 1970s, but also became a manufacturing juggernaut, turning out high-quality automobiles, televisions, and innovative electronics (like the Sony Walkman) that took the world by storm.

THE JAPANESE MARKET BUBBLE

As a result of these achievements, the Japanese stock market caught fire. In the 1970s and 1980s, Japanese stock returns averaged more than 10 percentage points per year above US returns and surpassed those from every other country. The Nikkei Dow Jones Stock Average, which was set at the same level as the Dow Industrial Average when the Japanese average was founded on May 16, 1949, soared from 2,000 in 1970 to almost 39,000 by the end of 1989, reaching almost four times the level of the venerable US Dow. But that was not all; the Japanese yen appreciated almost threefold during that period, so dollar investors experienced nearly a 6,000 percent return on their money, 12 times what they would have experienced in US stocks.

The superior returns in the Japanese market during the great bull market attracted billions of dollars of foreign investment. By the end of the 1980s, valuations of many Japanese stocks reached stratospheric levels. Nippon Telephone and Telegraph, or NTT, the Japanese version of America's former telephone monopoly AT&T, sported a P/E ratio above 300. This company alone had a market value that dwarfed the aggregate stock values of all but a handful of countries. Valuations exceeded those attained in the great US technology and internet stock bubble of 2000.

The bull market in Japan was so dramatic that by the end of 1989, for the first time since the early 1900s, the market value of the American stock market was no longer the world's largest. It was astounding that Japan, a country whose economic base was destroyed in World War II and had only half the population and 4 percent of the landmass of the United States, housed the world's biggest stock market with a 40 percent share of worldwide equities compared to just 29 percent for the United States.

During his travels to Japan in 1987, Leo Melamed, president of the Chicago Mercantile Exchange, asked his hosts how such remarkably high valuations could be warranted. "You don't understand," they responded. "We've moved to an entirely new way of valuing stocks here in Japan." And that is when Melamed knew Japanese stocks were doomed.[3] It is when investors cast aside the lessons of history that the past comes back to haunt them.

When the bubble burst and the Nikkei Dow Jones fell sharply in the following years, the mystique of the Japanese market was broken. The Nikkei average fell to 7,000 in 2008, less than 20 percent of its value at the peak of the bull market two decades earlier. In 2020, Japan's share of world equities fell to a measly 7 percent, while the US share was back again over one-half.

Some people point to the Japanese market as a refutation of the thesis that in the long run, stocks will always be the superior investment. But there were glaring warnings of the Japanese bubble. At the peak of the market, Japanese stocks sold for well over 100 times earnings, more than three times the level that US market sold at the top of its biggest bubble in 2000.

What goes around, comes around. The outperformance of the Japanese market disappeared in the following decades. As shown in Figure 4.1, which plots the Japanese Dow in dollar terms, the US Dow caught up to the Nikkei Dow by 2021. Reversion to the mean dominates.

FIGURE 4.1

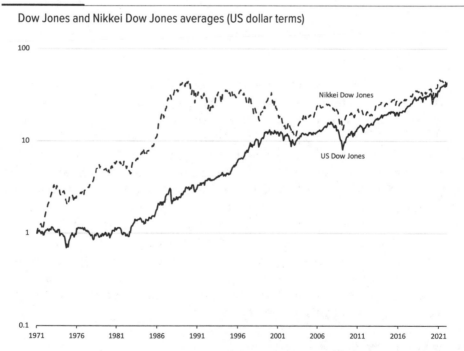

Dow Jones and Nikkei Dow Jones averages (US dollar terms)

EMERGING MARKETS BUBBLE

Soon after the collapse of the Japanese market, international investors turned their attention to the *emerging markets*, those economies such as China, India, and others that had lagged behind the United States, Europe, and Japan but held great promise for the future.

In 2001, James O'Neill, an economist at Goldman Sachs, wrote an article "Building Better Global Economic BRICs," that lit a fire for investors seeking new market opportunities.[4] BRIC was an acronym for Brazil, Russian, India, and China, the four countries that O'Neill felt would be leaders in the new century.

Two years later, two other Goldman economists wrote an even more enthusiastic piece, "Dreaming with BRICs: The Path to 2050."[5] In it they said:

> The results [of our research] are startling. If things go right, in less than 40 years, the BRICs economies together could be larger than the G6 (US, Japan UK, Germany, France, and Italy) in US dollar terms. If the BRICs come anywhere close to meeting the projections set out here, the implications for the pattern of growth and economic activity could be large [and] the weight of the BRICs in investment portfolios could rise sharply.[6]

Certainly the years immediately following the O'Neill article were kind to those who followed Goldman's advice. The Dow index of 50 BRIC stocks went up by an astonishing 600 percent between the beginning of 2003 and the end of 2007, far outperforming the 60 percent rise in the S&P 500 Index. Since then, BRICs stalled. As Figure 4.2 shows, the BRIC Index at the end of 2021 was below the high it reached 14 years earlier, and despite the surge from 2003 to 2007, over the whole period the dollar returns in these countries lagged or barely matched the return of the S&P 500 Index over the same period. Mean reversion once again ruled.

The Japanese and emerging market bubbles, as well as the strong outperformance of US stocks since the financial crisis, soured many investors on international investing. But there is much to like about international investing for those seeking not only superior returns but also diversification from the US market.

THE WORLD OF EQUITIES 2021

Figure 4.3 shows the current distribution of world equity values. In December 2021, the total market value of all world stocks was $70 trillion. The United States' share stands at 61.2 percent of that total. Developed Europe, which includes Austria, Belgium, Denmark, Finland, France, Germany, Ireland, Italy, Netherlands, Norway, Portugal, Spain, Sweden,

FIGURE 4.2

Morgan Stanley Capital International (MSCI) Country Index returns

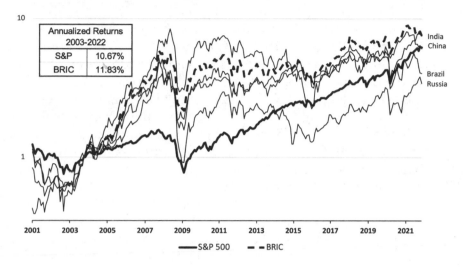

FIGURE 4.3

Distribution of global equity market capitalization, 2021

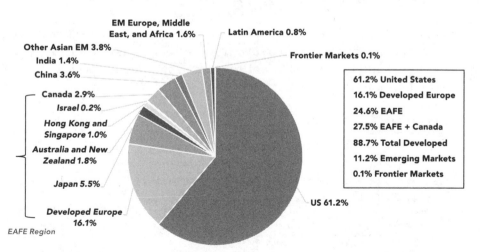

Switzerland, and the United Kingdom, comprise 16.1 percent; Japan is at 5.5 percent; Australia and New Zealand are at 1.8 percent, respectively; Hong Kong and Singapore are at 1.0 percent, respectively; and Israel is

at 0.2 percent. All the aforesaid, excluding the United States, comprise a group of countries called EAFE (an acronym for *Europe, Australasia,* and the *Far East*) and are the most popular index of the non-US-developed world markets. EAFE comprises 24.6 percent of the total world market equity. Canada is not part of EAFE (although included in some other developed market indexes such as FTSE) and is 2.9 percent of the world market. Adding Canada to EAFE and the United States means the total developed world has 88.7 percent of the world's equity values.

Outside the developed world there are the emerging markets. The MSCI index of Emerging Markets contains 25 countries,[7] of which the 5 largest—China (32 percent), Taiwan (16 percent), South Korea[8] and India, (each 12 percent), and Brazil (4 percent)—comprise a total of 78 percent of the index.[9] The total market value of emerging markets on December 2021 was $7.8 trillion, 11.2 percent of the global equity.

A final group that has recently emerged is the "frontier" market, which comprises developing countries with smaller capitalizations. The MSCI index of frontier markets contains 28 of these countries[10] of which Vietnam at 30 percent and Morocco at 10 percent are the largest. The aggregate market value of these stocks is $103 billion, or about 0.1 percent of the world's total.

INTERNATIONAL STOCK RETURNS

Table 4.1 displays the historical risk and returns for dollar-based investors in the international markets from 1970 through 2021 (1989 for emerging markets). Over the entire period, the dollar returns among different regions do not differ greatly.

TABLE 4.1

Dollar returns and risks in stocks, from January 1970 through December 2021

Country or Region	US $ Returns 1970-2021	US $ Returns 1988-2021	Domestic Risk	Exchange Risk	Total Risk	Correlation Coefficient*
World	10.00%	8.72%	13.82%	4.10%	14.77%	89.43%
EAFE	9.36%	6.03%	14.23%	8.10%	16.75%	64.80%
USA	10.83%	11.61%	15.25%	- - -	15.25%	- - -
Europe	9.86%	9.00%	14.99%	9.09%	17.34%	69.99%
Japan	9.07%	2.13%	18.24%	10.77%	20.30%	38.60%
Em Mkts**	- - -	10.50%	20.93%	8.14%	22.20%	60.22%

*Correlation between US equity market and foreign markets US dollar returns.
**Data for emerging markets is from 1988 to 2021.

Over the 51 years from 1970 through 2021, investors in US stocks realized 10.83 percent compound returns; those in EAFE (non-US-developed countries) had a slightly lower 9.36 percent return. The correlation between EAFE and US returns was 65 percent, with a slightly higher correlation with Europe, but a meaningfully lower correlation with Japan. Emerging market returns since 1988 virtually match those in the United States, with a correlation that is slightly lower than with the rest of the world. As we shall see, it is these imperfect correlations that are a key reason to maintain an international-oriented portfolio.

DIVERSIFICATION IN WORLD MARKETS

Given the disappointing performance of international investing during the decade of the 2010s, many have considered abandoning the global approach and maintaining investments in the more dynamic US economy. There are three reasons why this advice can be faulted.

The first is that the definition of a "foreign" firm is quite arbitrary: it is entirely based on where the headquarters of the firm is based, not where it produces or sells. For example, if a firm based in London both produces and sells 99 percent of its products in the United States, it is designated a "UK" firm. I have long advocated that a better way to do geographic-based investing is to determine the location where the country produces and sells its output, not where its headquarters is physically located.

Unfortunately, such an approach has never caught on. Despite the increase in globalization over time, geographic investing has gone in the opposite direction, so most country-based indices purged all foreign firms. In the early 1990s Standard and Poor's announced that no new non-US companies would be added to its benchmark S&P 500 Index and in 2002 removed the remaining seven foreign-based firms, including such giants as Royal Dutch Petroleum and Unilever, from the index.[11] Supporters of this approach argue that government regulations and legal structures of a particular country do matter, even when most of the firm's sales, earnings, and production come from abroad.

These headquarter influences may diminish if globalization advances. In fact, there is evidence that it has already happened. In 2011, Jose Menchero and Andrei Morozov published research that measured the relative importance of "industries versus countries." In the early 1990s, countries dominated industries by a wide margin.[12] The technology bubble of 2000 thrust industries into the forefront, but even after the bubble burst, *industry* influences have matched or exceeded country influences. Since the introduction of the euro, industry factors have become much more important within Europe. For emerging markets, country differences still dominate, but have also become less important.

It is likely that this trend will continue. I envision the possibility of *international* corporations, where firms choose to be governed by a set of international rules agreed upon among nations and where the headquarters of the company resides will be of very little or no importance. International incorporation standards will be similar to the growing popularity of the worldwide accounting standards promulgated by the International Accounting Standards Board (IASB).

If international incorporation gained prominence, there would be no meaning to "headquartered country," and investment allocations would have to be made on the basis of global sectors, or by production and distribution locations. In this future, investing only in the United States would be very narrow indeed. Even if international incorporations do not come to pass, the arbitrariness of the current classification system warns that a US-only portfolio may be insufficiently inclusive.

A second reason to invest globally is that many goods and services bought in the United States are produced by firms that are headquartered abroad. Total imports into the United States at the end of 2021 totaled nearly $3.5 trillion. The appetite of Americans for foreign automobiles, imported foods, and other luxury goods is enormous. If these goods and services are in demand in the United States, then there is reason that the companies that produce these should be in your portfolio.

Some claim that investing in US-based stocks alone is sufficient to gain global exposure. To be sure, the percentage of revenues of the S&P 500 Index that come from outside the United States has been rising sharply in recent decades, reaching 41 percent in 2021. Nevertheless, the United States still imports far more than it exports. Even if you believe America will house growth leaders in this new century, that does not argue for excluding firms that provide products to our economy.

The third and most important reason to hold international stocks is *diversification*, the ability to spread the risk of holding equities among an even greater selection of firms. Figure 4.4 displays the rolling 10-year returns of the United States, EAFE, and the emerging markets. Note that these markets are not synchronous and often move in opposite direction. This is the essence of diversification.

FIGURE 4.4

10-year rolling period returns

Foreign investing provides diversification in the same way that investing in different sectors of the domestic economy provides diversification. It would be poor investment strategy to pin your hopes on just one stock or one sector of the economy. Similarly, it is not a good strategy to buy the stocks only in your own country, no matter how well it has performed in the recent past.

International diversification reduces risk because the stock prices of different countries do not rise and fall in tandem, and this asynchronous movement of returns dampens the volatility of a globally-diversified portfolio. As long as two assets are not perfectly correlated, then combining these assets will lower the risk of your portfolio for a given return, or alternatively, raise return for a given risk.

Should You Hedge Foreign Exchange Risk?

The risks for dollar investors in foreign stocks are measured by the standard deviation of annual dollar returns. There are two components of this risk: fluctuations of stock prices calculated in their local currencies and fluctuations in the exchange rate between the dollar and the local currency. In Table 4.1, these are described as the domestic risk and the exchange risk.

Since foreign exchange risk generally adds to the local risk, it may be desirable for investors in foreign markets to hedge against currency movements. *Currency hedging* means entering into a currency contract or purchasing a security that offsets unexpected changes in the price of foreign currency relative to the dollar. In recent years, a number of firms have offered portfolios that partially or fully hedge foreign exchange risk, so that investors do not have to undertake additional currency transactions.

But hedging against foreign currency depreciation is not always the right strategy. The cost of hedging depends on the difference between the interest rate in the foreign country and the dollar interest rate, and if a country's currency is expected to depreciate (typically because of high inflation), the cost of hedging could be quite high.

For example, even though the British pound depreciated from $4.80 to about $1.60 over the past century, the cost of hedging this decline exceeded the depreciation in the pound. Thus the dollar returns to British stocks were higher for investors who did not hedge the decline in the pound than for those who did.

For investors with long-term horizons, hedging currency risk in foreign stock markets may not be important. In the long run, exchange-rate movements are determined primarily by differences in inflation between countries, a phenomenon called *purchasing power parity*. Since equities are claims on real assets, their long-term returns have compensated investors for changes in inflation and thus protected investors from exchange depreciation caused by higher inflation in the foreign countries.

But over shorter periods of time, investors may reduce their dollar risk by hedging exchange risk. Often, bad economic news for a country depresses both its stock market and currency value, and investors can avoid the latter by hedging. Furthermore, if it is the policy of the central bank to lower the currency value in order to stimulate exports and the economy, hedged investors can take advantage of the latter without suffering the losses of the former. For example, investors who took hedged positions in Japanese stocks late in 2012, when Prime Minister Shinzo Abe advocated yen depreciation to stimulate the economy, far outpaced the gains made by those who did not hedge the depreciating yen.

In fact, currency hedging has served to increase returns and reduce volatility for dollar-based investors in developing markets. Over the

33-year period from December 1988 through December 2021, the Morgan Stanley Capital Index EAFE (non-US-developed) return was 5.0 percent per year. However, hedged against the dollar, the return rose to 5.4 percent, while the standard deviation of annual returns fell from 16.7 percent to 14.7 percent.[13]

Sector Allocation Around the World

Let's take a closer look at the importance of these industrial sectors by region and by country. The 10 Global International Classification (GIC) industrial sectors in five geographic regions (United States, EAFE, Europe, Japan, and the emerging markets) are shown in Table 4.2 by the respective weight of each industrial sector in 2013 and 2021. This table shows the significant sector shifts that have occurred over the last eight years.

TABLE 4.2

Sector weights around the world, 2021

Sector	S&P 500		Europe		Japan		EAFE		Em Mkts		Global	
	2013	2021	2013	2021	2013	2021	2013	2021	2013	2021	2013	2021
Cons Discr	11.8%	12.5%	9.6%	11.4%	21.4%	19.4%	11.4%	12.5%	8.2%	13.5%	11.4%	12.4%
Cons Staples	10.6%	5.9%	14.6%	w	6.6%	6.6%	11.9%	10.3%	9.3%	5.9%	10.6%	6.8%
Energy	10.6%	2.7%	9.7%	4.6%	1.2%	0.7%	7.1%	3.4%	11.6%	5.6%	10.1%	3.4%
Financials	16.7%	10.7%	21.4%	15.8%	20.7%	9.1%	25.2%	16.9%	27.9%	19.4%	21.2%	13.9%
Health Care	12.6%	13.3%	12.8%	14.7%	6.3%	9.6%	10.4%	12.8%	1.3%	4.2%	10.2%	11.7%
Industrials	10.1%	7.8%	11.4%	15.4%	18.9%	22.4%	12.5%	16.2%	6.4%	5.1%	10.5%	9.6%
Materials	3.3%	2.6%	8.4%	7.9%	6.0%	4.8%	8.3%	7.6%	9.7%	8.6%	6.1%	4.7%
Real Estate		2.8%		1.2%		3.3%		2.8%		2.0%		2.7%
Technology	18.0%	29.2%	2.8%	8.5%	10.9%	15.8%	4.4%	9.7%	14.6%	22.7%	12.2%	23.6%
Telecom	2.8%	10.2%	5.3%	3.5%	4.9%	7.6%	5.1%	4.5%	7.6%	10.7%	4.3%	8.6%
Utilities	3.2%	2.5%	4.0%	4.2%	3.0%	0.8%	3.7%	3.4%	3.5%	2.4%	3.3%	2.7%

Data as of December 31, 2021

What we see in Table 4.2 is the rise and dominance of technology in the United States. This is despite the shift of Alphabet (formerly Google) and Meta platforms (formerly Facebook) from the technology sector to the communication services sector in 2018. A number of US firms in the consumer discretionary sector, such as Tesla and Amazon.com, have huge components that are technology. All told, one could say that over 50 percent of the value of US stocks at the end of 2021 were in technology, and if we include biotech, which is in health care, the percentage is even higher.

No other region of the world approaches US dominance in equity valuations in the technology sector. This is the major reason why valuations in the United States exceed those in the rest of the world. These global technology giants are growing faster, both in revenues and earnings, than most of firms in the other sectors. The communications services sector has also increased significantly, but this is primarily a result of shifting such huge firms as Alphabet, Meta, Disney, and Comcast to that sector.

TABLE 4.3

World's largest US and non-US firms, 2013

#	American Companies	Sector	Market Cap
1	APPLE	Information Technology	$415
2	EXXON MOBIL	Energy	$407
3	MICROSOFT	Information Technology	$298
4	GENERAL ELECTRIC	Industrials	$247
5	JOHNSON & JOHNSON	Health Care	$239
6	CHEVRON	Energy	$236
7	GOOGLE	Information Technology	$291
8	IBM	Information Technology	$229
9	PROCTER & GAMBLE	Consumer Staples	$213
10	BERKSHIRE HATHAWAY	Financials	$284
11	JPMORGAN CHASE	Financials	$205
12	PFIZER	Health Care	$200
13	WELLS FARGO	Financials	$218
14	AT&T	Telecom Services	$191
15	COCA-COLA	Consumer Staples	$184
16	CITIGROUP	Financials	$157
17	PHILIP MORRIS Int	Consumer Staples	$151
18	MERCK	Health Care	$146
19	VERIZON COMMUNICATIONS	Telecom Services	$144
20	BANK OF AMERICA	Financials	$144

#	Foreign Companies	Country	Sector	Market Cap
1	PETROCHINA	CHINA	Energy	$243
2	IND & COMM BK OF CHINA	CHINA	Financials	$237
3	NESTLE	SWITZERLAND	Consumer Staples	$218
4	ROCHE	SWITZERLAND	Health Care	$213
5	ROYAL DUTCH SHELL	NETHERLANDS	Energy	$211
6	HSBC HOLDINGS	BRITAIN	Financials	$205
7	CHINA MOBILE	HONG KONG	Telecom Services	$204
8	CHINA CONSTRUCTION BANK	CHINA	Financials	$196
9	NOVARTIS	SWITZERLAND	Health Care	$194
10	TOYOTA	JAPAN	Consumer Discretionary	$194
11	SAMSUNG	SOUTH KOREA	Information Technology	$188
12	BHP BILLITON	AUSTRALIA	Materials	$160
13	ANHEUSER-BUSCH	BELGIUM	Consumer Staples	$152
14	VODAFONE	BRITAIN	Telecom Services	$145
15	AG BANK OF CHINA	CHINA	Financials	$143
16	SANOFI	FRANCE	Health Care	$142
17	BP	BRITAIN	Energy	$136
18	BANK OF CHINA	CHINA	Financials	$129
19	GLAXOSMITHKLINE	BRITAIN	Health Care	$127
20	TOTAL SA	FRANCE	Energy	$119

Data as of December 31, 2013

TABLE 4.4

World's largest US and non-US firms, 2021

#	American Companies	Sector	Market Cap
1	APPLE	Information Technology	$2,935
2	MICROSOFT	Information Technology	$2,527
3	ALPHABET	Communication Services	$1,931
4	AMAZON.COM	Consumer Discretionary	$1,689
5	TESLA	Consumer Discretionary	$1,046
6	META PLATFORMS	Communication Services	$948
7	NVIDIA	Information Technology	$735
8	BERKSHIRE HATHAWAY	Financials	$677
9	UNITEDHEALTH GROUP	Health Care	$473
10	JPMORGAN CHASE	Financials	$473
11	VISA	Information Technology	$461
12	JOHNSON & JOHNSON	Health Care	$450
13	HOME DEPOT	Consumer Discretionary	$438
14	WALMART	Consumer Staples	$405
15	PROCTER & GAMBLE	Consumer Staples	$397
16	BANK OF AMERICA	Financials	$374
17	MASTERCARD	Information Technology	$355
18	PFIZER	Health Care	$331
19	DISNEY	Communication Services	$281
20	BROADCOM	Information Technology	$273

#	Foreign Companies	Country	Sector	Market Cap
1	SAUDI ARABIAN OIL	SAUDI ARABIA	Energy	$1,907
2	TAIWAN SEMICON MFG	TAIWAN	Information Technology	$576
3	TENCENT HOLDINGS	CHINA	Communication Services	$562
4	SAMSUNG ELECTRONICS	KOREA	Information Technology	$442
5	LVMH MOET HENNESSY	FRANCE	Consumer Discretionary	$417.
6	KWEICHOW MOUTAI	CHINA	Consumer Staples	$404
7	NESTLE	SWITZERLAND	Consumer Staples	$393
8	ROCHE HOLDING	SWITZERLAND	Health Care	$364
9	ASML HOLDING	NETHERLANDS	Information Technology	$332
10	ALIBABA GROUP HOLDING	CHINA	Consumer Discretionary	$330
11	TOYOTA MOTOR	JAPAN	Consumer Discretionary	$298
12	L'ORÉAL	FRANCE	Consumer Staples	$264
13	NOVO NORDISK	DENMARK	Health Care	$259
14	ICBC	CHINA	Financials	$244
15	CONTEMPORARY AMPEREX TECH	CHINA	Industrials	$214
16	NOVARTIS	SWITZERLAND	Health Care	$214
17	RELIANCE INDUSTRIES	INDIA	Energy	$201
18	CHINA MERCHANTS BANK	CHINA	Financials	$193
19	TATA CONSULTANCY SERVICES	INDIA	Information Technology	$186
20	HERMES INTERNATIONAL	FRANCE	Consumer Discretionary	$184

Data as of December 31, 2021

In contrast, note the fall in the energy and financial sectors over the past decade. Globally, the energy sector is only one-third the percentage today as it was eight short years ago. The financial sector, which in 2013 was twice as large as the next largest sector (consumer staples), has also significantly shrunk in size, although it still looms large among nonglobal firms.

Tables 4.3 and 4.4 display the 20 largest firms by market value headquartered in and outside the United States in 2013 and 2021. In the United States in 2021, the top seven—Apple, Microsoft, Alphabet, Amazon.com, Tesla, Meta, and NVIDIA—are heavily involved with technology. In 2013, four of the top seven were not in technology: ExxonMobil was number two, General Electric number four, Johnson & Johnson number five, and Chevron was number six.

While five US firms topped $1 trillion at the end of 2021, there was only one outside the United States. When Saudi Arabia's Aramco, its national oil company, became public in 2019, it was by far the largest capitalization firm in the world. At the end of 2021 it was no longer, as it had been eclipsed by both Apple and Microsoft. In 2021 in the United States 11 out of the top 20 firms are in technology or communications services; elsewhere there are only 5.

But the price of such dynamic growth is not cheap. The estimated P/E ratio of the seven-trillion-dollar US companies based on estimated 2022 earnings is almost 50, with Apple, Microsoft, and Google averaging a more modest 30, Amazon.com at 69, and Tesla at 90. In contrast, Saudi Aramco sells at 18 times earnings with a dividend yield near 4 percent. It is likely that many of these top tech companies will fall from their exalted heights.

CONCLUSION

Despite the rise in geopolitical tensions in 2021, I do not believe that globalization is dead. The inexorable trend toward integration of the world's economies and markets will certainly continue in this new millennium. No country will be able to dominate every market, and industry leaders are apt to emerge from any place on the globe. The globalization of the world economy means that the strength of management, product lines, and marketing will be far more important factors in achieving success than where the firm is headquartered.

Sticking only to US equities is a risky strategy for investors. No advisor would recommend investing only in those stocks whose name begins with the letters A through L. But sticking only to US equities would be just such a bet, since US-based equity constitutes only one-half of the world equity market. Only those investors who have a fully diversified world portfolio will be able to reap the best returns with the lowest risk.

II

STOCK RETURNS:
MEASUREMENT
AND VALUATION

Stock Indexes

Proxies for the Market

It has been said that figures rule the world.

—Johann Wolfgang Goethe, 1830

MARKET AVERAGES

"How's the market doing?" one stock investor asks another.

"It's having a good day—it's up over 500 points."

For those who follow the markets, no one would ask, "What's up 500 points?" Everyone knows the answer: the Dow Jones Industrial Average, the most quoted stock average in the world. This index, popularly called the Dow, is so renowned that the news media often called the Dow "the stock market." No matter how imperfectly the index describes the movement of share prices—and virtually no money manager pegs his or her performance to it—the Dow is the way all investors think of the stock market.

But today there are many other, more inclusive indexes. The S&P 500, created by Standard & Poor's in March 1957, has become the uncontested benchmark index for large US stocks.[1] The Nasdaq is an automated electronic market that began in 1971, which started out as the exchange of choice for technology companies. The Nasdaq index measures the performance of large technology firms, such as "FAANG" stocks: Facebook (now Meta), Amazon.com, Apple, Netflix, and Google (now Alphabet). The performance of the Nasdaq is often quoted right along with the Dow and the S&P 500 as the triumvirate of US stock indices.

Although the term *industrials* conjures up old line manufacturing companies, the Dow has become much more representative of firms that dominate today's landscape. In 1999, the Dow Industrials entered the technological age when, for the first time, the company selected two Nasdaq stocks—Microsoft and Intel—to join its venerable list of 30 stocks. Later, Apple joined the list, and in 2020, a firm whose name was unrecognizable by most Americans, Salesforce.com, was added to the index for the first time. This chapter tells the story of these three very different indexes, each with unique reflections of the stock market.

THE DOW JONES AVERAGES

Charles Dow, one of the founders of Dow Jones & Co., which also publishes the *Wall Street Journal*, created the Dow Jones averages in the late nineteenth century. On February 16, 1885, he began publishing a daily average of 12 stocks (10 railroads and 2 industrials) that represented active and highly capitalized stocks. Four years later, Dow published a daily average based on 20 stocks—18 railroads and 2 industrials.

As industrial and manufacturing firms succeeded railroads in importance, the Dow Jones Industrial Average was created on May 26, 1896, with the original 12 stocks shown in Table 5.1. The old index created in 1889 was reconstituted and renamed the Rail Average on October 26, 1896. In 1916, the Industrial Average was increased to 20 stocks, and in 1928 the number was expanded to 30, its present size. The Rail Average, whose name was changed to the Transportation Average in 1970, is composed of 20 stocks, as it has been for over a century.

The early Dow firms were centered on commodities: cotton, sugar, tobacco, lead, leather, rubber, and so on. Six of the 12 companies have survived in much the same form, but none has retained membership in this elite index.[2]

Many of the original Dow stocks have continued to thrive as large and successful firms, even if they were eventually removed from the index (see this chapter's appendix for historical details). The only exception was U.S. Leather Corp., which was liquidated in the 1950s. Shareholders received $1.50 plus one share of Keta Oil & Gas, a firm it had acquired earlier. But in 1955, the president, Lowell Birrell, who later fled to Brazil to escape US authorities, looted Keta's assets. Shares in U.S. Leather, which in 1909 was the seventh-largest corporation in the United States, became worthless.

TABLE 5.1

Firms in the Dow Jones Industrial Average

1896	1916	1928	1965	2021
American Cotton Oil	American Beet Sugar	Allied Chemical	Allied Chemical	3M
American Sugar	American Can	American Can	Aluminum Company of America	American Express
American Tobacco	American Car & Foundry	American Smelting	American Can	Amgen Inc
Chicago Gas	American Locomotive	American Sugar	American Tel. & Tel.	Apple
Distilling & Cattle Feeding	American Smelting	American Tobacco	American Tobacco	Boeing Co
General Electric	American Sugar	Atlantic Refining	Anaconda Copper	Caterpillar Inc
Laclede Gas	American Tel & Tel	Bethlehem Steel	Bethlehem Steel	Chevron Corp
National Lead	Anaconda Copper	Chrysler	Chrysler	Cisco Systems Inc
North American	Baldwin Locomotive	General Electric	Dupont	Coca-Cola
Tennessee	Central Leather	General Motors	Eastman Kodak	Dow
Coal & Iron	General Electric	General Railway Signal	General Electric	Goldman Sachs
U.S. Leather Pfd.	Goodrich	Goodrich	General Foods	Home Depot
U.S. Rubber	Republic Iron & Steel	International Harvester	General Motors	Honeywell Intl
	Studebaker	International Nickel	GoodYear	IBM
	Texas Co.	Mack Trucks	International Harvester	Intel
	U.S. Rubber	Nash Motors	International Nickel	Johnson & Johnson
	U.S. Steel	North American	International Paper Company	JPMorgan Chase
	Utah Copper	Paramount Publix	Johns-Manville	McDonald's Corp
	Westinghouse	Postum, Inc.	Owens-Illinois Glass	Merck
	Western Union	Radio Corp.	Procter & Gamble	Microsoft Corp
		Sears, Roebuck	Sears, Roebuck	Nike
		Standard Oil (N.J.)	Standard Oil of California	Procter & Gamble
		Texas Corp.	Standard Oil (N.J.)	Salesforce.com
		Texas Gulf Sulphur	Swift & Company	Travelers Companies Inc
		Union Carbide	Texaco Incorporated	UnitedHealth Group
		U.S. Steel	Union Carbide	Verizon Communications
		Victor Talking Machine	United Aircraft	Visa
		Westinghouse Electric	U.S. Steel	Walgreens Boots Alliance
		Woolworth	Westinghouse Electric	Wal-Mart Stores
		Wright Aeronautical	Woolworth	Walt Disney Co

Computation of the Dow Index

The original Dow Jones averages were simply the sum of the prices of the component shares divided by the number of stocks in the index. This divisor has to be adjusted over time to prevent discontinuities in the index when there were changes in the companies that constituted the average or stock splits

The Dow Industrials is unique in that it is a *price-weighted index*, which means that the prices of the component stocks are added together and then divided by the number of firms in the index. Before the computer, this was the fastest way to calculate the performance of the market. As a result, proportional movements of high-priced stocks in the Dow averages have a much greater impact than movements of lower-priced stocks, regardless of the size of the company. In February 2022, UnitedHealth Group constituted 9 percent of the index, with a market price of $460 a share, while Intel, the lowest-priced stock had a weight of less than 1 percent.[3] This price-weighting construction is becoming a more serious flaw in recent years, as high-priced stocks such as Tesla and Amazon.com must be excluded because their price is so much higher than others. When Google announced a 20-to-1 split in February 2022, there was immediate speculation that their motive was to be included in the Dow. One solution to the price problem with the Dow Industrials would be to switch to an equally weighted index that would not be dependent on prices.

Yet despite the odd construction of the Dow Jones Industrial Average, the return over the past 50 years (1971–2021) of 11.26 percent per year has beat the 11.14 percent annual return of the S&P 500 and the 10.85 percent return of the tech-heavy Nasdaq! Notwithstanding the stodgy image of the Dow Industrials, and the fact that the market value of their members stands at less than one-quarter of all stocks in the United States, the Dow Committee has through the years chosen their members wisely and few money managers have outperformed the index in the long run.

Long-Term Trends in the Dow Jones Industrial Average

Figure 5.1 plots the monthly high and low of the Dow Jones Industrial Average from its inception in 1885, corrected for changes in the cost of living. The inset shows the Dow Industrial Average uncorrected for inflation.

A *trendline* and a *channel* are created by statistically fitting the Dow on a time trend. The upper and lower bounds are 1 standard deviation, or 50 percent, above and below the trend. The slope of the trend line, 1.94 percent per year, is the average compound rate at which the Dow stocks have appreciated after inflation, since 1885. The Dow Jones average, like most other popular averages, does not include dividends, so the rise in the index greatly understates the total return on the Dow stocks. Since the average dividend yield on all stocks was about 4.3 percent over this period, the total annual real compound return on the Dow stocks was at least 6.2 percent per year over this period, particularly since the dividend yield on Dow stocks have generally been above the average stock.

The inflation-corrected Dow average has stayed within the channel about three-quarters of the time. When the Dow broke out of the channel to the upside, as it did in 1929, in the mid-1960s, and in 2000, stocks subsequently suffered poor short-term returns. Likewise, when stocks penetrated the channel on the downside, they subsequently experienced superior short-term returns.

FIGURE 5.1

Real and nominal Dow Jones Industrial Average, February 1885–December 2021, nominal inset

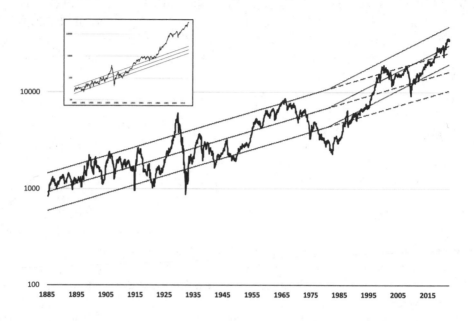

When Are Times *Really* Different?

Using past price movements to predict the future, however tempting, can be misleading. We often laugh when someone says, "This time is different!" But sometimes it is true.

Longstanding trends have been broken for good economic reasons. Uncorrected for inflation, the Dow Industrials broke and stayed above the trendline in the mid-1950s, as shown in the inset of Figure 5.2. This is because chronic inflation, caused by the shift to a paper money standard, propelled nominal stock prices justifiably above their previous trend. Those who used trendline analysis and who failed to plot stock prices in *real* instead of nominal terms would have sold in 1955 and *never* reentered the market.[44]

There is another economic justification why the channel, even defined in real terms, has shifted upward once more. As noted, stock indexes track only capital appreciation and therefore understate total returns, which include dividends. However, firms have been paying an ever-lower fraction of their earnings as dividends, using the difference to buy back their shares and invest capital in their firm; in recent years, a greater part of the return on stocks now comes through capital gains instead of dividend income. Since the average dividend yield on stocks has fallen 1.5 percentage points since 1980, a new channel has been drawn in Figure 5.1 with a slope that is 1.5 percentage points higher to represent the increase in the expected growth of capital gains. At the end of 2021, the Dow was slightly above the midpoint of the new channel.

VALUE-WEIGHTED INDEXES

Standard & Poor's Index

Although the Dow Jones Industrial Average was published in 1885, it was certainly not a comprehensive index of stock values, covering at most 30 stocks. In 1906 the Standard Statistics Company was formed, and in 1918 it began publishing the first index of stock values based on each stock's performance weighted by its capitalization, or market value, instead of its price as Dow Jones did. Capitalization weighting is now recognized as the best indication of the return on the overall market, and it is almost universally used in establishing market benchmarks.[5] In 1939, Alfred Cowles, founder of the Cowles Commission for Economic Research, constructed indexes of stock values back to 1871 that consisted of all stocks listed on the NYSE, using Standard Statistical Company's market-weighting techniques.

The Standard & Poor's stock price index began in 1923, and in 1926 it became the Standard & Poor's Composite Index, containing 90 stocks. The index was expanded to 500 stocks on March 4, 1957, and it became the S&P 500 Index. At that time, the value of the S&P 500 Index comprised about 90 percent of the value of all NYSE-listed stocks. The 500 stocks contained exactly 425 industrial, 25 railroad, and 50 utility firms. Before 1988, the number of companies in each industry was restricted to these guidelines, but since that date there are no industry restrictions on the firms selected.

A base value of 10 was chosen for the average value of the S&P Index from 1941 to 1943, so when the S&P 500 Index was first published in 1957, the average price of a share of stock (which stood between $45 and $50) was approximately equal to the value of the index. An investor at that time could easily identify with the changes in the S&P 500 Index, since a one-point change approximated the price change for an average stock.

The S&P 500 does not just contain the 500 firms (headquartered in the United States) that are the largest in market capitalization. There are stringent criteria for being admitted.[6] Since the S&P 500 Index does not update its members continuously, the index contains a few firms that are quite small, representing companies that have fallen in value and have yet to be replaced. As of the end of 2021, the total value of all S&P 500 companies was about $42 trillion, this constitutes about 90 percent of the value of all US stocks, not much different from the percentage that prevailed when the index was first formulated more than a half century earlier. A history of the S&P 500 Index and the insights that come from analyzing the stocks in this world-famous index are described in the next chapter.

Nasdaq Index

On February 8, 1971, the method of trading stocks underwent a revolutionary change. On that date, an automated quotation system called the Nasdaq (for National Association of Securities Dealers Automated Quotations) provided up-to-date bid and asked prices on 2,400 leading "over-the-counter" (OTC) stocks. Formerly, quotations for these unlisted stocks were submitted by the principal trader or by brokerage houses that carried an inventory. The Nasdaq linked the terminals of more than 500 market makers nationwide to a centralized computer system.

In contrast to the Nasdaq, stocks traded on the New York or American Stock Exchanges were assigned to a single specialist, who is charged with maintaining an orderly market in that stock. The Nasdaq changed the way quotes were disseminated and made trading these issues far more attractive to both investors and traders.

At the time that the Nasdaq was created, it was clearly more prestigious to be listed with an exchange (and preferably the NYSE) than be traded on the Nasdaq. Nasdaq stocks tended to be small or new firms that had recently gone public or did not meet the listing requirements of the larger exchanges. However, many young technology firms found the computerized Nasdaq system to be a natural home. Nasdaq has lower costs of listing and less stringent membership requirements.[7] Some tech firms, such as Intel and Microsoft, chose not to migrate to the Big Board, as the NYSE was termed, even when they qualified to do so.

The Nasdaq Index, which is a capitalization-weighted index of all stocks traded on the Nasdaq, was set at 100 on the first day of trading in 1971. It took almost 10 years to double to 200 and another 10 years to reach 500 in 1991. It reached its first major milestone of 1,000 in July 1995. As the interest in technology stocks grew, the rise in the Nasdaq Index accelerated, and it doubled its value to 2,000 in just three years. In the fall of 1999, the technology stock boom sent the Nasdaq into orbit. The index increased from 2,700 in October 1999 to a peak of 5,048.62 on March 10, 2000.

The increase in popularity of technology stocks resulted in a tremendous increase in volume on the Nasdaq. In 1971, the volume on this electronic exchange was a small fraction of that on the NYSE. By 1994, share volume on the Nasdaq exceeded that on the NYSE, and five years later, dollar volume on the Nasdaq surpassed the NYSE as well.[8]

No longer was the Nasdaq the home of small firms waiting to qualify for Big Board membership; by 1998, the capitalization of the Nasdaq had already exceeded that of the Tokyo Stock Exchange. At the market peak in March 2000, the total market value of firms traded on the Nasdaq reached nearly $6 trillion, more than one-half that of the NYSE, and more than any other stock exchange in the world. At the beginning of the millennium, Nasdaq's Microsoft and Cisco had the two largest market values in the world, and Nasdaq-listed Intel and Oracle were also among the top 10 in market capitalization.

When the technology bubble burst, trading and prices on the Nasdaq sunk rapidly. The Nasdaq Index declined from over 5,000 in March 2000 to 1,150 in October 2002, before rebounding to 3,000 at the end of 2012. Trading also fell off from an average of over 2.5 billion shares when prices peaked, to approximately 2 billion shares in 2007. But the strong showing of technology stocks in recent years sent the Nasdaq to a record of over 16,000 by the end of 2021.

Nevertheless, the significance of individual exchanges is declining rapidly, and the importance of floor trading has declined precipitously, as the overwhelming percentage of shares listed on the NYSE are now traded electronically. In 2008, the NYSE bought the American Stock Exchange, and in late 2012, the Intercontinental Exchange (ICE) acquired the NYSE. Even though it may sound exciting for news reporters to broadcast from the floor of the NYSE, built in 1903 to trade the world's largest and most important stock companies, the colonnaded building may soon turn dark.

Other Stock Indexes: The Center for Research in Security Prices (CRSP)

In 1959, Professor James Lorie of the Graduate School of Business of the University of Chicago received a request from the brokerage house Merrill Lynch, Pierce, Fenner & Smith. The firm wanted to investigate how well people had done investing in common stock and could not find reliable historical data. Professor Lorie teamed up with colleague Lawrence Fisher to build a database of securities data that could answer that question.

With computer technology in its infancy, Lorie and Fisher created the Center for Research in Security Prices (CRSP, pronounced "crisp") that compiled the first machine-readable file of stock prices dating from 1926; it was to become the accepted database for academic and professional research. The database contains all stocks traded on the New York and American Stock Exchanges and the Nasdaq. At the end of 2021, the market value of the 4,317 stocks in the database was over $50 trillion.

Figure 5.2 shows the size breakdown and total market capitalization of the stocks in this index. The top 500 firms, which closely mirror the S&P 500 Index, constitute 84.8 percent of the market value of all stocks. The top 1,000 firms in market value, which are virtually identical to the Russell 1000 published by the Russell Investment Group, comprise nearly 94 percent of the total value of equities. The Russell 2000 contains the next 2,000 largest companies, which adds an additional 6.3 percent to the market value of the total index. The Russell 3000, the sum of the Russell 1000 and 2000 indexes, comprises 99.9 percent of the value of all US stocks. The remaining 1,317 stocks constitute just 0.1 percent of the value of stocks traded.[9]

FIGURE 5.2

CRSP total market index, December 31, 2021

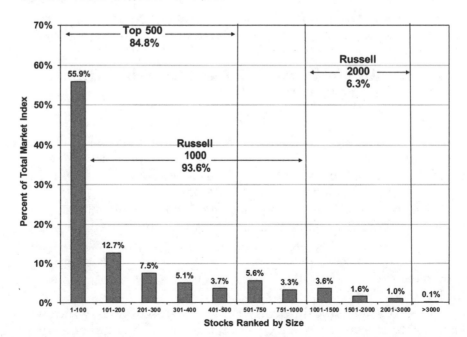

RETURN BIASES IN STOCK INDEXES

Because stock indexes such as the S&P 500 Index constantly add new growing firms and delete old dying ones, some investors believe that the return calculated from these indexes will be biased higher than the returns that investors can achieve in the overall market.

This is not the case. It is true that the best-performing stocks will stay in the S&P 500 Index, but this index misses the powerful upside move of many small and mid-sized issues. For example, Microsoft was not added to the S&P 500 Index until June 1994, eight years after going public, or Tesla, which was not admitted in October 2020, when it was an over-$500-billion company, the fifth largest company in the index. While small stock indexes are the incubators of some of the greatest growth stocks, they also contain those "fallen angels" that have dropped out of the large-cap indexes and are headed downward.

An index is *not* biased if investors can replicate or match its performance. To replicate an index, the date of additions and deletions to the index must be announced in advance so that new stocks can be bought, and deleted stocks can be sold. This is particularly important for issues that enter bankruptcy: the post-bankrupt price (which is usually zero) must be factored into the index. All the major stock indexes, such as Standard & Poor's, Dow Jones, and the Nasdaq, can be replicated by investors. Consequently, there is no statistical reason to believe that capitalization-based indexes give a biased representation of the return on the market.

WHY THE AVERAGE STOCK IS A LOSER WHILE THE STOCK MARKET IS A WINNER

As noted previously, there are over 3,000 stocks in the US database that researchers analyze to choose factors that beat the market. The average investor believes that if he or she picks one or two of those stocks at random, on average, they will realize the average rate of return, which has been almost 7 percent per year after inflation.

This is wrong, both on empirical and theoretical grounds. A simple example will suffice: suppose that each period there is an equal probability that a stock will go up 10 percent or down 10 percent, and there are thousands of stocks to pick from. For simplicity, you are planning two periods ahead, although the experiment makes the point even stronger for longer periods.

One-quarter of the time you will pick a win-win stock, which will go from 100 to 110, and then 121. One-half the time you will pick a win-lose or a lose-win stock, which will end at 99 (either by the path 100-110-99 or the path 100-90-99). And one-quarter of the time you will choose a lose-lose stock, which will go to 81. In other words, three-quarters of the time you will pick a losing stock, even those where the return to the market is, as constructed, zero. If we add a positive expected return to each stock's return, the results don't change: in this simple example you will underperform the market three-quarters of the time. Only by buying *all* the stocks will you realize the market rate of return.

Indeed researchers have found this is exactly true of the stock market. Henrik Bessembinder of Arizona State College has written a paper entitled, "Do Stocks Outperform T-bills?"[10] He found that slightly more than one-half of common stocks that have appeared in the CRSP database since 1926 have positive lifetime buy-and-hold returns and only about one out of four has beat Treasury bills. He concludes:

> While a slight majority (50.8 percent) of single stock strategies generated a positive 90-year return, the median 90-year return is only 9.5 percent, compared to a buy-and-hold return on Treasury bills of 1,928 percent. Only 27.5 percent of single stock strategies produced an accumulated 90-year return greater than one-month Treasury bills. That is, the data indicates that in the long term (defined here as the 90 years for which CRSP and Treasury bill returns are available) only about one-fourth of individual stocks outperform Treasuries. Further, only 4.0 percent of single stock strategies produced an accumulated return greater than the value-weighted market.[11]

Although Bessembinder attributes this to the "skewness" in stock returns, the preponderance of losers would be expected if stocks follow a perfectly symmetric percentage change, often called *geometric Brownian motion*, which is by far the most popular way to describe the motion of stock prices. There may indeed be skewness and "fat tails" in individual stock returns, but that is not a necessary condition for the average stock to underperform the market.

This study has been echoed by research done by JP Morgan. By looking at all the stocks in the Russell 3000 from 1980 through 2020, they found that the median stock had a return between zero and −10 percent most of the time, and this included reinvested dividends.[12]

The takeaway from these studies is simple. Broad diversification is the *only* guaranteed way to approximate the superior returns that stocks have historically offered investors. Putting together a narrow portfolio of stocks may be a big winner, but usually is a loser.

APPENDIX: WHAT HAPPENED TO THE 1896 ORIGINAL 12 DOW INDUSTRIALS?

None of the original 12 Dow companies or their successors now belong to the Dow Industrials. General Electric, booted out in 2018 after 122 years, was the last to exit. Only one stock (General Electric) retained its original name; five (American Cotton, American Tobacco, Chicago Gas, National Lead, and North American) became large public companies in their original industries; one (Tennessee Coal and Iron) was merged into U.S. Steel; and two (American Sugar and U.S. Rubber) went private— both in the 1980s. Surprisingly, only one (Distilling and Cattle Feeding) changed its product line (from alcoholic beverages to petrochemicals, although it still manufactures ethanol), and only one (U.S. Leather) liquidated. Here is a rundown of the original 12 stocks (market capitalizations as of December 2012):

American Cotton Oil became Best Food in 1923, Corn Products Refining in 1958, and finally, CPC International in 1969—a major food company with operations in 58 countries. In 1997, CPC spun off its corn-refining business as Corn Products International and changed its name to Bestfoods. Bestfoods was acquired by Unilever in October 2000 for $20.3 billion. Unilever (UN) is headquartered in the Netherlands. With a market value (2021) around $100 billion, it is the most highly valued successor of any of the original Dow 12 stocks.

American Sugar became Amstar in 1970 and went private in 1984. In September 1991 the company changed its name to Domino Foods, Inc., to reflect its world-famous Domino line of sugar products.

American Tobacco changed its name to American Brands (AMB) in 1969 and to Fortune Brands (FO) in 1997, a global consumer product holding company with core business in liquor, office products, golf equipment, and home improvements. American Brands sold its American Tobacco subsidiary, including the Pall Mall and Lucky Strike brands, to one-time subsidiary B.A.T in 1994 and remains a publicly traded company. In 2011 Fortune Brands changed its name to Beam Inc (BEAM), which operates as a distribution company in the spirits industry. In 2014, Beam was purchased by Suntory, a Japanese distillery and consumer products manufacturer and has remained private.

Chicago Gas became Peoples Gas Light & Coke Co. in 1897 and then Peoples Energy Corp., a utility holding company, in 1980. Peoples Energy Corp. (PGL) was bought by WPS Resources and changed its name in 2006 to Integrys Energy Group (TEG). In 2015 the firm was taken over by WEC Energy Group. PGL was a member of the Dow Jones Utility Average until May 1997.

Distilling and Cattle Feeding went through a long and complicated history. It changed its name to American Spirits Manufacturing and then to Distiller's Securities Corp. Two months after the passage of prohibition, the company changed its charter and became U.S. Food Products Corp. and then changed its name again to National Distillers and Chemical. The company became Quantum Chemical Corp. in 1989, a leading producer of petrochemicals and propane. Nearing bankruptcy, it was purchased for $3.4 billion by Hanson PLC, an Anglo-American conglomerate. It was spun off as Millennium Chemicals (MCH) in October 1996. Lyondell Chemical (LYO) bought Millennium Chemicals in November 2004. In 2007 Lyondell was taken over by the Dutch firm, which renamed itself LyondellBasell Industries (LYB).

General Electric (GE), founded in 1892, was in the Dow Jones Industrial Average for 122 years until it was removed in June 2018. GE was a huge manufacturing, broadcasting, and financial conglomerate that had the largest market value of any US stock for many months in the 1990s and early 2000s. Its value declined about 70 percent during the stewardship of Jeffrey Immelt, who followed the legendary Jack Welch in 2001. Immelt was removed from his position in 2017.

Laclede Gas (LG) changed its name to Laclede Group, Inc., and it is a retail distributor of natural gas in the St. Louis area. In 2017 Laclede changed its name to Spire Inc.

National Lead (NL) changed its name to NL Industries in 1971. The firm manufactures products relating to security, precision ball bearings, as well as titanium dioxide and specialty chemicals. It is still operating although it was removed from the Dow Jones Industrial Average in 1916.

North American became Union Electric Co. (UEP) in 1956, providing electricity in Missouri and Illinois. In January 1998, UEP merged with Cipsco (Central Illinois Public Service Co.) to form Ameren (AEE) Corp.

Tennessee Coal and Iron was bought out by U.S. Steel in 1907, and it became USX-U.S. Steel Group (X) in May 1991. In January 2002, the company changed its name back to U.S. Steel Corp. U.S. Steel was removed from the index in 1991.

U.S. Leather, one of the largest makers of shoes in the early part of this century, liquidated in January 1952, paying its shareholders $1.50 plus stock in an oil and gas company that was to become worthless.

U.S. Rubber became Uniroyal in 1961, and it was taken private in August 1985. In 1990 Uniroyal was purchased by the French company Michelin Group.

6

The S&P 500 Index

More Than One-Half Century of US Corporate History

Nearly 94% of all domestic active stock fund managers had underperformed their respective S&P benchmarks in the past 20 years.

—S&P Global, analysis as of mid-2021

The market is a device of transferring money from the inpatient to the patient.

—Warren Buffett

Out of the three major US stock market indexes—the Dow, the Nasdaq, and the S&P 500—only one became the standard for measuring the performance of large-cap US stocks. And as we shall learn in later chapters, it became a standard that very few active fund managers could beat.

The Standard & Poor's 500 Index was born on February 28, 1957, and it grew out of Standard & Poor's Composite Index, a capitalization-weighted index begun in 1926 that contained 90 large stocks. Ironically, the 1926 index excluded the largest stock in the world at that time, American Telephone and Telegraph, because S&P did not want to let the performance of such a large firm dominate the index. To correct this omission and to recognize the growth of new firms in the postwar period, Standard & Poor's compiled an index of 500 of the largest industrial, rail, and utility firms that traded on the NYSE.

The S&P 500 Index comprised nearly 90% percent of the total value of firms traded on the Big Board in 1957. It rapidly became the standard for comparing the performance of institutions and money managers investing in large US stocks. The S&P 500 Index originally contained exactly 425 industrial, 25 rail, and 50 utility firms, but these groupings were abandoned in 1988 in order to maintain, as S&P claimed, an index that included "500 leading companies in leading industries of the economy."

Since its creation, the index has been continually updated by adding new firms that meet Standard & Poor's criteria for market value, earnings, and liquidity while deleting an equal number that fall below these standards.[1] The number of new firms added to the S&P 500 Index from its inception in 1957 is about 1,360, an average of about 20 per year. These new firms constitute on average about 5 percent of the market value of the index.

The highest number of new firms added to the index in a single year occurred in 1976, when Standard & Poor's added 60 stocks, including 15 banks and 10 insurance carriers. Until that year, the only financial stocks in the index were consumer finance companies, because banks and insurance companies were traded in the over-the-counter (OTC) market, and timely price data were not available until the Nasdaq exchange began in 1971. In 2000, at the peak of the technology bubble, 49 new firms were added to the index, the highest since 1976, when for the first time Nasdaq stocks were included. In 2003, just after the technology bubble collapsed, the number of additions fell to a record-tying low of eight.

SECTOR ROTATION IN THE S&P 500 INDEX

The evolution of the US economy during the past half-century has brought about profound changes in its industrial landscape. Steel, chemical, auto, and oil companies dominated our economy in the middle of the last century. Today health care, technology, finance, and other consumer firms hold sway.

Increasingly, active investors use sector analysis to allocate their portfolios. The most popular industry classification system was formulated in 1999 when Standard & Poor's joined Morgan Stanley to create the Global Industrial Classification Standard (GICS). This system arose from the earlier Standard Industrial Code (SIC) system devised by the US government, which had grown less suited to our service-based economy.[2]

The GICS divides the economy into 10 sectors: *materials* (chemicals, papers, steel, and mining), *industrials* (capital goods, defense, transportation, and commercial and environmental services), *energy* (exploration, production, marketing, refining of oil and gas, and coal), *utilities* (electric, gas, water, and nuclear generating or transmission firms), *telecommunication services* (fixed line, cellular, wireless, and bandwidth), *consumer discretionary* (household durables, autos, apparel, hotels, restaurants, media, and retailing), *consumer staples* (food, tobacco, personal products, retailing, and hypermarkets), *health care* (equipment producers, health care providers, pharmaceuticals, and biotechs), *financial* (commercial and investment banking, mortgages, brokerage, insurance), and *information technology* (software services, Internet, home entertainment, data processing, computers, and semiconductors). In 2016 the *real estate* sector (real estate investment trusts, or REITs) was broken out from the financials to form an 11th sector.

FIGURE 6.1

Sector weights of S&P 500, 1957–2021

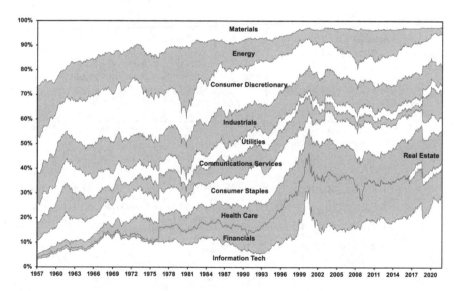

The share of the market value of each of these sectors in the S&P 500 Index from 1957 through 2021 is displayed in Figure 6.1. Many of the changes have been dramatic. The materials sector, by far the largest with a 26.6 percent market share in 1957, has become one of the smallest (along with utilities) by the end of 2021. In fact, the materials and energy sectors made up almost one-half of the market value of the index in 1957, but by 2021 these two sectors together constituted only 5.3 percent of the index. On the other hand, the financial, health care, and technology sectors, which started off as the three smallest sectors and comprised only 6 percent of the index in 1957, commanded more than one-half of the market value of all S&P 500 firms by 2021.

Although there is a positive correlation between the share of a sector in the S&P 500 and the return to that sector, the relation is not strong. Take a look at Table 6.1, which shows the beginning and ending weights of each sector and the difference, or "excess" return, of each sector relative to the S&P 500 Index.

TABLE 6.1

S&P 500 sector weight and return

Sector	1957 Weight	2021 Weight	Weight Change	Excess Return
Information Tech	3.1%	29.2%	26.1%	1.5%
Health Care	1.2%	13.3%	12.1%	2.6%
Financials*	5.9%	10.7%	4.8%	-1.5%
Telecom Svc	7.6%	10.2%	2.6%	-1.2%
Consumer Staples	5.9%	5.9%	0.0%	1.8%
Consumer Discretionary	14.9%	12.5%	-2.3%	0.7%
Industrials	12.2%	7.8%	-4.4%	-0.7%
Utilities	7.7%	2.5%	-5.2%	-0.9%
Energy	20.0%	2.7%	-17.3%	-0.8%
Materials	26.6%	2.6%	-24.1%	-2.2%

*Financials added to S&P 500 in July 1976, weight went from <1% to 6%.
Excess returns for financials from 12/31/76

To be sure, technology and health care—which grew dramatically—did well, and materials—which shrunk the most—did the poorest. But look at financials, telecoms, and especially energy; despite the fact that the energy sector shrank by more than 85 percent, energy stocks trailed the return on S&P by less than 1 percent. Financials and telecommunications, which grew rapidly, actually lagged behind the returns of the "disappearing" energy sector!

The reason why the rising or falling market shares do not necessarily correlate with good or poor returns to investors is because change in sector weights often reflects the change in the *number* of firms, not just the change in the *value* of individual firms. Furthermore, return depends on the price you pay. In this book we will see repeatedly that valuation—paying a low price relative to earnings—is generally more important than growth for long-term investors. That is why the oils have done surprisingly well.

This strength of the oil sector is brought home by the surprising results shown in Table 6.2, which ranks the returns of the 20 *largest* (not the *best-performing*) companies that Standard & Poor's included in their first list in 1957. One feature that stands out is that all 9 oil companies on the list finished in the top 10, and the returns on all but one of the oil companies beat the S&P 500 over the subsequent 64 years.[3]

The returns are calculated by assuming that the shares were bought when the index was created, all dividends were reinvested, and in the event that firms were spun off from the original firm, the spin-offs were also held with dividends reinvested. That's why three of the four firms that went bankrupt had positive total returns. General Motors spun off Raytheon, Eastman Kodak spun off Eastman Chemical, and Sears spun off Allstate and Morgan Stanley, which have proved so successful that the total return to Sears did not fall that far behind the S&P 500 Index despite the fact the Sears shares went to zero. Alas, Bethlehem Steel, which had no spin-offs, had a zero return.

TABLE 6.2

Returns of the 20 largest original S&P 500 firms

Return Rank	1957 Name	3/1/1957-2/4/2022 Return	1957 Market Cap Rank
1	Gulf Oil	11.90%	6
2	Socony Mobil Oil	11.66%	13
3	Standard Oil Co CA	11.52%	10
4	Royal Dutch Petroleum	11.46%	12
5	Standard Oil Co NJ	11.24%	2
6	Shell Oil	11.10%	14
7	Texaco	11.01%	8
8	Phillips Petroleum	10.95%	20
9	Standard Oil Co Ind	10.32%	16
10	Union Carbide	10.30%	7
11	IBM	10.18%	11
12	Sears	9.96%	15
13	AT&T	9.50%	1
14	General Electric	8.19%	5
15	Dupont	7.75%	4
16	Eastman Kodak	7.49%	19
17	Aluminum Co of America	6.14%	17
18	General Motors	5.05%	3
19	United States Steel Corp	4.99%	9
20	Bethlehem Steel	-100.00%	18
	Average Top 10	11.22%	
	Average Top 20	10.33%	
	S&P 500	10.85%	

The Performance of the S&P 500 Index Versus the Original Stocks

Many investors, as well as professionals, are likely to believe that the superior performance of the S&P 500 Index over time is due to the continual inflow of new firms into the index. That is not necessarily the case. In 2005, Jeremy Schwartz and I published an article, "Long-Term Returns on the Original S&P 500 Companies," that demonstrated that if an investor bought and held the original 500 companies that comprised the index when it was founded in March 1957, and held them until the end 2006, that investor would have outperformed the actual S&P 500 by nearly 1 percentage point a year![4]

Why did this happen? How could the new companies that fueled US economic growth and made America the preeminent economy in the world underperform the original firms? The answer is twofold: First, we shall see that many of the original companies were acquired by stronger companies that became long-term winners. Second, although the earnings and sales of many of the newer firms grew faster than those of the older firms, the price that investors paid for these stocks was often too high to generate superior returns. In fact, over the period from 1957 through 2006, only the consumer discretionary sector added firms that have outperformed the original firms put into the index.

The outperformance of the original companies to the S&P 500 Index continued until the mid-2010s, but it ended when some of the new technology companies that had been added, such as Google, Apple, Amazon.com, and Microsoft, began their unprecedented run. Can the superior performance of these tech giants continue? Before we address that question, it is important to analyze which stocks have been the biggest winners since the inception of the S&P 500.

TOP-PERFORMING FIRMS

The 25 best-performing firms of the original S&P 500 that have survived with their corporate structure intact are shown in Table 6.3. All of them have outperformed the 10.78 percent annual return of the index itself.

By far the best-performing stock was Philip Morris, which in 2003 changed its name to Altria Group and in 2008 spun off its international division (Philip Morris International).[5] Philip Morris introduced the world to the Marlboro Man, one of the world's most recognized icons, two years before the formulation of the S&P 500 Index. Marlboro cigarettes subsequently became the world's bestselling brand, propelling Philip Morris stock upward.

TABLE 6.3

Returns on the top-performing original S&P 500 firms

Ticker	Original Name	Current Name	Annualized Returns 03/1957–12/2021
MO	PHILIP MORRIS INC	ALTRIA GROUP INC	18.02%
ABT	ABBOTT LABS	ABBOTT LABORATORIES	15.76%
SPGI	MCGRAW HILL PUBLISHING INC	S & P GLOBAL INC	14.72%
PEP	PEPSI COLA CO	PEPSICO INC	14.03%
BMY	BRISTOL MYERS CO	BRISTOL MYERS SQUIBB CO	13.77%
KO	COCA COLA CO	COCA COLA CO	13.75%
DE	DEERE & CO IL	DEERE & CO	13.74%
CL	COLGATE PALMOLIVE CO	COLGATE PALMOLIVE CO	13.61%
HSY	HERSHEY CHOCOLATE CORP	HERSHEY CO	13.60%
PFE	PFIZER CHAS & CO INC	PFIZER INC	13.52%
CR	CRANE CO	CRANE CO	13.47%
KR	KROGER COMPANY	KROGER COMPANY	13.40%
MRK	MERCK & CO INC	MERCK & CO INC NEW	13.36%
CVS	MELVILLE SHOE CORP	C V S HEALTH CORP	13.27%
PG	PROCTER & GAMBLE CO	PROCTER & GAMBLE CO	13.00%
ETN	EATON MFG CO	EATON CORP PLC	12.99%
ITT	INTERNATIONAL TEL & TELEG CORP	I T T INC	12.76%
GIS	GENERAL MILLS INC	GENERAL MILLS INC	12.59%
MSI	MOTOROLA INC	MOTOROLA SOLUTIONS INC	12.57%
CCK	CROWN CORK & SEAL INC	CROWN HOLDINGS INC	12.44%
ADM	ARCHER DANIELS MIDLAND CO	ARCHER DANIELS MIDLAND CO	12.11%
BA	BOEING AIRPLANE CO	BOEING CO	12.05%
KMB	KIMBERLY CLARK CORP	KIMBERLY CLARK CORP	11.63%
PPG	PITTSBURGH PLATE GLASS CO	P P G INDUSTRIES INC	11.37%
TT	INGERSOLL RAND CO	TRANE TECHNOLOGIES PLC	11.31%

The average annual return on Philip Morris over the past almost 65 years, at 18.02 percent per year, is almost double the 10.78 percent return on the S&P 500 Index. This return means that $1,000 invested in Philip Morris on March 1, 1957, would have accumulated to over $45 million by the end of 2021, about 600 times the $750,000 accumulation in the S&P 500 Index.

Philip Morris's bounty did not extend to only its own stockholders. Philip Morris eventually became the owner of *10* other original S&P 500 firms, such as General Foods, Del Monte, Standard Brands, National Dairy, and Nabisco, among others. Many investors became enormously wealthy because the shares of their firms were exchanged for Philip Morris shares. Riding on the coattails of such winners has become an unexpected windfall for many stockholders. The source of the superior returns to Philip Morris is discussed in more detail in Chapter 11.

TOP-PERFORMING SURVIVOR FIRMS

As can be seen from Table 6.3, many of the most successful original S&P companies kept their own name, brand, and industry. There were two exceptions. McGraw Hill Publishing transformed into S&P Global and spun off its book operations. And the most surprising high performer was Melville Shoe Corporation, founded in 1892.

Shoe companies have been among the worst investments over the past century; even Warren Buffett bemoans his purchase of Dexter Shoe in 1991. Melville Shoe was fortunate enough to buy a few small retail stores specializing in personal health products in 1969 called Consumer Value Stores. The chain quickly became the most profitable division of the company, and in 1996 Melville changed its name to CVS. As a result, a woeful shoe manufacturer turned into the largest and most successful retail pharmacy chain in the United States through management's fortuitous (and serendipitous) purchase of a small retail drug chain.

WHAT HAPPENED TO "TOP DOGS" OF THE MARKET?

Eleven firms have occupied the position of the highest market value, or "top dog" since the CRSP records on individual stocks were created in 1926; they are shown in Table 6.4, which includes how many months they have been top dog, when they first and last appeared, and the maximum number of consecutive months they occupied the top position. All 11 of these firms have also been top dog in the S&P 500 Index.

TABLE 6.4

Highest capitalization stocks, 1926–2021, monthly appearances

Rank	Company Name	Frequency	Max Number of Consecutive Mo	First Date Top Cap	Last Date Top Cap
1	A T & T CORP	456	251	Dec-26	Oct-94
2	INTERNATIONAL BUSINESS MACHS COR	236	89	Jul-67	Feb-91
3	GENERAL ELECTRIC CO	117	46	Sep-93	Dec-05
4	STANDARD OIL OF NJ	116	68	Jan-57	Jul-13
5	APPLE INC	103	63	Sep-11	Dec-21
6	GENERAL MOTORS CORP	69	24	Jul-27	Nov-58
7	MICROSOFT CORP	40	17	Sep-98	Oct-21
8	DU PONT E I DE NEMOURS & CO	1	1	Jun-55	Jun-55
9	PHILIP MORRIS COS INC	1	1	Mar-92	Mar-92
10	WAL MART STORES INC	1	1	Nov-92	Nov-92
11	AMAZON COM INC	1	1	Jan-19	Jan-19

American Telephone and Telegraph (AT&T), the private regulated phone company that served as the primary phone provider to the nation until it was broken up in 1984, has been top dog for 436 months, including 251 consecutive months over a 21-year period from 1929 to 1950. The next most frequent was IBM, followed by General Electric, and then ExxonMobil, which first took the reins from AT&T just two months before the S&P 500 Index was founded.

The fifth most frequent top dog is Apple, which entered top position in September of 2011 and still reigned supreme at the end of 2021. Since 2011, Apple has dropped from first place a number of times, as ExxonMobil and Microsoft, took the highest honors. General Motors, which was on top for 40 months, rounds out the top seven. There are four "single month" top dogs Dupont, Philip Morris, Wal-Mart, and Amazon.com, which just nosed ahead of Apple for one month in January 2019.

Table 6.5 shows the subsequent 1-year, 10-year, 20-year, 30-year, and lifetime returns on these top dogs after they have first achieved the status of the most valuable company in the United States.

TABLE 6.5

Subsequent returns to highest cap stocks

First Date Top Cap	Company Name	Next 1 Year		Next 10 Years		Next 20 Years		Next 30 Years		Return Until Dec 2021		
		Stock	Market	Stock	Market	Stock	Market	Stock	Market	Stock	Market	No. of Months
Dec-26	A T & T CORP	25.6%	32.6%	10.6%	6.0%	8.0%	5.7%	7.7%	9.2%	7.7%	10.1%	947
Jul-67	INTERNATIONAL BUSINESS MACHS COR	34.5%	8.5%	4.8%	3.6%	9.2%	10.7%	8.2%	11.9%	7.3%	10.6%	653
Sep-93	GENERAL ELECTRIC CO	3.4%	2.4%	16.4%	9.6%	8.6%	8.9%			4.2%	10.8%	339
Jan-57	STANDARD OIL OF NJ	-8.2%	-2.3%	5.4%	10.8%	8.4%	7.8%	12.4%	10.7%	10.5%	10.8%	779
Sep-11	APPLE INC	75.6%	29.9%	28.3%	16.9%					30.4%	17.4%	123
Jul-27	GENERAL MOTORS CORP	81.0%	23.6%	8.9%	4.2%	7.9%	4.9%	13.5%	8.8%			983
Sep-98	MICROSOFT CORP	64.6%	27.7%	1.4%	3.9%	9.7%	8.0%			13.6%	9.3%	279
Jun-55	DU PONT E I DE NEMOURS & CO	-5.0%	16.0%	8.1%	11.0%	2.7%	7.7%	4.8%	9.7%	7.8%	10.3%	747
Mar-92	PHILIP MORRIS COS INC	-12.7%	15.6%	12.9%	12.6%	14.5%	8.7%			13.1%	10.9%	357
Nov-92	WAL MART STORES INC	-10.6%	11.0%	13.5%	9.6%	9.0%	8.3%			9.5%	10.8%	349
Jan-19	AMAZON COM INC	16.9%	20.1%							25.5%	23.3%	35
Average		24.1%	16.8%	11.0%	8.8%	8.7%	7.9%	9.3%	10.1%	13.0%	12.1%	508.3
Average (excluding DuPont, Philip Morris, Amazon, and Walmart)		39.5%	17.5%	10.8%	7.9%	8.6%	7.7%	10.4%	10.1%	12.3%	11.2%	586.1

If you look at the averages (either including or excluding the last four firms that had single-year appearances), it appears that becoming top dog is not the same curse as being on the cover of *Sports Illustrated*![6] In fact, the average subsequent 1-, 10-, and 20-year average returns have beat the S&P 500 Index itself, although the outperformance definitely fades over time. For 30-year and longer horizons, the average performance of these top dogs closely mimics the S&P 500 Index.

But these averages mask very uneven individual performances. Virtually all the older firms, save Philip Morris and Standard Oil of NJ, significantly underperformed in the long run. AT&T and General Motors alternated number-one status from the 1920s until the mid-1950s, until Standard Oil of NJ (now ExxonMobil) reached the top in January 1957. Both AT&T and General Motors outperformed the market for the next 20 years after becoming top dog, and General Motors outperformed for the next 30 years. Over time, both firms faded, and General Motors eventually went bankrupt.

Standard Oil of NJ performed very differently than most of the other top dogs, generally continuing to outperform the market after reaching the top. The oil company underperformed the index for years after reaching the top, but then surged in the 1980s, and its long-term returns virtually matched that of the S&P 500. The sad story of General Electric is well known, although for the 10-year period after reaching the top in 1993, its performance also far exceeded the market. The current technology giants—Microsoft, which debuted as top dog in 1998; Apple, which made the list in September 2011; and Amazon.com, which topped Apple and Microsoft for one month in January 2019—have, like most other top dogs, subsequently far outpaced the market.

The longer-term history of these tech giants is yet to be written. IBM is a cautionary tale, having entered this elite group in 1967. Big Blue hugely outperformed the market for one year and then faltered, ultimately significantly underperforming the index. Philip Morris, although it spent only one month as top dog in March 1992, has been the only true long-term winner.

CONCLUSION

The history of the S&P 500 Index offers a view of the changes in American industry since the middle of the last century. It also provides insights into the firms that can offer investors superior returns. The fact that the performance of the original S&P 500 firms outperformed the continuously updated index for many decades surprises most investors. The growth of a sector's market value over time in no way guarantees that investors will earn superior returns in that sector. The fact that since 1957 investment in the oil industry has virtually matched the performance despite the massive shrinkage of that sector is testament to that fact.

This chapter also shows that reaching the pinnacle of market value is not a death knell for the stock of firms that reach that status, and these often continue to outperform for years, if not decades, afterward. But do not hold these winners too long; many eventually lose their mojo and begin to underperform the market.

Is this a warning for the current set of big tech stocks that crowd the top of the S&P 500 Index? Perhaps it is. In the long run, there is an old Wall Street expression: "No tree grows to the sky and no bull market lasts forever."

Sources of Shareholder Value

Earnings and Dividends

The importance of dividends for providing wealth to investors is self-evident. Dividends not only dwarf inflation, growth, and changing valuations levels individually, but they also dwarf the combined importance of inflation, growth, and changing valuation levels.[1]

—**Robert Arnott, 2003**

It is just after 4 p.m. eastern time and the major US stock exchanges have just closed. The anchor of one of the major financial networks excitedly proclaims: "Tesla just out with its earnings! It beat the Street by 80 cents and its price has jumped 5 percent in after-hours trading."

Earnings drive stock prices, and their announcements are eagerly awaited by Wall Street. But exactly how should we calculate earnings, and how do firms turn earnings into stockholder value? This chapter addresses these questions.

DISCOUNTED CASH FLOWS

The fundamental source of asset values derives from the expected cash flows that can be obtained from owning that asset. For stocks, these cash flows come from dividends or other cash distributions resulting from earnings or the sale of the firm's assets. Stock prices also depend on the rate at which these future cash flows are discounted. Future cash flows are *discounted* because cash received in the future is not valued as highly as cash received in the present. The discount rate is composed of two factors: (1) the *risk-free rate of interest*, a yield on a safe alternative asset such as government or other AAA-rated securities, and (2) the risk associated with the *realization* of expected cash flows, which induces stock investors to demand an additional premium to the risk-free rate. For stocks, the total discount rate is also called the *required return on equity* or the *cost of equity*.

SOURCES OF SHAREHOLDER VALUE

Earnings are the source of cash flows to shareholders. *Earnings* (also called *profits* or *net income*) are the difference between the revenues to the firm and the costs of production. The costs of production include all labor and material costs, interest on debt, taxes, and allowances for depreciation on tangible and intangible assets.

Firms can transform these earnings into cash flows for shareholders in a number of ways. The first, and historically the most important, is:

- Payment of cash dividends

Earnings that are not used to pay dividends are called *retained earnings*. Retained earnings, in turn, can create value by raising future cash flows through:

- Retirement of debt, which reduces interest expense
- Investment in securities or other assets, which raises future cash flows
- Investment in capital projects designed to increase future profits
- Importantly, repurchase of the firm's own shares, which is known as a *buyback* and raises future per share earnings

The last source of value, buybacks, deserves some elaboration. Clearly, shareholders who sell their shares to the company engaged in buybacks receive cash for their stock, and in this way, buybacks are quite like selective cash dividends. But those shareholders who do not sell will realize greater *per share* earnings and *per share* dividends in the future, as the firms' earnings are divided among a smaller number of shares. For these shareholders, a buyback is similar to an automatic reinvestment of cash flows into the firms. It should be noted that buybacks do not, in theory, change the *current* price of shares, since the present value of future cash flows does not change.[2] Nevertheless, we shall show that *over time* buybacks increase the growth rate in per share earnings and thus increase the future price of shares, generating capital gains that replace the dividends the shareholders would have received.

In recent years, there has been significant controversy and opposition to share buybacks.[3] Most of this opposition is based on fundamental misunderstandings. Some believe that buybacks substitute for capital investment, and somehow if buybacks were restricted, firms' capital investment would increase.

This belief is incorrect. Buybacks are a direct alternative to paying dividends and are motivated primarily by the way our tax system treats cash dividends. As noted previously, buybacks, implemented in lieu of cash dividends, increase share prices over time. However, these price increases, in contrast to dividends, are not taxed until a shareholder sells his or her shares, and then favorable capital gains taxes are applicable. A change in the tax code that allows the tax on dividends that are immediately reinvested in shares (such as is done in automatic dividend reinvestment plans) to be deferred until the shares are sold would, in my opinion, significantly reduce the motivation for buybacks and increase cash dividends.

A secondary reason for the increase in buybacks in recent years is the increase in management and employee stock options. Since most options are usually based on share price alone (not including dividends), it is in the interest of management to follow a low-dividend policy, which boosts future share prices. Changes in regulations that encourage (or require) corporations to base options on *total return*, which includes dividends paid instead of price alone, would help correct this bias against dividends.

Buybacks also do not stifle investment. Ironically, there is evidence that the market believes firms undertake *too many* capital projects, as we will see in Part III. Investors routinely penalize firms with high investment levels. Firms should only undertake capital projects when the promised return on the project exceeds the cost of equity capital. Therefore, restricting buybacks would do little to increase a firm's capital expenditures. Instead it would lead to an increase in cash dividends and more likely, the investment in other securities that generate attractive returns. A change in our tax code would be the most efficient way to reduce the level of buybacks.

HISTORICAL TRENDS IN EARNINGS AND DIVIDENDS

Figure 7.1 plots the real stock price index, real per share reported (GAAP) earnings, and real per share dividends in the United States from 1871 through 2021. Over the whole period, earnings have supported the rise in stock prices, although prices have gone up more than earnings, reflecting a rise in the valuation, or price-to-earnings (P/E) ratio, of the market. The reason for this increase in valuation will be discussed in Chapter 10. Real dividends per share have lagged behind earnings, but this is because firms are buying back more shares, depressing dividend growth in the 1980s and 1990s, but as noted above raising the growth rate of dividends subsequently.

FIGURE 7.1

Real per share reported earnings, dividends, and prices

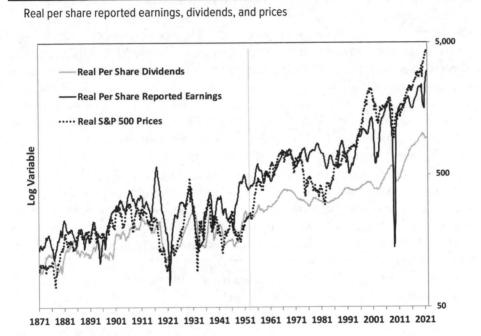

The Gordon Dividend Growth Model of Stock Valuation

To show how dividend policy impacts the price of a stock, it is useful to understand the *Gordon dividend growth model* developed by Roger Gordon in 1962.[4] A little math is required to derive this important but often misused formula.

The price of a stock P is the discounted value of all future cash flows, which we shall call dividends. In this case, it can be shown that if future dividends per share grow at a constant rate g and the discount rate on these future dividends is r, then the price per share of a stock P can be written as follows:

$$P = d/(1+ r) + d(1+ g)/(1+ r)^2 + d(1+ g)^2/(1 + r)^3 + \ldots \text{ or}$$

$$\textbf{Price} = d/(r - g)$$

The price of a stock is the level of dividends divided by the discount rate, minus the growth rate of those dividends. For example, if the dividend is $5 per share, the discount rate for the stock is 10 percent, and the growth rate of these dividends is 5 percent per year, the price of the stock would be $100 per share.

Since the Gordon model formula is a function of the per share dividend and the per share dividend growth rate, it appears that dividend policy is crucial to determining the value of the stock, but this is not necessarily so. As long as one specific condition holds—*that the firm is expected to earn the same return on its retained earnings as the return on its other assets*—then dividend policy, or what fraction of earnings are paid in dividends, *does not* impact the price of the stock or the market value of the firm.[5] This is because dividends that are not paid today become retained earnings that generate higher dividends in the future, and as it will be shown, the present value of those dividends is unchanged no matter when they are paid.

The management can, of course, influence the time *path* of dividends. The lower the *dividend payout ratio*, which is the ratio of dividends to earnings, the smaller the current dividends will be. But because a lower dividend today increases retained earnings, future dividends will rise and eventually exceed the level of dividends that would have prevailed if the dividend payout ratio was not cut. Assuming the firm earns the same return on its retained earnings as it does on its equity capital, the present value of these dividend streams will be identical no matter what payout ratio is chosen.

This equivalence can be shown by using the Gordon dividend growth model. Let us assume that the required equity return (the discount rate) r is 10 percent, all earnings are paid as dividends, there is no dividend growth ($g = 0$), and the dividend level d is $10 per share. In this case the price of the shares, by the Gordon model, would be $100.

Now assume that firm lowered its dividend payout ratio from 100 percent to 90 percent, thereby reducing its per share dividend (d) to $9, and increased its retained earnings by $1. If the firm earns 10 percent on its retained earnings (the same as its other capital), then earnings per share next year will be $10.10, and the dividend, at a 90 percent payout ratio, will be $9.09. If the firm maintains this payout ratio, the growth rate in per share dividends will be 1 percent. Setting $g = 0.01$ and $d = $9 into the Gordon growth model yields the same $100 price of the stock as before. As long as r remains at 10 percent, the price per share of the stock will rise at 1 percent a year, identical to the growth of per share earnings and per share dividends, and the total return to shareholders will remain at 10 percent, with 9 percentage points of the return coming from the dividend yield and 1 percentage point coming from stock appreciation. The firm can choose any proportion of the return that comes from dividends and capital gains by varying the dividend payout ratio from zero to 100 percent, but the return to stockholders remains at 10 percent.

The exact same result would hold if the firm used its retained earnings to buy back shares. In the preceding case, the $1 not used to pay dividends would be used to purchase 1 percent of the shares per year. The 1 percent reduction in the number of shares would mean that *per share* dividends (and *per share* earnings) will rise by 1 percent per year. Again, the buyback policy, like the dividend policy, will not change the value of the firm.

This theory is borne out by the long-run data shown in Table 7.1, which summarizes the historical growth rate of dividends and earnings, and their relation with the dividend payout ratio. Over the whole period, dividends are by far the most important source of shareholder return. From 1871, the real return on stocks has averaged 7.1 percent, composed of an average dividend yield of about 4.3 percent and real capital gains of 2.5 percent.[6] The capital gains have been generated mostly by the growth of per share earnings, which have increased at an annual rate of 2.05 percent over the past 150 years.

TABLE 7.1

Long-term real stock market variables

	Reported EPS Growth	Real Dividend Growth	Dividend Yield	Real Capital Gains	Real Stock Returns	Payout Ratio
1871-2021	2.05%	1.56%	4.29%	2.59%	7.1%	57.2%
1871-1945	0.67%	0.74%	5.31%	1.32%	6.8%	66.8%
1946-2021	3.43%	2.38%	3.28%	3.85%	7.4%	49.0%

There has been a significant change in dividend and earnings growth since World War II. The growth rate of per share earnings has increased, while the dividend payout ratio and the dividend yield have decreased. Before World War II, firms paid two-thirds of their earnings as dividends (and an even higher proportion in the nineteenth century). Since retained earnings were too small to fund expansion, firms issued more shares to obtain needed capital, reducing per share earnings growth. However, in the postwar period, firms reduced dividends and generated sufficient earnings so that the need to issue new shares to finance growth declined. This is why in the postwar period, per share earnings and dividend growth increased significantly.

The historical statistics confirm these results. Before World War II, the average dividend payout ratio was 66.8 percent and since then it has fallen to 49 percent. This reduced the dividend yield from 5.31 percent to 3.28 percent, more than 2 percentage points. The lower dividend yield has resulted in an acceleration of per share earnings growth from 0.67 percent to 3.43 percent, and the rate of growth of capital gains has risen accordingly by more than 2 percentage points. The reduction in the dividend yield, combined with an increase in the growth rate of dividends and earnings, is completely consistent with orthodox financial theory. Also consistent is the fact that the total return to stocks after World War II is only marginally higher than before the war.

It should be noted that although the rate of growth of the forward-looking dividend per share increases after the dividend payout ratio is cut, the *realized* rate of growth of dividends, which includes the period of the cut, will for many years be less than the previous growth rate of dividends. This is indeed what the historical data show in Table 7.1, as the rate of growth of dividends per share has lagged behind that of per share earnings or price appreciation as firms substituted buybacks and other forms of creating value for cash dividends. However, if the dividend payout ratio remains steady at these levels, theory dictates that future dividend growth will be higher relative to past trends.

Discount Future Dividends, Not Earnings

Although earnings determine the level of dividends paid by the firm, the price of the stock is always equal to the present value of all future *dividends*, and not the present value of future earnings. Earnings not paid to investors can have value only if they are paid as dividends or other cash disbursements at a later date. Valuing stock as the present discounted value of future *earnings* is manifestly wrong and overstates the value of a firm.

John Burr Williams, one of the greatest investment analysts of the early part of the last century and the author of the classic *Theory of Investment Value*, argued this point persuasively in 1938:

> Most people will object at once to the foregoing formula for valuing stocks by saying that it should use the present worth of future earnings, not future dividends. But should not earnings and dividends both give the same answer under the implicit assumptions of our critics? If earnings not paid out in dividends are all successfully reinvested at compound interest for the benefit of the stockholder, as the critics imply, then these earnings should produce dividends later; if not, then they are money lost. Earnings are only a means to an end, and the means should not be mistaken for the end.[7]

One may ask how investors should value a firm such as Warren Buffett's Berkshire Hathaway, which pays no dividends. Berkshire Hathaway generates substantial cash flows, which, if they are not invested in new businesses, are used to buy back shares. These cash flows could be used to pay future dividends. At any time, if the firm's value falls below the value indicated by these cash flows, an investor group could tender the shares, obtain control, and either pay dividends or sell the individual companies that comprise Berkshire Hathaway. It is the *potential* that either current or future owners of a firm *could* sell their assets (or pay dividends) that keeps share value at true market value, even though no dividends are being paid now.[8]

EARNINGS CONCEPTS

Clearly, dividends cannot be paid on a sustained basis unless the firm is profitable. As a result, it is critical that a definition of earnings be developed that gives investors the best possible measure of the sustainable cash that the firm can generate for the payment of dividends.

Earnings are the difference between revenues and costs. But the determination of earnings is not just a "cash-in minus cash-out" calculation, since many costs and revenues, such as capital expenditures, depreciation, and contracts for future delivery, extend over many years. Furthermore, some expenses and revenues are one-time or "extraordinary" items, such as capital gains and losses or major restructurings, and they do not add meaningfully to the picture of the ongoing profitability or sustainability of earnings that are so important in valuing a firm. Because of these issues, there is no single "right" concept of earnings.

Earnings Reporting Methods

There are two principal ways that firms report their earnings. *Net income* (or *reported earnings*) is those earnings sanctioned by the Financial Accounting Standards Board (FASB), an organization established in 1973 to establish accounting standards. These standards are called the *generally accepted accounting principles* (GAAP), and they are used to compute the earnings that appear in the annual report and are filed with government agencies.[9]

The other, often more generous, concept of earnings is called *operating earnings*, which often excludes one-time events such as restructuring charges (expenses associated with a firm's closing a plant or selling a division), investment gains and losses, inventory write-offs, expenses associated with mergers and spin-offs, and depreciation or impairment of "goodwill," among others. But *operating earnings* is not a concept defined by FASB, and this gives firms latitude to interpret what is and what is not excluded. There are circumstances where a similar charge may be included in operating earnings for one company and omitted from another.

There are several versions of operating earnings. Standard & Poor's calculates a very conservative version, which differs from GAAP reported earnings only by excluding asset impairments (including inventory write-downs) and severance pay associated with such impairments. However, when firms report their earnings, they frequently exclude many more items, such as litigation costs, pension costs associated with changing market rates or return assumptions, stock option expenses, and so on. We shall call the earnings that are reported by firms *firm operating earnings*, although the terms *non-GAAP, pro forma,* or *earnings from continuing operations* are also used.

Table 7.2 summarizes items that are generally included and excluded from earnings for nonfinancial companies. For financial companies, virtually all these items are included in both S&P operating earnings and the earnings reported by the firms, as well as GAAP earnings.

TABLE 7.2

Inclusionary and exclusionary items in earnings definitions

	GAAP EPS	S&P Operating EPS	Non-GAAP EPS
Asset impairments	Included	Excluded	Excluded
Severance costs	Included	Included	Excluded
Cash plant closing costs	Included	Included	Excluded
Litigation	Included	Included	Excluded
Pension fair value charges	Included	Included	Excluded
Stock option expense	Included	Included	Usually Included*

Historical Earnings Trends: A Comparison

Figure 7.2 plots these GAAP, S&P, and firm operating earnings per share for S&P 500 companies from 1974 through 2021. S&P operating earnings are available from 1988.

One can see from Figure 7.2 that firm operating earnings are highest, close behind are S&P operating earnings, and GAAP earnings are lowest. FASB mark-to-market rules, put in place since the 1980s, have caused GAAP earnings to drop far below the other measures, especially during recessions.

FIGURE 7.2

Real per share earnings, 1974–2021

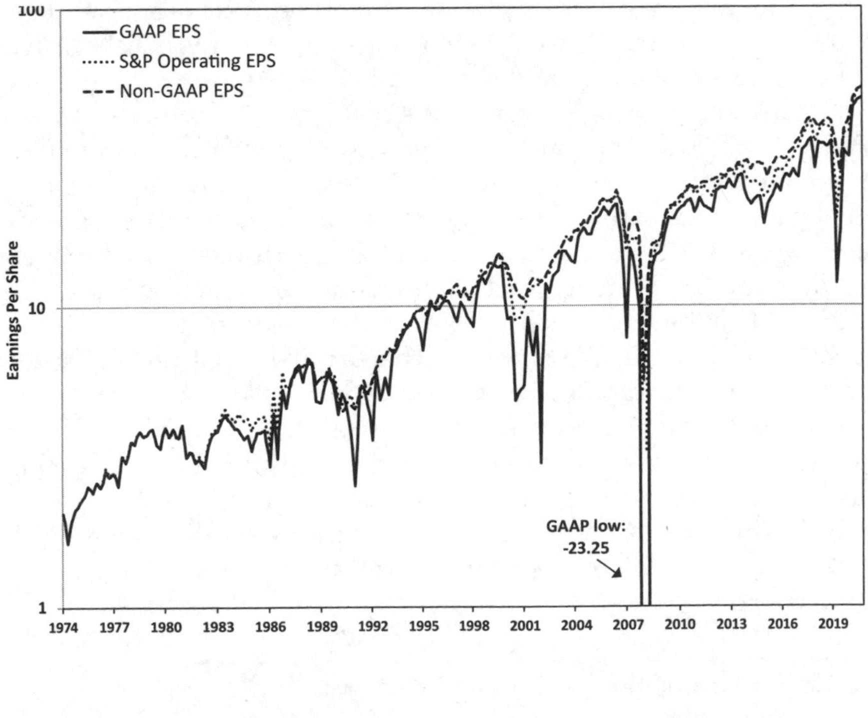

It is often assumed that "reported" or "GAAP earnings" better represent the true earnings of a firm than operating earnings. But that is not necessarily true. In fact, the increasing conservatism of FASB standards, especially as related to the required write-down of asset values, has resulted in severe downward biases to reported earnings. These write-downs were mandated by SFAS (Statement of Financial Account

Standard) Rules 142 and 144 issued in 2001, which required any impairments to the value of property, plant, equipment, and other intangibles (such as goodwill acquired by purchasing stock above book value) to be marked to market, and previously by Rule 115, which was issued in 1993, which stated that securities of financial institutions held for trading or "available for sale" were required to be carried at fair market value.[10] These new standards required firms to "write down" asset values regardless of whether the asset was sold or not. These rules are especially severe in recessions when market prices are depressed.[11] On the other hand, firms are not allowed to write tangible fixed assets back up, even if they recover from a previous markdown, unless they are sold and recorded as "capital gain" income.[12]

Recently FASB has pushed mark-to-market even further. In ASU No. 1920-01 issued in 2016, the board sharply expanded the application of mark-to-market accounting to bottom-line reported earnings. This ruling drew a sharp rebuff from many CEOs that had marketable investments on their balance sheet. They argued that fluctuations in market value, especially caused by the volatility of market sentiment, did not represent the ongoing profitability of the firm.

Warren Buffett was especially critical, saying that the new rule would cause "wild and capricious swings" in Berkshire Hathaway's earnings statements and that "for analytical purposes [because of the new rules], Berkshire Hathaway's bottom line will be worthless."[13] This is noteworthy criticism from an investor who for years criticized CEOs for using lax accounting standards. In Chapter 10 we shall see how these FASB changes, causing the increased volatility of reported earnings, distorted the predictive power of the P/E ratios, especially the CAPE ratio that has been used by many sophisticated investors.

GAAP, Operating Earnings, and NIPA Profits

The increasing volatility of GAAP earnings over time is also apparent from viewing Figure 7.3. In the Great Depression of the 1930s, corporate profits computed by the Bureau of Economic Analysis National Income and Product Accounts (NIPA) showed a much sharper drop than reported profits. In every recession before 1990 except 1937–1938, the decline in S&P reported earnings was *less than* the decline in NIPA profits. In fact, the average magnitude of the decline in S&P reported earnings in recessions before 1990 averaged just slightly over one-half that reported by NIPA profits. Since then, the change has been dramatic; GAAP profits have since fallen by more than twice the drop in NIPA profits.

FIGURE 7.3

Real per share GAAP, operating, and national income profits

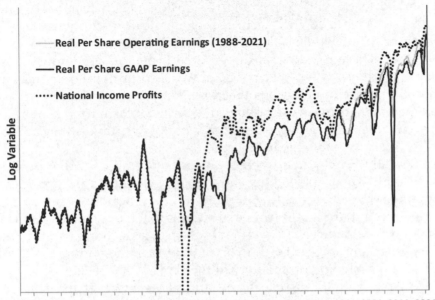

It is particularly striking that the decline in GAAP earnings in the 2008–2009 recession, where the maximum decline in GDP was just over 5 percent, was much greater than the 63 percent decline in earnings during the Great Depression, where the decline in GDP was five times as deep. These disparities confirm that recent FASB rulings have resulted in much lower reported earnings, particularly in economic downturns, and it is necessary for investors to take this fact into account when valuing the market.[14]

The Quarterly Earnings Report

Let us end this chapter by shifting from the long-term view of earnings to the short-term view that we illustrated at the onset of this chapter. What drives stock prices during the "earnings season," which occurs in the month that follows the end of each quarter, is the *difference* between the operating results that a firm reports and what traders expect, and usually "operating earnings" is the key variable investors watch. When we hear that XYZ Corporation "beat the Street," it invariably means that its earnings came in above the consensus forecast.[15]

But the published consensus estimates do not always match the expectations built into the price of the stock at the time the announcements are made. This is because analysts and traders who monitor companies closely often come up with estimates that differ from the consensus. These estimates, often referred to as the *whisper estimates* because they are not widely disseminated, are the ones that influence the price of the stock prior to the announcement. More often than not, these whisper estimates are higher than the ones that circulate as the "consensus," particularly for technology stocks, which often must beat the Street by a wide margin to send their stock price higher.

One reason whisper estimates are higher than consensus estimates is that a firm's *earnings guidance* prior to the announcement is often tilted to the pessimistic side, in order for the firm to "surprise" the Street on the upside and beat the consensus. How else can one explain that over the past 10 years approximately 65 percent of the quarterly earnings reports (and more recently 70 to 75 percent) beat the consensus estimate? Furthermore, a large number of firms beat the Street by exactly one penny, far higher than one would calculate on a statistical basis.

Earnings, although very important, are not the only data that traders act on in the quarterly reports. Revenue is generally considered the next most important indicator, and some traders consider it more important than earnings. When the revenue data is combined with the earnings data, one can compute the profit margin on sales, another important piece of data.

Finally, investors are influenced by any earnings and revenue *guidance* that firms give over the next quarter or year. Forward guidance below earlier forecasts will certainly influence the stock price negatively. Years ago, management would often tip off analysts when unexpected good or bad news impacted the firm. But after tough new fair disclosure (FD) laws were adopted by the US Securities and Exchange Commission (SEC) in 2000, such selected disclosure is no longer permitted. The quarterly conference call is an ideal time for management to release all the important information to shareholders.

CONCLUSION

The fundamental determinants of stock values are the future expected cash flows to investors and the discount rate that discounts these cash flows. These cash flows, called dividends, are derived from the earnings. If a firm earns the same rate of return on its retained earnings that it does on the rest of its corporate capital, then the dividend policy of a firm will not influence the current stock price, although it will influence the future growth rate of per share earnings and dividends.[16] Historical data confirm these results.

There are many earnings concepts. Firm operating earnings are what are calculated and forecast by analysts, and are the most important data in the quarterly reports. These operating earnings are almost always higher than reported or GAAP earnings. But recent rulings by the FASB have led to both a greater volatility and a downward bias in reported earnings that has sharply reduced their significance to investors. The implications of earnings for the valuation of the stock market are the subject of Chapter 10. In the next two chapters we shall discuss the impact of interest rates and inflation on stock prices.

8

Interest Rates and Stock Prices

It all comes down to interest rates. As an investor, all you're doing is putting up a lump-sum payment for a future cash flow.

—Ray Dalio, hedge fund manager and founder of Bridgewater Associates

One of the most surprising developments over the last several decades has been the persistent and steep decline in *real* interest rates. Certainly *nominal*, or *market*, interest rates, which include a premium for expected inflation, have declined because inflation (until the Covid-19 pandemic) fell over this period. But real, after-inflation interest rates have also fallen dramatically. And this decline in real interest rates has occurred not only in the United States, but around the world. Figure 8.1 shows the history of after-inflation, real interest rates in the United States and other developed countries. All have dropped from 2 to 4.5 percent at the turn of the century into negative territory in 2021.

REAL INTEREST RATES AND STOCKS

As noted in the previous chapter, the fundamental theorem of finance specifies that the price of any asset is the present discounted value of its expected future cash flows. The discount rate used for these cash flows is the nominal rate of interest on risk-free assets, such as Treasury securities, plus a risk premium related to the riskiness of these future cash flows. For real assets, that is, assets whose future cash flows rise with the general rate of inflation, it can be shown that the price of real assets can be expressed as the present value of expected *real* cash flows discounted at the *real* (inflation corrected) discount rate. For stocks and other real assets, a fall in the real interest rate, *holding all other variables constant*, will have a positive impact on the price.

FIGURE 8.1

Real yields on 10-year government bonds

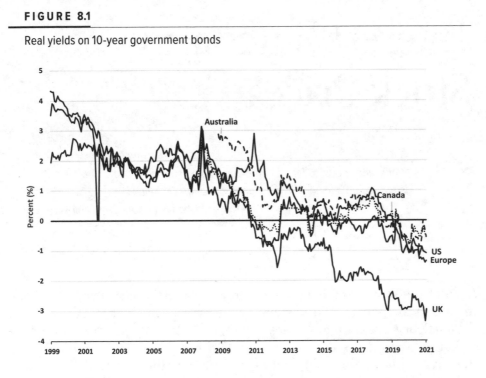

But other variables are rarely constant. This is because changes in real rates are almost always associated with changes in future cash flows and risk premiums. This is why to fully understand the impact of interest rates on stock prices, we need to understand the factors that have led to the decline in real rates.

DETERMINANTS OF REAL INTEREST RATES

A popular explanation for the persistent decline in real interest rates is the "easy money" policy of world central banks, particularly during the financial crisis of 2008–2009 and continuing through the Covid-19 pandemic, but that explanation is largely mistaken. Although central banks play an important role in setting *short-term* market interest rates, the overwhelming determinants of real rates, especially those on the longer-term securities, are determined by *real* not *monetary* forces.

The basic theory of interest rates was laid out more than a century ago by the Austrian economist Eugen von Böhm-Bawerk, the Swedish economist Knut Wicksell, and the American economist Irving Fisher.[1] All of them showed real interest rates were primarily impacted by (1) *economic growth*, (2) *time preference*, and (3) *risk*.

Economic Growth

Economic growth consists of three components: population growth, the share of the population in the labor force, and productivity, which measures the increase in output per hour worked, the most determinant factor of the standard of living. All three of these measures have been trending downward in recent years, some dramatically so. A reduction in the growth of the workforce or productivity reduces the demand for capital by firms and the incentive to borrow against future income by individuals. Both of these factors work together to lower the rate of interest.

The impact of economic growth on interest rates is confirmed by the reactions of financial markets: When stronger-than-expected data on the economy are released, bond prices fall and interest rates rise. The reverse happens when weaker-than-expected numbers are announced.

Population Growth

Population growth is strongly related to the *fertility rate*, or the number of children born to a female in her lifetime. Figure 8.2 shows historical trends of the fertility rate of major regions around the world.

The fall in the world's fertility rate in the post–World War II era is precipitous and has surprised most demographers. Outside of Africa, the world's fertility rate has dropped to or below the 2.1 level (termed the "replacement level") required to keep the population from falling.

The fertility rate of Europe, Japan, and much of East Asia has been below the replacement level for years and is still falling. Even in the United States, which before the Covid-19 pandemic had a fertility rate above the replacement level, grew by just 393,000 between July 2020 and July 2021—the lowest rate of annual population increase in history and the smallest numeric gain in more than 100 years.

FIGURE 8.2

Trends in worldwide fertility rates, 1960–2021

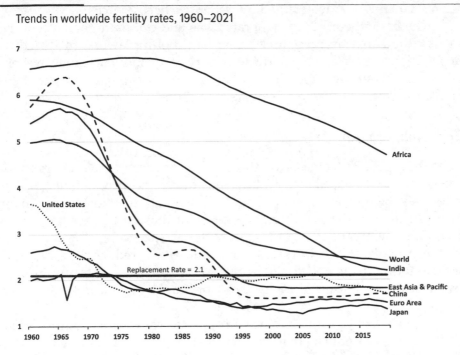

Fertility has also fallen precipitously in the world's two largest countries: China and India. The fertility rate in China fell precipitously after the country imposed the one-child policy in 1979. Even with recent easing restrictions and the institution of new policies encouraging children, the fertility rate in China has remained below the replacement level.[2]

In 1960, the fertility rate in India was approximately six, and even in 2000 it was above three. But in the last 20 years, the number of children born to the average woman in India has fallen rapidly. Although the official International Monetary Fund (IMF) numbers still show India above the replacement level in 2021, the National Family Health Survey in India indicated that the rate has dropped to 2.0 overall and is only 1.6 in cities.[3]

Aging of Population

The aging of the world's population arises from two factors: the increase in life expectancy and the drop in the birth rate. The aging of the world's population means that the share of the population that is active in the labor market is shrinking, while the share of retirees is rising. The aging of the population reinforces the decline in the fertility rate and decreases the growth rate of the working population. Aging also has important implications for the demand for bonds.

The degree of aging is frequently measured by computing the old-age dependency ratio, defined as those aged 65 years as a percentage of the total population. This ratio is rising sharply in all countries and will continue to rise over the next 30 years. Table 8.1, taken from the UN World Population Prospects, shows the dependency ratio for a number of key countries in 1950, 2020, and a forecast for 2050.

TABLE 8.1

The old age dependency ratio

Country	1950	2020	2050
United States	8%	15%	22%
Germany	10%	22%	30%
Italy	8%	22%	37%
Japan	5%	29%	37%
China	4%	10%	26%
South Korea	3%	15%	38%

The sharpest increases in the dependency ratio have occurred in Asia. China, which had an age-dependency ratio of only 4 percent in 1950, has risen to 10 percent today, which is still low by international standards. Because of the one-child policy, its dependency ratio is expected to climb to 26 percent in 2050, far more than forecast for the United States. South Korea, which had the lowest dependency ratio in 1950, is expected to jump to 38 percent by 2050, the highest among the countries shown in Table 8.1. The United States, in comparison to Europe and Asia, is expected to show the smallest rise in the dependency by the middle of this century, but to still experience a significant increase from the level today and nearly three times the level in 1950.

Productivity

One factor that can offset the fall in population growth and increase in the dependency ratio is a rise in productivity. Unfortunately, productivity growth, which rose strongly in developed countries in the half century following the World War II, has fallen over the last two decades.

Table 8.2 summarizes the average annual productivity growth of the 38 OECD (Organization for Economic Cooperation and Development) countries,[4] the G7 countries,[5] as well as the United States, the Eurozone,[6] and Japan. In the last decade, productivity growth has fallen in all major developed countries in the world, particularly in the United States. Despite the tremendous gains in technology developed over this period, growth in output per hour worked has not accelerated.

TABLE 8.2

Productivity growth

Geographic Area	2000–2010	2010–2020
United States	2.2%	0.9%
Japan	1.1%	1.0%
G7 Countries	1.5%	1.0%
Eurozone	1.2%	1.0%
OECD	1.3%	1.2%

Decline in Growth of Per Capita GDP

The decrease in the working-age population, combined with the stagnation of productivity growth, has contributed to a slowdown in the growth rate of per capita GDP. Table 8.3 shows the growth of per capita income in the world, the United States, the Eurozone, Japan, as well as China and India over the 50 years since 1970. Despite the strong growth in China and India from 1970 to 2010, both countries have experienced slow growth in the last 10 years. The slowdown in per capita GDP has been especially sharp in Europe, Japan, and the United States in the last 20 years.

TABLE 8.3

Per Capita GDP Growth

Region/Country	1970–2000	2000–2020	2000–2010	2010–2020
World	1.59%	1.47%	1.74%	1.21%
United States	2.21%	0.92%	0.81%	1.04%
Eurozone	2.32%	0.53%	0.73%	0.33%
Japan	2.70%	0.45%	0.47%	0.42%
China	7.06%	8.11%	9.92%	6.33%
India	2.48%	4.41%	5.09%	3.75%

Other Impacts of Slower Economic Growth

Slower economic growth, in addition to lowering the real rate of interest, does have benefits. It reduces the pressure on the world's natural resources. Furthermore, an increase in the retirement period and a reduction in the hours worked do increase leisure time. Leisure is not directly valued in GDP (although the activities taking place during this time do add to GDP), so economic welfare may be increasing at a faster rate although GDP growth may be slowing. Nevertheless, slower economic growth reduces the demand for capital, and slower productivity growth reduces the demand for borrowing against the future, both of which lower the real rate of interest.

Time Preference

Time preference is another factor influencing real interest rates. Time preference refers to the psychological trait that given a choice, most individuals prefer a unit of consumption today to an identical unit of consumption in the future. That means that to persuade someone to defer consumption today, one has to offer a greater quantity of consumption tomorrow. The higher the time preference for today's consumption, the higher the interest rate required to entice consumers to invest, or defer today's consumption for the promise of more in the future. This variable is difficult to measure, and there is no evidence of a trend in one direction or another.

Risk Aversion

We have shown that slower growth has a negative effect on real interest rates. But risk also influences interest rates, specifically (1) the changing risk behavior of investors and (2) the shifting risk characteristics of bonds. These two factors are caused by the aging of the population and the increasing ability of bonds to hedge short-term risks in the equity market.

As we showed in Chapter 3, as individuals age, their portfolios become more conservative and the proportion of their assets in bonds rise. This occurs because mean reversion of equity returns means that the riskiness of stocks compared to bonds rises as the time horizon gets shorter. Furthermore, older investors have a lower opportunity to offset losses in one's portfolio by increasing labor income, increasing their conservatism. This incentivizes older individuals to hold more bonds in their portfolio relative to stocks, a factor that lowers real rates of interest.

Hedge Qualities of Bonds

The most ignored, yet I believe one of the most powerful, factors driving down real interest rates is the increasingly negative correlation between bonds and risk assets. We touched on this phenomenon in Chapter 3.

Finance theory predicts and data confirm that one of the most important factors determining forward-looking return on any asset is its ability (or inability) to hedge other risks in the market. A hedge asset is one whose price moves in the *opposite* direction of the prices of other risk assets; in other words, a hedge asset rises in price when risk assets (such as stocks) fall, and vice versa. These counter-cyclical assets are valuable because they offset, or hedge, the volatility in the rest of an investor's portfolio. As a result, hedge assets are highly priced and offer a lower expected return. If the hedge asset is particularly effective, its expected return can fall to zero or even become negative.

Hedge assets are like insurance policies; one doesn't expect to profit on buying insurance, but these policies are bought because of their ability to offset negative shocks to your wealth. One of the most important developments over the last several decades has been the transformation of long-term bonds, especially US Treasury bonds, into excellent hedge assets.

FIGURE 8.3

Five-year rolling correlation between stocks and bonds

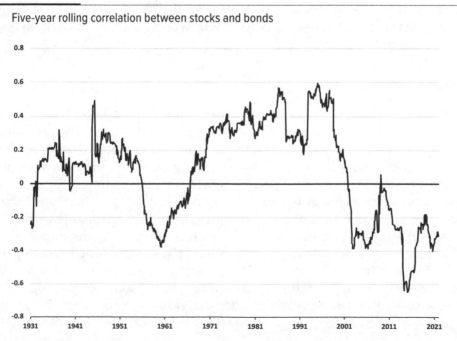

Figure 8.3 displays a rolling five-year correlation between monthly bond and stock returns from 1931 onward. These correlations show that during most of the 1960s and early 1970s, long-term Treasuries had little hedge characteristics; that is, they were basically uncorrelated with stocks. But in the 1980s and 1990s, the correlation of bond prices with risky assets increased dramatically, and Treasury bonds became very poor hedge assets—in other words, stock and bond prices moved in the same direction. During that period, bondholders required a higher expected return to hold these assets in their portfolio, because they did not hedge against stock price movements.

One of the reasons for the increase in the stock-bond correlation in the 1970s and early 1980s was that the US economy was buffeted by supply-side shocks, mostly emanating from oil shocks, such as OPEC oil embargoes and other supply disruptions. These energy shocks caused inflation to increase, which lowered the real value of Treasury bonds and also harmed the real economy, sending stock prices lower. Bond and stock returns moved in the same direction. This undesirable characteristic of bonds forced interest rates upward as investors required a substantial premium to hold bonds that offered them no diversification.

This trend changed in the 1990s and especially the early years of the twenty-first century. As oil shocks waned, different risks emerged; the "emerging market" crisis of 1997 and most importantly, the financial crisis of 2008 amplified fears of banking and monetary collapse. These crises brought about the specter of the Great Depression of the early 1930s, a period when nominal Treasury bonds provided an excellent hedge against the collapsing real economy. History has shown that one of the best-performing assets during the period 1929 to 1932 was long-term US Treasury bonds.

Negative Beta Assets

In the finance literature, these hedge assets are called *negative beta* assets, where "beta" is a measure of the correlation between the price of the assets and the price of the entire portfolio. Other negative beta assets are the VIX volatility index, discussed in Chapter 22, as well as put options on stocks, or options to sell stocks at a given price. Products based on VIX indexes, as well as puts on stocks, have negative expected returns since they insure against price drops. Figure 8.4 shows the five-year rolling beta of bonds versus stocks, and a retirement portfolio that contains 75 percent stocks and 25 percent bonds.

FIGURE 8.4

Five-year rolling beta: Bonds vs stocks and bonds vs 75/25 stock bond portfolio

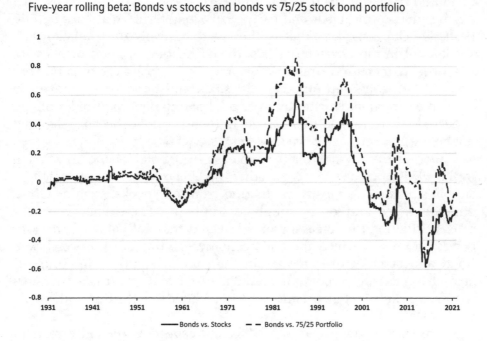

One cannot overemphasize the importance of the transformation of Treasury bonds from a poor hedge in the 1970s and 1980s to an effective hedge from 1990. In a key study, John Campbell concluded that "from peak to trough, the change in correlation, implies that the term premium on a ten-year (zero coupon) would decline by 60% of the equity risk premium."[7] If the equity risk premium is 5 percent, the change in correlation could account for as large as a 3-percentage point decline in long rates.

Richard Clarida, vice chair of the Board of Governors of the Federal Reserve System from 2018–2022, claimed in an international banking conference in Zurich in November 2019 that the hedging characteristic of the long bond is a significant source of the drop in their yields and referenced the 38 percent gain in the 30-year Treasury bond during the financial crisis, while the S&P 500 Index plunged 37 percent.[8]

The Role of the Monetary Authority

What may be striking about this discussion of forces that have driven real interest rates downward is that no mention has been made about the Federal Reserve, central banks, or any aspect of monetary policy.

The omission of central banks does not at all mean they have no role in interest rate determination. For any given inflation rate, there is no question that the central bank can set the *short-term* real interest rate by either controlling the supply of reserves of the banking system or setting the interest rate paid on those reserves. This power impacts spending and the economy.

Over longer periods, however, the Fed's influence on real rates is far more tenuous. To be sure, the Fed's tightening in early 2022 did send the 10-year TIPs yield up substantially, but that surge, in my opinion, is unlikely to last. It was Knut Wicksell who coined the term *natural rate* of interest, referring to the interest rate determined by productivity, time, and risk preferences, which are outside the control of the central bank. If the central bank tried to keep the real rate below this natural rate for a lengthy period, inflation would erupt and force the central bank to tighten policy. On the other side, if the monetary authority tried to keep rates above the natural rate, deflation and economic contraction would occur, again forcing the central bank to ease.

To be sure, the central bank, even in the long run, can control the *nominal* interest rate by controlling the rate of inflation. Excessive monetary issuance on a long-term basis leads to chronic inflation, which would force borrowers to add an inflation premium to the natural rate in order to be compensated for the decline in the purchasing power of the currency. The high interest rates in the 1970s, both in the United States and around the world, were primarily caused by this inflation premium, in addition to the poor hedging quality of bonds. Nevertheless, real, after-inflation long-term interest rates are primarily determined by real economic forces.

INTEREST RATES AND STOCK PRICES

The previous discussion implies that the relation between interest rates and stock prices is far more complicated than it first appears. As noted at the beginning of this chapter, stock prices are determined by the present value of future cash flows. It is true that if the interest rate falls and all other variables remain unchanged, stock prices will rise.

But all other variables do not stay the same. If the fall in interest rates is caused by a decline in growth, then future cash flows are reduced, and the impact on stock prices is ambiguous. If the fall in interest rates is due instead to increased risk aversion, then the decline in the risk-free rate would need to offset higher risk aversion in order for stock prices to rise. If the fall in interest rates is due to the improved hedging characteristics of bonds, the demand for bonds will rise, lowering interest rates, but this may not be accompanied by an increase in demand for stocks.

In the short run, one can say that a decrease in interest rates caused by central banks *is* generally positive to stocks, as long as such a move does not signal excessive, unexpected weakness in the economy. Easing monetary conditions provides economic stimulus and reduces the borrowing costs of firms. If the easing does not become excessive and cause inflation, which could destabilize the economy and force the central bank to tighten in the future, the lowering of the short-term interest rates (such as the Fed funds rate in the United States) usually has a strong positive impact on stock prices.

CONCLUSION

The long-term decline in interest rates over the last several decades has more to do with fundamental economic factors than with central bank policies. This does not deny the importance of central banks in stabilizing the economy nor their power to impact both the fixed income and stock markets. But the forces that impact real interest rates reveal that there is no simple relation between the rate of interest and the price of stocks, and one has to understand the economic factors underlying the movement in interest rates to determine the impact on the stock market.

Inflation and Stock Prices

By a process of inflation, government can confiscate, secretly and unobserved, the wealth of their citizens.

—John Maynard Keynes

Inflation is taxation without legislation.

—Milton Friedman

MONEY AND PRICES

In 1950, President Truman startled the nation in his State of the Union address with a prediction that the typical American family income would reach $12,000 by the year 2000. Considering that median family income was about $3,300 at the time, $12,000 seemed like a princely sum and implied that America was going to make unprecedented economic progress in the next half-century. In fact, President Truman's prediction proved too low. The median family income in 2000 was $41,349. However, in 2000 that sum bought less than $6,000 in 1950 prices, about one-half of what the president predicted and a testament to the inflation of the last half of the twentieth century. Instead of the typical family income soaring over 12 times, from $3,300 to $41,349, real incomes only doubled.

Inflation and deflation have characterized history as far back as economists have gathered data. However, since 1955, there has never been a single year in which the US CPI has declined.[1] What has changed over the past 70 years that makes inflation the rule rather than the exception? The answer is simple: control of the money supply has shifted from gold to the government. Because of this, the government can always provide enough liquidity so prices do not decline.

We analyzed the overall price levels in the United States and Great Britain over the last two centuries in Chapter 2. There was virtually no increase in the price level from 1802 until World War II, and then there was protracted inflation after the war. Before the Great Depression, inflation occurred only because of war, crop failures, or other crises. But the behavior of prices in the postwar period has been entirely different. Inflation is now endemic: the only question is whether it will be stable around the 2 percent goal set by most developed economies or higher.

Money and Inflation

Economists have long known that one variable is paramount in determining the price level: the amount of money in circulation. The robust relation between money and inflation is strongly supported by the evidence. Take a look at Figure 9.1, which displays money and prices in the United States since 1830. The overall trend of the price level has closely tracked that of the money supply normalized for the level of output.

The strong relation between the money supply and consumer prices is a worldwide phenomenon. No sustained inflation is possible without money creation, and every hyperinflation has been associated with an explosion of the money supply. The evidence is overwhelming that countries with high monetary growth experience high inflation, while countries with restrained money growth have low inflation.

Why is the quantity of money so closely connected to the price level? Because the price of money, like any good, is determined by supply and demand. The supply of money is closely controlled by the central bank. The demand for dollars is derived from the demand of households and firms transacting billions of dollars of goods and services in a complex economy. If the supply of dollars increases more than the quantity of goods produced, this leads to inflation. The classic description of the inflationary process, "too many dollars chasing too few goods," is as apt today as ever.

One might wonder why the huge increase in the balance sheet of the Federal Reserve (and other central banks) that followed the Great Financial Crisis did not turn into inflation. Milton Friedman in *The Monetary History of the United States* determined that the quantity of deposits plus currency, which he defined as M2, had the closest link with inflation, not the balance sheet of the central bank, which constitutes bank reserves and currency, called the *monetary base*. The monetary base in the United States did triple from 2007 to 2013, but almost all the increase went into excess reserves in the banking system, which were not lent out and therefore did not create deposits. To be sure, the Fed must monitor the quantity of reserves closely to prevent excess credit creation from turning into inflation. But the low inflation from 2007 to 2021, despite the expansionary policies of the world central banks, has not contradicted the historical link between money and prices.

FIGURE 9.1

Money and prices in the United States, 1830–2021

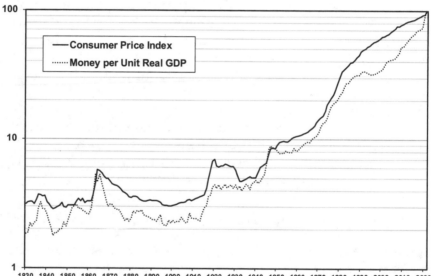

The situation is very different since the Covid-19 pandemic hit in March 2020. As discussed in detail in Chapter 24, the Federal Reserve purchased the debt issued by the government to fund pandemic relief, and so the bank accounts of individuals, businesses, and state and local governments soared, leading to an unprecedented jump in the money supply. In fact, the M2 money supply increased by over 20 percent in 2020, the greatest single annual increase in the 150 years that we have data. M2 continued to increase rapidly in 2021, and inflation surged to 7 percent, the highest in 40 years. The relation between money and prices was confirmed once again.

STOCKS AS HEDGES AGAINST INFLATION

Although the central bank has the ability, through lowering short-term interest rates and providing liquidity to the financial sector, to moderate (but not eliminate) the business cycle, in the long run central bank policy has the most significant influence on inflation. The inflation of the 1970s was due to the overexpansion of the money supply, when the central bank mistakenly thought it could offset the impact of the OPEC oil supply restrictions. This expansionary policy brought inflation to double-digit levels in most industrialized economies, peaking at 13 percent per year in the United States and exceeding 24 percent in the United Kingdom.

In contrast to the returns of fixed-income assets, the historical evidence is overwhelming that the returns on stocks *over long time periods* have kept pace with inflation. Stocks are claims on the earnings of real assets, particularly physical capital, land, and intellectual property. The value of these assets is intrinsically related to the price of the goods and services produced, and therefore should not be impacted by inflation in the long run. For example, the period since World War II has been the most inflationary period in our history, and yet the real return on stocks has actually exceeded that of the previous 150 years. The ability of stock to maintain its purchasing power during periods of inflation makes equities an excellent long-term *inflation hedge*.

Why Stocks Fail as a Short-Term Inflation Hedge

Despite the robustness of the returns to stock against inflation in the long run, the evidence is not as favorable for shorter periods of time. The annual compound returns on stocks, bonds, and Treasury bills against inflation over 1-year and 30-year holding periods from 1871 through 2021 are shown in Figure 9.2.

As expected, stocks serve as excellent long-term hedges against inflation. But the data indicate that neither stocks nor bonds nor bills are good *short-term* hedges against inflation. Short-term real returns on these financial assets are highest when the inflation rates are low, and their returns fall as inflation increases.

If stocks represent real assets, why do they fail as a short-term inflation hedge? A popular explanation is that inflation increases interest rates on bonds, and higher interest rates on bonds depress stock prices. In other words, inflation must send stock prices down sufficiently to increase their future return to match the higher rates available on bonds.

FIGURE 9.2

Holding period returns and inflation, 1871–2021

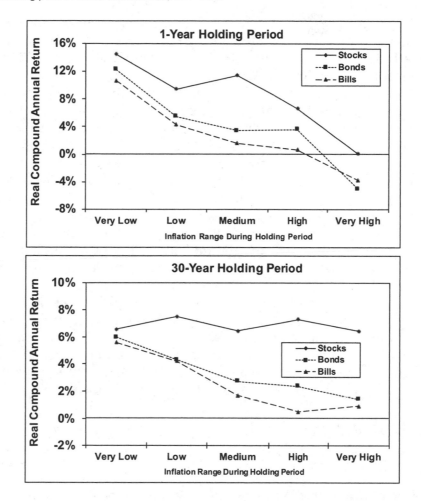

However, this explanation is largely incorrect. Certainly, expectations of rising prices do increase interest rates. Irving Fisher, the famous
early twentieth-century American economist, noted that lenders seek to
protect themselves against inflation by adding the expected inflation to
the real interest rate that they demand from borrowers. This proposition
has been called the *Fisher equation*, after its discoverer.[2]

Higher inflation also raises the expected future cash flows to stockholders. Stocks are claims on the earnings of real assets, whether these
assets are the products of machines, labor, land, or ideas. Inflation is

defined as a rise in the prices of outputs, and as long as the price of inputs does not rise more than those outputs, profits will rise at least as much as inflation.

It can be shown that when inflation impacts input and output prices equally, the present value of the future cash flows from stocks is unaffected by inflation even though interest rates rise. This can be understood by recalling the Gordon formula we derived in Chapter 7. That formula showed the price of a stock can be represented at the level of the dividend divided by the difference between the discount rate and the expected growth rate in dividends. Inflation will raise interest rates and hence the discount rate on stocks, but it will also raise the growth rate of future dividends by the same amount. Those two effects cancel, leaving stock prices unchanged. Over time, the price of stocks—as well as earnings and dividends—will all rise at the rate of inflation. In theory, the returns from stocks will be an ideal inflation hedge.

However, inflation may also lower stock prices when it increases investors' anticipation that the central bank will take anti-inflationary action by raising short-term *real* interest rates. As we learned in the last chapter, it is real rates, not nominal rates, that are the proper discount rate for real assets such as stocks. The central bank can set short-term real rates through controlling the rate of interest on reserves. When inflation exceeds the central bank's target, the central bank raises real short-term rates that may then depress stock prices. Furthermore, such restrictive monetary policies may be followed by an economic slowdown that depresses future cash flows and therefore stock prices.

NONNEUTRAL INFLATION

Supply-Side Effects

The invariance of stock prices to the inflation rate holds when inflation is purely monetary in nature, influencing costs and revenues equally. However, there are many circumstances in which earnings cannot keep up with inflation. Stocks declined during the 1970s because the restriction in OPEC oil supplies dramatically increased energy costs. Firms were not able to raise the prices of their output by as much as the soaring cost of their energy inputs, depressing earnings.

US manufacturers, who for years had thrived on low energy prices, were totally unprepared to deal with surging energy costs. The recession that followed the first OPEC oil squeeze pummeled the stock market. Productivity plummeted, and by the end of 1974 real stock prices, measured by the Dow Jones Industrial Average, had fallen 65 percent from the January 1966 high—the largest decline since the crash of 1929. Pessimism ran so deep that nearly half of all Americans in August 1974 believed the economy was heading toward a depression such as the one the nation had experienced in the 1930s.[3]

In some economies, especially in less-developed countries, chronic inflation is also closely linked with large government budget deficits and excessive government spending. Inflation therefore may signal that the government is taking too large a role in the economy, which often leads to lower growth, lower corporate profits, and lower stock prices. In short, there are a number of economic reasons why stock prices should not keep up with inflation.

TAXES

Economic factors are not the only reason stocks are not good short-run hedges against inflation. The US tax code also penalizes investors during inflation. There are two significant areas in which the tax code works to the detriment of shareholders: capital gains taxes and corporate profits.

Capital Gains Taxes

In the United States, capital gains taxes are paid on the difference between the price of an asset when it is purchased (its *nominal price*) and the value (price) of that asset when it is sold, with no adjustment made for inflation. This means that an asset that appreciates by less than the rate of inflation—resulting in a loss of purchasing power—will nevertheless be taxed upon sale.

Although the appreciation of stock prices generally compensates investors for increases in the rate of inflation, especially in the long run, a tax code based on *nominal* prices penalizes investors in an inflationary environment. Because of the tax code, the "inflation tax" for various inflation rates and various holding periods is displayed in Figure 9.3.[4]

For a given real return, even a moderate inflation rate of 3 percent causes an investor with a five-year average holding period to lose 60 basis points per year compared with the after-tax return that would result if the inflation rate were zero. If the inflation rate rises to 6 percent, the decline in return increases to 112 basis points.

As Figure 9.3 shows, the inflation tax has a far more devastating effect on after-tax real returns when the holding period is short than when it is long. This is because the more frequently an investor buys and sells assets, the more frequently the government can tax the nominal capital gain, which might not be a real, after-inflation gain at all.

FIGURE 9.3

After-tax stock return and inflation

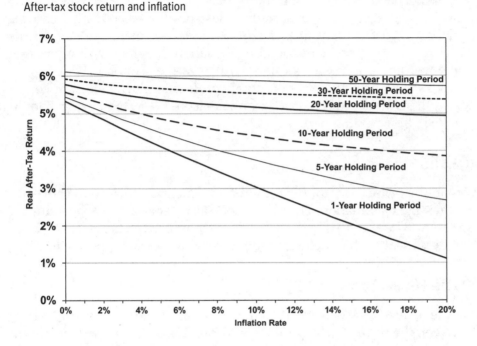

There is considerable support, both inside the government and in the financial community, to make an adjustment for inflation in the capital gains tax, as is done in many other parts of the tax code.[5] Under these proposals, investors would pay taxes on only that portion of the gain (if any) that exceeded the increase in the price level over the holding period of the asset. Since inflation has remained low, there has been less pressure in recent years to adjust the capital gains tax for inflation, although this may change with the inflation associated with the Covid-19 pandemic.

Corporate Tax Distortions

Earnings can also be distorted by standard and accepted accounting practices that do not properly consider the effects of inflation on corporate profits. This distortion shows up primarily in the treatment of depreciation, inventory valuation, and interest costs.

Depreciation of plant, equipment, and other capital investments is based on *historical* costs. These depreciation schedules are not adjusted for any change in the price of capital that might occur during the life of the asset. Inflation increases the cost of the capital but reported depreciation does not make any adjustment for inflation. Therefore, depreciation allowances are understated and taxable earnings are overstated, leaving corporations with higher tax bills.

Inventory accounting is another source of bias. In calculating the cost of goods sold, firms must use the historical cost: generally, either "first in, first out" or "last in, first out" methods of inventory accounting. In an inflationary environment, the gap between historical costs and selling prices widens, producing inflationary profits for the firm. These "profits" do not represent an increase in the real earning power of the firm; instead, they represent just that part of the firm's capital— namely, the inventory—that turns over and is realized as a monetary, not real profit. However, since these inventory profits are reported to the tax authorities, they force the corporation to pay higher taxes. Note that the accounting for inventories differs from the firm's other physical and intellectual assets, which are not revalued on an ongoing basis for the purpose of determining taxable earnings.

The Department of Commerce, the government agency responsible for gathering economic statistics, is well aware of these distortions and has computed both a depreciation adjustment and an inventory valuation adjustment in the national income and product accounts. Unfortunately, the Internal Revenue Service does not recognize any of these adjustments for tax purposes; firms are required to pay taxes on reported profits, even when these profits are biased upward by inflation and therefore increase the effective tax rate on capital.

There are other accounting practices that are more favorable to corporations during inflationary periods. As noted previously, an increase in expected inflation through the Fisher equation, will raise the nominal discount rate on future cash flows, and that will be offset by the expected increase in nominal future cash flows.

But *reported* profits will fall when inflationary expectations cause interest rates to rise. That is because corporations are required to deduct *nominal*, not *real*, interest expenses from the revenues to determine profits. Corporations do not report the imputed income resulting from the decline in the real value of debt when inflation occurs. Conceptually, inflation increases interest expense but that is exactly offset by the decline in the real value of debt. These two effects will cancel each other, leaving real corporate profits unchanged.

Because corporate taxes are based on the increased nominal interest expense, but for the nonreporting of the corresponding reduction in real indebtedness, this accounting distortion makes a difference. Lower reported profits mean lower taxes, which implies that true after-tax corporate profits are higher than what is reported. This is a positive for stock prices, as it effectively lowers the effective corporate tax rate.

In summary, because our tax code is based on nominal values, an increase in inflation, even if it raises cash flows by the same amount, can impact stock prices. A large negative effect comes from the lack of inflation indexation for capital gains. On the corporate side, there are three effects of higher inflation: depreciation allowances are understated, inventory profits are overstated, and interest expenses are also overstated. The first two effects are a negative for the firms, and the last is a positive. For corporations, the balance of all three of these factors depends on the leverage of the firm.[6]

CONCLUSION

In the case of pure inflation, where input and output prices rise at exactly the same rate, inflation has no impact on the real value of stock prices and the real returns on stocks will not be affected. The historical evidence overwhelmingly supports this contention. The price level has increased more than twentyfold since the end of World War II, yet real stock returns have not only held their own, but actually increased from the noninflationary period of the nineteenth and first half of the twentieth centuries.

But the short run is far more complicated. Input and output prices may increase at different rates, depending on whether supply shocks or demand shocks impact the economy. Furthermore, inflation may prompt the Fed to increase real rates to slow the rate of price increases down to their target levels. Finally, our tax system, not adequately indexed to inflation, causes a higher effective tax rate on real capital gains and potentially higher taxes on corporations. For that reason, in the short term, real stock returns are often depressed by inflation.

Yardsticks to Value the Stock Market

*Even when the underlying motive of purchase [of common stocks]
is mere speculative greed, human nature desires to conceal
this unlovely impulse behind a screen of apparent logic and
good sense.*

—Benjamin Graham and David Dodd, 1940[1]

AN "EVIL OMEN" RETURNS

In the summer of 1958, an event of great significance took place for investors who followed long-standing yardsticks of the stock market valuation. For the first time in history, the interest rate on long-term government bonds rose decidedly above the dividend yield on common stocks.

BusinessWeek noted this event in an August 1958 article "An Evil Omen Returns," warning investors that when yields on stocks approached those on bonds, a major market decline was likely coming.[2] The stock market crash of 1929 occurred in a year when stock dividend yields fell to the level of bond yields. The stock crashes of 1891 and 1907 also followed episodes when the yield on bonds came within 1 percent of the dividend yield on stocks.

Until 1958, the yearly dividend yield on stocks had always been higher than long-term interest rates (as Figure 10.1 indicates), and financial analysts taught that this was the way it was supposed to be. Stocks were riskier than bonds and therefore should yield more in the marketplace. Under this criterion, whenever stock prices went too high and sent dividend yields below the yields on bonds, it was time to sell.

But in this case, things did not work that way. Stocks boomed after the dividend yield fell below the bond yield, and stocks returned over 30 percent in the next 12 months and continued to soar into the 1960s.

FIGURE 10.1

Dividend and nominal bond yields, 1870–2021

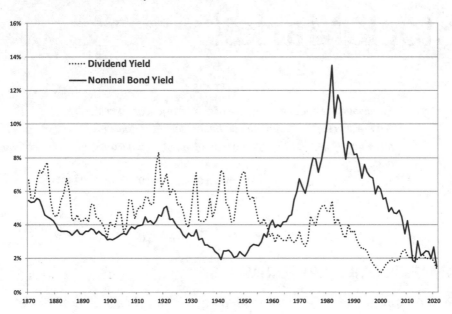

It is now understood that there were good economic reasons why this well-respected valuation indicator fell by the wayside. Inflation increased the yield on bonds to compensate lenders for rising prices, while investors bought stocks against the eroding value of money. As early as September 1958, *BusinessWeek* noted, "The relationship between stock and bond yields was clearly posting a warning signal, but investors still believe inflation is inevitable and stocks are the only hedge against it."[3]

Despite the good economic reason to be wary of the relation between the dividend yield and the bond yield, many on Wall Street were puzzled by the "great yield reversal." Nicholas Molodovsky, vice president of White, Weld & Co. and editor of the prestigious *Financial Analysts Journal*, observed:

> Some financial analysts called [the reversal of bond and stock yields] a financial revolution brought about by many complex causes. Others, on the contrary, made no attempt to explain the unexplainable. They showed readiness to accept it as a manifestation of providence in the financial universe.[4]

Imagine the investor who followed this well-regarded indicator and pulled all his or her money out of the stock market in August 1958 and put it into bonds, vowing never to buy stocks until dividend yields rose once again above bond yields. Such an investor would have to wait another 50 years to get back into stocks, as it was not until the financial crisis of 2007–2009 that the dividend yield on stocks once again rose above the yield on long-term Treasury bonds. Yet over that half-century, real stock returns averaged over 6 percent per year and overwhelmed the returns on fixed-income securities.

This episode illustrates that valuation yardsticks are valid only if underlying economic and financial conditions do not change. Chronic postwar inflation, resulting from a switch to a paper money standard, forever changed the way investors judged the investment merits of stocks and bonds. Stocks were viewed as claims on real assets whose prices rose with inflation, while bonds were not. Those investors who clung to the old ways of valuing equity never participated in one of history's greatest bull markets.

Dividend Yield and Buybacks

Except for a brief period in the 1970s and 1980s, the dividend yield has continued to decline since the great yield reversal. A major reason for this decline was the increase in share buybacks, which, as discussed in Chapter 7, are a tax-efficient way to return cash to the shareholder. In fact, buybacks have become as important as dividends in recent years. Figure 10.2 shows the dividend yield and the buyback yield (the value of shares that are bought back divided by the total market value of the shares) from 1960 through the present, and the sum of both, sometimes called the *shareholder yield*.

Buybacks became important in the early 1980s when regulations were significantly eased on their implementation. Figure 10.2 shows that the sum of the dividend yield and the buyback yield, often called the *shareholder yield*, has been remarkably stable since 1960 and in fact is slightly upward. One can also see that the buyback yields went to zero during and shortly after the financial crisis of 2008–2009. This was due almost entirely to the radical changes in the financial sector: the issuance of shares by stronger firms to purchase weaker firms (Bank of America purchasing Merrill Lynch, J.P. Morgan purchasing Bears Stearns) and the issuance of common and preferred shares to several lenders to bolster their balance sheet. The bottom line is the dividend yield alone is a poor indicator of the valuation of the overall market.

FIGURE 10.2

Dividend, buyback, and shareholder yields

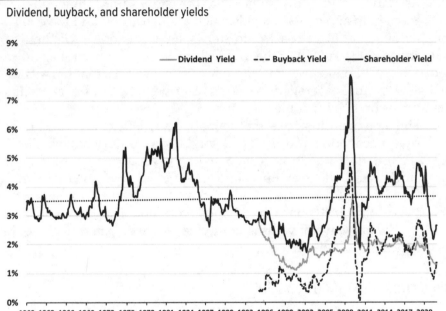

YARDSTICKS FOR VALUING THE MARKET

Many valuation yardsticks measure the market value of the shares outstanding relative to economic *fundamentals*, such as earnings, dividends, and book values, or to some economic aggregate, such as GDP, interest rates, or profit margins.

P/E Ratio

The most basic yardstick for valuing stocks is the *price-earnings ratio* (or *P/E ratio*). The current P/E ratio of a stock is simply the ratio of its value of its stock to its annual earnings, measured either on an aggregate or (equivalently) on a per share basis. The P/E ratio measures how much an investor is willing to pay for a dollar's worth of annual earnings.

FIGURE 10.3

GAAP Reported and Operating P/E Ratios 1871–2021

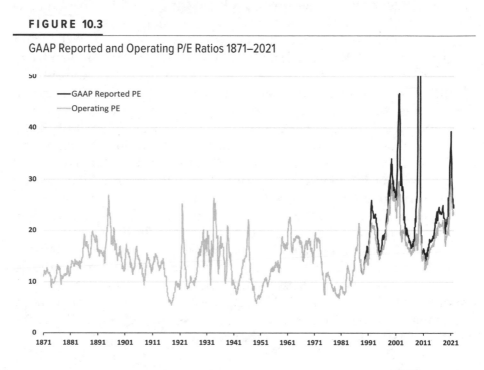

Figure 10.3 shows the historical P/E ratio of the market from 1871 through December 2021, based on the last 12 months of GAAP reported earnings and operating earnings of the S&P 500 Index. The P/E ratio based on GAAP reported earnings is marked by spikes in the last four recessions, especially the 2008–2009 recession that followed the financial crisis. Although P/E ratios naturally increased in earlier recessions because of the drop in earnings, the magnification of these spikes in recent years were caused by changes in FASB mark-to-market accounting rules that are detailed in Chapter 7.

The spikes in the P/E ratio overstate the aggregate P/E ratio of the market for another reason. The traditional way of calculating the P/E ratio of an index is by adding the earnings of each firm in the index and dividing the sum by the total market value of the firms in the index. But when one or more firms reports a large loss, as happens during recessions, such a methodology can greatly overstate the P/E ratio of the index.

As a simple example, take two firms, A and B. Assume A is a firm with earnings of $10 billion and is selling for a P/E of 20, giving it a market value of $200 billion. Assume firm B reports a $9 billion loss and has a market value of only $10 billion. A capitalization-weighted portfolio, which is the basis of all popular indexes, such as the S&P 500, would consist of over 95 percent of firm A and less than 5 percent of firm B.

Yet, because the aggregate earnings of the firms in the index is only $1 billion while the total market value is $210 billion, the P/E ratio of the index is computed as 210 even though over 95 percent of the index is composed of a firm with a 20 P/E ratio. The method of computing the P/E ratio of an aggregation index therefore leads to an upward distortion in the P/E ratio of the index that I call the *aggregation bias* and makes the P/E ratio of the market appear much higher than it is.[5] The reason why adding together profits and losses and then dividing the sum into aggregate market value does not produce the right P/E is that losses in one firm do not cancel the profits of another firm. Individual stocks are not like divisions of a single firm, where it is proper to aggregate profits no matter the size. In contrast, equity holders have unique rights to the profits of their firms, unsullied by the losses in others. The aggregation bias has been magnified by large losses reported by firms due to the changes in mark-to-market rules. In recessions, aggregate P/E ratios greatly overstate the valuation of the market.

Earnings Yield

The reciprocal of the P/E ratio, which is called the *earnings yield*, measures the annual earnings generated per dollar of stock market value. The earnings yield is important, since this statistic gives us a good predictor of the long-run real return on stocks. If all earnings were paid as dividends, then the earnings yield on a stock would be identical to the dividend yield.

The median P/E ratio over the 150 years from 1870 through 2021 is 14.9 using GAAP earnings and 14.8 using operating earnings. That means that the median earnings yield is 6.7 percent, just a few tenths of a percentage point below the long-run real return on stocks.

The very close correspondence between the earnings yield and the long-term real return on the market is significant. The P/E ratio and the earnings yield, corrected for any cyclical effect, can serve as a predictor of future real returns on stocks. That is precisely what Robert Shiller surmised when he created the CAPE ratio.

The CAPE Ratio

In 1998, Robert Shiller and his coauthor, John Campbell, published a path-breaking article, "Valuation Ratios and the Long-Run Stock Market Outlook."[6] This article, following up on some of their earlier work on stock market predictability, established that long-term stock market returns were not random walks but could be forecast by a valuation measure called the *cyclically adjusted price-earnings ratio*, or *CAPE ratio*. The CAPE ratio was calculated by taking a broad-based index of stock market prices, such as the S&P 500, and dividing by the average of the last 10 years of aggregate earnings, all measured in real terms. The use of 10-year average earnings instead of 1-year is to dampen the volatility of earnings associated with the business cycle.

The CAPE ratio predicted about one-third of the variation in future 10-year real returns, which is high for stock market prediction models that have had notoriously low success. When the CAPE ratio is above its long-run average, the model predicts below-average real returns for stocks over the next 10 years and above-average returns when the CAPE ratio is below its average. Figure 10.4 shows the Shiller CAPE ratio based on GAAP and operating earnings.

FIGURE 10.4

Shiller CAPE ratio: GAAP reported and operating P/E ratios, 1881–2021

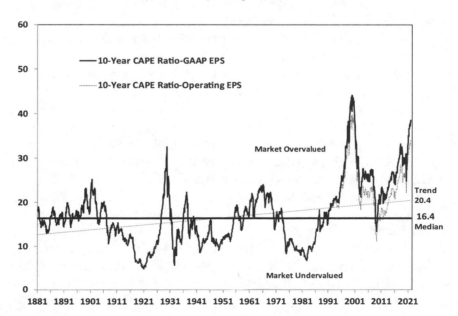

The CAPE ratio gained the attention of the investment community when Campbell and Shiller presented a preliminary version of their research at the Board of Governors of the Federal Reserve on December 3, 1996, and warned that stock prices in the late 1990s were running well ahead of earnings. Greenspan's "Irrational Exuberance Speech," delivered one week later, was said to have been based, in part, on their findings.[7] At the top of the bull market in 2000, the CAPE ratio hit an all-time high of 43, more than twice its historical average, and correctly forecast the below average equity returns over the next decade.

Historically, the CAPE ratio has had some notable successes, predicting poor returns after the 1929 peak and 2000 technology bubble, as well as predicting above-average returns during the Depression and the bear markets of the late 1970s. But in recent years the CAPE ratio has given excessively bearish forecasts. Figure 10.4 shows that over the past three decades the CAPE ratio has almost always been above its long-run average, forecasting below-average returns for stocks. In contrast, stock returns during this period have almost always been above average. In all but four months over the last 40 years (from 1981 through 2021), the actual 10-year real returns in the stock market have exceeded forecasts using the CAPE model. The model has been dramatically too bearish since the Great Financial Crisis, indicating the market moved into overvalued territory in May 2009, just a few months after the market bottom, which marked the beginning of one of the greatest bull markets in history.

The unwarranted bearishness of the CAPE model in recent years can be attributed to several sources: First, the decline in the dividend yield accelerated the growth of earnings, which altered the past 10-year earnings average.[8] Second, for reasons discussed at the end of the chapter, increased liquidity and reduced transaction costs for equities do justify an upward trend in P/E ratios, as noted in Figure 10.4.

The most important source of the bearishness of the CAPE ratio was the change in the FASB rules about reporting losses, which overstated the decline in earnings during recessions. These outsized losses remain in the CAPE earnings for 10 years and make P/E ratios higher than they would be if previous GAAP rules had been used.

Since firm operating earnings do not include as many write-downs as GAAP reported earnings, the CAPE ratio based on operating earnings, which is also plotted in Figure 10.4, does not give as much of a bearish cast to the recent CAPE ratio as based on GAAP earnings. I detailed these issues in my academic paper "The CAPE Ratio: A New Look," which examines why the CAPE indicator has been far too bearish in recent years.[9]

In 2020 Shiller modified his CAPE ratio by considering the fall in real interest rates, terming the new model *the excess CAPE yield*, or *ECY*.[10] In this model, Shiller takes the earnings yield from the standard CAPE model and instead of looking at this yield in isolation, subtracts the real interest rate from the CAPE earnings yield and compares this with the historical average.

Since real interest rates have fallen dramatically over recent years, the ECY is far less bearish on equities than the standard CAPE model. The model in 2021 does predict that the future return on equities will be lower than their historical average, but since the real yield on bonds is so much lower than their historical average, the CAPE forecast for future equity returns is not that far from the historical average.

In February 2022 Jason Zweig interviewed Shiller about the poor performance of the CAPE ratio over the last decade.[11] Shiller emphasized that even with 150 years of data, one still has only 15 nonoverlapping observations, which lowers its statistical significance. When asked what the right CAPE ratio is, he responded, "We don't know. We're constantly moving into a new era." Sometimes there are sound reasons for ignoring historical warnings, as noted at the beginning of this chapter. The much-mocked phrase, "this time is different," may sometimes be true.

The Fed Model, Earnings Yields, and Bond Yields

In early 1997, in response to Federal Reserve Chairman Alan Greenspan's increasing concern about the impact of the rising stock market on the economy, three researchers from the Federal Reserve produced the paper "Earnings Forecasts and the Predictability of Stock Returns: Evidence from Trading the S&P."[12] This paper documented the remarkable correspondence between the earnings yields on stocks and the 30-year government bond rates.

Greenspan supported the results of this paper and suggested that the central bank regard the stock market as "overvalued" whenever this earnings yield fell below the bond yield and "undervalued" whenever the reverse occurred. The analysis showed that the market was most overvalued in August 1987, just before the October 1987 stock market crash, and most undervalued in the early 1980s, when the great bull market began. This research has been dubbed the "Fed model."

The basic idea behind the Fed model is like the dividend yield versus bond yield model discussed at the beginning of this chapter, but it does so more accurately because it compares the *earnings* yield and not the *dividend* yield to the Treasury bond rate. The idea is that when the bond yields rise above the earnings yield, stock prices fall because investors shift their portfolio holdings from stocks to bonds. On the other hand, when the bond yields fall below the earnings yields, investors shift to stocks from bonds. Figure 10.5 shows the earnings yield on stocks and the nominal and real interest rates on bonds from 1871 through 2021.

FIGURE 10.5

Earnings yields versus bond yields, 1871–2021

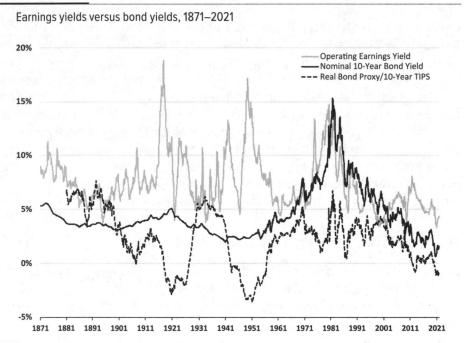

Indeed, the earnings yield on stocks and the nominal interest rate on bonds did display a close relation between 1960 and 2000. Outside that period, however, the correlation is very weak. Furthermore, the Fed model has a major conceptual shortcoming: We have noted that stocks are real assets whose prices will rise with inflation. The proper comparison should be between the earnings yield on stocks and the real, after-inflation interest rate on bonds, not the nominal interest rate. In fact, that is the basis of the Shiller ECY model. But outside that 40-year period, these correlations are extremely weak. As noted earlier, many factors changing the real rate of interest do not have corresponding impact on stock valuation.

Nevertheless, when earnings yields and real bond yields are at extremes, that often signals a turning point. At the peak of the dot-com bubble in 2000, the earnings yield on stock was just over 3 percent, while the 10-year TIPs bond yielded over 4 percent. This led to an extraordinarily rate negative risk premium (earnings yield minus TIPS yield) and reliably signaled the subsequent decline in equity prices.

Stock Market Value, GDP, and Profit Margins

Another indicator of stock market valuation is the ratio of aggregate stock market value to gross domestic product (GDP). This indicator was introduced in 2001 by Warren Buffett as his favorite indicator of the valuation of the market.[13] This ratio is shown in Figure 10.6. Buffett indicated in 2001 that when this indicator fell to 70 percent or 80 percent, the stock market was a "buy," but when it soared, as it did in 1999 to 200 percent, the market was very "dangerous." In 2021, the ratio rose to an all-time high, signaling a very overvalued market.

FIGURE 10.6

Buffett indicator: market cap to GDP ratio

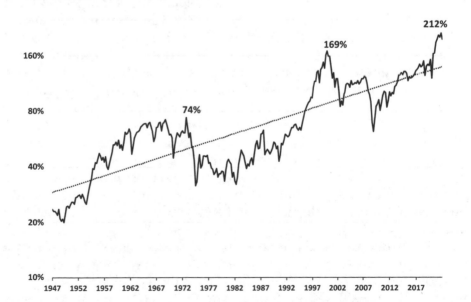

However, the ratio of the market value of stocks to GDP is not a good stock market indicator. For one, the indicator does not account for a change in the number and size of firms that are public compared to those that are private. Over this period, many partnerships, especially in the financial sector, have turned into corporate entities, enhancing market value.

But more important, as we noted in Chapter 4, the fraction of revenues that have come from overseas sales has increased dramatically in the post–World War II years and now comprises almost one-half of the revenues and profits. As the US economy shrinks relative to the size of the world economy, the corporate profits and market valuation of US multinational corporations should rise relative to the GDP. The upward trend of the Buffett ratio is easily explained by this factor.

Book Value, Market Value, and Tobin's Q

The *book value* of a firm is often used as a valuation yardstick. The book value is the value of a firm's assets minus its liabilities, evaluated at historical costs. A major shortcoming of this measure is that book value uses *historical* prices and thus ignores the effect of changing prices on the value of the assets. If a firm purchased a plot of land for $1 million that is now worth $10 million, examining the book value will not reveal this.

To help correct these distortions, James Tobin, former professor at Yale University and a Nobel laureate, adjusted the book value for inflation and computed the "replacement cost" of the assets and liabilities on the balance sheets of US corporations.[14] He proposed that the "equilibrium" or "correct" market price of a firm should equal the book value of its assets and liabilities corrected for inflation. If the aggregate market value of a firm exceeds this inflation-corrected book value, it would be profitable for management to sell shares to finance further investment, reaping a profit from the difference in market price and underlying value. If the market value falls below the replacement cost, then it would be better for a firm to dismantle and sell its capital, or stop investment and cut production.

Tobin designated the ratio of the market value of the aggregate stock market to the inflation-corrected book value with the letter Q, and he indicated that the ratio should be unity if the stock market was properly valued. In 2000 Andrew Smithers and Stephen Wright of the United Kingdom published the book *Valuing Wall Street*, which maintained that Tobin's Q was the best measure of the value of the stock market. They asserted that the US markets as well as the UK and many other European markets were extremely overvalued by this criterion.[15] A graph of the Q value is not shown here, but its historical level virtually matches that of the original Shiller CAPE ratio, and predictions using the Q ratio have suffered similar failures over the past decade.

There are sound criticisms of the Q theory, as they are mostly about book-value-based criteria for stock valuation. Capital equipment and structures lack a good secondary market, and hence there is no realistic way to value much of the physical capital stock. But the most important shortcoming is the inability of book value to value intellectual capital. Research and development costs are not capitalized and therefore do not appear in market value.

This is particularly severe for the technology companies that have increasingly dominated the market. For example, in February 2022 the book value of Microsoft was $22 per share and its market value was $300. Apple had a book value of only $4.40, while it had a market value of about $160. We shall discuss book value as a criterion for valuing individual stocks in more detail in Chapter 12. The bottom line is that book value is a construct of the past; market value derives from prospective earnings and looks to the future.

Profit Margins

Another ratio that has generated concern in recent years is the level of profit margins, the ratio of corporate profits to revenues. Figure 10.7 plots the profit margins on S&P 500 firms' reports for the average profit margin of S&P 500 firms since 1967. One can see that margins have recently risen to the highest levels in at least 50 years. Bears claim that these margins are unsustainable, and if margins retreat, it could lead to a significant decline in corporate profits and market prices.

But there are several reasons why corporate margins are high and are not likely to retreat significantly. These include low nominal and real interest rates, the decline in the corporate tax rate, and most importantly, the sharply increasing share of technology companies and the increasing share of profits coming from foreign sales, which historically have had higher margins than domestic sales.

As can be seen in Figure 10.7, technology stocks have much higher margins due to their intellectual capital and worldwide dominance. Excluding technology stocks, corporate margins in 2021 are reduced from 13.1 percent to 10.6 percent. Although this is still higher than the historical average, higher margins can be mostly accounted for by the increase in foreign sales and decline in the tax rate over the last three decades.

FIGURE 10.7

S&P 500 profit margins

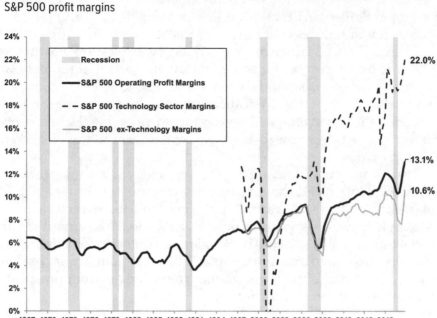

WHAT IS THE RIGHT VALUATION OF THE MARKET?

We have noted that over the last 150 years, the median P/E ratio of the market has been about 15, but there has been a trend to higher valuations in more recent years. Given current and prospective economic circumstances, what is the right P/E ratio of the market?

This question has bedeviled economists for decades. More than a half-century ago, Nobel Prize–winning economist Paul Samuelson wrote in *Newsweek*:

> I doubt that the devil himself knows what is the equilibrium P/E ratio on stocks. Eighteen to 1, as so long held? Fifteen to 1, as [Treasury] Secretary Douglas Dillon once rashly averred? Twenty-five to 1. Or 14 to 1, as the tape enunciates now . . . No one knows.[16]

Yet there are persuasive economic reasons why the trend of P/E ratios should be upward over time. One of the most important, but least cited, is the dramatic decrease in the cost of investing in equities and achieving a fully diversified portfolio.

A Fall in Transaction Costs

Historical data confirms that the real return on equity *as measured by stock indexes* was between 6 and 7 percent after inflation over the past two centuries. But over the nineteenth century and the early part of the twentieth century, it was extremely difficult, if not impossible, for an investor to replicate the stock returns calculated from these stock indexes.

Charles Jones of Columbia University has documented the decline in stock trading costs over the last century.[17] These costs include both the fees paid to brokers and the bid-asked spread, or the difference between the buying and selling costs for stocks. His analysis shows that the average one-way cost to either buy or sell a stock has dropped from over 1 percent of value traded as late as 1975 (before the deregulation of brokerage fees) to under 0.18 percent in 2002 and even lower today.

The fall in transaction costs implies that the price of obtaining and maintaining a diversified portfolio of common stocks, which is necessary to replicate index returns, could have easily cost from 1 to 2 percent per year over much of the nineteenth and early twentieth centuries. Because of these costs, investors in earlier years were less diversified and assumed more risk than implied by stock indexes. Alternatively, if investors attempted to buy all the stocks to replicate a broad-based index, their real returns could have been as low as 5 percent per year after deducting transaction costs. If the required real return on equity for investors is only 5 percent, then a P/E ratio of 20, corresponding to an earnings yield of 5 percent, will produce that return for today's investors, and this would become the equilibrium P/E ratio for the market today.

Other Factors Raising Valuation Ratios

Another factor frequently cited justifying the increase in P/E ratio is the sharp reduction in real rates. To be sure, in pivoting to his new excess CAPE yield, Robert Shiller has radically reduced the bearishness of his equity forecast because of the decline in rates. However, we have sounded caution with this approach. Many of the reasons for the decline in real yields, particularly slower growth and higher risk aversion, do not necessarily raise the price of equities. Nevertheless, fixed-income assets are the most important alternative to stocks, and the precipitous drops in their yields have certainly kept many investors in equities despite their higher valuation.

The Equity Risk Premium

The decline in transaction costs or the decline in discount rates may each be used to justify a higher P/E ratio. Yet another reason is that the equity risk premium itself may shrink. In the mid-1980s, economists Rajnish Mehra and Edward Prescott published "The Equity Premium: A Puzzle."[18] In their paper, they showed that given the standard models of risk and return that economists had developed over the years, one could not explain the large gap between the returns on equities and fixed-income assets found in the historical data. They claimed that economic models predicted that either the rate of return on stocks should be lower, or the rate of return on fixed-income assets should be higher, or both. In fact, according to their studies, an equity premium as low as 1 percent or less could be justified.[19]

There is much literature that attempts to justify the high 3 to 4 percent premium that equities offer over fixed income.[20] Some of these are based on very high aversion by individuals to lowering their consumption. Others are based on the myopic behavior of those who dislike taking short-term losses on their investments, even when they have substantial long-run gains. Perhaps one explanation of the equity premium lies with the ignorance of the investing public of the magnitude of the outperformance of equities. Furthermore, given the uncertainty of inflation, most investors do not recognize that in the long run, fixed-income investments are not safer than stocks. If these factors were fully recognized, the demand for stocks would rise and P/E ratios would increase substantially from historical levels.

Nearly a century ago Professor Chelcie Bosland of Brown University made this very observation. In 1936, he stated that one of the consequences of the spread of knowledge of superior stock returns, generated by Edgar Lawrence Smith's 1925 *Common Stocks as Long-Term Investments*, was a higher valuation ratio. He stated:

> Paradoxical though it may seem, there is considerable truth in the statement that widespread knowledge of the profitability of common stocks, gained from the studies that have been made, tends to diminish the likelihood that correspondingly large profits can be gained from stocks in the future. The competitive bidding for stocks which results from this knowledge causes prices at the time of

purchase to be high, with the attendant smaller possibilities of gain in the principal and high yield. The discount process may do away with a large share of the gains from common stock investment and returns to stockholders and investors in other securities may tend to become equalized.[21]

CONCLUSION

Despite more than eight decades of continued outperformance of stocks, valuation levels of equities have risen little from their long-term historical average. The irony is that if stocks rise to a level that sends the equity risk premium down to the lower level deemed appropriate by many macroeconomic models, then the forward-looking returns on stocks will be reduced. In other words, a future reduction in the equity risk premium would first send stock prices higher, benefiting the older generation of stockholders who wish to consume from their retirement portfolios, but the younger generation of investors would experience lower long-term returns from equities.

III

MARKET EFFICIENCY AND VALUE VERSUS GROWTH

Which Stocks for the Long Run?

It ain't what you don't know that gets you in trouble. It's what you know for sure that just ain't so.

—Mark Twain[1]

A great company is not a great investment if you pay too much for the stock.

—Benjamin Graham[2]

WHICH STOCK?

If an investor wants to beat the market in the *short run*, there are two strategies to pursue: (1) invest in firms that will surpass market expectations on earnings or other growth metrics, or (2) buy stocks that you think that *other* investors, for whatever reason, (justified or unjustified) will also buy, sending their price higher. In other words, anticipate the crowd.

If you want to be a winner in the long run, you must pursue a very different strategy. Surprisingly, earnings growth is not the primary consideration for better long-run returns, and in fact, faster growth often leads to overvaluation that results in long-term *under*performance. History shows that the most important criterion for long-term investors is to buy and hold stocks that stay reasonably priced relative to their fundamentals, not to pursue those firms that grow the fastest.

Standard Oil and IBM

Imagine that you are transported back to the beginning of 1950 and a recently deceased uncle has just bequeathed $10,000 to your newborn daughter. The bequest has specific strings attached: With this money you must buy either Standard Oil of New Jersey (now ExxonMobil) or a much smaller, but promising new-economy company called IBM. You are also instructed to reinvest all dividends back into the stock you choose and to put your investment under lock and key, only to be opened when your daughter reaches the age of 60 in 2010.

Which Firm Should You Buy?

To aid your decision, let us assume a genie appears and tells you the actual annual revenue, earnings, dividend growth rates of each of these two firms over the next six decades, and the change in the market capitalization of the technology and energy sectors. Furthermore, the genie tells you that IBM will develop the first commercial computer in two years and will dominate technology over the next two decades like no other firm has before or since. None of IBM's fabulous growth was anticipated in 1950. The data on earnings, dividends, and revenue growth over this 60-year period is presented in Table 11.1.

TABLE 11.1

IBM and Standard Oil of New Jersey, 1950–2010

Growth Measures	IBM	Standard Oil of NJ	Advantage
Revenue Per Share	10.59%	7.99%	IBM
Dividends Per Share	9.73%	6.83%	IBM
Earnings Per Share	11.26%	7.63%	IBM
Annual Sector Change*	3.43%	-0.98%	IBM

*Change in Market share of technology and energy sectors 1957-2010

Valuation Measures	IBM	Standard Oil of NJ	Advantage
Average Price-Earnings ratio	22.48	12.92	Standard Oil of NJ
Average Dividend Yield	2.17%	4.21%	Standard Oil of NJ

Return Measures	IBM	Standard Oil of NJ	Advantage
Annual Return	12.98%	14.48%	Standard Oil of NJ
Price Appreciation	10.66%	9.18%	IBM
Dividend Return	2.13%	4.94%	Standard Oil of NJ

Returns measured year end 1949-2010

You can see that IBM beat Standard Oil by wide margins in *every* growth measure that Wall Street professionals use to choose stocks. IBM's earnings per share growth, the Street's favorite stock-picking criterion, surpassed the oil giant's growth by more than 3 percentage points per year over the next six decades. Furthermore, the oil industry's share of the market shrunk dramatically over this period. Oil stocks comprised about 20 percent of the market value of all US stocks in 1950, but fell to nearly half that value in 2010 while the share of the technology sector increased more than sixfold.

With all this information, you confidently choose IBM shares. The decision looks like a slam dunk.

But IBM turned out to be the wrong choice. In 2010, when the lock-box is opened, your daughter would probably be pleased to see almost $15 million worth of IBM stock, but had you purchased Standard Oil instead, the investment in the oil giant would be worth more than $33 million. By the way, both IBM and Standard Oil beat the market over that time period, as an investment in a capitalization-weighted index fund would have accumulated to only under $5 million.

This conclusion does not change if we extend the data another 11 years to the end of 2021. Although both IBM and Standard Oil significantly lagged behind the S&P 500 Index from 2010 through 2021, an investment in ExxonMobil beat IBM and the oil company still beat the market over the 71-year period. The graph of the accumulation of these two stocks since 1950 is shown in Figure 11.1.

FIGURE 11.1

Standard Oil vs IBM: Total Return

Why did Standard Oil beat IBM when it fell far short in every growth category? Certainly, right after 1950, IBM surged ahead of Standard Oil. The excitement caused by IBM's new products caused IBM's valuation to rise markedly, and although it continued to churn out superior growth, the average price investors paid for IBM shares during those six decades was just too high. As you can see from Table 11.1, the average P/E ratio of Standard Oil was about half of IBM's ratio, and the oil company's average dividend yield was almost 3 percentage points higher. Because Standard Oil's price was lower and its dividend yield much higher than IBM, those who bought its stock and reinvested the oil company's dividends would have accumulated to 11.87 times the number of shares they started out with, while investors in IBM accumulated only 3.63 times their original shares. Although the price of Standard Oil's stock appreciated at a rate that was almost 2 percentage points below that of IBM, its higher dividend yield made the oil giant the winner for long-term investors.

WHICH COUNTRY?

In 2020, about one-half of the world's equity capital was located in the United States. With the surge in the value of the US-based tech giants, that fraction, which had been steadily declining for years, has held steady or even grown slightly in recent years. Nevertheless, as we learned in Chapter 4, because of diversification, international investment should be an important component of portfolio planning.

If you choose to invest abroad, which countries or regions should you pick? Europe, Japan, or the emerging markets? And what about China?

To decide, let us pose the following question: You have a choice of investing in country A or country B. The only information you are offered is that over the coming decades the GDP of country B will grow faster than that of country A. Which one would you invest in? The vast majority who are confronted with this question will respond "country B."

But on the basis of long-term historical data, that is the wrong answer. Figure 11.2 shows the total real stock returns and real per capita GDP growth for 21 countries from 1900 to 2020. The results are striking. The average relation between GDP growth and real stock returns is *negative*. In fact, the countries with the highest real return, South Africa, Australia, the United States, and New Zealand, have the very lowest per capita GDP growth rates.

I first reported this seemingly puzzling result in the second edition of *Stocks for the Long Run*. I found that from 1970 to 1997, the correlation between stock returns and GDP growth was −0.32 for 17 developed countries and −0.03 for 18 emerging markets. These negative correlations were later confirmed by Jay Ritter, as well as Elroy Dimson, Mike Staunton, and Paul Marsh over much longer periods of time.[3]

FIGURE 11.2

Global equity return versus real per capita GDP growth, 1900–2020

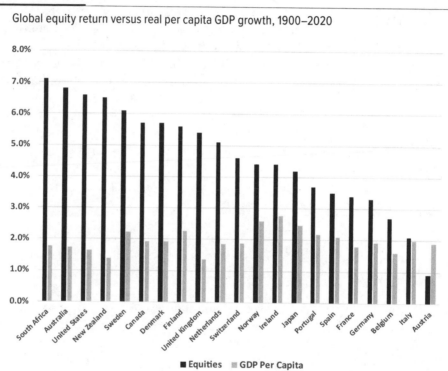

The results are the same if you examine stock returns and GDP growth around the world in the last half-century, from 1971–2020. Among developed world economies (excluding the city-states of Singapore and Hong Kong), the country with the highest return has been Denmark, whose 13.5 percent compound annual return exceeds the United States by almost 3 percentage points. Yet Denmark ties Germany for the second lowest GDP growth rate over the past one-half century, almost 1 percentage point behind the United States.

The last 30 years provide an even more striking example. From 1992 through 2020, China, the world's second largest economy, has generated the fastest GDP growth by far, averaging 9.3 percent per year. Yet the annual return on Chinese stocks has been only 2.7 percent, the absolute lowest among 18 emerging markets. In contrast, the highest stock market returns over this period among developing economies have been in Peru and Brazil, although they are near the bottom of GDP growth.

There are several reasons why faster economic growth does not automatically bestow greater returns to shareholders. Firms require capital, and faster growth requires firms to float more shares to achieve greater production, diluting existing shareholders. In the long run, the fruits of faster productivity growth have accrued to the benefit of workers in the form of higher wages. Since the Industrial Revolution, real wages (return per hour worked) have steadily risen, but the return to a dollar's worth of invested equity capital, although higher than the growth of real wages, has remained remarkably constant.

The most important reason for the inverse relation between growth and return is the same as why Standard Oil beat IBM; investors pay too much for growth, undervaluing low-growth countries, and overvaluing high-growth countries.

GOAT: GREATEST OF ALL TIME

GOAT, greatest of all time, has become a popular acronym. It is usually applied to sports figures or teams. Who is the best—Simone Biles, Rafael Nadal, Tom Brady, or the New York Yankees? Fans love to rank these sports icons.

In the equity market, we can calculate GOAT by computing the stock with the highest total return over the greatest number of years that we have comprehensive data on individual stock returns, as compiled by the CRSP data series beginning in 1926. Table 11.2 shows the best-performing original stocks since 1926.

But the GOAT stock, in contrast to the GOATs in the sports world, is admired by few and shunned by many. The winner is Philip Morris, a leading manufacturer of tobacco products, the same company that we reported in Chapter 6, was also the best-performing stock since March 1957, when it became one of the original companies in the new S&P 500 Index.

Its superior performance goes back even further than 1957. For the 95-year period from the end of 1926 through the end of 2021, Philip Morris delivered a 16.02 percent compound annual return, almost 6 percentage points greater than the market. Had your grandmother bought 40 shares (at a cost of $1,000) of Philip Morris in 1925 and joined their dividend investment plan, her shares, handed down through the generations, would be worth over $1.33 *billion* by the end of 2021! With reinvested dividends, the original 40 shares would grow to over 25 million shares and would constitute more than 1 percent ownership of this global giant.

TABLE 11.2

Best performing stocks from 1926–2021

Ticker	Original Name	Current Name	Annualized Returns from 12/1926-12/2021
MO	PHILIP MORRIS INC	ALTRIA GROUP INC	16.02%
KSU	KANSAS CITY SOUTHERN RY CO	KANSAS CITY SOUTHERN	14.50%*
VMC	VULCAN MATERIALS CO	VULCAN MATERIALS CO	14.21%
ETN	EATON MFG CO	EATON CORP PLC	13.08%
IBM	INTERNATIONAL BUSINESS MACHS COR	INTERNATIONAL BUSINESS MACHS COR	12.97%
KO	COCA COLA CO	COCA COLA CO	12.89%
PEP	PEPSI COLA CO	PEPSICO INC	12.84%
GD	GENERAL DYNAMICS CORP	GENERAL DYNAMICS CORP	12.51%
ADM	ARCHER DANIELS MIDLAND CO	ARCHER DANIELS MIDLAND CO	12.07%
TR	SWEETS CO AMER	TOOTSIE ROLL INDS INC	11.75%
TT	INGERSOLL RAND CO	TRANE TECHNOLOGIES PLC	11.53%
XOM	STANDARD OIL CO N J	EXXON MOBIL CORP	11.29%
TXN	TEXAS INSTRUMENTS INC	TEXAS INSTRUMENTS INC	11.04%
CVX	STANDARD OIL CO CALIFORNIA	CHEVRON CORP NEW	10.75%
ADX	ADAMS EXPRESS CO	ADAMS EXPRESS CO	10.56%

*KSU returns measured until merger with Canadian Pacific Railway Limited (CP) on 12/13/2021

Source of Philip Morris Outperformance

Ironically, one of the best things to happen to Philip Morris investors that wished to hold for the long run was a financial calamity for the company. This paradox has been well noted by value investors. Warren Buffett has said, "The best thing that happens to us is when a great company gets into temporary trouble. We want to buy them when they're on the operating table."[4]

And for many years, Philip Morris was not only on the operating table but on life support in the ICU! A slew of federal and state lawsuits against cigarette manufacturers cost Phillip Morris nearly $100 billion and threatened the cigarette manufacturer with bankruptcy. This caused the price of the stock to remain depressed for nearly a decade.

However, the company continued to churn out cash and pay dividends, and the low price of its stock enabled stockholders to use their dividends to buy more shares on the cheap. These reinvested dividends have turned its stock into a pile of gold for those who stuck with Philip Morris.

The stellar returns of Philip Morris have been true of the entire tobacco industry. Dimson, Marsh, and Staunton from the London Business School have compiled historical returns on US industries dating back to 1900. A dollar invested in the market from 1900 to the end of 2014 would have produced a return of 9.6 percent per year. However, a dollar invested in the tobacco industry during that time period, would have returned 14.6 percent, over 160 times as much as the market.[5]

OTHER "NEAR-DEATH EXPERIENCES" THAT TURNED TO GOLD

We have already noted how Melville Shoe Corporation was transformed into CVS, one of the big long-term winners in the S&P 500. Melville Shoe just missed Table 11.2 by being listed two years later in 1928. Yet its annual return from that listing until the end of 2021 is 12.48 percent, versus 9.88 percent for the market.

Another fascinating example is the Thatcher Glass Corporation, the leading milk bottle manufacturer in the early 1950s. As the baby boom turned into the baby bust, and glass bottles were replaced by cardboard cartons, Thatcher's business sank drastically. Fortunately for Thatcher shareholders, in 1966 the firm was purchased by Rexall Drug, which became Dart Industries, then merged with Kraft in 1980, and was eventually bought by Philip Morris in 1988. Although glass bottles went the way of the buggy whip, an investor who purchased 100 shares of Thatcher Glass in 1957 and reinvested the dividends would be worth more than $40 million at the end of 2021.

A final example of how winners can rise from the seeming abyss is the railroad industry. Railroads dominated the capital markets in the late nineteenth and early twentieth centuries. During the Great Depression, rails suffered a steady decline as planes and highways provided more efficient travel. As a result, dozens of railroads went bankrupt or were taken over by governments.

It is the height of irony that virtually tied with Philip Morris as the *best*-performing of the original 500 stocks that comprised the S&P 500 Index and the second-best stock from 1926 through 2021 is a railroad: Kansas City Southern (KSU), founded in 1887. KSU was not bought by another successful firm, nor did management transform the firm into a very different company. KSU stayed almost exclusively in the rail business and for more than a century has churned out superior profits. Yet after 134 years of existence, it was purchased in December 2021 by Canadian Pacific, and KSU was dropped from the CRSP database. KSU had great management, but investors never put high valuations on the rail business, and the low prices helped keep KSU near the top of the best returns list.

It's What You Know for Sure That Ain't So

Near the height of the dot-com mania in 1999, I was invited to join the board of a new firm that planned to offer advice to investors using algorithms derived from finance theory. I flew to San Francisco to attend the opening meeting. I was most impressed by the management team, programmers, and business strategy.

At the beginning of the meeting, the CEO passed out a list of new internet-oriented companies. He asked the participants to guess which in 20 years would be the most successful and which would fail. The winners would be announced at the postmeeting get-together.

There were at least 30 companies on the list. The favorite suffix for many of these aspiring firms was "dot-com," much like "blockchain" and "crypto" during the bull market 20 years later. The candidates contained some companies that were already public, like Pets.com, Webvan. com, eToys.com, theGlobe.com, and Flooz.com. There were also a few communications giants on the list such as WorldCom and JDS Uniphase, as well as Yahoo and AOL, the internet giants that had just been listed on the S&P 500 Index.

I do not recall the firm that received the votes as "most likely to succeed," but I do remember the overwhelming choice of the company that would fail and would not be around in 2020. In fact, its announcement during the postmeeting happy hour elicited snickers of agreement from virtually everyone assembled: it was the bookseller Amazon.com.

CONCLUSION

Amazon.com doubters had good company in 2000. Around the same time when I went to San Francisco, *Barron's* magazine, one of the oldest and most influential weeklies on Wall Street, came out with what has become one of the most mocked lead stories of all time. Splashed over the cover page one was the title "Amazon.bomb."

Has history rendered *Barron's* projection wrong? Yes, and no. Amazon.com closed at $59 on the day before the *Barron's* article was published nearly a year and a half later, the stock sold for $5.51 per share, a stunning collapse of over 90 percent. It took nearly 10 more years before the stock surpassed its 1999 high. If you exercised a little patience in

2000, you were able to buy more than 10 times the number of shares of Amazon.com as you would just have been able to buy at the top of the bubble.

Although very long-term Amazon.com holders who bought in 2000 were eventually bailed out, this episode illustrates a fundamental principle for long-term investors: *Don't fall in love with a company, fall in love with its price.*

Is Value Investing Dead?

Benjamin Graham's [the father of value investing] book, The Intelligent Investor, *changed my life. If I hadn't read the book, I'd probably still be delivering newspapers.*[1]

—Warren Buffett, 2019

Value investing is dead.

—Bank of America/Merrill Lynch memo, September 2020

VALUE INVESTING

For decades, *value investing*, the strategy of buying stocks with a low price relative to the firm's fundamentals—such as dividends, earnings, assets, or cash flows—was the hallmark of virtually all successful long-term investors. The acknowledged founder of value investing was Benjamin Graham, a British-born New Yorker who linked up with Columbia University Professor David L. Dodd to write *Security Analysis*, the classic 1934 book that laid out the principles of value investing. Graham developed a methodology for determining the intrinsic value of a firm by using disciplined financial analysis. He believed that investors could beat the market by taking advantage of the difference between the market price of a stock and its intrinsic value.

By following his principles, Graham became an extremely successful investor, gained a wide following, and generated returns that regularly beat the market. He published his strategies in a 1949 book entitled *The Intelligent Investor*, which sold millions of copies and was translated into dozens of languages.

The best-known disciple of Benjamin Graham is Warren Buffett, who enrolled in Columbia Business School to study under Graham and learn the principles of value investing. Other highly successful value investors include Walter Schloss, William Ruane, and Tweedy Browne Partners. These and others are highlighted in Buffett's 1984 article, "The Super-investors of Graham-and-Doddsville." Buffett demonstrated that these investors' superior performance could not be due to chance, but reflected a disciplined application of the principles of value investing.[2] More recent protégées of the Graham and Dodd approach include Mario Gabelli, Bill Ackman, and Michael Bury (featured in Michael Lewis's *The Big Short*).

In his teachings, Graham introduced one of the most famous characters to the investing literature: Mr. Market, an emotional, manic-depressive personality who offers to buy or sell shares of the firm he is representing at prices that are frequently disconnected from fundamentals. Graham showed that the intelligent investor can take advantage of Mr. Market's moodiness, buying shares that Mr. Market offers below intrinsic value and selling those priced too high. Stocks whose prices are low relative to a firm's fundamentals, called *value* stocks, would in the long run offer investors superior risk-adjusted returns to *growth* stocks, whose prices are high, relative to fundamentals.[3] The advantages of growth versus value investing became an enduring topic debated among investment professionals.

Yet from 2007 through 2021, value investing has not proved to be a successful strategy. In fact, by virtually every measure, value investing has lagged behind growth investing by the largest margin in the nearly century-long data set on stocks used for analyzing the performance of investment strategies.

What has happened? Is value investing dead, as some proclaim? Or is it just a run of bad luck for this investing style? To answer these questions, we shall define the various criteria used for value investing and then review and interpret the data.

Earnings, Dividends, and Book Value

Graham and Dodd emphasized the importance of price relative to earnings (P/E ratio) as a key variable determining whether a firm's stock should be bought and warned that purchasing high P/E stocks was a losing strategy. In their classic 1934 edition of *Security Analysis*, they state:

> Hence, we may submit, as a corollary of no small practical impor-
> tance, that people who habitually purchase common stocks at more
> than about 16 times their average earnings are likely to lose consid-
> erable money in the long run.[4]

Refraining from buying stocks over 16 times earnings was very limiting, even though the average stock in those days sold below 15 times earnings. Interestingly, in their second edition published six years later, Graham and Dodd gave a nod to the possibility that firms with higher earnings growth deserved higher valuation, and they substituted 20 as the upper limit of a "reasonable P/E ratio."[5] Nevertheless, they maintained that buying stocks with higher P/E multiples would often lead to lower future returns.

The importance of the P/E ratio to future returns was confirmed by academic research. In the late 1970s, Sanjoy Basu, building on the work of S. F. Nicholson in 1960, confirmed that stocks with low P/E ratios have significantly higher risk-adjusted returns than stocks with high P/E ratios.[6] Later analysis of extensive data on stocks from 1926 onward confirmed that firms with lower P/E ratios outperformed those with higher ratios.

Figure 12.1 shows the cumulative returns for all firms in the United States from 1950 through 2021, ranked by their E/P ratios, or *earnings yield* (the inverse of the P/E ratio) on December 31 of each year. I divided the earnings yields of all stocks into five quintiles, from the highest (top 20 percent) to the lowest (bottom 20 percent), and computed their subsequent return over the next 12 months.[7]

FIGURE 12.1

Earnings-to-price (E/P) ratio by quintiles

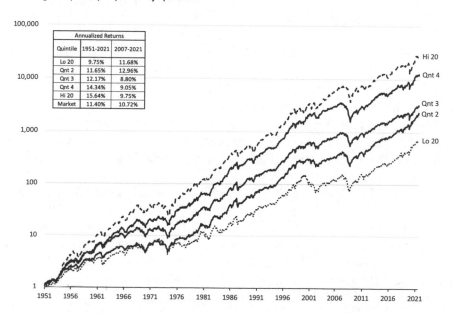

	Annualized Returns	
Quintile	1951-2021	2007-2021
Lo 20	9.75%	11.68%
Qnt 2	11.65%	12.96%
Qnt 3	12.17%	8.80%
Qnt 4	14.34%	9.05%
Hi 20	15.64%	9.75%
Market	11.40%	10.72%

One can see that over the entire period, stocks with the highest earnings yields (lowest P/E ratios) outperformed those with the lowest earnings yields (highest P/E ratios). However, as the inset shows, the maximum gain from pursuing this strategy occurred before 2006, prior to the financial crisis. Since that date, low P/E stocks have underperformed high P/E stocks, although they still maintained their outperformance over the entire period.

Dividends

A second important factor used by value investors is dividend yield. In *Security Analysis*, Graham and Dodd stated:

> Experience would confirm the established verdict of the stock market that a dollar of earnings is worth more to the stockholder if paid him in dividends than when carried to surplus. The common-stock investor should ordinarily require both an adequate earning power and an adequate dividend.[8]

Once investors take account of earnings, it is right to ask why dividends should be an additional factor that might motivate investors to buy a stock. In Chapter 7, we showed that earnings that are *not* paid as dividends can create value for shareholders in several ways, such as buying back stock, increasing investments, or paying down debt. In fact, we demonstrated that *if* firms earn the same return on internally held funds as investors demand for holding the stock, then the price of shares does not depend on whether earnings are retained or paid as dividends.

Benjamin Graham believed that firms frequently did not use internal funds efficiently. In fact, some of his most profitable investments involved taking over firms and distributing unproductive surpluses (often held in cash or other liquid assets) to shareholders. Furthermore, value investors believe that a steady commitment by management to pay cash dividends (and increase these dividends over time) incentivizes managers to undertake productive and profitable investments that will increase shareholder return.

As in the case of P/E ratios, early research confirmed Graham and Dodd's conviction. In 1978, Krishna Ramaswamy and Robert Litzenberger found a significant correlation between dividend yield and subsequent returns.[9] Well-known market advisors such as James O'Shaughnessy showed that in the period 1951 through 1994, the 50 highest-dividend-yielding large-capitalization stocks had a 1.7 percentage point higher return than the market.[10]

Share Repurchase

Dividends are just one way for a firm to distribute earnings directly to shareholders. As discussed in Chapters 7 and 10, buybacks, or management's purchase of a firm's own shares in the open market (often called *share repurchases*), are an important source of shareholder return. Before 1982, the government strongly restricted the ability of a firm to engage in buybacks, concerned that management could use such purchases to manipulate the market. But in 1982, the SEC issued a set of rules (10b-18) that greatly liberalized the conditions that allow firms to repurchase their own shares.

From a tax standpoint, share repurchases, which increase the price of a stock, are superior to dividends. This is because dividends are taxed when paid, while capital gains are only taxed when the shares are sold, a decision that is under the control of the investor. As a result, an investor can defer the tax on shareholder returns, perhaps indefinitely, if the shares are eventually donated to charity or placed in a tax-exempt trust.

Indeed, researchers have found that firms that repurchase shares outperform the market, while those that issue shares underperform. Figure 12.2 shows the cumulative and annualized returns of those firms that have engaged in share repurchase, as well as the returns from dividend yields (sorted by quintiles) from 1950 through 2021. During that period, firms that repurchased shares outperformed even the highest dividend payers.[11] Although the long-term data support the case for using dividend yields alone to achieve higher stock returns, a dividend yield strategy is not nearly as successful as using either P/E ratios or buybacks. The cumulative returns from 1951, sorted by quintiles, are shown in Figure 12.2.

Although portfolios with higher dividend yields offered investors higher total returns than the market, the *second* highest quintile of dividend-paying stocks actually provided slightly higher returns than the highest dividend yielders. This may be because the highest dividend yielders represented firms that ran into financial difficulty and were forced to cut their dividends in subsequent years.

As was the case with P/E ratios, the performance of higher-dividend-yield stocks has deteriorated markedly since 2006. In contrast, the outperformance of firms that engaged in share repurchase continued over that period. From 2007 through 2021, firms that repurchased their shares returned 11.22 percent per year against 10.72 percent for the market. Although high-dividend-yield stocks alone have not outperformed the market in recent years, the combination of high-dividend yield and share repurchases has done quite well.[12]

FIGURE 12.2

Dividend yield by quintiles and share buybacks

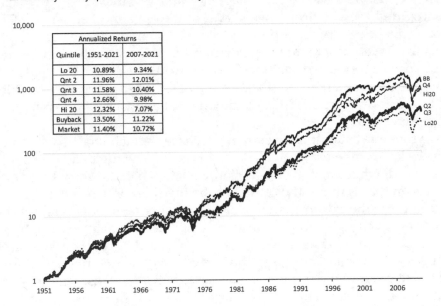

The Dow 10 Strategy

Another high-dividend-yield strategy that has outperformed the market over the long run is called the "Dow 10 strategy" or the "Dogs of the Dow." This strategy involves investing each year in the 10 highest-yielding stocks in the Dow Jones Industrial Average.

The Dow 10 strategy has been regarded by some as one of the simplest and most successful investment strategies of all time. James Glassman of the *Washington Post* claimed that John Slatter, a Cleveland investment advisor and writer, invented the Dow 10 system in the 1980s.[13] Harvey Knowles and Damon Petty popularized the strategy in their book *The Dividend Investor*, written in 1992, as did Michael O'Higgins and John Downes in *Beating the Dow*. These high-yielding stocks are often those that have fallen in price and are out of favor with investors. For this reason, the Dow 10 strategy is often called the Dogs of the Dow.

Figure 12.3 confirms the superiority of the Dow 10 strategy. The Dow 10 strategy outperforms both the overall Dow Jones Industrial

Average, composed of all 30 stocks, and the S&P 500 from 1957 to 2021. Over that 68-year period, the annualized return of the Dow 10 strategy has been 12.40 percent, against 11.45 percent for the Dow 30 and 11.03 percent for the S&P 500. However, the gap has narrowed in recent years as the Dogs of the Dow, like other value-based strategies, have underperformed the market.

FIGURE 12.3

Dow 10, Dow Jones Industrial Average, and S&P 500

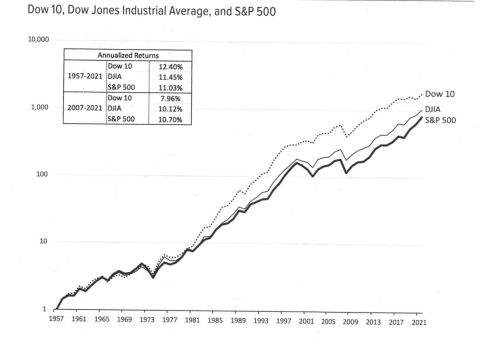

Annualized Returns		
	Dow 10	12.40%
1957-2021	DJIA	11.45%
	S&P 500	11.03%
	Dow 10	7.96%
2007-2021	DJIA	10.12%
	S&P 500	10.70%

Book Value

One of the biggest boosts to value investing, at least in the eyes of academics and money managers, came from analyzing the extensive data collected by CRSP for all listed stocks since 1926. In 1992, Eugene Fama and Ken French published "The Cross Section of Expected Stock Market Returns" in the *Journal of Finance*, which became one of the most cited articles in finance literature.[14]

In this research, Fama and French showed that the ratio of the book value to market value could be used to choose stocks that displayed superior returns relative to their risk. In fact, their original research showed that price-to-book ratios were better than P/E ratios in predicting future cross-sectional stock returns.[15]

To be sure, Graham and Dodd also considered book value to be an important factor in determining returns:

> [We] suggest rather forcibly that the book value deserves at least a fleeting glance by the public before it buys or sells shares in a business undertaking. . . . Let the stock buyer, if he lays any claim to intelligence, at least be able to tell himself, first, how much he is actually paying for the business, and secondly, what he is actually getting for his money in terms of tangible resources.[16]

Figure 12.4 shows that dividing stocks by quintiles according to book value is an effective way to increase returns. Even with the severe downturn in the fortunes of this strategy in recent years, the return on the lowest quintile of price-to-book stocks beats the highest quintile by more than 3 percentage points per year over the last 70 years. Nevertheless, the recent poor performance of book value has dropped this strategy behind the P/E ratio when judged over the entire period. Since 2006, it has trailed the market by almost 3.5 percentage points per year.

Despite the emphasis on the book value in the research by Fama and French, the use of this factor to estimate the true market value of a firm is fraught with difficulties, as discussed in Chapter 10. *Book* value, which records firm assets at historical cost, does not correct for changes in the *market* value of those assets, nor does it adequately include research and development (R&D) or other expenditures related to intellectual property.

The deterioration of book value as a signal for investors is hardly surprising. The growing importance of intangible assets, such as intellectual property in the transformation of the US economy, has been confirmed by recent research. Cate Elsten and Nick Hill have shown that in 1975 only 17 percent of the market value of the S&P 500 firms was comprised of intangible assets. By 1985 this had nearly doubled to 32 percent and by 1995 had exceeded two-thirds. In 2015 the percentage had risen further to 84 percent.[17] Indeed, when researchers have included intangible assets in the book calculations, this improves the recent performance of the book-to-value ratio.[18]

There is a second important reason why book value is a poor indicator of the intrinsic value of the firm. A firm that engages in a stock buyback is taking cash out of its treasury and buying its stock at the market price rather than book value. As long as the market value is greater than book value (which it usually is), this will decrease its book value. As noted in Chapter 10, the book value of Apple stock is just a few dollars a share, although the market value is many times this number. The growing popularity of share buybacks further reduces the effectiveness of book value as an indicator of intrinsic value.

FIGURE 12.4

Book to market by quintiles

Annualized Returns		
Quintile	1951-2021	2007-2021
Lo 20	9.46%	14.09%
Qnt 2	9.87%	11.07%
Qnt 3	10.82%	9.06%
Qnt 4	10.58%	4.52%
Hi 20	12.73%	7.30%
Market	11.40%	10.72%

UNDERPERFORMANCE OF VALUE STOCKS

The period since 2007 is not the first time that value stocks have underperformed growth stocks. During the early 1970s a group of firms with superior earnings growth dubbed "the Nifty Fifty" caught the attention of Wall Street professionals and pension funds. These included long-time winners such as Philip Morris, Pfizer, Bristol-Myers, Gillette, and Coca-Cola, but also embraced losers such as MGIC Investment Co, Sears, Polaroid, Burroughs, and Kresge. Institutional buying pushed the average P/E ratio of these stocks over 40 by December 1972, well more than twice that of the S&P 500.[19] During this period value stocks underperformed substantially until most of these nifty stocks crashed, enabling value investing to reassert its supremacy.

An even more notable run of growth stocks occurred at the turn of the last century, called the dot-com bubble. This buying focused on technology firms involved in the creation of the internet. The surge in the prices of firms such as Oracle, MCI WorldCom, Sun Microsystems, and EMC sent the P/E ratios of these stocks far higher than those reached during the Nifty Fifty mania.[20] The crash of the dot-com and tech stocks, which caused the Nasdaq market index to fall by nearly 80 percent in the following year, again resurrected the value strategy, which continued to outperform the market until it reached its peak performance in 2006.

But the poor performance of the value strategy during the Nifty Fifty and dot-com mania did not approach the severity or duration of its downfall since 2006. Using the Fama and French book value criteria the decline in a portfolio that went long in stocks with the lowest price-to-book ratios and short stocks with the highest price-to-book ratios (called the long-short portfolio) was 55 percent, the deepest fall on record. [21]

Among large-capitalization stocks, the drawdown of the long-short portfolio was an even deeper 61 percent, which is unusual since large-cap value stocks had done better than small-cap value stocks during previous value downturns. To be sure, using other value criteria, such as the P/E ratio or book value adjusted for intellectual property, the declines were not as severe.[22] Nevertheless, the 13.5-year duration of the underperformance that followed the financial crisis was unprecedented, far eclipsing the previous record of 2.5 years that followed the dot-com bubble.

Explanations for the Post-2006 Value Downturn

One explanation of the disappearance of the premium to value investing is that value stocks had been bought by so many investors that the advantage of this strategy has been arbitraged out of the market. As we shall see in Chapter 17, many phenomena, particularly calendar anomalies, that had been found in earlier data have faded or completely disappeared in recent years.

Has the Premium Been Arbitraged?

Is it possible that so many investors may have acted on Benjamin Graham's thesis that there is no longer any advantage to pursuing the value strategy? If this were the case, then value stock would have risen, not fallen, relative to growth stocks in recent years. Once value stocks reach their new, and higher price equilibrium, their forward-looking returns would drop to those commensurate with growth stocks. However, the evidence does not support that hypothesis. Although the P/E ratios of value stocks have risen modestly, the P/E ratios of growth stocks, particularly big-cap growth stocks have risen even more.

Instead, value stocks were hit with the "perfect storm" between 2006 and 2021. First, growth stocks, particularly technology stocks, proved to be undervalued following the collapse of the 2000 tech bubble, as their subsequent earnings far outstripped expectations. In addition, their valuation ratios rose substantially over this period, giving their returns a further boost.

Furthermore, important value sectors suffered severe losses during this period. First, the financial sector fell dramatically during the Great Financial Crisis and never fully recovered. Then the oil sector collapsed, due to both the sharply increased supply from fracking and the increasingly restrictive environmental regulations. Last, the Covid-19 pandemic greatly increased the demand for technology. Given these blows, it is not surprising that value stocks experienced record underperformance.

In fact, recent research by Ľuboš Pástor, Robert Stambaugh, and Lucian Taylor claims that a good part of the underperformance of value stocks is related to the surge in environmental, social, and governance (ESG) investing, the topic of Chapter 15.[23] This is particularly true with respect to investing trends that are linked to environmental risks. ESG investors' avoidance of certain sectors that are viewed as harming the environment, particularly oil, and their preference for technology firms that are viewed as environmentally friendly, have contributed both to the earnings and valuations changes of these sectors that have harmed value investors.

The largest increase in valuations since 2006 has occurred in the largest firms, which almost exclusively reside in the technology sector. Figure 12.5 displays the average P/E ratios of stocks with the highest 30 percent, middle 40 percent, and lowest 30 percent of the market value spectrum from 1962 through 2021. It is readily apparent that the largest stocks experienced the greatest rise in valuation ratios, while the P/E ratios of the middle and smaller stocks rose far more modestly. In 2021 the P/E ratios of low P/E stocks were about the same as in the early 1960s, while those of the high P/E stocks nearly doubled.

FIGURE 12.5

P/E ratios and market capitalizations

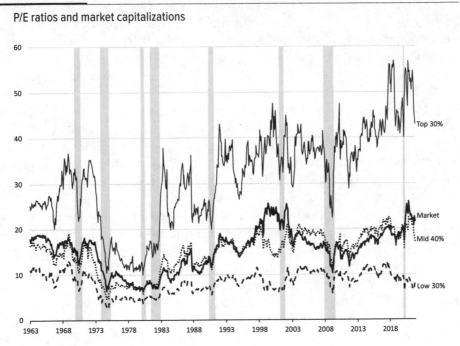

Discount Rate

Another explanation for the outperformance of growth stocks centers around the fall in the interest rate used to discount future cash flows. Value stocks provide cash flows sooner than growth stocks. *Duration* is a term that the finance profession uses to describe the average time that it takes for an investor to receive an asset's expected cash flows. The duration of value stocks is shorter than that of growth stocks.

It can be easily shown that the price of assets with longer durations is impacted more by a given change in interest rates than by the price of assets of shorter duration. For example, a 1 percentage point drop of interest rates will cause a greater increase in the price of a 30-year bond than in a 10-year bond. As we have seen in Chapter 8, over the past 20 years there has been a marked and persistent drop in both real and nominal interest rates. Therefore, it is reasonable to expect that the valuation of growth stocks would rise relative to the valuation of value stocks and provide one explanation for the underperformance of value stocks since 2006.

Arguing against this explanation is the historical data, which shows very little impact of interest rates on the valuation of growth stocks relative to value stocks. One of the greatest bursts in growth stocks occurred during the internet and dot-com bubble of 1999 to 2000, when real interest rates were extremely high. It could be argued that the excitement about the development of the internet was so intense that it offset these higher interest rates, and this episode should not count against the interest rate explanation. If so, it is not unreasonable to assign some of the underperformance of value stocks in recent years to the significant decline in interest rates.

Technology

When growth stocks outpace value stocks, it must be because (1) the earnings of growth stocks, relative to value stocks, exceeded investors' expectations, or (2) the valuation that investors assign to growth stocks rose relative to value stocks.

In fact, both conditions have prevailed in recent years. In 2007, the information technology and communications services sectors (whose firms are closely linked to technology) were 19 percent of the market capitalization of the S&P 500. In 2021, that proportion reached 40 percent, and if you add Amazon.com and Tesla, which have been switched from technology to the consumer discretionary sector, technology-dominated firms comprise nearly one-half of the market value of all US firms. In the nearly 70-year history of the S&P 500, the only other time that approached this concentration was the dominance of the material and energy sectors when the index was born in 1957.

As previously mentioned, since 2007, most technology firms in the S&P 500 have outperformed earnings expectations and have increased their price relative to those sharply rising earnings. In 2012, the P/E ratio of the information technology sector was about 14, slightly lower than that of the entire S&P 500 Index. In retrospect, this valuation clearly undervalued growth stocks. Since that time, tech earnings per share grew at a 12.7 percent rate over the next 10 years, more than 5 percentage points more than other firms in the index, while their P/E ratio nearly doubled.

Big-Cap Growth Stocks

Most visible is the growing dominance of the technology giants, such as Meta (formerly Facebook), Apple, Amazon.com, Netflix, Google (now

Alphabet), and Microsoft, a group originally dubbed FANG by television host Jim Cramer in 2013.[24] In that year, the aggregate value of these six firms was just over $1 trillion, which constituted 8 percent of the market value of the S&P 500. By 2021 their value approached $10 trillion, and their market value comprised over one-quarter of the S&P 500. Their earnings grew quickly, but nonetheless their aggregate P/E ratios went from the low 20s to the mid-30s over this period. In 2021 these six stocks added approximately three points to the P/E ratio of the S&P 500.

It should be noted that the tech giants of 2021 were nowhere nearly as expensive, as tech stocks were at the top of the dot-com bubble in 2000. Figure 12.6 shows the P/E ratio of the tech sector and the largest five tech stocks of that sector from 1962 through 2021. Not only are the P/E ratios of these stocks lower in 2021 than during the dot-com bubble, but they are not much higher in 2022 than during the 1960s. During both of these periods, interest rates were significantly higher than they were in 2020. This argues that the current valuation of technology stocks may not be unreasonable, and *if* they maintain their superior earnings growth, the valuation may continue to rise relative to the market.

FIGURE 12.6

P/E ratios sorted by firm equity value

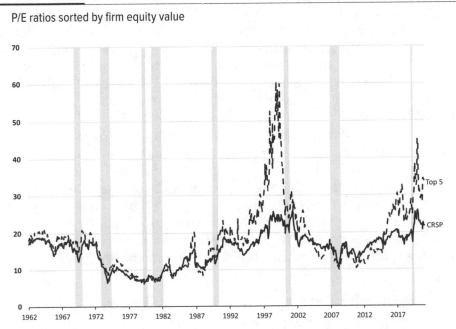

THE FUTURE OF VALUE VERSUS GROWTH

In the debate between value and growth, those advocating the abandonment of value investing argue that the world has permanently changed. Economics 101 teaches that profits are maximized when marginal cost, the cost of producing an additional *widget*, the economist's term for an arbitrary unit of output, is equated to the marginal revenue earned by selling that widget. But in today's digital world, the cost of producing one more digital widget is virtually zero. The whole world can be flooded with digital products at virtually no cost.

Nevertheless, not all output is digital. Apple must produce physical phones, Netflix must produce real content, and Tesla must produce real cars. Amazon.com is the second-largest private labor employer in the United States. The traditional economic models cannot be completely abandoned.

There have been many times in the past when one industry has dominated the economic landscape and capital markets. In the nineteenth century it was the railroads; in the early twentieth century it was oil, steel, and then autos. During the middle of the twentieth century, AT&T, the government-protected monopoly of all US telephone services, was so large that it was excluded from the S&P stock indexes, for fear that its size would distort index returns.

Will the next dominant industries be entertainment, climate mitigation, pure air and water, fintech, biotech, virtual and augmented reality, or something we cannot imagine today? It is possible that a technology giant will grow from an industry that now has a meager market value. Look how Elon Musk transformed the sleepy auto industry, and how Jeff Bezos turned low-margin retailing into a juggernaut that has devastated the brick-and-mortar retailing industry. No one can tell from whom or where the next breakthrough will come.

CONCLUSION

The basis of value investing goes far beyond the mood swings of Mr. Market that Benjamin Graham so colorfully described a century ago. It is also based on the fact that prices do not, and in fact cannot, always equal their true market value. Why that happens and how investors might take advantage of "noisy" markets is the subject of our next chapter.

Market Efficiency or Noisy Markets?

*Security analysis cannot presume to lay down general rules as to
the "proper value" of any given common stock. . . . The prices of
common stocks are not carefully thought out computations, but the
resultants of a welter of human reactions.*

—Benjamin Graham and David Dodd, 1940[1]

THE EFFICIENT MARKET HYPOTHESIS

Chapter 1 showed that the equity market has delivered consistent and
significantly positive long-term real returns to shareholders. The last
two chapters analyzed value investing, which once was the leading
strategy of successful investors but has significantly underperformed
because of the surge in growth stocks in the early 2020s. Are there any
strategies that investors can use to choose stocks that can deliver better
returns than a simple capitalization index fund?

"No!" responded those economists who in the mid-1960s and early
1970s supported the *efficient market hypothesis* or *EMH*. EMH was a term
coined by Harry Roberts in 1967 and popularized by Eugene Fama of
the University of Chicago in the early 1970s.[2] The EMH maintains that
all the criteria that influence stock returns, such as earnings, dividends,
and cash flows, are already incorporated into prices, so investing on the
basis of these factors (or any others) will not improve the risk-return performance of a simple capitalization-weighted investor portfolio.

The ascendancy of the EMH followed (but is not necessarily
implied by) the development of the *capital asset pricing model*, or *CAPM*,

in the 1950s by William Sharpe, John Lintner, and others and the pioneering work of Harry Markowitz on portfolio selection.[3] The CAPM demonstrated that the measure of an individual stock's risk most relevant to investors is not the volatility of the stock's price itself, as many advisors had believed, but the *correlation* of its return with the overall market, a number that can be estimated from historical data.[4] This correlation, which is known as *beta*, measures the risk of an asset's return that cannot be eliminated through diversification. The volatility of an individual stock that is not correlated with the market, which is called *diversifiable, residual,* or *idiosyncratic risk,* does not warrant a higher return in a well-diversified portfolio.

The CAPM, coupled with the EMH, implied that the best risk-return trade-off that investors could achieve was to hold the "market" portfolio, specifically a capitalization-weighted, fully diversified portfolio of stocks, often called an *index fund.*[5] Investors with higher risk tolerance would hold a higher proportion of their assets in the stock index fund (and a lower proportion in safe assets, such as bonds or cash), and those with lower risk tolerance would hold a lower proportion in the index fund. Whatever the risk preferences of investors, the capitalization-weighted index fund would be the optimal portfolio of stocks, for every investor.[6]

The EMH received support from studies undertaken by Irwin Friend, Jack Treynor, and Michael Jensen in the 1960s, which showed that "managed money," measured from the performance of mutual funds, systematically failed to beat the market represented by the popular indexes.[7] Early studies in the 1970s confirmed that higher beta stocks did, in fact, have higher returns.[8] As a result of these findings, the EMH and the CAPM dominated the way that academics, and indeed most Wall Street professionals, viewed financial markets from the 1960s through the 1980s.

But in the 1980s and 1990s, empirical evidence contrary to CAPM and the EMH began to emerge. As more data on individual stocks were analyzed, beta did not prove effective at explaining their returns. In 1992, Eugene Fama and Ken French, strong early supporters of CAPM and EMH, wrote an article that showed that two other factors, one relating to firm *size* (measured by market capitalization) and the other to the *valuation* (measured by book-to-market ratio), were far more important than beta in determining a stock's return.[9]

Subsequently, many other factors, such as "momentum" and others related to a firm's financial variables, were found to have a significant impact on returns and are discussed in the next chapter. These pricing "anomalies," as they were called, prompted Fama and French to state that the evidence against beta was "compelling" and that "the average return anomalies . . . are serious enough to infer that the [CAPM] model is not a useful approximation" of a stock's return. In fact, Fama and French suggested researchers investigate "alternative" asset pricing models or even "irrational asset pricing stories."[10]

THE NOISY MARKET HYPOTHESIS

The discovery that size and valuation factors could significantly improve returns for investors, above that achieved by a capitalization-weighted portfolio, implied that some of the assumptions underlying either the EMH or the CAPM are violated. Questioning the validity of the EMH was furthered by the research of Sanford Grossman and Joseph Stiglitz. They proved that asset prices must at times deviate from fundamental value in order to motivate analysts to undertake costly research to bring stock prices back to levels justified by fundamental factors.[11] Perfectly efficient markets, they claimed, are in fact an impossibility.

One reason why prices deviate from fundamentals is the presence of "noise traders," who trade on the basis of information that is either imperfectly or completely unrelated to the valuation of the firm, or investors who buy or sell stock for personal financial reasons unrelated to fundamental factors.[12] Many noise traders misinterpret financial data, chase "trends" or other technical signals, or invest on the basis of "gurus" who they perceive to have special knowledge about the valuation of certain stocks.

Whatever the reason, these noise traders drive the price of the shares away from their "fundamental" or "intrinsic" value, which is defined as the value that the stock would trade based on the *actual* rather than conjectured distribution of future earnings.

In 2006, I coined the term *noisy market hypothesis* to describe a market environment that I thought was more realistic than the one represented by the EMH.[13] It is not easy to find strategies that beat popular broad-based capitalization-weighted stock indexes, but that does not mean that opportunities to beat these indexes do not exist. When noise traders drive prices to deviate from fundamentals, there may be opportunities for fundamentally based investors to profit.

One way of taking advantage of a noisy market is by weighting stocks by fundamental financial factors, such as earnings or dividends, a strategy often called *fundamentally weighted* indexing or *smart beta*.[14] This strategy involves reducing the weight of stocks whose market price rises more than (or falls less than) fundamentals, and increasing weights on firms whose stock price falls relative to such fundamentals in a predetermined manner. These portfolios automatically tilt toward value stocks, without engaging in financial analysis or analyzing individual firms.

DEVIATIONS FROM MARKET EFFICIENCY

In order for such strategies to be superior to capitalization-weighted indexing, the existence of noise traders must be established, and their importance has been hotly debated. In the 1950s, Milton Friedman, making the case for flexible, market-driven foreign exchange rates, claimed that deviations from fundamental values would not be large, because such speculators who had bought "too high" and sold "too low" would suffer financial losses and become a minor factor in the markets.[15]

Others showed that may not be the case. In the late 1980s, Bradford de Long and others showed that noise traders can cause prices to diverge significantly from fundamental values, even when all the future cash flows that determine the price of a security are known. Furthermore, these noise traders may even earn higher returns than investors who base their decision on fundamentals.[16] The question became, "How far from 'fundamental value' do prices have to go before the market can be described as 'inefficient' and induce fundamental investors to take opposing positions to profit from price discrepancies?"

Fischer Black, codeveloper of the famous Black-Scholes model of option pricing and a strong supporter of the EMH, surprised many economists when he stated in his 1986 presidential address to the American Finance Association, "We might define an efficient market as one in which the price is within a factor of 2 of [fundamental] value, that is, the price is more than half of value and less than twice value." He followed up stating, "By this definition, I think almost all markets are efficient almost all the time. 'Almost all' means at least 90%."[17]

IRRATIONALITY VERSUS LIQUIDITY

If prices often deviate by a factor of two from fundamental value, this appears to leave easy pickings for fundamental investors who strive to beat the market. But even with a discrepancy of this magnitude, significantly mispriced stocks (and markets) may become even more mispriced before they eventually return to fundamentals.

Nearly a century ago John Maynard Keynes warned that speculators who followed the "crowd" may overwhelm the impact of fundamental investors and send prices further from equilibrium. He maintained that "Investment based on genuine long-term expectation is so difficult . . . as to be scarcely practicable. He who attempts it must surely . . . run greater risk of [speculators] who tried to guess better than the crowd how the crowd will behave."[18] In more modern times, Keynes's words have been summarized, "Markets can stay irrational longer than investors can remain solvent."[19]

In recent years, we have seen examples of markets driven to extremes that topple fundamental investors. Many investors began shorting the dot-com stocks in the late 1990s, but were forced to cover their position at great losses as these stocks continued to soar before they collapsed in 2000 and 2001. Similarly, 20 years later, "meme" stocks, which became popular on financial chat sites such as Reddit's r/WallStreetBets, soared in price, forcing many fundamentally based investors, and even some well-financed hedge funds, to reverse their positions at a great loss.

When prices fall *below* intrinsic values, fundamental investors have an easier time maintaining their investment position, but even in that case they may not avoid liquidity constraints. Individual investors can borrow up to 50 percent of the value of stock on margin, while institutional investors can often borrow much more. If the price falls by one-half, which still settles within that range of what Fischer Black called an efficient market, an individual investor who borrowed 50 percent on margin would be on the edge of forced liquidation. If such liquidation occurs, fundamentally based investors will lose even if their stock later rises in price.

In addition to liquidation risk, there are psychological obstacles to pursuing a strategy that deviates from the market. If prices continue to move away from fundamentals, fundamental investors will underperform those with simple capitalization-weighted indexed portfolios. Even indexed investors are frequently spooked by bear markets. If one has entrusted money to a fundamentally based strategist, staying the course is even more difficult. As one well-known fundamental fund manager confided to me, even if your strategy is vindicated in the longer run, the large number of clients who abandon you during the tough times will never come back or even acknowledge that your strategy was ultimately proved sound. Indeed, Andrei Shleifer and Robert Vishny have argued that the risks of engaging in strategies that deviate from the market loom large for institutional managers, whose career paths often depend heavily on short- and not long-term performance.[20]

RESTRICTIONS ON SHORT SELLING

One of the reasons why prices may exceed fundamental values for extended periods of time is restrictions on short selling. One of the assumptions of the CAPM is it is as easy for investors to short a stock as to acquire a long position, but there are practical and psychological reasons why this assumption is violated. Shorting a stock requires an investor to locate shares that can be borrowed and sold, and then to hold funds or "margin" against a short sale, which provides security to those who loaned the stock. More important, short sellers are exposed to potentially unlimited losses if prices rise. In contrast, a long-only investor can lose, at most, 100 percent of the amount invested.

Restrictions on short selling are particularly significant in order to pursue strategies that attempt to beat the market. Many of the pricing anomalies that are pursued by sophisticated investors, such as hedge funds, are called "long-short" strategies. These strategies involve not only buying the stocks (called the "long leg" of the strategy) that have historically outperformed, but also selling short stocks at the other end of the spectrum (called the "short" leg). Robert Stambaugh, Jianfeng Yu, and Yu Yuan did an extensive study of 11 different anomalies for the period 1965 to 2008 and found that nearly 70 percent of the return from the long-short strategy came from the short leg of the portfolio.[21]

The profits from the short leg of the long-short strategy are significantly influenced by the level of "market sentiment," that is, whether investors are bullish or bearish about stocks. Malcolm Baker and Jeffrey Wurgler developed such a sentiment index. It demonstrated that the size and value anomalies identified by Fama and French were particularly profitable when market sentiment was high, since during those periods investors are bullish and many stocks are priced above their fundamental value.[22]

Stambaugh, Yu, and Yuan also found that nearly 80 percent of the profits that originated from long-short strategies occurred during periods of high market sentiment. In contrast, they found that the profitability of the long leg of the portfolio is not significantly influenced by market sentiment. This is consistent with the theory that "undervalued" securities have an easier time attracting capital that goes long than attracting capital for overvalued securities that must go short. Their results tended to confirm the hypothesis that restrictions on short selling are an important source of these anomalies and are most profitable when stocks are priced above their fundamentals.

THE MARKET PORTFOLIO

The presence of noise traders and the risks and restrictions on short selling help explain why prices deviate from fundamental value, and such mispricing opens up the possibility that certain strategies may outperform the market. But noise traders are not the only reason why CAPM based on analyzing the universe of traded stocks does not explain individual stock returns.

One of the difficulties in empirically verifying the CAPM is that it is not well-defined which assets constitute the "market portfolio." Should the market portfolio consist of only US stocks, or should it be all global stocks, or should one include bonds and perhaps also real estate? And importantly, should one include *human capital*, which is perhaps the largest part of many investors' current wealth, especially for young people? This ambiguity limits the testability of the CAPM and is termed the *Roll critique* after Richard Roll who emphasized this problem in the 1970s.[23]

For example, if the return of a stock or group of stocks is correlated with one's labor income, then these stocks should be underweighted in one's portfolio. Advisors strongly caution against the once-common practice of holding the company's stock that you work for in your pension fund. If bad luck befalls your firm or industry, you will suffer the double whammy of stock and employment losses.

More generally, if value stocks (those with low prices relative to fundamentals) have a higher correlation with labor income than growth stocks, then investors in value stocks would require a higher expected return than computed by the CAPM that excludes human capital. But this higher return does not imply that investors with labor income should over-weight value stocks in their portfolio, since that would put their total wealth, defined to include their real assets and labor income, at greater risk. In a similar vein, Leonid Kogan, Dimitris Papanikolaou, and Noah Stoffman have constructed a model where investors buy growth stocks to participate in the part of the economy that is involved in "creative destruction" and may adversely affect their employment.[24] Growth stocks then become a hedge against losses in labor income, leading growth stocks to have a lower return. This is yet another reason why value stocks outperform in a simple CAPM context.

INTERTEMPORAL RISKS

Originally CAPM models were designed for one-period portfolio recommendations. Under the assumption that stock fluctuations are random walks, the CAPM portfolio recommendations can then be extended to multiple periods. But if stock prices are mean reverting, stock portfolios constructed from one-period standard deviations may not lead to the best longer-term allocations.

Bonds are particularly troublesome assets to include in static one-period models. In the 1970s, Robert Merton showed that when you extend the CAPM to many periods—called the *intertemporal capital asset pricing model* (ICAPM)—long-term bonds serve as an effective hedge against shifting investing opportunities, and their single-period volatility overstates their true risk.[25] In other words, single-period variability in prices that result from shifting discount rates may hedge against long-term fluctuations in the return from one's portfolio.

Similar arguments may be applied to stocks. Fluctuations caused by changing discount rates are not as detrimental to long-term portfolio performance as are fluctuations caused by changing perceptions of future cash flows. If fluctuations in the price of *growth stocks* are caused more by changes in discount rates, because their valuations are based on cash flows that extend further into the future, then growth stocks may be less risky for a long-term portfolio, and hence offer lower returns based on a simple-one period CAMP model. In his article "Good Beta, Bad Beta," John Campbell separates market fluctuations into changes in interest rates (which he called "good beta") and the beta related to business cycles (which he called "bad beta") and finds the latter does a better job at explaining returns than the beta taken from static CAPM models.[26]

SKEWED RESPONSE TO GAINS AND LOSSES

Another set of conditions that may cause the failure of the CAPM model to predict returns arises from behavioral responses. The CAPM assumes that individuals care only about expected return and risk, the latter defined as the standard deviation of their portfolio returns. *Prospect theory*, a concept pioneered by Nobel Prize–winning economist Daniel Kahneman and Amos Tversky (discussed in more detail in Chapter 25 on behavioral economics), maintains that investors experience greater pain from absorbing losses than they receive pleasure by realizing gains.[27] This may lead investors to dispose of winners too early and hold on to losers for too long, a characteristic that might lead to a momentum factor described in the next chapter. In fact, cognitive biases may be responsible for quite a few return anomalies found in the historical data.

CONCLUSION

The preceding discussion focuses on conditions that deviate from the EMH and the CAPM that may cause certain portfolios to perform better than the "plain vanilla" fully diversified, capitalization-weighted index fund.

But beating the market indexes might be too narrow a goal. Investors must ask how their stock portfolio correlates with their other non-stock assets, such as real estate and particularly their labor income. Furthermore, some stocks do better at hedging against future risks (including climate risk) than others, and some individuals may wish to reward certain companies that comply with ESG standards (as we shall see in Chapter 15), even though doing so will not optimize the risk-return trade-offs of their market portfolio. Outperforming the major market indexes, so prized by the vast majority of stockholders and money managers, may not lead to the best economic or even financial outcome for many investors.

The "Factor Zoo"

Size, Value, Momentum, and More

> *The rate of factor production [criteria to "beat the market"]
> in the academic research is out of control. Academic journals
> overwhelmingly publish papers with positive results that support
> the hypothesis being tested. . . . Authors figure this out. To
> maximize the chance a paper is published, the paper needs a
> positive result. Hence, the data mining begins.*[1]
>
> **—Campbell Harvey and Yan Liu, 2019**

MAJOR MARKET FACTORS

The CAPM predicted there was one factor that dictated whether a stock had an expected return above or below the market. It was *beta*, the sensitivity of the stock's return to the market. Those stocks with higher correlations were supposed to have higher expected returns, and those with lower correlations had lower expected returns. If the correlation was zero, the expected return was the same as the risk-free rate, as this risk could be diversified away. Those with negative correlations were called *hedge assets* and had even lower, possibly negative expected returns.

Later the empirical work of Eugene Fama and Ken French confirmed that two other factors significantly impacted returns and were far more important than beta: valuation (based on price-to-book ratios) and size, where small stocks outperformed large stocks. Unlike beta, these factors were not derived from the EMH but were found by empirically examining individual stock returns. Nonetheless, these three

193

factors became known as the Fama-French *three-factor model* and dominated quantitative stock-picking strategies in the late 1980s and 1990s.

Finding criteria to improve market performance did not end with the three-factor model. Fama and French themselves later added two more factors, "profitability" and "investment," to produce the *five-factor model*.[2] Meanwhile, other researchers discovered a slew of other factors, including quality of earnings, stock issuance, liquidity, volatility, and especially "momentum," which has outperformed all the others. In his 2011 presidential address to the American Finance Association, John Cochrane called the explosion of factors a veritable "zoo," and some worried that data mining was involved in this eternal search to beat the market.[3] The returns on just some of these factors, which will be discussed later in the chapter, are shown in Figure 14.1.

FIGURE 14.1

The factor zoo

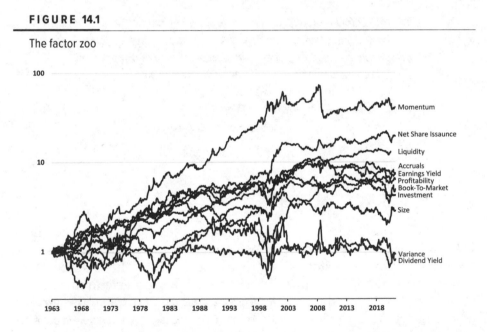

LONGER-RUN VIEW OF SIZE, VALUATION, AND MOMENTUM FACTORS

Figure 14.2 displays the cumulative returns from forming portfolios that take advantage of the factors *valuation*, *size*, and *momentum*, the latter being the tendency for stocks that have gone up or down in the previous 12 months to continue in the same direction in the following year. These factor strategies, which are designed to enhance the return on a market portfolio, are constructed by taking a long position in the top 30 percent of the stocks ranked by each factor (lowest price to book, smallest market cap, and highest momentum) and a short position in the bottom 30 percent of the stocks of each category.[4] These are self-financing portfolios insofar as the revenues from shorting stocks finance the long purchases, although margin funds must be held against the short position. All stocks traded on the NYSE, Amex, and NASDAQ from 1926 through 2021 are included. Also displayed are the cumulative returns on the entire market and the risk-free asset.

FIGURE 14.2

Major market factors: size, value, and momentum, the whole market, and the risk-free rate

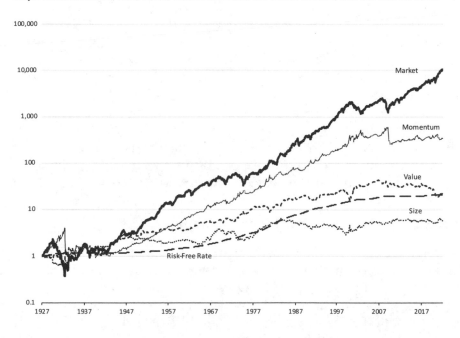

Several broad trends are notable. Despite significant volatility in the 1930s, the graph of these factor returns and the overall market returns go back to nearly the same position in the early 1940s as where they began in 1926. Second, the strength and persistence of the momentum factor dominates the other factors. Third, all these factors, even momentum, have faded significantly, adding little or nothing to the return on the stock market in the last 20 years. In fact, the size factor has added nothing to returns for almost 40 years.

SIZE FACTOR

The discovery of the size factor came well before the Fama and French research. In 1981, Rolf Banz, a graduate student at the University of Chicago, investigated the returns on stocks using the database that had been recently compiled by CRSP, located at the university. He found that small stocks systematically outperformed large stocks, even after adjusting for risk as defined within the framework of the CAPM.[5] Indeed from 1926 through 1980, the annual return to the smallest 20 percent of the stocks exceeded those of the largest 20 percent of the stocks by about 4 percentage points per year, far in excess of what would have been predicted on the basis on the smaller stocks' somewhat higher volatility.

Why should small stocks outperform large stocks? Some economists maintained that the superior performance was compensation for the higher transaction costs of acquiring and selling these securities, especially in the earlier years of the sample. Others asserted that because there is relatively less information and far too few analysts covering small stocks, there is more uncertainty surrounding their true valuation. This in turn requires a higher return for investors who take a position in these stocks. Furthermore, buy-side managers likely needed a larger incentive to justify a significant position in a small stock compared to a position in a large firm represented in an index such as the S&P 500.[6]

Unusual Features of Small Stock Premium

Unfortunately for investors trying to beat the market, the outperformance of small stocks is not consistent. The magnitude of the outperformance of small-cap stocks has waxed and waned unpredictably over the past 95 years, as shown in Figure 14.3, which displays the cumulative returns on the smallest 20 percent stocks on the CRSP database with those of the S&P 500 Index (the top 90 stocks before 1957) from 1926 through 2021.[7]

Small stocks recovered smartly from their beating during the Great Depression and experienced a surge during World War II. From 1946 until 1974, small stock performance lagged behind the S&P 500. But between 1975 and the end of 1983, small stocks exploded. During these years, small stocks averaged a 35.3 percent compound annual return, more than double the 15.7 percent return on large stocks. Cumulative returns in small stocks during these nine years exceeded 1,400 percent. That period is unusual; Figure 14.3 shows that if the years 1975 through 1983 are eliminated, the total return from owning small stocks virtually matches that of the S&P 500.

FIGURE 14.3

Small stocks and S&P returns, 1926–2021 (including and excluding 1975–1983)

One explanation for the strong outperformance during that period was the enactment of the Employee Retirement Income Security Act (ERISA) by Congress in 1974, making it far easier for pension funds to diversify into small stocks. Another was the turn by investors to buy small stocks following the collapse of the big-cap Nifty Fifty stocks earlier in the decade.

An even more unusual characteristic of the small firm effect is that shortly after its discovery, it was found that virtually all the excess returns of small firms occurred during the month of January. The so-called January effect is discussed in detail in Chapter 17 on calendar anomalies. This January effect has disappeared in recent years and may have contributed to the poorer performance of the small stocks.

Some economists question if a true size factor ever existed, and whether it was other characteristics associated with small stocks that explained small stock outperformance. As noted earlier, stocks with high correlations to the market (high-beta stocks), which characterize many small stocks, have lower returns than predicted by the CAPM model. When this factor is considered, the small stock outperformance completely disappears.[8] Others claim that you can restore the small stock effect if you screen these stocks for severe financial stress or use some "quality" of earnings factor.[9] The debate about the outperformance of small stocks still rages.[10]

Small Stocks and Value Stocks

Although small stock outperformance is in question, it has long been recognized that value investing is more profitable in small stocks than in large stocks. Table 14.1 shows the compound realized returns for stocks ranked both according to size and price-to-book quintiles. Over the entire period from 1926 through 2021, small value stocks, defined as the smallest 20 percent, have experienced a compound rate of return of 16.24 percent per year, against only 2.83 percent for small growth stocks. Among large stocks, the value effect has been far smaller, as large growth stocks have edged out large value stocks by less than 1 percentage point per year.

TABLE 14.1

Size/value returns

1926-2021		Size Quintiles				
		Small	2	3	4	Large
Book-to-Market Quintiles	Value	16.24%	14.97%	13.39%	12.29%	10.93%
	2	14.53%	13.57%	13.55%	12.85%	8.97%
	3	11.39%	12.79%	12.67%	11.91%	10.53%
	4	7.05%	12.15%	12.46%	11.27%	9.89%
	Growth	2.83%	7.77%	9.45%	10.53%	10.20%

2006-2021		Size Quintiles				
		Small	2	3	4	Large
Book-to-Market Quintiles	Value	10.53%	8.13%	8.89%	6.97%	8.37%
	2	8.79%	8.72%	10.65%	8.85%	3.47%
	3	7.68%	11.05%	10.74%	8.43%	9.84%
	4	9.67%	12.76%	12.86%	12.41%	11.26%
	Growth	5.43%	11.83%	11.28%	13.96%	14.19%

As noted earlier, there has been a sharp decline in the performance of value stocks in recent years. Although the *smallest* value stocks have still beaten the *smallest* growth stocks from 2006 through 2021, growth stocks have outperformed value stocks in every other quintile except the smallest 20 percent over those 15 years. In fact, among the largest 20 percent of stocks, which approximates the stocks in the S&P 500 Index, large growth stocks have beat large value stocks by almost 6 percentage points per year. Value investing still works best in the smallest stocks, but the magnitude of the outperformance has dwindled significantly.

There are a number of reasons why small value stocks outperform small growth stocks. Small stocks in general have a much smaller group of analysts who follow them, and therefore their price can deviate from intrinsic value for a longer period of time before they attract the attention of value investors. Furthermore, small growth stocks have very high volatility and attract investors that wish to hit a home run with their investment, much like those who buy lottery tickets. Because the volume and *float* (the number of shares traded) of small stocks is small, noise traders have a disproportionate effect on these stocks. As noted earlier, the activity of noise traders, by sending prices away from fundamentals, favors value investors.

International Size and Value Investing

Small value stocks' outperformance also prevails internationally. Table 14.2 summarizes these findings. From 1990 to 2021, small value stocks have outperformed large growth stocks in every major region in the world. The small value stock outperformance is the smallest in the United States and the largest in the emerging markets. Nevertheless, the outperformance of value stocks has shrunk from 2006 through 2021 in all regions. In the United States and Europe, large growth stocks have outperformed small value stocks over that period. However, in Japan, Asia, and the emerging markets, small value stocks have still outperformed large growth stocks. The underperformance of value investing has not been as severe outside the developed countries, especially outside of the United States, where the surge of technology stocks has fueled growth stocks' performance.

TABLE 14.2

International size and value

Region	1990-2021			2006-2021			Switch
	Small Value	Large Growth	Difference	Small Value	Large Growth	Difference	
US	13.48%	12.00%	1.49%	8.13%	13.37%	-5.25%	-6.74%
Developed	10.62%	8.36%	2.26%	6.89%	11.19%	-4.30%	-6.56%
Developed Ex US	9.06%	4.87%	4.20%	6.47%	7.38%	-0.91%	-5.11%
Europe	10.17%	7.25%	2.92%	6.29%	8.82%	-2.53%	-5.45%
Japan	3.89%	1.08%	2.80%	5.11%	3.86%	1.25%	-1.55%
Asia Pacific Ex Japan	10.86%	8.38%	2.48%	7.86%	6.68%	1.18%	-1.30%
Emerging Markets	15.00%	6.63%	8.37%	11.85%	7.50%	4.35%	-4.02%

MOMENTUM

In 1985, Werner De Bondt and Richard Thaler showed that portfolios of stocks that have done well relative to the market over the past five years underperformed over the next three to five years and vice versa. They concluded, "Thirty-six months after portfolio formation, the losing stocks have earned about 25 percent more than the winners, even though the latter are significantly riskier."[11]

This whopping difference was strictly contrary to the random walk theory of stock market prices and the EMH. Such findings, many claimed, could be explained by behavioral finance: excessive optimism when stocks are doing well, which drives their price well above fundamentals, and excessive pessimism when these stocks are doing poorly.

De Bondt and Thaler's findings opened a floodgate of additional research into whether past stock behavior can predict the future. Two years later, they wrote a follow-up article that corroborated their earlier findings and showed their results were not related to the size or value factors found by Fama and French.[12] They also gave evidence that these reversals were caused by investors who extrapolated recent earnings trends too far into the future. Sustained rises in stock valuations did not predict a comparable rise in future earnings, contrary to the EMH. [13]

But these long-run reversals in stock prices that De Bondt and Thaler found were not detected in the short run. On the contrary, in 1990, Narasimhan Jagadeesh found that stocks that have outperformed that market over the previous 12 months continued to outperform in the next 12 months, while losers continued to lag the market.[14] These excess returns were large and more significant than any other factor and extended beyond US markets.[15] In fact, researchers have found evidence of a "super momentum" strategy that sorts momentum stocks on the basis of the individual stock's volatility. Choosing the most volatile of the momentum stocks produces returns that are about double the already powerful returns of the standard momentum strategy.[16]

Buying stocks that are appreciating and selling those that are declining could not be furthest from the principles of value investing. In the *Intelligent Investor*, Benjamin Graham states, "Never buy a stock because it has gone up or sell one because it has gone down." And Warren Buffett, Graham's disciple, has more forcefully warned "The dumbest reason in the world to buy a stock is because it's going up."[17] In fact, Fama admitted that "Of all the potential embarrassments to market efficiency, momentum is the primary one."[18]

The explanation for the success of the momentum strategy is very likely based on behavioral explanations. Investors initially react too slowly to earnings surprises (sometimes called the "conservative bias") and then when subsequent surprises occur (in the same direction), these same investors overreact, extrapolating earnings growth (or earnings shortfalls) further in the future than warranted. This type of behavior can produce trends or serially correlated price behavior that gives rise to the momentum phenomenon.[19]

Another behavioral explanation relies on the self-reinforcing impact of traders who predict the direction of stock prices correctly. If a trader makes a bullish prediction on a stock and the stock indeed moves up, this reinforces the conviction of the trader and causes other investors to shift their expectations in a bullish manner, reinforcing the upward trend.[20]

The existence of runs in the price of stocks is not by itself inconsistent with an efficient market. Economists have long noted that market efficiency does not require that price movements exhibit a random walk where the probability of the next price change being up or down is equal, but rather a *martingale*, which allows for short-term serially correlated price movements. However, a martingale pattern cannot be exploited for profit since such correlated price movements are followed by sharp, and unpredictable reversals in the other direction.

There is an old saying on Wall Street, "up a staircase, down the elevator," that illustrates the pattern of stock prices. Despite the unpredictability of when a stock experiencing a sustained upward or downward movement in price will reverse, there are many trend followers who believe that they are skillful enough to avoid these reversals.

"Make the trend your friend" or "Ride the wave" is familiar trader lingo, voiced by traders who confidently believe they can jump off the train before it goes over the cliff.

Despite the enormous returns to the momentum strategy, there are downsides. The strategy does involve more portfolio churning than any other strategy, and if transaction costs are large, this consumes some of the profits. Furthermore, as can be seen from Figure 14.1, the momentum strategy does experience some very sharp downturns, especially near the bottom of bear markets. For investors sensitive to such drawdowns, the profits from pursuing this strategy may not be worth the extra volatility.

Nevertheless, some money managers, such as Cliff Asness of AQR Associates, have maintained that the downsides of the momentum strategy do not nullify its significant long-term returns.[21] However, like all the other factor strategies, the momentum strategy has not added much to market returns over the past two decades.

INVESTMENT AND SHARE ISSUANCE

In 2015 Fama and French added two more factors to their famous three-factor model that they rolled out in 1993.[22] One was the level of capital expenditures (investment) that a firm undertakes and the other is based on a measure of profitability. Based on the research of Sheridan Titman and others,[23] they showed that firms that expand their capital had lower shareholder returns than firms that were conservative with their capital investment. I also demonstrated in my 2005 book *Future for Investors*, in the chapter "Capital Pigs," that the returns of S&P 500 firms that spent the most on capital relative to their sales lagged badly behind those firms that spent the least.

This observation coincides with the views of the most famous value investor, Warren Buffett. In his 1985 report to Berkshire Hathaway shareholders, he explained his decision not to undertake capital expenditures in an effort to improve the profitability of his money-losing textile firm. He said each proposal looked like an "immediate winner," but he never accepted a single one because he knew that other textile firms would engage in the same behavior, neutralizing the gain, and cause more losses.

Excessive capital expenditures arise from projects that promise but do not deliver profit. Some CEOs are intent on building empires, and if they have cash on hand they will deploy it. Overexpansion often causes management to lose focus. Jim Collins, author of the bestselling book

Good to Great, asked CEOs, "Do you have a 'to do' list? Do you also have a *'stop* doing' list?" He regarded the latter to be equally important as the former.[24]

Another factor related to excessive investment, *share issuance*, first identified by Jay Ritter in the early 1990s, has been shown to be followed by lower returns, and this was confirmed by Fama and French.[25] Since excessive investment causes lower than expected returns, it is not surprising that a related characteristic, share issuance, which is often used to finance such investment, also leads to lower returns. We have already seen that firms that engage in buybacks (negative share issuance) have superior returns to firms that do not buy back their shares. On the flip side, those firms that issue the most shares have substantially lower returns to the market.

PROFITABILITY

The second factor added by Fama and French to their three-factor model is *operating profitability*, defined as annual revenues minus the cost of goods sold and interest divided by the book equity.[26] In 2013 Robert Novy-Marx concluded that profitability is a strong predictor of a company's future growth, as well as of earnings and free cash flow. Of particular interest, Novy-Marx noted that adding a profitability factor worked especially well when combined with the value factor.[27] The profitability factor was confirmed for out of sample data by Sunil Wahal, further increasing its credibility.[28]

The profitability factor was justified by the claim that this earnings measure better indicated true value and more accurately forecasted future earnings than the "net income" figure that Wall Street used. Of course, that either capital investment or profitability, well-publicized metrics, can be utilized to achieve superior returns is further evidence against the efficiency of the market.[29]

OTHER QUALITY OF EARNINGS FACTORS

The *profitability* variable defined by Fama and French is not the only factor about a firm's earnings that appears ignored by investors. Financial measures that ascertain *failure probability* or financial *distress* have also been found to be inadequately considered by investors who overpay for distressed assets. Richard Sloan has found that *accruals*, which are revenues earned or expenses incurred that impact a company's net income, but have not yet actually occurred, significantly impact returns.[30] Such accruals do not always translate into the revenues that firms expect, leading to unexpected write-offs. He showed that firms with higher-than-normal accruals have lower forward returns.

Combining factors in a single measure can also produce significant results. Cliff Asness, Andrea Frazzini, and Lasse Pedersen have combined prominent quality and profitability factors into a single measure called *quality minus junk*.[31] And Robert Stambaugh and Yu Yuan combined 11 prominent factors into a single factor that outperforms the Fama and French five-factor model.[32]

These quality factors are based on well-publicized data that are known to investors. No strategist implementing these factors makes any judgment about the future prospects of the firm or industry, or whether management is executing well or not. Furthermore, no widely accepted explanation of why these factors are significant is consistent with EMH.

LOW VOLATILITY INVESTING

What could sound better than investing in a low volatility portfolio and beating the market? There is a theory and, until recently, there was good evidence to back this approach.[33] The reason why low volatility stocks have higher returns is that restrictions on and aversion to short selling make it more difficult for value traders to short these stocks and bring them back down to their true fundamental value. As a result, these stocks are more likely to trade above, rather than below, their intrinsic value, thereby generating lower long-term returns. These restrictions, discussed in the last chapter and noted by Fischer Black in the early stages of development of the CAPM, are linked to reasons why high beta stocks have lower returns than predicted by the CAPM.

Low volatility investing is correlated with several other factors, such as quality of earnings, and some researchers have questioned whether it is a strong independent factor. Certainly, its name is extremely attractive to investors who wish to avoid market volatility.[34] Nevertheless, its return has suffered substantially in recent years. Because of the downdraft of low volatility funds in 2020 and 2021, risk-adjusted return of the volatility factor from 1963 through 2021 has fallen below zero.

LIQUIDITY INVESTING

Another factor that generates excess returns is the liquidity of a stock. Liquidity is a property of an asset that measures the discount that sellers would encounter if they were forced to sell on short notice. Assets with high liquidity generally have low discounts, while assets with low liquidity have high discounts.

In 1986 Yakov Amihud and Haim Mendelson showed that less liquid stocks, characterized by high bid-asked spreads, outperformed liquid stocks.[35] More recently Roger Ibbotson and others, using stock turnover ratio (the ratio of average daily volume compared to total number of shares outstanding), have confirmed those results.[36] Analyzing all New York, Amex, and Nasdaq stocks from 1972 through 2010, Ibbotson determined that stocks with the lowest quartile (25 percent) of turnover have a compound annual return of 14.5 percent per year, approximately double the return of stocks in the highest turnover quartile.

There are good economic reasons for a liquidity effect. It has been long recognized that among assets with identical, or near identical, risk-return profiles, those that are higher liquidity trade at a higher price. In the US Treasury market, the "on-the-run" long-term government bonds, which are considered benchmarks and are most actively traded, command a higher market price—and hence lower yield—than bonds with virtually identical maturities. Traders and speculators are willing to pay a premium for assets that they can buy and sell in quantity with low transaction costs. Investors value flexibility—the ability to respond to altered circumstances quickly without paying a substantial discount or premium. Furthermore, many large mutual funds would not be able to purchase large quantities of relatively inactive stocks, since to do so would require driving up their price to a point where the return is no longer attractive. This research implies that investors that do not value liquidity should tilt their portfolios toward less liquid stocks.

Robert Stambaugh and Ľuboš Pástor have shown that there is a liquidity effect related to the conditions in the *overall* stock market, not only related to the liquidity of the individual stocks.[37] They construct a measure of how individual stocks react when there are liquidity-wide market disturbances, such as occurred during the Lehman financial crisis in 2008, the Long-Term Capital Management bailout of 1998, or the volatility during the recent Covid-19 pandemic. Their hypothesis is that stock that can be bought or sold most easily during these crises will be preferred by investors, sending their prices to a premium and lowering their long-term return.

Indeed, they found that from 1966 through 1999, the average return on stocks with high sensitivities to liquidity exceeded that for stocks with low sensitivities by 7.5 percent annually, adjusted for beta, size, value, and momentum factors. Furthermore, they claim that such a liquidity risk factor accounts for half of the profits to a momentum strategy over the same 34-year period. Marketwide illiquidity can be viewed as a risk factor that is priced in the market, much like the climate risk factor discussed in the next chapter. This work implies that investors that do not value liquidity in a crisis should tilt toward stocks that are more sensitive to marketwide liquidity shocks.

INTERNATIONAL FACTOR INVESTING

Although the dollar market returns of most foreign countries have not measured up to those in the United States in recent years, most foreign countries have recorded an even greater advantage from factor investing than those recorded for US stocks.[38] Table 14.3 summarizes the returns to five factors: size, valuation (based on book-to-market ratios), profitability, capital investment, and momentum from 1990 through 2021 and from 2006 through 2021, when factor investing became less effective.. It shows that in every region except Japan, the average of these five factors is larger than in the United States. The small stock effect is not a significant factor in any region over this period, similar to what we have found in the United States. Valuation based on book value has a moderate impact, particularly in the Asia Pacific, excluding Japan. The quality of earnings is strong in every region and to a lesser extent so is the capital expenditure factor.

The biggest surprise is the strength of the momentum factor. In every region (excluding Japan[39]), momentum is the most important factor, and in some regions, it is the most important factor by a wide margin. Figure 14.3 implies that following a factor approach, particularly a momentum approach, can yield superior returns from foreign investing. The factor approach, if pursued, is greater than the diversification benefits gained through international investing. Furthermore, since 2006, although the net effect of factor investing has faded in the United States, it still remains positive, albeit at a lower level than existed before.

The one region where factor investing is not very successful is Japan. Not only does it have a sum of factor investing that is less than one-half of any other region, but its return to momentum investing, so powerful in every other geographical region, is actually negative![40]

TABLE 14.3

International factor investing

1990-2021		International Market						
		US	Developed	Developed Ex US	Europe	Japan	Asia Pacific Ex Japan	Emerging Markets
Factor	Domestic Returns	10.99%	8.23%	5.92%	7.67%	2.15%	8.89%	8.14%
	Size	1.15%	0.41%	0.85%	0.65%	0.43%	-1.71%	1.26%
	Value	0.94%	1.85%	3.10%	2.18%	2.29%	5.64%	7.22%
	Profitability	4.08%	4.40%	4.31%	4.68%	1.61%	3.54%	2.22%
	Capex	2.16%	1.83%	1.14%	0.88%	0.16%	2.90%	2.74%
	Momentum	3.52%	6.11%	7.33%	10.00%	-0.37%	9.39%	9.98%
	Avg of Factors	2.37%	2.92%	3.35%	3.68%	0.83%	3.95%	4.68%

2006-2021		International Market						
		US	Developed	Developed Ex US	Europe	Japan	Asia Pacific Ex Japan	Emerging Markets
Factor	Domestic Returns	10.90%	8.20%	5.42%	5.95%	3.46%	6.79%	6.54%
	Size	-0.13%	-1.03%	0.27%	1.66%	0.78%	-1.02%	0.58%
	Value	-3.37%	-2.52%	-0.55%	-2.91%	-0.09%	2.06%	4.34%
	Profitability	4.07%	4.33%	4.00%	4.97%	1.80%	3.52%	2.61%
	Capex	0.28%	-0.07%	0.06%	-1.12%	0.73%	1.71%	2.79%
	Momentum	-1.37%	3.03%	5.72%	8.02%	-1.24%	9.13%	8.31%
	Avg of Factors	-0.10%	0.75%	1.90%	2.12%	0.40%	3.08%	3.72%

This is no ready explanation for the absence of return from momentum investing in Japan. However, since most explanations of momentum are based on behavioral factors, such as under-reaction to news events or trend-following behavior of individual or institutional investors, the absence of momentum in Japan might suggest that these aberrational behavioral characteristics are absent from Japanese investors in recent years. Perhaps their market bust of 1989 to 1993, when the Japanese stock market fell 80 percent, the largest of any major country in the post–World War II era, has dissuaded Japanese investors from "following the trend," which so many had during their unsustainable boom.

CONCLUSION

Figure 14.4 displays some of the most important factor returns over the last half-century.[41] Momentum is by far the strongest factor over the entire period, yet most have faded or disappeared completely over the period from 2006 to 2021. Many of these factors have been ineffective over much longer periods.

FIGURE 14.4

Primary factors, 1963–2021

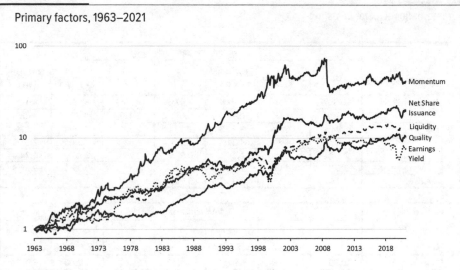

In a noisy market, where stock prices are deflected by various forces from equilibrium, a tilt toward stocks with lower valuations, especially based on earnings quality, valuation, and share buybacks, seems warranted.

But patience must be exercised. Strategies can run dry for years, or even decades, before they reassert themselves, if they ever do. Never embrace a single strategy. Wide diversification should always be the core of an investor's portfolio.

IV

STYLES, TRENDS, AND THE CALENDAR

ESG Investing

"The Social Responsibility of Business Is to Increase Its Profits."
—Milton Friedman, September 1970

[Friedman's essay] influenced—I'd say brainwashed—a generation of CEOs.

—Marc Benioff, CEO of Salesforce, September, 2020

On September 13, 1970, Professor Milton Friedman wrote the lead article in the *New York Times* magazine section that rocked the corporate world. In response to increasing demands that CEOs be "socially responsible," Friedman claimed:

> In a free-enterprise, private-property system, a corporate executive is an employee of the owners of the business. He has direct responsibility to his employers. That responsibility is to conduct the business in accordance with their desires, which generally will be to make as much money as possible while conforming to the basic rules of the society, both those embodied in law and those embodied in ethical custom.[1]

PROFITS VERSUS VALUE

By ending his essay with the emphatic statement that the "one and only social responsibility" of business is to increase its profits, the "Friedman doctrine," as his philosophy became known, served as a motif for generations of corporate leaders. The *New York Times* claimed the landmark essay "changed the course of capitalism."[2]

But by the time the golden anniversary of the Friedman doctrine came around, the stated goals of corporate America decidedly changed. A year earlier, in 2019, the Business Roundtable, an influential organization of business leaders, issued a new statement of purpose; the Roundtable declared that firms should make a fundamental commitment to all stakeholders, not only shareholders. These new goals included compensating employees fairly, fostering diversity, and protecting the environment by embracing sustainable production practices.[3]

The next year, the *Times* published an eight-page special insert exactly 50 years to the day that Friedman's original article was printed. The editors solicited comments from more than 20 prominent individuals, comprised of academicians, leading corporate executives, and other professionals.[4] Almost all were sharply critical of Friedman's original essay. Some, such as Marc Benioff, CEO of Salesforce, claimed that Friedman brainwashed a generation of CEOs. Others asserted the Friedman doctrine encouraged excessive "short-termism," the erosion of employee and environmental protections, and other evils. Many implied the Friedman doctrine led to a "greed is good" philosophy of corporate America, famously voiced by Gordon Gekko in the 1987 film *Wall Street*.[5]

What if Friedman had said that the purpose of management was to pursue policies that maximize *shareholder return* instead of corporate profits? Back in 1970, these two goals would have been considered one and the same.

However, today's research strongly suggests that this might not be the case.[6] By pursuing a broader set of goals, corporations may actually increase their profits; even if they do not, these actions might boost share value.

ESG INVESTING

A trio of categories: environmental, social, and governance, which goes by the acronym ESG, has become one of the fastest growing styles of investing.[7] According to the US SIF (Social Investment Forum) Foundation, professional investors considering ESG factors reached $17 trillion in 2020, a 42 percent increase since 2018. Funds committed to this strategy have increased sevenfold from 2012 to 2020 and the upward trend is accelerating.[8]

There are many agencies, most prominently MSCI (formerly Morgan Stanley Capital International) but also FTSE Russell and Sustainalytics, that evaluate each firm based on hundreds of criteria related to ESG, and post-composite ratings for each firm in each category. With the demand for ESG investing surging, the importance of ESG ratings now rivals the traditional stock and bond ratings of Standard & Poor's and Moody's, which for decades have dominated the investing landscape.

CORPORATE EARNINGS AND ESG RATING

The direct implementation of ESG policies may enhance corporate profits; better working conditions improve morale and productivity; encouraging diversity recruits better talent and brings a wider perspective to the boardroom. Good corporate practices, such as an independent board of directors or the establishment of a compensation committee, may also directly increase earnings.

Another way that implementing ESG criteria may increase profits is when customers are willing to purchase goods from firms that follow ESG practices, even if the products they make cost more than those from firms that do not pursue such practices. Many customers will pay more for goods that are "fair trade," meaning they do not violate labor laws or are produced with environmentally sustainable methods. A large number of automobile buyers demand electric vehicles, even if purchasing standard combustion engines would be more cost-efficient.

Achieving ESG objectives may also enhance the valuation investors place on corporate earnings, particularly by pursuing best practices in the governance category. Firms that establish tight auditing standards or increase the transparency of the decision-making process may sell at a higher earnings multiple than those that do not.

VALUATION ENHANCEMENT AND ESG STATUS

Notwithstanding the foregoing, there are many firms for which the cost of pursuing ESG objectives will exceed the direct monetary benefit, discouraging management from taking actions to enhance ESG goals. Yet implementing ESG objectives may increase share price, even if these pursuits decrease profits. There are two mechanisms through which this could occur: (1) The *psychic pleasure* that some investors receive through owning ESG stocks and (2) the *risk hedging* that environmentally friendly firms offer against adverse climate changes.

If there are investors that derive "psychic pleasure" from buying firms with high ESG rankings (as they do from buying products from these firms), then that preference will send the price of these firms higher than similar firms with lower ESG rankings.[9] This does mean that high ESG firms, after their price has risen, will deliver lower *forward-looking* returns than non-ESG firms. ESG investors are willing to forgo this diminished monetary return in exchange for the psychic satisfaction of owning companies that are good for the environment, value their employees, or pursue other ESG criteria that they value.[10]

There is evidence that demand for ESG characteristics, particularly related to the environment, send firms that pursue ESG objectives to premium valuations. In the environmental realm, Bank of America Global Research has analyzed all firms in the S&P 500 and found that those with below-median carbon emission, relative to all other firms in their sector, sell at 5.1 times that book value, versus 4.2 for those with above-median emissions.[11]

The establishment of carbon-neutral emission targets may send valuations higher. For the three largest carbon-emitting S&P 500 sectors (utilities, energy, and industrials), the forward P/E ratio of the firms where management has set such targets sported 50 percent higher P/E ratios than those who did not.[12] Of course, other factors, such as differences in expected profit growth, could explain the results instead of the preference by investors to own these firms. Yet, more specific evidence of the "psychic demand" for ESG investing is found in Germany. The German government floated two identical bonds: one funding ESG projects and the other not. Both are identically backed by the German government, yet the ESG bond sells for a higher price and thus has a lower yield than the non-ESG bond.[13]

FUTURE RETURNS FOR ESG STOCKS

The fact that ESG stocks may command a premium because of the psychic demand for holding these stocks does not imply that investors should overweight these stocks in their portfolios. The future return on ESG stocks is composed of three components: (1) unexpected changes in the future demand for ESG investing, (2) unexpected changes in the future profitability of ESG firms, and (3) the lower-than-expected long-run return to these stocks due to their premium valuation.

This last factor comprises a "headwind" for investors in ESG stocks. In order for ESG stocks to outperform non-ESG stocks on a pure risk-return basis, their earnings or the popularity of ESG investing must grow significantly faster than anticipated. Note that the current premium for ESG stocks already includes the expected future growth of ESG investing. The forecast that ESG investing will grow in popularity is not sufficient to conclude these stocks will outperform the market, even if their profitability matches expectations.

ESG AND PORTFOLIO SELECTION

This analysis allows us to determine whether an investor should *over-weight* or *underweight* ESG stocks in his or her portfolio, compared to the market-neutral, or capitalization-weighted indexed, portfolio. First, we shall consider the case where the investor has no independent opinion of the growth of ESG investing or its profitability—meaning, their expectations match the market.

If such an investor does not receive any psychic benefit from holding ESG stocks, then ESG firms should be underweighted in his portfolio. If the psychic benefit of this investor from holding ESG stocks matches the average, ESG firms should be held at market weight, that is, holding a capitalization-weighted, standard indexed fund will be optimal.

It should be noted that investors who own the standard market-weighted index fund are not getting the best risk-return trade-off from their portfolio, measured by monetary returns. A better monetary trade-off would be achieved by underweighting ESG stocks, no matter what your ESG preferences are. But when the psychic benefit of an investor with average ESG preferences is factored in, a market-neutral, capitalization-weighted indexed portfolio is optimal.

Finally, if the investor values ESG stocks more than the average investor, then they should overweight ESG stocks. Such an investor's risk-return trade-off will suffer further, but the investor's total satisfaction, which includes the psychic benefit from holding ESG stocks, will be enhanced.

PAST IS *NOT* ALWAYS PROLOGUE

There is little doubt, by most measures, that the stocks with strong ESG criteria have outperformed the popular averages in recent years. Casey Clark and Harshad Lalit of Rockefeller Asset Management have created a list of returns of those firms that have improved their ESG ranking versus those that have not and have analyzed their returns over the past decade.[14] As Figure 15.1 shows, those who have improved their ranking have outperformed the market.

There has indeed been a very strong shift toward ESG stocks in recent years. The faster-than-expected rise in ESG investing combined, in many cases, with their faster-than-expected profit growth has been the source of much ESG outperformance through 2021. If an investor can detect which firms are or will implement ESG criteria *before* the rest of the market, investing in those firms is likely to outperform. But future outperformance of any stock or any sector depends, as it always has, on *better-than-expected* future developments, not past realization.

FIGURE 15.1

ESG improvers and decliners vs. broad market

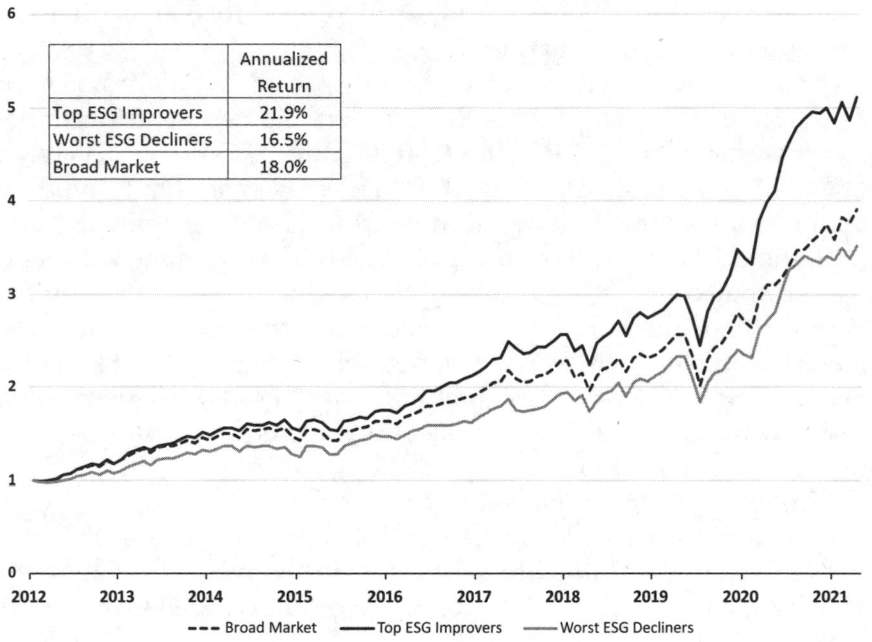

	Annualized Return
Top ESG Improvers	21.9%
Worst ESG Decliners	16.5%
Broad Market	18.0%

Despite the recent surge in demand for ESG investments, the long term tells a cautionary tale. In Chapter 6, we discussed that the best long-term stock in the United States has been Philip Morris, which would not score high on any ESG list. Additionally, as noted in Chapter 11, Dimson, Marsh, and Staunton, in their long-term study of industry returns in the United States, show that the tobacco industry outperformed all other industries and the markets from 1900 to the present by a large margin.[15] For the United Kingdom over the same period, firms involved in the production of alcoholic beverages beat all other sectors. Virtuous stocks may be winners in the short run, but through history, sinner stocks have taken first place.

ESG AS CLIMATE RISK HEDGES

Investor preference derived from the psychic pleasure of owning ESG stocks may not be the only rationale to hold these stocks despite their lower forward-looking returns. Standard finance theory dictates that portfolios should be chosen to achieve the best return subject to an investor's risk preferences. But if the state of the climate is a concern for an investor, then there is a case to hold the stocks of some firms—which we shall call "green" firms (environmental of the ESG categories)—that will provide larger payoffs in a situation where the environment deteriorates more rapidly than anticipated.[16] This case holds notwithstanding any psychic return investors may or may not receive from holding such firms.

Another way of understanding this source of green firm demand is that the holding of green stocks serves as an insurance policy against bad climate outcomes, and therefore these stocks qualify as a hedge asset. Hedge assets have higher prices and subsequently lower returns than the nonhedge assets, since hedge assets offset other risks that impact investors.

Viewing green stocks as hedge assets does *not* imply that they should be automatically overweighted in one's portfolio. Green stocks should be overweighted in an investor's portfolio only if the quality of the environment is of greater importance to that investor than to an average investor, or an investor who cares about climate change perceives the threat posed by unexpected worsening of the environment to be greater than that perceived by the market.[17]

In the case where green stocks hedge climate risk, the same conditions are required for green stocks to outperform the market on a pure risk-return basis, as the case we discussed where investors derive psychic income from holding these stocks. For green stocks to outperform the market, they must overcome the headwind of higher valuation through faster-than-anticipated profit growth, worse-than-anticipated climate change, or greater-than-anticipated growth in the demand for green stocks.

Some enthusiasts of ESG investing may be disappointed that high-rated ESG stocks may (and in equilibrium, are expected to) underperform low-rated ESG stocks because of their higher valuation. ESG advocates should be comforted that the higher price of ESG stocks reduces these firms' cost of capital. This allows for the flow of resources from weak-ESG firms to strong-ESG firms, allowing high-rated ESG firms to gain a stronger footing in the marketplace.

REFLECTIONS ON THE FRIEDMAN DOCTRINE

In 1970, the maximization of profits was synonymous with the maximization of shareholder value. More sophisticated models of stock valuation now suggest that they are not necessarily the same. If management spends time and resources implementing ESG criteria instead of solely maximizing corporate profits, this may actually increase the returns to shareholders.

If one reads the words of Friedman's 1970 article carefully, he emphasizes that the CEO is an employee of the business owners, who are the shareholders. He claimed management should conduct the business "in accordance with [the shareholders] desires." If the CEO is charged with maximizing shareholder *value*, a goal that I am sure Friedman would be in complete agreement with, the pursuit of ESG goals may be fully justified in a free-market, capitalistic economy that Friedman so admired.

CONCLUSION

For investors who believe that ESG investing will become much more popular than currently anticipated, overweighting those stocks is justified. If, in addition, one gets psychic value by owning these stocks, then one should overweight these firms even more.

For those who get no such psychic value from holding ESG stock and do not believe environmental risk is significant, holding these ESG stocks at a market-neutral level is only justified if you believe they will become far more popular than currently expected and the subsequent rise in price of ESG shares will overcome their higher valuation. If you do not believe this will happen, such an investor should underweight ESG stocks, correctly expecting to attain a better risk-return trade-off than holding a market-neutral, capitalization-weighted portfolio.

For investors who believe the future growth of ESG investing is already built into the market, your position in ESG stocks depends on your preferences, specifically the psychic pleasure from holding ESG firms and the desire to hedge climate risk. If these preferences approximate those of the average investor, you should hold the old-fashioned market-weighted, fully indexed portfolio. You must realize that this portfolio will not give you the best *monetary* return for the risk you are taking (you will be off the efficient CAPM frontier), but you will be maximizing the sum of your pecuniary and nonpecuniary (psychic) benefits.

And by giving ESG firms higher valuation and enabling them to grow faster, society may be better off.

The Friedman doctrine, which emphasized the duty of management to their owners, may not, after all, be inconsistent with the pursuit of ESG goals. By doing "good," corporate executives might, indeed, do very "well" for their shareholders.

Technical Analysis and Investing with the Trend

Many skeptics, it is true, are inclined to dismiss the whole procedure [chart reading] as akin to astrology or necromancy; but the sheer weight of its importance in Wall Street requires that its pretensions be examined with some degree of care.

—Benjamin Graham and David Dodd, 1934[1]

THE NATURE OF TECHNICAL ANALYSIS

Flags, pennants, saucers, and *head-and-shoulders formations. Stochastics, moving-average convergence-divergence indicators,* and *candlesticks.* Such is the arcane language of the technical analyst, an investor who forecasts future returns using past price trends. Few areas of investment analysis have attracted more critics; yet no other area has a core of such dedicated, ardent supporters.

Technical analysis has often been dismissed by academic economists as being as useful as astrology. Professor Burton Malkiel of Princeton University has been quite clear in his denunciation of technical analysis. In 1990 in his bestselling book *A Random Walk Down Wall Street,* he proclaimed:

Technical rules have been tested exhaustively by using stock price data on both major exchanges, going back as far as the beginning of the 20th century. The results reveal conclusively that past movements in stock prices cannot be used to foretell future movements. The stock market has no memory. The central proposition of charting is absolutely false, and investors who follow its precepts will accomplish nothing but increasing substantially the brokerage charges they pay.[2]

Yet this opinion, once supported by the great majority of academic economists, is changing. Recent research has shown that such simple trading rules as 200-day moving averages or short-term price momentum may be used to improve the risk-return profile for investors.[3] In this chapter we shall review the pros and cons of technical analysis.

FUNDAMENTALS OF TECHNICAL ANALYSIS

Technical analysts, or *chartists* as they are sometimes called, stand in sharp contrast to *fundamental analysts*, who use such variables as dividends, earnings, and book values to forecast stock returns. Chartists ignore these fundamental variables, maintaining that information important to predicting future price movements can be gleaned by analyzing past price patterns. Some of these patterns are the result of shifts in market psychology that repeat themselves, whereas others are caused by informed investors who have special knowledge of the prospects of the firm. If these patterns are read properly, chartists maintain, investors can use them to outperform the market and share in the gains of those who are more knowledgeable about a stock's prospects.

CHARLES DOW, TECHNICAL ANALYST

The first well-publicized technical analyst was Charles Dow, the creator of the Dow Jones Industrial Average. But Charles Dow did not analyze only charts; in conjunction with his interest in market movements, Dow founded the *Wall Street Journal* and published his strategy in editorials in the early 1900s. Dow's successor, William Hamilton, extended Dow's technical approach and published the *Stock Market Barometer* in 1922. Ten years later, Robert Rhea formalized Dow's concepts in a book entitled *Dow Theory*.

Charles Dow likened the ebb and flow of stock prices to waves in an ocean. He claimed that there was a *primary wave*, which like the tide determined the overall trend. Upon this trend were superimposed secondary waves and minor ripples. Dow claimed you could identify which trend the market was in by analyzing a chart of the Dow Jones Industrial Average, the volume in the market, and the Dow Jones Rail Average (now Dow Jones Transportation Average).

Those who follow Dow's theory acknowledge that the strategy would have gotten an investor out of the stock market before the October 1929 stock crash. Martin J. Pring, a noted technical analyst, argues that starting in 1897, investors who purchased stock in the Dow Jones Industrial Average and followed each Dow theory buy-and-sell signal would have seen an original investment of $100 reach over $116,000 by January 1990, as opposed to less than $6,000 with a buy-and-hold strategy (these calculations exclude reinvested dividends).[4] But confirming profits that come from trading based on the Dow theory is difficult, because the buy-and-sell signals are purely subjective and cannot be determined by precise numerical rules.

THE RANDOMNESS OF STOCK PRICES

Although the Dow theory might not be as popular as it once was, technical analysis is still alive and well. The idea that you can identify the major trends in the market, riding bull markets while avoiding bear markets, is still the fundamental goal of technical analysts.

Yet most economists still attack the fundamental tenet of the chartists—that stock prices follow predictable patterns. To these academic researchers, the movements of the market more closely conform, especially in the short term, to a pattern called a *random walk* than to special formations that forecast future returns.

The first economist to come to this conclusion was Frederick Mac-Cauley, an economist in the early part of the twentieth century. His comments at a 1925 dinner meeting of the American Statistical Association on the topic of "forecasting security prices" were reported in the association's official journal:

> Macauley observed that there was a striking similarity between the fluctuations of the stock market and those of a chance curve which may be obtained by throwing dice. Everyone will admit that the course of such a purely chance curve cannot be predicted. If the stock market can be forecast from a graph of its movements, it must be because of its difference from the chance curve.[5]

More than 30 years later, Harry Roberts, a professor at the University of Chicago, simulated movements in the market by plotting price changes that resulted from completely random events, such as flips of a coin. These simulations looked like the charts of actual stock prices, forming shapes and following trends that are considered by chartists to be significant predictors of future returns. But since the next period's price change was, by construction, a completely random event, such patterns could not logically have any predictive content. This early research supported the belief that the apparent patterns in past stock prices were the result of completely random movements.

Does the randomness of stock prices make economic sense? Factors influencing supply and demand do not occur randomly and are often quite predictable from one period to the next. Shouldn't these predictable factors make stock prices move in nonrandom patterns?

In 1965, Professor Paul Samuelson of MIT showed that the prices of *securities* based on prospective cash flows would be unpredictable even if the forces influencing supply and demand were not.[6] In fact, such unpredictability was a result of a free and efficient market in which investors had already incorporated all the known factors influencing the price of the stock. This is the crux of the *efficient market hypothesis.*

If the market is efficient, prices will change only when new, unanticipated information is released to the market. Since unanticipated information is as likely to be better as it is to be worse than expected, the resulting movement in stock prices is random. Price charts will therefore look like a random walk and cannot be predicted.[7]

SIMULATIONS OF RANDOM STOCK PRICES

If stock prices are indeed random, their movements should not be distinguishable from simulations generated randomly by a computer. Figure 16.1 extends the experiment conceived by Professor Roberts 60 years ago. Instead of generating only closing prices, I programmed the computer to generate intraday prices, creating the popular high-low-close bar graphs that are found in most chart publications.

There are eight charts in Figure 16.1. Four have been generated by a random-number generator. In these charts, there is absolutely no way to predict the future from the past, because future movements are designed to be totally independent from the past. The other four charts were chosen from actual data of the Dow Jones Industrial Average. Before reading further, try to determine which four are actual historical prices and which are computer generated.

The task is quite difficult. In fact, most of the top brokers at a leading Wall Street firm found it impossible to tell the difference between the real and counterfeit data. In the mid-1990s, two-thirds of brokers did correctly identify Figure 16.1D, which depicts the period around the October 19, 1987, stock crash. For the remaining seven charts, the brokers showed no ability to distinguish actual from computer-generated data. The true historical prices are represented by charts B, D, E, and H, while the computer-generated data are charts A, C, F, and G.[8]

FIGURE 16.1

Real and simulated stock indexes

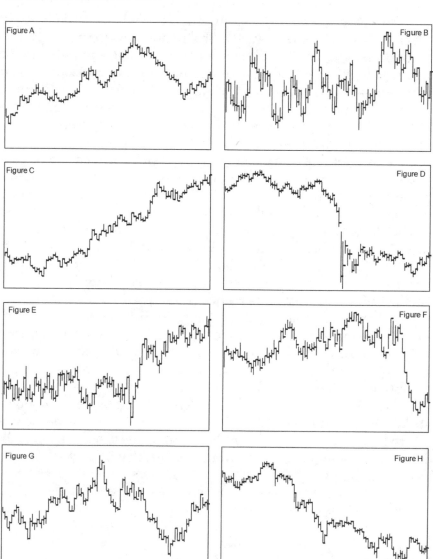

TRENDING MARKETS AND PRICE REVERSALS

Even though many trends are in fact the result of the totally random movement of stock prices, many technical traders will never invest against a trend that they believe they have identified. Two of the most well-known sayings of market timers are "Make the trend your friend" and "Trust the thrust."

Martin Zweig, a well-known market timer who used fundamental and technical variables to forecast market trends, forcefully stated: "I can't overemphasize the importance of staying with the trend of the market, being in gear with the tape, and not fighting the major movements. Fighting the tape is an open invitation to disaster."[9] We have seen in Chapter 14 that momentum traders have been successful in outperforming the market by holding individual stocks that have established a trend.

When a trend appears, technical analysts often draw *channels* consisting of parallel upper and lower bounds within which the price has traded. The lower bound of a channel is frequently called a *support level* and the upper bound a *resistance level*. When the market breaks the bounds of the channel, a large price changes often follow.

The very fact that many traders believe in the importance of trends can induce behavior that makes trend-following popular. While the trend is intact, traders sell when prices reach the upper end of the channel and buy when they reach the lower end, attempting to take advantage of the fluctuations of stock prices within the channel. If the trendline is broken, many of these traders will reverse their positions: buying if the market penetrates the top of the trendline or selling if it falls through the bottom. This behavior often accelerates the movement of stock prices and reinforces the importance of the channel.

Options traders reinforce the behavior of trend followers. When the market is trading within a channel, traders will sell put and call options at strike prices that represent the lower and upper bounds of the channel. If the market remains within the channel, these speculators collect premiums as the options expire worthless. If the market penetrates the resistance or support levels, these options writers "run for cover," or buy back their options before they experience large losses, accelerating the movement of prices.

MOVING AVERAGES

Successful technical trading requires not only identifying the trend but, more importantly, identifying when the trend is about to reverse. A popular tool for determining when the trend might change is based on the relation between the current price and a moving average of past price movements, a technique that goes back to at least the 1930s.[10]

A *moving average* is simply the arithmetic average of a given number of past closing prices of a stock or index. The most popular moving average uses the average prices for the past 200 trading days, and it is therefore called the *200-day moving average*. For each new trading day, the oldest price is dropped, and the most recent price is added to compute the average.

Moving averages are far less volatile than daily prices. When prices are rising, the moving average is below the market price, and technical analysts claim this forms a support level for stock prices. When prices are falling, the moving average is above current prices and forms a resistance level. Analysts assert that a moving average allows investors to identify the basic market trend without being distracted by the day-to-day volatility of the market. When prices penetrate the moving average, this indicates that powerful underlying forces are signaling a reversal of the basic trend.

The 200-day moving average is frequently plotted in investment letters as a key determinant of investment trends. One of the early supporters of this strategy was William Gordon, who stated that, over the period from 1897 to 1967, buying stocks when the Dow broke above the moving average produced nearly seven times the return as buying when the Dow broke below the average.[11] Robert Colby and Thomas Meyers claim that for the United States the best time period for a moving average of weekly data is 45 weeks, just slightly longer than the 200-day moving average.[12]

TESTING THE DOW JONES MOVING-AVERAGE STRATEGY

To test the 200-day moving-average strategy, I examined the entire daily record of the Dow Jones Industrial Average from 1885 through 2020. In contrast to the previous studies on moving-average strategies, the holding-period returns include the reinvestment of dividends when the strategy calls for investing in the market, and short-term interest-bearing securities when one is not invested in the stock market. Annualized returns are examined over the entire period as well as the subperiods.

I adopted the following criteria to determine the buy-sell strategy: whenever the Dow Jones Industrial Average closed by *at least* 1 percent above its 200-day moving average (not including the current date), stocks were purchased at these closing prices; and whenever the Dow Industrials closed by *at least* 1 percent below its 200-day moving average, stocks were sold at the closing prices. When sold, the proceeds were invested in Treasury bills.

There are two noteworthy aspects of this strategy: The 1 percent band around the 200-day moving average is used to control the number of times an investor would have to move in and out of the market. The smaller the band, the greater the number of times a trader moves in and out of the market.[13] A very small band would cause traders to be frequently "whipsawed," a term used to describe the alternate buying and then selling of stocks in an attempt to beat the market. Whipsawing dramatically lowers investor returns because investors find themselves buying high and selling low a great number of times.

The second aspect of this strategy assumes that an investor buys or sells stocks at the *closing* price, rather than during the trading day. Only in recent decades has the exact intraday level of the popular averages been computed. Using historical data, it is impossible to determine times when the market average penetrated the 200-day moving average during the day. By specifying that the average must close above or below the average of the 200 preceding closes, I present a theory that could have been implemented in practice through the entire 135-year period.[14]

THE DOW INDUSTRIALS AND THE 200-DAY MOVING AVERAGE

Figure 16.2 displays the daily and 200-day moving averages of the Dow Jones Industrial Average during two select periods: from 1924 to 1936 and from 2001 through 2020. The shaded time periods are when investors are out of the stock market (and in short-term bonds); otherwise, investors are fully invested in stocks.

FIGURE 16.2

Dow Jones 200-day moving-average strategy

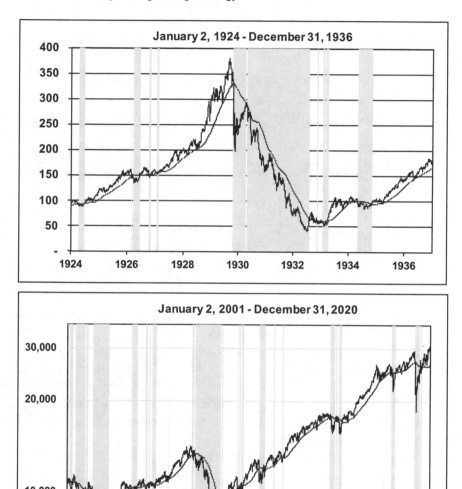

Shaded areas = out of market

The returns from the 200-day moving-average strategy and a buy-and-hold strategy over the whole period are summarized in Table 16.1.

TABLE 16.1

Timing and holding strategy annualized returns, January 1886–December 2020

Period	Holding Strategy		Timing Strategy			
	Return	Risk	Return	Risk	% in Market	# of Switches
1886 - 2020	9.62%	20.9%	9.66%	16.4%	63.6%	402
Subperiods						
1886 - 1925	9.08%	23.7%	9.77%	17.7%	56.6%	122
1926 - 1945	6.25%	31.0%	11.13%	21.8%	62.2%	60
1946 - 2020	10.82%	15.8%	9.21%	14.1%	68.5%	220
1990 - 2020	10.52%	14.8%	5.85%	15.2%	74.1%	126
2001 - 2020	7.68%	15.2%	4.16%	13.5%	70.5%	84
2012 - 2020	12.96%	11.7%	8.10%	14.0%	86.1%	30
Excl. 1929 - 1932 Crash						
1886 - 2020	10.76%	19.7%	9.84%	16.1%	64.8%	384
1926 - 1945	13.94%	24.5%	12.38%	20.3%	70.8%	42

From January 1886 through December 2020, the 9.66 percent annual return from the timing strategy just eked out a win over the 9.62 percent return of the buy-and-hold strategy. Looking at Figure 16.2, one can see that the timing strategy had a huge success avoiding the 1929–1932 crash. If that period is excluded, the returns of the timing strategy are 92 basis points per year behind the holding strategy, although the timing strategy has more than 4 percentage points lower standard deviation than the buy-and-hold strategy.

Looks can be deceiving. When examining the returns from 2001 onward in Figure 16.2, it appears as if the returns from the timing strategy would swamp the buy-and-hold strategy. But that is not the case; the buy-and-hold strategy from 2001 to 2020 beats the timing strategy by more than 3 percentage points per year. This is because an investor was whipsawed by buying and selling many times in the early 2010s. Poor returns from the timing strategy occur when markets are not in a strong uptrend or downtrend and the market crosses the 200-day moving average many times. By buying when the market is 1 percent above the moving average, and selling when it is 1 percent below, frequent crossings of the moving average incur large costs.

AVOIDING MAJOR BEAR MARKETS

Although the returns from the timing strategy may fall behind that of a buy-and-hold investor, the major advantage from the timing strategy is that the investor experiences lower volatility. Since the market timer is in the market less than two-thirds of the time, the standard deviation of returns is reduced by about one-quarter compared to a buy-and-hold investor. This means that on an annual risk-adjusted basis, the return on the 200-day moving-average strategy is impressive. Another major gain from the timing strategy comes from the avoidance of bear markets.

The 200-day moving-average strategy had its greatest triumph during the boom and crash of the 1920s and early 1930s. Using the criteria outlined previously, investors would have bought stocks on June 27, 1924, when the Dow was at 95.33 and, with only two minor interruptions, ridden the bull market to the top at 381.17 on September 3, 1929. Investors would have exited the market on October 19, 1929, at 323.87, just 10 days before the Great Crash. Except for a brief period in 1930, the strategy would have kept investors out of stocks through the worst bear market in US history. Investors would have finally reentered the market on August 6, 1932, when the Dow was 66.56, just 25 points higher than its absolute low.

Investors following the 200-day moving-average strategy would also have avoided the October 19, 1987, crash, selling out at the close of the previous Friday, October 16. However, in contrast to the 1929 crash, stocks did not continue downward. Although the market fell 23 percent on October 19, investors would not have reentered the market until the following June when the Dow was only about 5 percent below the exit level of October 16. Nonetheless, following the 200-day moving-average strategy would have avoided October 19 and 20, traumatic days for many investors who held stocks.

Moreover, investors using the 200-day moving average did avoid most of the devastating 2007–2009 bear market, as timing investors exited stocks on January 2, 2008, when the Dow Industrials was about 8 percent below its October 2007 peak, and did not reenter the market until July 15, 2009, when the Dow was about 40 percent lower. And the moving-average strategy would have kept investors out of the bear market associated with the Covid pandemic, exiting on February 26, 2020 while the Dow continued to fall more than 30 percent before reaching bottom in the following month.

Nevertheless, in 2010, 2011, and 2012, timing investors were frequently whipsawed, switching in and out of stocks 20 times, which caused about 20 percentage points to be clipped from their returns. This is the downside to the strategy.

The moving-average strategy does keep investors out of the worst declines during declining markets. Since the Dow was created in 1886, the average drawdown during bear markets (declines of 20 percent or more) from using the moving-average strategy is only 13.25 percent, far less than one-half the 32.73 percent drawdown from peak to trough for the buy-and-hold investor. Although those gains are eventually nullified by switching into and out of stocks when the market is trendless, it was certainly comforting to be out of stocks during the worst part of *every* bear market over the last 135 years!

DISTRIBUTION OF ANNUAL RETURNS

Figure 16.3 shows the distribution of yearly gains and losses of the timing and the holding strategy for the Dow Industrials. As noted previously, the timing strategist participates in most bull markets and avoids bear markets, but the losses suffered when the market has little trend are significant.

FIGURE 16.3

Distribution of gains and losses from timing versus holding strategy

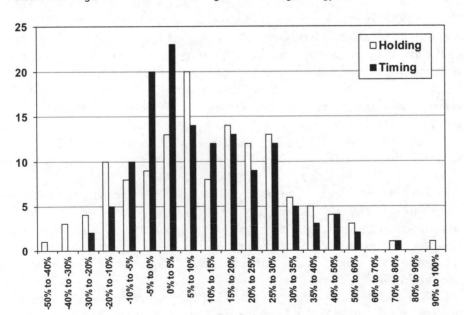

The distribution of gains and losses is like that of a buy-and-hold investor who has purchased index puts to cushion market declines. As will be noted in Chapter 26, purchasing index puts is equivalent to buying an insurance policy on the market. If the market does not decline, the cost of buying puts drains returns. Similarly, the timing strategy involves many small losses that come from moving in and out of the market. That is why the modal annual return for the timing strategy is from zero to −5 percent, while the modal return for a buy-and-hold investor is plus 5 to 10 percent. The most negative yearly return from the timing strategy occurred in 2000, when investors had to execute 16 switches and suffered a negative return that exceeded 33 percent, far less than the negative 5 percent return realized by the buy-and-hold investor.

CONCLUSION

Proponents claim that technical analysis can identify the major trends of the market and determine when those trends might reverse. Yet there is considerable doubt about whether such trends exist or whether they are the result of random price movements.

Despite the ongoing academic debate, technical analysis has a huge number of adherents on Wall Street and among many savvy investors. The analysis in this chapter gives a cautious nod to these strategies, but as I have noted throughout this book, actions by investors to take advantage of the past may change returns in the future. As Benjamin Graham stated so well 80 years ago:

> A moment's thought will show that there can be no such thing as a scientific prediction of economic events under human control. The very "dependability" of such a prediction will cause human actions which will invalidate it. Hence thoughtful chartists admit that continued success is dependent upon keeping the successful method known to only a few people.[15]

A final word: technical analysis requires the full-time attention of traders. On October 16, 1987, the Dow fell below its 200-day moving average at the very end of trading on the Friday before the crash. But if you failed to sell your stocks that afternoon, you would have been swept downward by the 22 percent nightmare of Black Monday, the single greatest stock market decline in history.

17

Calendar Anomalies

October. This is one of the peculiarly dangerous months to speculate in stocks. The others are July, January, September, April, November, May, March, June, December, August, and February.

—Mark Twain

The dictionary defines *anomaly* as something inconsistent with what is naturally expected. What is more unnatural than to expect to beat the market by predicting stock prices based solely on the day or week or month of the year? Yet it appears that you can. Research has revealed that there are predictable times during which the stock market, or certain stocks in the market, do particularly well.

The analysis in the first edition of *Stocks for the Long Run*, published in 1994, was based on long data series analyzed through the early 1990s. The calendar anomalies reported in that edition invited investors to outperform the market by adopting strategies related to these unusual calendar events. However, as more investors learn of and act on these anomalies, the prices of stocks may adjust so that much, if not all, of the anomaly is eliminated. Certainly, that would be the prediction of the efficient market hypothesis.

In this edition of *Stocks for the Long Run*, I look at the evidence since 1994 to determine whether the anomaly survived or not. The results are surprising; some anomalies have weakened and even reversed, while others remain strong. Here is a rundown.

SEASONAL ANOMALIES

The most important historical calendar anomaly is that small-capitalization stocks had far outperformed large stocks in the month of January. This effect is so strong that without January's return, small stocks would have a *lower* return than large stocks since 1925 even though over the whole period small stocks have outperformed the capitalization-weighted market.

The January effect might be the granddaddy of all calendar anomalies, but it is not the only one. Stocks generally do much better in the first half of the month than the second half, do well before holidays, and plunge in the month of September. Furthermore, they do exceptionally well between Christmas and New Year's Day, and until very recently, they have soared on the last trading day of December, which is the day that launches the January effect.

THE JANUARY EFFECT

The outperformance of small stocks in January has been dubbed the *January effect*. It was discovered in the early 1980s by Donald Keim,[1] based on research he did as a graduate student at the University of Chicago. It was the first significant finding that flew in the face of the efficient market hypothesis, which claimed there was no predictable pattern to stock prices.

Of all the calendar-related anomalies, the January effect has been the most studied. From 1925 through 2021, the average arithmetic return on the S&P 500 Index in the month of January was 1.29 percent, while the average returns on the small stocks came to 4.93 percent. The 3.64 percentage-point difference in January far more than explains the superior total returns to small stocks over this 96-year period.

Table 17.1 shows how important the January effect is. If an investor just held small stocks in January and the S&P 500 for the remaining 11 months, they would have beaten the buy-and-hold S&P 500 by almost 4 percentage points per year, a spectacular return. On the other hand, holding small stocks from February through December and the S&P in January, they would have fallen more than 2 percentage points a year behind the market. Nevertheless, since 1995, the January effect has disappeared, and returns from all these strategies are nearly the same.

The January effect was strongest during the most powerful bear market in our history, the Great Depression. It is astounding that from August 1929 through the summer of 1932, when small stocks lost over 90 percent of their value, small stocks posted consecutive January monthly returns of plus 13 percent, plus 21 percent, and plus 10 percent in 1930, 1931, and 1932, respectively. It is testimony to the power of the January effect that investors could have increased their wealth by 50 percent during the worst bear market in history by buying small stocks at the end of December in those three years and selling them at the end of the following month, putting their money in cash during the other months.

TABLE 17.1

The January effect of small stocks

Indexes	Return 1926–2021	Return 1995–2021
S&P 500	10.1%	10.4%
Small Stocks	11.3%	9.4%
Small Stocks with January S&P 500 Returns	7.7%	9.8%
S&P 500 with January Small Stocks Returns	13.8%	10.0%

When researchers turned to foreign markets, they found that the January effect was not just a US phenomenon. In Japan, the world's second-largest capital market, the excess returns on small stocks in January came to 7.2 percent per year, more than in the United States.[2] As you shall see later in the chapter, January had the best month for both large and small stocks in many other countries of the world.[3]

Causes of the January Effect

Why had investors favored small stocks in January? No one knows for sure, but there are several hypotheses. Individual investors hold a disproportionate share of small stocks, and in contrast to most institutions, they are more sensitive to the tax consequences of their trading. Small stocks, especially those that have declined in the preceding 11 months, are subject to tax-motivated selling in December. This selling depresses the price of individual issues. In January after the selling ends, these stocks bounce back in price.

There is some evidence to support this explanation. Stocks that have fallen throughout the year fall even more in December and then often rise dramatically in January. Furthermore, there is some evidence that before the introduction of the US income tax in 1913, there was no

January effect. In Australia, where the tax year runs from July 1 through June 30, there are abnormally large returns to small stocks in July.

If taxes were a factor, however, they cannot be the only one, for the January effect holds in countries that do not have a capital gains tax. Japan did not tax capital gains for individual investors until 1989, but the January effect existed prior to that date. Furthermore, capital gains were not taxed in Canada before 1972, and yet there was a January effect in that country as well. Finally, stocks that have risen throughout the previous year and should not be subject to tax-loss selling still rise in January, although not by as much as stocks that have fallen the previous year.

The January Effect Has Disappeared

We should not be surprised that the January effect has not lasted. If money managers know that small stocks will surge in January, these stocks should be bought well before New Year's Day to capture these spectacular returns. That would cause the price of small stocks to rise in December, which would prompt other managers to buy them in November, and so on. In the process of acting on the January effect, the price of stocks would be smoothed out over the year, and the phenomenon would disappear. Perhaps all the publicity about the January effect has motivated investors and traders to take advantage of this calendar anomaly and caused it to disappear from the market.

Predictive Power of January

It is often said, "As the market goes in January, so goes the rest of the year." There actually is some predictive power to this statement. Table 17.2 summarizes the returns to January, the average of the return in the following 11 months, and how many times the movement in January matches that of the rest of the year.

From 1928 through 2021, when the January return has been negative, the average return for the rest of the year has been less than one-half what it has been if January's return is positive. Furthermore, if January is negative, the rest of the year is negative more than one-third of the time, while if January is positive, the rest of the year is negative just over 20 percent of the time.

The January predictive effect like the January Effect itself, has been weakening, however, and before 1995, a negative January return was more foreboding. Since 1995, negative January returns are only slightly, and not significantly, different from the next 12 months. From 1995 through 2021, there have been 12 negative January returns, yet only in three years were the remainder of the months negative.

TABLE 17.2

January predictive power

1928–2021				
	Jan	Feb - Dec	Years	# Same Direction
Negative January	-3.64%	0.35%	36	13
Positive January	4.22%	0.74%	58	45
All Months	1.21%	0.59%	94	

1928–1994				
	Jan	Feb - Dec	Years	# Same Direction
Negative January	-3.66%	0.18%	24	10
Positive January	4.46%	0.65%	43	33
All Months	1.55%	0.48%	67	

1995–2021				
	Jan	Feb - Dec	Years	# Same Direction
Negative January	-3.61%	0.70%	12	3
Positive January	3.53%	0.99%	15	12
All Months	0.36%	0.86%	27	

MONTHLY RETURNS

The monthly price return on the Dow Industrials and monthly total return on the S&P 500 Index are displayed in Figure 17.1.

FIGURE 17.1

Monthly returns on the Dow and S&P 500

Figure A

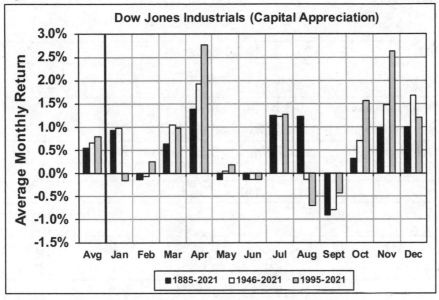

Figure B

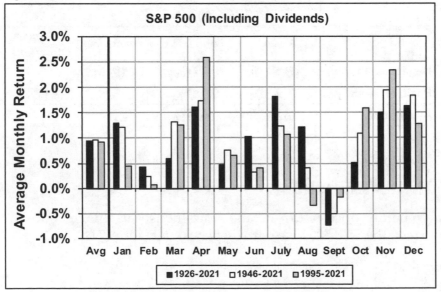

It can be seen that April is the best month of the year (spring is here!) and this effect is getting stronger through time for both for the Dow Industrials and the S&P 500. September is the worst month (winter is coming!) and November and December have been good months, and according to recent data, they continue to be. But January's return, even for large stocks, formerly one of the best months, has faltered in recent years. July continues to shine (summer is here!), but the expression "Sell in May and go away" certainly has some empirical justification. In fact, virtually all the gains in the market have been realized from October through April, as the good summer returns are largely negated by the autumn downdrafts.

THE SEPTEMBER EFFECT

While July has good returns, watch out for the beginning of fall, especially September. September is by far the worst month of the year, both in the United States and elsewhere in the world. It is the only month to have a negative return *including* reinvested dividends.

FIGURE 17.2

International calendar returns, 1970–2021

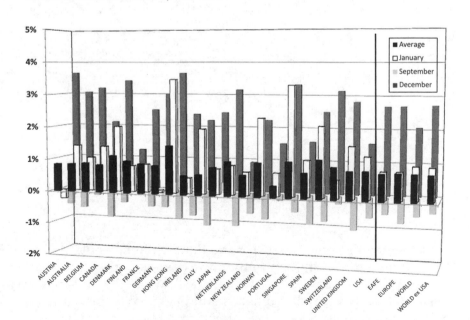

Figure 17.2 tracks the MSCI international calendar returns for January, September, and December, as well as the monthly average. Over this period, 21 of the 22 countries had negative returns in the month of September.

The data in the United States is quite striking. Figure 17.3 tracks the Dow Jones Industrial Averages from 1885 through 2021, both including and excluding the month of September. An investment of $1 in the Dow Jones Average in 1885 would be worth $1,428 by the end of 2021 (dividends excluded). On the other hand, if you put your money in the stock market every month *except* September, your dollar would have been worth $6,167 at the end of 2021. In contrast, $1 invested in the Dow only in the month of September since 1885 would today be worth only 23 cents!

FIGURE 17.3

The September effect: Dow Jones Industrial Averages, 1885–2021

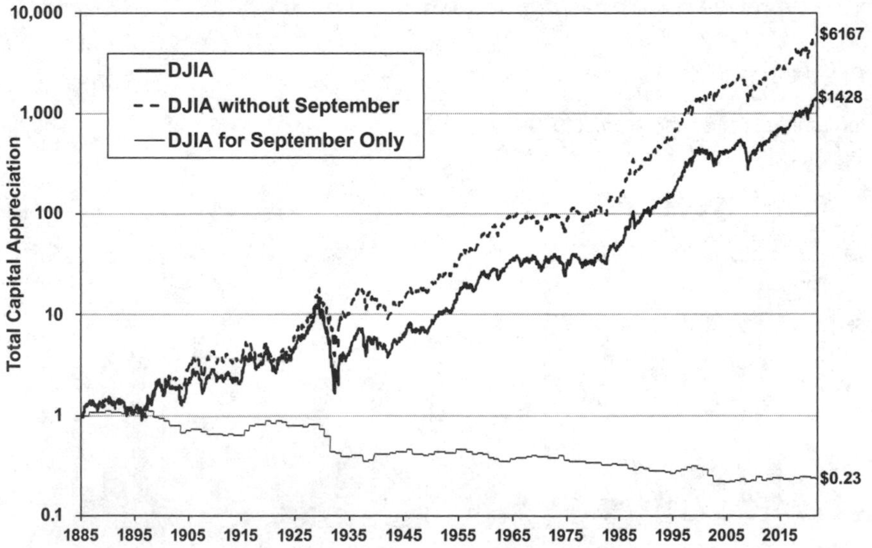

The September effect is so negative that investors would do better holding zero-interest cash than putting their assets in the stock market that month. In contrast to the January effect, which has disappeared in recent data, the September effect is still operative, although returns are not as negative as before. Since my first edition was published in 1994, 18 of the 21 countries still had negative returns in September. Since publication, traders may have tried to take advantage of the September downdraft as can be seen in Figure 17.1; August, and not September, has become the worst month of the year.

Reasons for the September Effect

Maybe the poor returns in September are related to the approach of winter and the depressing effect of rapidly shortening daylight. Psychologists stress that sunlight is an essential ingredient to well-being: recent research has confirmed that the NYSE does significantly worse on cloudy days than it does on sunny days.[4] But this explanation falters "down under," as September is also a poor month in Australia and New Zealand, where the month marks the beginning of spring and longer days in the Southern Hemisphere.[5]

Perhaps the poor returns in September are the result of investors liquidating stocks (or holding off buying more stocks) to pay for their summer vacations. As we will discuss soon, until recent years, Monday was by far the worst-performing day of the week. For many, September is the monthly version of Monday, the time you face work after a period of leisure.

OTHER SEASONAL RETURNS

Although psychologists say that many silently suffer depression around Christmas and New Year's, stock investors believe the last week of the year "'tis the season to be jolly." Table 17.3 displays the daily price returns, as measured by the Dow Jones Industrial Average, for various times in the year and in the month. Over the past 136 years, daily price returns, between Christmas and New Year's, have averaged nearly 10 times the average return.

Even more striking is the difference between stock returns in the first and second half of the month.[6] Over the entire 136-year period studied, the percentage change in the Dow Jones Industrial Average during the first half of the month—which includes the last trading day of the previous month up to and including the fourteenth day of the current month—is almost three times the gain that occurs during the second half, and this outperformance has even increased since 1995. This outperformance would be accentuated if we included dividends, as they are mostly paid in the first half of the month.[7] The average percentage changes in the Dow Jones Industrial Average over every calendar day of the month are shown in Figure 17.4.

TABLE 17.3

Daily price returns, February 1885–December 2021

	1885–2021	1885–1925	1926–1945	1946–1989	1946–2021	1995–2021
Overall Averages						
Whole Month	0.0250%	0.0192%	0.0147%	0.0273%	0.0318%	0.0398%
First Half of Month	0.0388%	0.0144%	0.0531%	0.0402%	0.0497%	0.0645%
Second Half of Month	0.0133%	0.0233%	-0.0173%	0.0163%	0.0166%	0.0185%
Last Day of Month	0.0736%	0.0875%	0.1633%	0.1460%	0.0426%	-0.1267%
Days of the Week						
Monday	-0.0831%	-0.0874%	-0.2106%	-0.1313%	-0.0470%	0.0561%
Tuesday	0.0442%	0.0375%	0.0473%	0.0307%	0.0469%	0.0850%
Wednesday	0.0569%	0.0280%	0.0814%	0.0909%	0.0659%	0.0265%
Thursday	0.0252%	0.0012%	0.0627%	0.0398%	0.0281%	0.0173%
Friday	0.0625%	0.0994%	0.0064%	0.0942%	0.0575%	0.0142%
With Sat	0.0539%	0.0858%	-0.0169%	0.0747%		
Without Sat	0.0695%	0.3827%	0.3485%	0.0961%	0.0565%	0.0142%
Saturday	0.0578%	0.0348%	0.0964%	0.0962%		
Holiday Returns						
Day before Holiday						
July 4th	0.2968%	0.2118%	0.8168%	0.2746%	0.2058%	0.1955%
Christmas	0.3153%	0.4523%	0.3634%	0.3110%	0.2288%	0.0921%
New Year's	0.2745%	0.5964%	0.3931%	0.2446%	0.0697%	-0.1719%
Day After New Year's	0.1457%	0.1114%	0.0363%	0.0779%	0.1926%	0.3552%
Holiday Avg	0.2955%	0.4201%	0.5244%	0.2767%	0.1681%	0.0386%
Christmas Week	0.2241%	0.3242%	0.2875%	0.1661%	0.1425%	0.0991%

FIGURE 17.4

Day of the month price change, 1885–2021

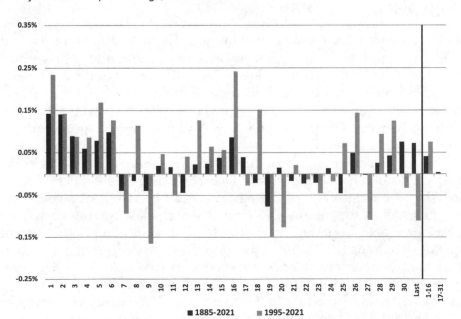

■ 1885-2021   ■ 1995-2021

Note how the pattern of returns has changed in recent years. Although the gains on the first six days of the month have become greater, the change on the last day of the month has turned sharply negative, while the first day of the month is even more positive than it had been.

The strong gains at the very beginning of the month are likely related to the inflow of funds into the equity market from workers who automatically have part of their pay invested directly into the market on the first day of the month. One notices another gain on the sixteenth of the month, where workers who are paid twice per month put funds into stocks and this effect has become larger over time.

DAY-OF-THE-WEEK EFFECTS

Many workers hate Mondays. After two days of relaxing, facing work on Monday is a drag. Stock investors have apparently felt the same way. Monday has been by far the worst day of the week for the market. Over the past 136 years, the returns on Monday have been decisively negative.

Although investors hate Mondays, they *used to* relish Fridays. At one time, TGIF—"Thank goodness it's Friday"—ruled the roost in the market, as Friday had been the best day of the week, yielding price returns about three times the daily average. Even when markets were open on Saturday (every month before 1946 and nonsummer months before 1953), Friday price returns were the best.

Since 1995, however, Friday has gone from the best to the worst day, and Monday has gone from the worst to second best, barely trailing the top day, Tuesday. One reason for this change may be that more stock traders now hedge their equity positions over the weekend and sell their long positions at or near Friday's close. Friday's negative returns might also be caused by traders who, having learned that Monday is usually a bad day, sell on Friday. Traders then reestablish their stock positions on Monday, causing returns to increase. Whatever the reasons, the change demonstrates that well-publicized anomalies are often arbitraged out of the market.

Another calendar anomaly is that stocks do very well before major holidays, as shown in Table 17.3. Price returns before the Fourth of July, Christmas, and New Year's Eve are, on average, almost 12 times the average daily price return. But some of these returns have also changed dramatically in recent years. Although stock returns on the day before July Fourth and Christmas have remained strong, returns on the last day of the trading year have switched from a strongly positive to a decisively negative since 1995. The negative returns on the last trading day in recent years are probably caused by many "sell-on-close" orders that are automatically executed at year-end to offset positions in stock index futures, ETFs, and other customized hedge instruments. Yet a lot of that downward pressure unwinds on the first trading day of the year, which has become significantly more positive since 1995.

Finally, there appears to be a diurnal pattern of stock returns. Evidence has shown that there is usually a sinking spell in the morning, especially on Monday. During lunch the market firms, then pauses or declines in the midafternoon before rising in the last half hour of trading. This often leads the market to close at the highest levels of the day.

CONCLUSION: WHAT'S AN INVESTOR TO DO?

Some of these anomalies are tempting for traders. Investors frequently hear pundits declare that this is or is not a good "seasonal time" to be in the market. But these seasonal patterns do not always occur, and as investors have become aware of these patterns, many have moderated, while others have disappeared altogether. The famous January effect has been mostly absent over the past two decades. Other anomalies have completely reversed, such as the returns of stocks on the last trading day of the year and the returns on Mondays and Fridays. The September effect has also moderated, although returns remain negative. But some anomalies, such as the large returns early in the month and the poor returns in the last half, have actually increased.

Trying to take advantage of these anomalies requires the buying and selling of stock, which incurs transaction costs and may realize capital gains taxes (unless you are trading within tax-sheltered funds). Nevertheless, investors who have already decided to buy or sell, but have some latitude in choosing the timing of such a transaction, might wish to take these calendar anomalies into account before making their trades. Remember, historically the edge in doing so is small, and no one can guarantee they will last.

V

THE ECONOMIC
ENVIRONMENT
FOR STOCKS

18

Money, Gold, Bitcoin, and the Fed

In the stock market, as with horse racing, money makes the mare go. Monetary conditions exert an enormous influence on stock prices.

—Martin Zweig, 1990[1]

If Fed Chairman Alan Greenspan were to whisper to me what his monetary policy was going to be over the next two years, it wouldn't change one thing I do.

—Warren Buffett, 1994[2]

On September 20, 1931, the British government announced that England was going off the gold standard. It would no longer exchange gold for deposits at the Bank of England or for British currency, the pound sterling. The government insisted that this action was only temporary, that it had no intention of permanently abolishing its commitment to exchange its money for gold. Nevertheless, it was to mark the beginning of the end of both Britain's and the world's gold standard—a standard that had existed for over 200 years.

Fearing chaos in the currency market, the British government ordered the London Stock Exchange closed. NYSE officials decided to keep the US exchange open, but also braced for panic selling. The suspension of gold payments by Britain, the second-greatest industrial power, raised fears that other industrial countries might be forced to abandon gold. Central bankers called the suspension "a world financial crisis of unprecedented dimensions."[3] For the first time ever, the NYSE banned short selling, in an attempt to shore up stock share prices.

Much to New York's surprise, stocks rallied sharply after a short sinking spell, and many issues ended the day higher. Clearly, British suspension was not seen as negative for American equities.

Nor was this "unprecedented financial crisis" a problem for the British stock market. When England reopened the exchange on September 23, prices soared. The Associated Press wire gave the following colorful description of the reopening of the exchange:

> Swarms of stock brokers, laughing and cheering like schoolboys, invaded the Stock Exchange today for the resumption of trading after the two-day compulsory close-down—and their buoyancy was reflected in the prices of many securities.[4]

Despite the dire predictions of government officials, shareholders viewed casting off the gold standard as good for the economy and even better for stocks. As a result of the gold suspension, the British government could expand credit by lending reserves to the banking system, and the fall in the value of the British pound would increase the demand for British exports.

The stock market gave a ringing endorsement to the actions that shocked conservative world financiers. In fact, September 1931 marked the low point of the British stock market, while the United States and other countries that stayed on the gold standard continued to sink into depression. The lessons from history: liquidity and easy credit feed the stock market, and the ability of the central banks to provide liquidity at will is a critical plus for stock values.

A year and a half later, the United States joined Britain in abandoning the gold standard, and finally every nation eventually went to a fiat, paper money standard. But despite the paper standard's inflationary bias, the world has become comfortable with the new monetary system, and the stock market enjoys the flexibility it accords policy makers.

HISTORY OF THE GOLD STANDARD

Britain was the first country to adopt the gold standard in 1821 and the United States followed in 1834. By the beginning of the twentieth century, virtually all developed nations had adopted the standard.

The only times the gold standard was suspended were during crises, such as wars. Great Britain suspended the gold standard during both the Napoleonic Wars and World War I, but in both cases, it returned to the gold standard at the original exchange rate. The United States suspended the gold standard during the Civil War, but it returned to the standard after the conflict ended.[5]

The adherence to the gold standard is the reason why the world experienced no overall inflation during the nineteenth and early twentieth centuries, but overall price stability was not achieved without cost. Since the money in circulation had to equal the quantity of gold held by the government, the central bank essentially relinquished control over monetary conditions. This meant that the central bank was unable to provide additional money during economic or financial crises. In the 1930s, adherence to the gold standard, which had restrained the US government from pursuing inflationary financial policies, turned into a straitjacket from which the government sought to escape.

The Establishment of the Federal Reserve

Periodic liquidity crises caused by strict adherence to the gold standard prompted Congress in 1913 to pass the Federal Reserve Act, creating the Federal Reserve System. The responsibilities of the Fed were to provide an "elastic" currency, which meant that in times of banking crises the Fed would become the lender of last resort. In trying times, the central bank would provide currency to enable depositors to withdraw their deposits without forcing banks to liquidate loans and other assets.

In the long run, money creation by the Fed was still constrained by the gold standard since the government's paper currency, or Federal Reserve notes, promised to pay a fixed amount of gold. In the short run, the Federal Reserve was free to create money if it did not threaten the convertibility of Federal Reserve notes to gold at the exchange rate of $20.67 per ounce that prevailed before the Great Depression. Yet the Fed was never given any guidance by Congress or by the Federal Reserve Act on how to conduct monetary policy and determine the right quantity of money.

The Fall of the Gold Standard

This lack of guidance had disastrous consequences just two decades later. In the wake of the stock crash of 1929, the world economies entered a severe downturn. Slumping asset prices and failing businesses made depositors suspicious of banks' assets. When word was received that some banks were having problems meeting depositors' withdrawals, a run on the banks ensued.

In an astounding display of institutional ineptitude, the Federal Reserve failed to provide extra reserves to stem the banking panic and prevent a crash of the financial system, even though the Fed had the explicit power to do so under the Federal Reserve Act. In addition, those depositors who did receive their money sought even greater safety by turning their notes back to the Treasury in exchange for gold, a process that put extreme pressure on the government's gold reserves. The banking panic soon spread from the United States to Great Britain and Continental Europe.

To prevent a steep loss of gold, Great Britain took the first step and abandoned the gold standard on September 20, 1931, suspending the payment of gold for sterling. Eighteen months later, on April 19, 1933, the United States also suspended the gold standard as the Depression and the financial crisis worsened.

Investors loved the government's newfound flexibility, and the reaction of the US stock market to gold's overthrow was even more enthusiastic than that in Great Britain. Stocks soared over 9 percent on the day the government left the gold standard and almost 6 percent the next day. This constituted the greatest two-day rally in US stock market history. Investors felt the government could now provide the extra liquidity needed to stabilize commodity prices and stimulate the economy, which they regarded as a boon for stocks. Bonds, however, fell, as investors feared the inflationary consequences of leaving the gold standard. *BusinessWeek*, in an editorial issued immediately following the suspension of dollar convertibility, asserted:

> With one decisive gesture, [President Roosevelt] throws out of the window all the elaborate hocus-pocus of "defending the dollar." He defies an ancient superstition and takes his stand with the advocates of managed money. . . . The job now is to manage our money effectively, wisely, with self-restraint. It can be done.[6]

POSTDEVALUATION MONETARY POLICY

Ironically, while the right to redeem dollars for gold was denied to US citizens, it was soon reinstated for foreign central banks at the devalued price of $35 per ounce. As part of the Bretton Woods Agreement, which set up the rules of international exchange rates after the close of World War II, the US government promised to exchange all dollars for gold held by foreign central banks at the fixed rate of $35 per ounce if these countries fixed their currency to the dollar.

In the postwar period, as inflation increased, gold seemed more and more attractive to foreigners. US gold reserves began to dwindle, despite official claims that the United States had no plans to change its gold exchange policy at the fixed price of $35 per ounce. As late as 1965, President Johnson stated unequivocally in the *Economic Report of the President*: "There can be no question of our capacity and determination to maintain the gold value of the dollar at $35.00 per ounce. The full resources of the Nation are pledged to that end."[7]

This was not so. As the gold reserves dwindled, Congress removed the gold-backing requirement for US currency in 1968. In the next year's *Economic Report of the President*, President Johnson declared: "Myths about gold die slowly. But progress can be made—as we have demonstrated. In 1968, the Congress ended the obsolete gold-backing requirement for our currency."[8]

Myths about gold? Obsolete gold-backing requirement? What a turnabout! The government finally admitted that domestic monetary policy would not be subject to the discipline of gold, and the guiding principle of international finance and monetary policy for almost two centuries was summarily dismissed as a relic of incorrect thinking.

Despite the removal of gold backing, the United States continued to redeem gold at $35 an ounce for foreign central banks, although individuals were paying over $40 in the private markets. Seeing that the end of this exchange option was near, foreign central banks accelerated their exchange of dollars for gold. The United States, which held almost $30 billion of gold at the end of World War II, was left with $11 billion by the summer of 1971, and hundreds of millions more were being withdrawn each month.

Something dramatic had to happen. On August 15, 1971, President Nixon, in one of the most extraordinary actions since Roosevelt's 1933 declaration of a bank holiday, announced the "new economic policy," freezing wages and prices and closing the "gold window" that was enabling foreigners to exchange US currency for gold. The link of gold to money was permanently—and irrevocably—broken.

Although conservatives were shocked at that action, few investors shed a tear for the gold standard. Nixon's announcement was coupled with wage and price controls and higher tariffs, and the stock market responded enthusiastically by jumping almost 4 percent on record volume. This should not have surprised those who studied history. Suspensions of the gold standard and devaluations of currencies have witnessed some of the most dramatic stock market rallies in history. Investors agreed that gold was a monetary relic.

POST-GOLD MONETARY POLICY

With the dismantling of the gold standard, there was no longer any constraint on monetary expansion, either in the United States or in foreign countries. The first inflationary oil shock from 1973 to 1974 caught most of the industrialized countries off guard, and all suffered significantly higher inflation as governments vainly attempted to offset falling output by expanding the money supply.

Because of the inflationary policies of the Federal Reserve, the US Congress tried to control monetary expansion by passing a congressional resolution in 1975 that obliged the central bank to announce monetary growth targets. Three years later, Congress passed the Humphrey-Hawkins Act, which forced the Fed to testify on monetary policy before Congress twice annually and establish monetary targets. It was the first time since the passage of the Federal Reserve Act that Congress instructed the central bank to take control of the stock of money. To this day, the financial markets closely watch the Fed chairman's biannual congressional testimony, which takes place in February and July.[9]

Unfortunately, the Fed largely ignored the money targets it set in the 1970s. The surge of inflation in 1979 brought increased pressure on the Federal Reserve to change its policy and seriously control inflation. On Saturday, October 6, 1979, Paul Volcker, who had been appointed in April to succeed G. William Miller as chairman of the board of the Federal Reserve System, announced a radical change in the implementation of monetary policy. No longer would the Federal Reserve only set interest rates to guide policy. Instead, it would exercise control over the supply of money. The market knew that this meant sharply higher interest rates, and indeed the Fed funds target was boosted to a record 20 percent.

The prospect of sharply restricted liquidity was a shock to the financial markets. Although Volcker's Saturday night announcement (later referred to as the "Saturday night massacre") did not immediately capture the popular headlines—in contrast to the abundant press coverage devoted to Nixon's 1971 new economic policy that froze prices and closed the gold window—it roiled the financial markets. Stocks went into a tailspin, falling almost 8 percent on record volume in the two and a half days following the announcement. Stockholders shuddered at the prospect of the sharply higher interest rates that would be necessary to tame inflation.

The tight monetary policy of the Volcker years eventually broke the inflationary cycle. European central banks and the Bank of Japan joined the Fed in calling inflation "public enemy number one," and they consequently geared their monetary policies toward stable prices. Restricting money growth proved to be the only real answer to controlling inflation. The movement to a monetary system based on central bank control and away from gold had significant consequences for our inflation and economy.

THE FEDERAL RESERVE AND MONEY CREATION

The process by which the Fed controls the money supply and credit conditions is not complicated. When the Fed wants to increase the money supply, it buys a government bond in the *open market*—a market where billions of dollars in bonds are transacted every day. What is unique about the Federal Reserve is that when it buys a government bond, called an *open market purchase*, it pays for them by crediting the reserve account of the bank of the customer from whom the Fed bought the bond—thereby creating money. A *reserve account* is a deposit a bank maintains at the Federal Reserve to satisfy reserve requirements facilitate check clearing, and maintain liquidity. Banks can request that these reserves be turned into currency—called Federal Reserve notes—at any time.

If the Federal Reserve wants to reduce the money supply, it sells government bonds from its portfolio. The buyer of these bonds instructs his or her bank to pay the seller from the buyer's deposit account. The bank then instructs the Fed to debit the bank's reserve account, and those reserves disappear from circulation. This is called an *open market sale*. Buying government bonds and selling them are called *open market operations*.

How the Fed's Actions Affect Interest Rates

There is an active market for the reserves created by the Federal Reserve. This market is called the *federal funds market*, and the interest rate at which these funds trade is called the *federal funds rate*.

If the Fed buys securities, then the supply of reserves is increased, and the interest rate on federal funds goes down because banks have more reserves to lend. Conversely, if the Fed sells securities, the supply of reserves is reduced, and the federal funds rate goes up because banks bid up the rate on the reduced reserve supply. The Federal Open Market Committee sets a *target rate* for the federal funds rate and engages in open market operations to keep the actual funds rate very close to that target.

During the Great Financial Crisis, the Federal Reserve engaged in *quantitative easing*, which involved large open market purchases that pushed the level of reserves far in excess of the banks' reserve requirements, and the rate of interest on Fed funds fell to zero. When this occurs, the situation is called an *ample-reserve regime*, and open market operations have very little effect on the federal funds rate. In this situation, the funds rate is set by the interest rate that the Fed *pays* on reserves, a right that was granted by Congress in 2009. This rate is called the *reserve deposit rate*. Federal funds trade very closely to this reserve deposit rate.

The interest rate on federal funds forms the anchor for all other short-term interest rates. These include the prime rate, which is the benchmark rate for most consumer lending, and rates on short-term Treasury securities, which are the basis of short-term commercial lending.[10] The federal funds rate directly or indirectly is the basis of literally trillions of dollars of loans and securities.

STOCK PRICES AND CENTRAL BANK POLICY

Given the influence that monetary policy has on interest rates, it is reasonable to expect that central bank policy impacts stock returns. Figure 18.1 plots the Fed funds target rate and the S&P 500 (measured as deviations from trend) from 1971 through 2021. Before 1990 there was little correlation between the two series, and to the extent that some can be detected, it is slightly negative. Since then, the correlation has been more positive. Stronger stock prices have been associated with rising rates, and weaker stock prices with falling rates. Empirically, the Fed funds rate lags the movement in stocks, as stock investors detect strength and weakness in the economy before the Fed changes the funds rate.

The switch from little or no correlation to a negative correlation is related to the factors discussed in Chapter 8. In the 1970s and 1980s, when supply shocks were predominant, especially those originating from oil disruptions, higher inflation led to lower stock prices. Nevertheless, the Fed was obligated to fight that higher inflation, so they raised the federal funds rate during those times. Since then, when demand shocks have become predominant, such as occurred during the Great Financial Crisis or the Covid-19 pandemic, the central bank lowered rates to stimulate demand.

Table 18.1 confirms that the price return of the S&P 500 Index is below average following the onset of a rate hiking cycle by the Federal Reserve.[11] The underperformance grows as the hiking cycle continues through the first two years, although it eases by year three. By far the most negative 3 month return followed the much-delayed March 2022 Fed rate hike designed to slow soaring post-pandemic inflation.

FIGURE 18.1

Fed funds target rate and normalized S&P 500

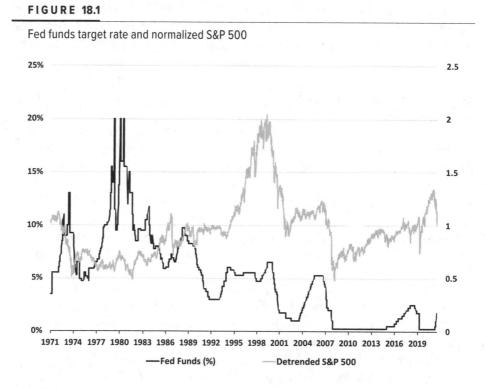

—Fed Funds (%)   —Detrended S&P 500

TABLE 18.1

Federal funds rate and subsequent S&P 500 price return

First Rate Hike	Last Rate Hike	3 mo	6 mo	9 mo	12 mo	2 yr	3 yr	Months From First to Last Hike	Total Hike
Mar-2022	NA*	-15.86%	NA*	NA*	NA*	NA*	NA*	NA*	NA*
Dec-2016	Dec-2019	5.46%	7.75%	10.72%	18.50%	15.14%	41.34%	36	2.00%
Jun-2004	Jun-2006	-2.30%	6.37%	3.56%	4.43%	11.34%	31.78%	24	4.25%
Jun-1999	May-2000	-6.56%	6.68%	8.39%	5.97%	-10.80%	-27.89%	11	1.75%
Feb-1994	Feb-1995	-3.85%	-2.43%	-1.60%	1.88%	35.34%	68.00%	12	3.00%
Mar-1988	Feb-1989	2.54%	0.13%	2.99%	8.05%	24.87%	36.69%	11	3.25%
Dec-1986	Sep-1987	15.27%	21.88%	25.92%	-0.78%	10.50%	40.00%	9	1.37%
May-1983	Aug-1984	-0.06%	1.68%	0.77%	-0.13%	10.43%	44.83%	15	3.25%
Aug-1980	Dec-1980	4.77%	5.92%	6.79%	6.85%	-15.89%	31.18%	4	10.50%
Dec-1976	Oct-1979	-1.79%	-5.42%	-5.52%	-7.61%	-6.06%	3.58%	34	10.75%
Average (Ex 1986 Hike)		-1.96%	2.59%	3.26%	4.74%	8.05%	28.69%		
Average		-0.24%	4.73%	5.78%	4.13%	8.32%	29.94%		
S&P 500 Average Return		2.34%	4.69%	7.03%	9.38%	18.76%	28.14%		

NA = Not Available at Time of Publishing

The reason that increases in the federal funds rate are often negative for stock prices is that these increases are implemented to prevent the economy from overheating and causing inflation. This means the Fed must raise the funds rate above inflation, which increases real interest rates and depresses the discounted value of future cash flows. The increase in rates also increases the probability of an economic downturn or recession, which will negatively impact corporate profits.

BITCOIN: THE NEW MONEY?

In recent years a new monetary asset has been born, created completely outside government control: *cryptocurrency*, of which Bitcoin is the most prominent. Can Bitcoin, or any other cryptocurrency, replace the dollar as the world's money of choice?

Bitcoin, the most prominent of many cryptocurrencies, is a decentralized digital currency invented in 2008. Bitcoins are created by solving increasingly difficult mathematical codes, a process called *mining*. The Bitcoin protocol calls for a maximum of 21 million Bitcoins, and approximately 19 million coins had been created by the end of 2021.

Bitcoins can be transferred between individuals without the need for a central bank or any other financial intermediary. Transactions are verified through a secure process, called cryptography, and recorded in a public ledger called a blockchain.

The price of a Bitcoin trades against all currencies in the world and became freely transferable in 2009. When Bitcoin first started trading, it could be purchased for 5 cents a coin, meaning a $1,000 investment would buy 20,000 Bitcoins. In December 2021, these coins were worth about $1 billion! There is no other publicly traded asset in history that has appreciated this much in such a short time.

What is the future of Bitcoin and other cryptocurrencies? To analyze this question, we must address the important characteristics of money, defined as a favored asset that is transferred between parties when goods and services (and assets) are exchanged.

CHARACTERISTICS OF MONEY

The following are the most important characteristics of money: (1) a *unit of account*, such that prices are quoted in units of this asset, (2) a *medium of exchange* that is widely accepted among individuals and used to facilitate transfers quickly and efficiently, (3) a *store of value*, an asset that will remain stable (or increase) in value relative to the price of goods and services and is a good hedge against other risks, and (4) *anonymity*, the ability to effect a transfer of wealth without being traced.

Four assets will be considered: (1) *national currency*, which are assets created by central banks (either in paper or digital form), (2) *deposits*, also called M2,[12] which are deposit accounts (checking, saving, etc.) in legally constituted financial intermediaries, often with authorization and implicit guarantees against any nominal losses by governments, (3) *gold*, which had once dominated the monetary system and has a history that goes back thousands of years, and (4) *cryptocurrencies*, of which Bitcoin is the most prominent.

Figure 18.2 summarizes the size of these monetary assets at the end of 2021, and Figure 18.3 reports the size of cryptocurrencies in February and June 2022. By far the largest monetary assets are deposits, or M2. The next largest are central bank assets (national currencies in the hands of the public, plus central bank reserves held by banking institutions), the next gold, and the smallest, cryptocurrencies. As of early 2022, Bitcoin comprises about one-half of all cryptocurrencies. Crypto enthusiasts often point to these data to show how much larger cryptocurrencies can become, if they can successfully rival these other monetary assets. Yet cryptocurrencies fell sharply in value in the first half of 2022, falling to less than $1 trillion by June of that year.

FIGURE 18.2

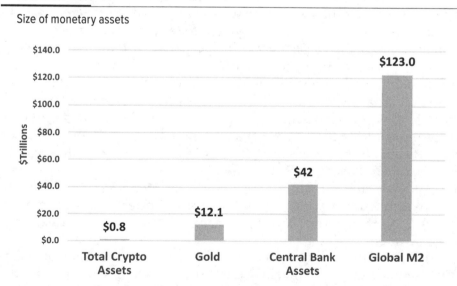

Size of monetary assets

FIGURE 18.3

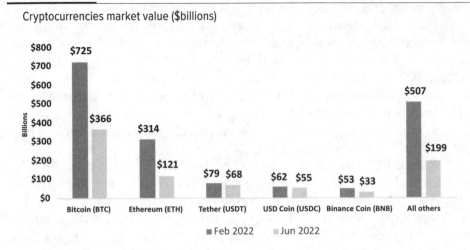

Cryptocurrencies market value ($billions)

■ Feb 2022   ■ Jun 2022

Assessing the Qualities of Monetary Assets

1. Currency

Currency has been issued by central banks for hundreds of years. The money issued by the central banks serves as a unit of account. In the United States, as in many other countries, currency is "legal tender," which means that the government can require and courts enforce individuals to accept these notes as payment for any debt.[13] That is why this money is often called *fiat currency*, that is, money by law.

    Since currency pays no interest, its real value depreciates at the rate of inflation. If inflation is low, currency is an acceptable store of value, although certainly not as remunerative as holding productive assets such as stocks or bonds. If the two parties engaged in a transaction are in close proximity, the cost of transfer is extremely low, and currency is very efficient. If the parties are separated, then the cost of transfer could be substantial. Furthermore, carrying fiat currency entails a risk of loss or theft. Nevertheless, fiat currency rates very highly for anonymity. In other words, currency is the ideal "traceless transfer," and as such, this money is often preferred for those engaging in illegal transactions or to avoid taxation.

    Recently, there has been much discussion about central banks creating digital currency. Digital currency overcomes the distance and the loss/theft disadvantages of holding physical currency, but digital currency loses its ability to become a traceless, anonymous transfer.

2. Bank Deposits

Bank deposits (or checks drawn on banks) can be transferred between buyers and sellers who hold accounts in financial institutions. Deposits are almost always denominated in the unit of account of the country in which they are based, although many banks do offer deposits in foreign currency. Debit transfers can be implemented very inexpensively, often at a charge of only 3 to 4 basis points (hundredths of a percentage point).

However, almost one-half of merchant transfers go through credit cards, which involves a substantial cost to such businesses of 2 to 3 percent, and then a remission of "rewards" to the purchaser at a slightly lower rate. Most merchants are reluctant to discount prices if the customer offers to undertake a more efficient debit transfer, and banks, which make large profits from credit cards, are in no hurry to encourage such transfers. Although banks may shield deposit information from the public, requisitions by government or other law-enforcement officials means that these transfers cannot be kept from the legal or tax authorities.

3. Gold

As noted at the onset of this chapter, gold and other precious metals, such as silver, were for centuries the benchmark of the world's monetary system. Gold and silver coins became the circulating media of exchange. Because these metals were limited in supply, they retained value better than fiat currencies that could be issued without limit. For this reason, most central banks linked their currency to either gold or silver, promising to exchange their notes for the precious metal at a fixed price.

Transfers of gold, like fiat currency, rate high for anonymity. But gold is no longer used as a medium of exchange, except occasionally among central banks to settle international transfers. Despite its current disuse, the long history of gold as a precious and valued medium of exchange cannot be denied. As one gold enthusiast asked me, if you were stranded on a desert island, which would you prefer: a debit card, a Bitcoin, or a gold coin?

4. Bitcoin

As of 2021, several companies and government agencies have declared that they will accept cryptocurrencies in payment for goods or taxes. But virtually no prices are quoted in Bitcoin, so Bitcoin is not yet a unit of account. Bitcoin, like gold, is limited in supply, so it cannot lose value by being overissued. In its short history, it has not been as good a hedge as gold (or currency) against other risk assets, such as the stock market.

Figure 18.4 shows the trailing three-year monthly correlations of gold and Bitcoin with the stock market. One can see that the correlation of Bitcoin with stock prices is substantially higher than gold. Furthermore, in the bear market brought on by the Covid-19 pandemic, Bitcoin fell by 50 percent in price, while the price of gold went up. Cryptocurrencies also fell when the stock market declined in early 2021 in response to anticipated tightening of the Federal Reserve. In its short history, Bitcoin has not yet served as an effective hedge asset against fluctuations in stocks.

FIGURE 18.4

Correlation between gold and Bitcoin with the S&P 500

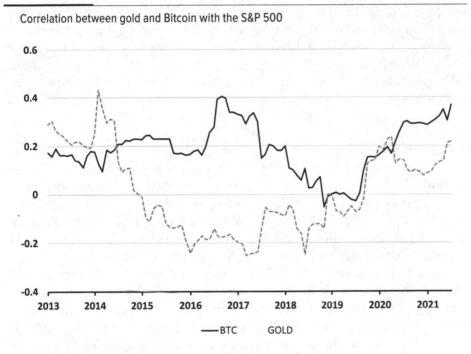

However, Bitcoin, at least in the early years of its existence, was an excellent medium for anonymous transfers. The infamous Silk Road, an Amazon.com-like website designed and run by Ross Uhlbricht, traded illegal goods like drugs, guns, and counterfeit currency, and would only allow transfer in Bitcoin, which could not be traced on the dark web. However, recent transfers, especially when they are connected through organized exchanges such as Coinbase and others, are not as anonymous.

Nevertheless, ransomware demands are almost always made in Bitcoin. In May 2021, Colonial Pipeline paid $4.3 million to a cyber-criminal group called Dark Side after they successfully hacked Colonials' computers and stopped their operations, impacting gas deliveries throughout the Southeast. However, a month later the government was able to recover almost 90 percent of the ransom, demonstrating that the anonymity of the system is penetrable. Furthermore, in the United States, the Internal Revenue Service has required individuals to reveal any crypto accounts on their taxes forms, making it harder to hide assets and transfers.

Bitcoin also has rather large transaction costs, at least compared to debit transfers, and a longer time delay to verify the transfer. Other cryptocurrencies have worked to make transfers faster, but it is too early to predict how successful this will be. One of the advantages of Bitcoin is that its transfer costs are often far lower than other methods for *international* transactions, which must go through foreign exchange markets and can be very costly.

Bitcoin, as well as other cryptocurrencies, can act as a "world money," just as the euro consolidated many of the European currencies in the 1990s. International transfers open a large opportunity for Bitcoin. Furthermore, in contrast to transfers between financial intermediaries, Bitcoin trades 24 hours a day, 365 days a year and transactions can be undertaken and verified at any time.

Macroeconomics of Cryptocurrencies

Cryptocurrencies present a threat to central bank money and bank deposits. The more the public holds cryptocurrencies, the lower will be the demand for central bank money. This reduced demand for central bank money would be inflationary, since central bank money is used as a unit of account. The reduction in the demand for central bank money also makes monetary control more difficult.

Instead, if goods and services are priced in cryptocurrencies, particularly Bitcoin, which is limited in supply, then the monetary system resembles the gold standard. As detailed at the beginning of this chapter, the gain from moving to such a standard is the absence of inflationary bias; but this advantage is offset by the inability to provide liquidity in times of crisis. Cryptocurrencies are certainly superior to gold for most transactions, but the lack of central bank control does create substantial downside risks.

Whether cryptocurrencies become widespread depends on the strengths and weaknesses of each asset as a medium of exchange. Although many central banks are considering a digital currency, few have implemented it and development in the United States is lagging.

Competition for effective monies is good for society, as competition spurs innovation. If countries wish to maintain control of their economy, it is incumbent on them to improve the efficiency of the payment system based on government money.

CONCLUSION

This chapter documented the role of money in the economy and financial markets. Before World War II, persistent inflation in the United States and other industrialized countries was nonexistent. But when the gold standard was dethroned during the Great Depression, the control of money passed to the central banks. With the dollar no longer pegged to gold, it was inflation and not deflation that proved to be the major problem that central banks sought to control.

The central bank controls the short-term interest rate by influencing the supply of reserves to the financial system and by setting the deposit rate on such reserves. Raising rates has a modestly negative impact on stock prices. In recent years, stock prices have anticipated changes in central bank policy rates.

Cryptocurrencies, most prominently Bitcoin, threaten the supremacy of government-backed money. Unless the private sector improves the ease and efficiency of electronic transfers among deposit accounts, cryptocurrencies could grow and take a significant share of transactions. This will reduce the demand for government money and make monetary control by the central bank more difficult. This implies that the central banks should move aggressively to make their currency attractive against competitors, by keeping inflation low and improving the efficiency of transactions.

19

Stocks and the Business Cycle

The stock market has predicted nine out of the last five recessions.

—Paul Samuelson, 1966[1]

I'd love to be able to predict markets and anticipate recessions, but since that's impossible, I'm as satisfied to search out profitable companies as Buffett is.

—Peter Lynch, 1989[2]

It is the summer of 1987. A well-respected economist is about to address a large group of financial analysts, investment advisors, and stockbrokers. There is obvious concern in the audience. The stock market has been surging to new all-time highs, driving down dividend yields to record lows and sending P/E ratios skyward. Is this bullishness justified? The audience wants to know if the economy is really going to do well enough to support these high stock prices.

The economist's address is highly optimistic. He predicts that the real GDP of the United States will increase over 4 percent during the next four quarters, a very healthy growth rate. There will be no recession for at least three years, and even if one occurs after that, it will be very brief. Corporate profits, one of the major factors driving stock prices, will increase at double-digit annual rates for at least the next three years. To boot, he predicts that a Republican will easily win the White House in next year's presidential election, a situation obviously comforting to the overwhelmingly conservative audience. The crowd likes what it hears.

The audience's anxiety is quieted, and many advisors are ready to recommend that their clients increase their stake in stocks.

But stocks were not the place to be. In just a few weeks, the market took one of its sharpest falls in history, including the record-breaking 23 percent decline on October 19, 1987. Three months after the address, most stocks could have been bought for half the price they were at the time of his speech. But the biggest irony of all is that the economist was dead right in each and every one of his bullish *economic* predictions.

STOCK RETURNS AND THE BUSINESS CYCLE

The lesson is that the markets and the economy are often out of sync. It is not surprising that many investors dismiss economic forecasts when planning their market strategy. The substance of Paul Samuelson's famous words, cited at the top of this chapter, remains true more than a half-century after they were first uttered.

However, do not think the business cycle is not important for the stock market. Stocks may often overreact, but they still respond powerfully to changes in economic activity. This is apparent from Figure 19.1, which displays the S&P 500 Index and the business cycle from 1871 onward. Stocks decline just before the shaded periods, which indicate recessions, and rally rigorously at signs of an impending economic recovery. *If* you can predict the business cycle, you can beat the buy-and-hold strategy that has been advocated throughout this book.

This is no easy task. To make money by predicting the business cycle, one must be able to identify peaks and troughs of economic activity *before* they actually occur, a skill very few, if any economists possess. Yet business cycle forecasting is a popular Wall Street endeavor, not because it is successful—most of the time it is not—but because the rewards are so large if you can identify the turning point of the business cycle.

WHO CALLS THE BUSINESS CYCLE?

It is surprising to many that the dating of business cycles is not determined by any of the myriad government agencies that collect data on the economy. Instead, the task falls to the National Bureau of Economic Research (NBER), a private research organization founded in 1920 for the purpose of documenting business cycles and developing a series of national income accounts. In the early years of its existence, the bureau's staff compiled comprehensive chronological records of the changes in economic conditions in many of the industrialized economies. In particular, the bureau developed monthly series on business activity for the United States and Great Britain back to 1854.

FIGURE 19.1

S&P 500 Index, earnings, and dividends, 1871–2021

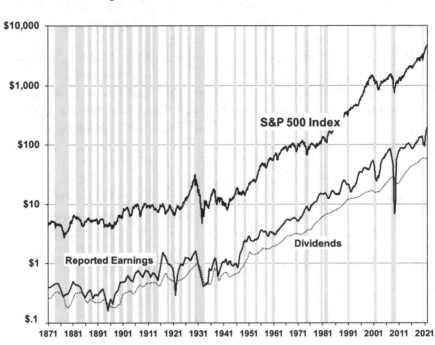

In a 1946 volume entitled *Measuring Business Cycles*, Wesley C. Mitchell, one of the founders of the bureau, and Arthur Burns, a renowned business cycle expert who later headed the Federal Reserve Board, gave the following definition of a *business cycle*:

> Business cycles are a type of fluctuation found in the aggregate economic activity of nations that organize their work mainly in business enterprises: a cycle consists of expansion occurring at about the same time in many economic activities, followed by similarly general recessions, or contractions, and revivals that merge into the expansion phase of the next cycle; this sequence of changes is recurrent but not periodic; in duration business cycles vary from more than one year to ten or twelve years and they are not divisible into shorter cycles of similar character.[3]

It is commonly assumed that a recession occurs when real GDP, the most inclusive measure of economic output, declines for two consecutive quarters. But this is not necessarily so. Although this criterion is a reasonable rule of thumb for indicating a recession, there is no single rule or measure used by the NBER. Rather, the bureau focuses on four different series to determine the turning points in the economy: employment, industrial production, real personal income, and real manufacturing and trade sales.

The Business Cycle Dating Committee of the NBER confirms the business cycle dates. This committee consists of academic economists who are associated with the bureau and who meet to examine economic data whenever conditions warrant. Over the entire period from 1802 through 2021, the United States has experienced 48 recessions, and these recessions have averaged nearly 19 months in length, while expansions have averaged 34 months.[4] This means that over these 220 years, the economy has been in a recession about one-third of the time. However, since World War II, there have been 12 recessions, averaging only 10 months in length, while the expansions have averaged 64 months. In the postwar period, the economy has been in a recession less than one-ninth of the time, far less than the prewar average. The longest expansion in US history lasted 10 years and eight months and only ended because it was cut short by the Covid-19 pandemic.

Dating the Business Cycle

The dating of the business cycle is of great importance. The designation that the economy is in a recession or an expansion has political as well as economic implications. For example, when the NBER called the onset of the 1990 recession in July rather than August, it raised quite a few eyebrows in Washington. The Bush administration had told the public that the Iraqi invasion of Kuwait and the surge in oil prices were responsible for the economic recession, an explanation that was undermined when the bureau dated the onset of the recession a month earlier. Similarly, the 2001 recession began in March when technology spending dropped sharply, well before the 9/11 terrorist attacks.

The Business Cycle Dating Committee is in no rush to call the turning points in the cycle. Never has a call been reversed because of new or revised data that become available—and the NBER wants to keep it that way. As Robert E. Hall, current chair of the seven-member Business Cycle Dating Committee, indicated, "The NBER has not made an announcement on a business cycle peak or trough until there was almost no doubt that the data would not be revised in light of subsequent availability of data."[5]

Recent examples of the NBER's dating make the point. The March 1991 trough was not called until 21 months later, in December 1992, and the November bottom of the 2001 recession was not called until July 2003. The peak of the 2002–2007 expansion was not called until December 2008, one year after it began and well after the Lehman crisis had paralyzed financial markets and sent stocks tumbling. The trough of the Covid-19 recession, which the bureau set as April 2020, was called in July. By that time, the market had recovered nearly all the sharp losses it experienced during the pandemic. Clearly, waiting for the bureau to designate business cycles is far too late to be of any use in timing the market.

STOCK RETURNS AROUND BUSINESS CYCLE TURNING POINTS

Almost without exception, the stock market turns down prior to recessions and rises before economic recoveries. In fact, out of the 48 recessions recorded from 1802 on, 44 of them—or more than 9 out of 10—have been preceded (or accompanied) by declines of 8 percent or more in the total stock returns index. Two exceptions followed World War II: the 1948–1949 recession that immediately followed the war, and the 1953 recession, when stocks fell just shy of the 8 percent criterion.

The returns during the 12 post–World War II recessions are summarized in Table 19.1. You can see that the stock return index peaked anywhere from 0 to 13 months before the beginning of a recession. The stock market gave no advance warning of a downturn for the recessions that began in January 1980 and July 1990, and the Covid-19 recession in February 2020.

As the Samuelson quote at the beginning of this chapter indicates, the stock market is also prone to false alarms, and these have increased in the postwar period. Declines greater than 10 percent in the Dow Jones Industrial Average during the postwar period that were not followed by recessions (false alarms) are listed in Table 19.2. The decline of 35.1 percent from August through early December 1987 is the largest decline in the 220-year history of stock returns when the economy did not subsequently fall into a recession.[6] The trough in the stock return index and the trough in the NBER business cycle are compared in Table 19.3.

TABLE 19.1

Peaks in the stock market and the economy

Recession	Peak of Stock Index (1)	Peak of Business Cycle (2)	Lead Time Between Peaks (3)	Decline in Stock Index From (1) to (2) (4)	Maximum 12 Month Decline in Stock Index (5)
1948 - 49	May 1948	Nov 1948	6	-8.91%	-9.76%
1953 - 54	Dec 1952	Jul 1953	7	-4.26%	-9.04%
1957 - 58	Jul 1957	Aug 1957	1	-4.86%	-15.32%
1960 - 61	Dec 1959	Apr 1960	4	-8.65%	-8.65%
1970	Nov 1968	Dec 1969	13	-12.08%	-29.16%
1973 - 75	Dec 1972	Nov 1973	11	-16.29%	-38.80%
1980	Jan 1980	Jan 1980	0	0.00%	-9.55%
1981 - 82	Nov 1980	Jul 1981	8	-4.08%	-13.99%
1990 - 91	Jul 1990	Jul 1990	0	0.00%	-13.84%
2001	Aug 2000	Mar 2001	7	-22.94%	-26.55%
2007 - 09	Oct 2007	Dec 2007	2	-4.87%	-47.50%
2020	Feb 2020	Feb 2020	0	0.00%	-33.67%
		Average	4.9	-7.24%	-21.32%

TABLE 19.2

False alarms by stock market: postwar declines of 10 percent or more in Daily Dow Jones Industrial Average when no recession followed within 12 months

Peak of Stock Index	Trough of Stock Index	% Decline
May 29, 1946	May 17, 1947	-23.2%
Dec 13, 1961	Jun 26, 1962	-27.1%
Jan 18, 1966	Sept 29, 1966	-22.3%
Sept 25, 1967	Mar 21, 1968	-12.5%
Apr 28, 1971	Nov 23, 1971	-16.1%
Aug 17,1978	Oct 27, 1978	-12.8%
Nov 29, 1983	Jul 24, 1984	-15.6%
Aug 25, 1987	Dec 4, 1987	-35.1%
Aug 6, 1997	Oct 27, 1997	-13.3%
Jul 17, 1998	Aug 31, 1998	-19.3%
Mar 19, 2002	Oct 9, 2002	-31.5%
Apr 26, 2010	Jul 02, 2010	-13.6%
Apr 29, 2011	Oct 03, 2011	-16.8%
May 19, 2015	Aug 25, 2015	-16.2%
Oct 03, 2018	Dec 24, 2018	-19.4%

TABLE 19.3

Troughs in the stock market and the economy, 1948–2020

Recession	Trough of Stock Index (1)	Trough of Business Cycle (2)	Lead Time Between Troughs (3)	Rise in Stock Index From (1) to (2) (4)
1948 - 1949	May 1949	Oct 1949	5	15.59%
1953 - 1954	Aug 1953	May 1954	9	29.13%
1957 - 1958	Dec 1957	April 1958	4	10.27%
1960 - 1961	Oct 1960	Feb 1961	4	21.25%
1970	Jun 1970	Nov 1970	5	21.86%
1973 - 1975	Sep 1974	Mar 1975	6	35.60%
1980	Mar 1980	Jul 1980	4	22.60%
1981 - 1982	Jul 1982	Nov 1982	4	33.13%
1990 - 1991	Oct 1990	Mar 1991	5	25.28%
2001	Sep 2001	Nov 2001	2	9.72%
2007 - 09	Mar 2009	Jun 2009	3	37.44%
March 2020	Mar 2020	Apr 2020	1	30.17%
		Average	4.3	24.34%
		Std. Dev.	2.02	9.25%

The average lead time between the bottom of the market and the bottom of an economic recovery has been 4.3 months. In the Covid-19 pandemic, the lead time was a record low of one month. These lead times compared to an average of five months that the peak in the market precedes the peak in the business cycle. The time between the peak of the market and the peak of the economy also has shown much greater variability than the time between the trough of the market and the trough of the economy.[7]

It is important to note that by the time the economy has reached the end of the recession, the stock market has already risen on average 25 percent from its low. Therefore, an investor waiting for tangible evidence that the business cycle has hit bottom has already missed a very substantial rise in the market. As noted previously, the NBER does not announce the dates when recessions end until months after the economy turns up.

GAINS THROUGH TIMING THE BUSINESS CYCLE

If investors could predict in advance when recessions will begin and end, they could enjoy superior returns to the returns earned by a buy-and-hold investor.[8] Specifically, if an investor switched from stocks to cash (short-term bonds) four months before the beginning of a recession and back to stocks four months before the end of the recession, he would gain almost 5 percentage points per year on a risk-corrected basis over the buy-and-hold investor. About two-thirds of that gain is the result of predicting the end of the recession, where as Table 19.3 shows that the stock market hits bottom between four and five months before the end of the economic downturn. The other third of the gain comes from selling stocks four months before the peak.

Investors who switch between stocks and bonds at peaks and troughs of the business cycle (which, as noted, are called many months after the fact) gain a mere half percentage point return over the buy-and-hold investor, and that gain is not statistically significant.

HOW HARD IS IT TO PREDICT THE BUSINESS CYCLE?

Clearly if one could predict in advance when recessions will occur, the gains would be substantial. That is perhaps why billions of dollars of resources are spent trying to forecast the business cycle. But the record of predicting business cycle turning points is extremely poor.

Stephen McNees, vice president of the Federal Reserve Bank of Boston, has done extensive research into the accuracy of economic forecasters' predictions. He claims that at business cycle turning points, forecasters' errors were "enormous."[9]

History of the Ability to Predict Recessions

The 1974–1975 recession was particularly tough for economists. Almost every one of the nearly two dozen of the nation's top economists invited to President Ford's anti-inflation conference in Washington in September 1974 was unaware that the US economy was in the middle of its most severe postwar recession to date. McNees, studying the forecasts issued by five prominent forecasters in 1974, found that the median forecast overestimated GNP growth by 6 percentage points and underestimated inflation by 4 percentage points. Early recognition of the 1974 recession was so poor that many economists jumped the gun on the next recession, which didn't strike until 1980—while most economists thought it had begun early in 1979.

From 1976 to 1995, Robert J. Eggert and subsequently Randell Moore documented and summarized the economic forecasts of a noted panel of economic and business experts. These forecasts were compiled and published in a monthly publication entitled *Blue Chip Economic Indicators*. In July 1979, the *Blue Chip Economic Indicators* reported that a strong majority of forecasters believed that a recession had already started—forecasting negative GNP growth in the second, third, and fourth quarters of 1979. However, the NBER declared that the peak of the business cycle did not occur until January 1980 and that the economy expanded throughout 1979.

Forecasters' ability to predict the severe 1981–1982 recession, when unemployment reached a postwar high of 10.8 percent, was no better. The headline of the July 1981 *Blue Chip Economic Indicators* report read, "Economic Exuberance Envisioned for 1982." Instead, 1982 was a disaster. By November 1981 the forecasters realized that the economy had faltered, and optimism turned to pessimism. Most thought that the economy had entered a recession (which it had done four months earlier), nearly 70 percent thought that it would end by the first quarter of 1982 (which it would not, instead tying the record for the longest postwar recession, ending in November 1982), and 90 percent thought that it would be mild, like the 1971 recession, rather than severe—wrong again!

In April 1985, with the expansion well under way, forecasters were queried about how long the economy would be in an expansion. The average response was for another 20 months, which would put the peak at December 1986, more than three and a half years before the cycle actually ended. Even the most optimistic forecasters picked spring 1988 as the latest date for the next recession to begin. This question was asked repeatedly throughout 1985 and 1986, and no forecaster imagined that the 1980s expansion would last as long as it did.

Following the stock market crash of October 1987, forecasters reduced their GNP growth estimates of 1988 over 1987 from 2.8 percent to 1.9 percent, the largest drop in the 11-year history of the survey. Instead, economic growth in 1988 was nearly 4 percent, as the economy grew strongly despite the stock market collapse.

HAS THE BUSINESS CYCLE BEEN CONQUERED?

As the post-crash expansion continued, the belief that a recession was imminent turned into the belief that prosperity was here to stay. There was a growing conviction that perhaps the business cycle had been conquered—by either government policy or the recession-proof nature of our service-oriented economy. Ed Yardeni, then senior economist at Prudential-Bache Securities, wrote a "New Wave Manifesto" in late 1988, concluding that self-repairing, growing economies were likely to continue to expand through the rest of the decade.[10] On the eve of one of the worst worldwide recessions in the postwar era, Leonard Silk, senior economics editor of the *New York Times*, stated in May 1990 in his article "Is There Really a Business Cycle?":

> Most economists foresee no recession in 1990 or 1991, and 1992 will be another presidential year, when the odds tip strongly against recession. Japan, West Germany, and most of the other capitalist countries of Europe and Asia are also on a long upward roll, with no end in sight.[11]

Yet by November 1990, *Blue Chip Economic Indicators* reported that most of the panel believed the US economy had already slipped, or was about to slip, into a recession. But in November, not only had the economy been in recession for four months, but the stock market had already hit its bottom and was headed upward. Had investors given in to the prevailing pessimism at the time when the recession seemed confirmed, they would have sold after the low was reached and stocks were headed for a strong three-year rally.

The 10-year expansion of the US economy from March 1991 through March 2001 again spawned talk of "new era economics" and economies without recession.[12] Even in early 2001, most forecasters did not see a recession. In fact, in September 2001, just before the terrorist attack, only 13 percent of the economists surveyed by *Blue Chip Economic Indicators* believed the United States was in a recession even though the NBER subsequently indicated that the US recession had begun six months earlier in March.[13] By February 2002, less than 20 percent thought the recession had ended in 2001, although the NBER eventually dated November 2001 as the end of the recession.[14] Once again, economists have been unable to call the turning point of the business cycle until well after the date has passed.

Forecasters did no better predicting the Great Recession of 2007 to 2009, which spurred on the financial crisis. The NBER did not actually call the beginning of the recession until December 2008, one year after it began, when the S&P 500 Index had already fallen more than 40 percent.

The Federal Reserve did begin easing interest rates in September 2007, three months before the onset of the recession, but had no concept that a recession was imminent. In the meeting of the Federal Open Market Committee on December 11, 2007, Fed economist Dave Stockton gave the following summary of the Federal Reserve forecast:

Obviously, we're not forecasting a business cycle peak. So in our forecast, we're not yet saying that we're on the downside of a business cycle. We have a "growth recession" [a slowdown in economic growth] in this forecast and nothing more than that.[15]

Alan Greenspan and the Fed, as well as almost all private forecasters, had no idea that the financial system was barreling headlong into the greatest financial calamity in almost a century.

CONCLUSION

Stock values are based on corporate earnings, and the business cycle is a prime determinant of these earnings. The gains of being able to predict the turning points of the economic cycle are large, and yet doing so with any precision has eluded economists of all persuasions.

The worst course an investor can take is to follow the prevailing sentiment about economic activity. That will lead investors to buy at high prices when times are good and everyone is optimistic, and to sell at the low.

The lessons to investors are clear. Beating the stock market by analyzing real economic activity requires a degree of prescience that forecasters do not yet have.

When World Events Impact Financial Markets

I can predict the motion of heavenly bodies, but not the madness of crowds.

—Isaac Newton

As the sun rose over New York City on a beautiful Tuesday morning, September 11, 2001, traders expected a dull day on Wall Street. There was no economic data coming out of Washington nor any earnings releases scheduled. The previous Friday the markets had fallen on a horrible employment report, but on Monday the markets had bounced back slightly.

The US equity markets had not yet opened, but contracts on the S&P 500 Index futures had been trading all night as usual on the electronic Globex exchange. The futures markets were up, indicating that Wall Street was expecting a firm opening. But then a report came at 8:48 a.m. on what was to be one of the most fateful days in world history: a plane crashed into the North Tower of the World Trade Center. The pattern of trading over the next 27 minutes is shown in Figure 20.1.

The news of the plane crash spread quickly, but few imagined what had really happened. Was it a large or small plane? Was it an accident? Or was there something more sinister going on? Although nobody knew the answers yet, immediately the stock index futures market traded down a few points, as it often does when uncertainty increases. Within a few minutes, however, buyers reappeared, and the index returned to its previous level, as most traders concluded that nothing significant had occurred.

FIGURE 20.1

S&P 500 futures market on Tuesday morning, September 11, 2001

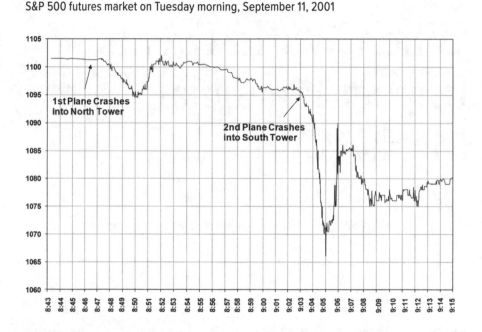

Fifteen minutes later, at 9:03 a.m., with news cameras focused on the World Trade Center and millions around the world watching, a second plane crashed into the South Tower. The entire world changed in that moment. Americans' worst fears had been realized. This was a terrorist attack. For the first time since World War II, America was under direct assault on its own soil.

Within two minutes of the second crash, the S&P futures plunged 30 points, about 3 percent, indicating that if the exchanges had been open, nearly $300 billion would have been wiped off US stock values. But then, miraculously, buyers did appear. Despite the enormity of the events unfolding, some traders bet that the market overreacted to these attacks and decided that this was a good time to buy stocks. The futures firmed and ended the session at 9:15 a.m. down about 15 points, gaining back one-half of the earlier loss.

Despite this comeback, the gravity of this attack quickly sank in. All the stock, bond, and commodity exchanges in the United States first delayed opening and then canceled trading for the day. In fact, stock exchanges in the United States would remain closed for the remainder of the week, the longest closing since Franklin D. Roosevelt declared a bank holiday in March 1933 to try to restore America's collapsing banking system.

Foreign stock exchanges, however, remained open. It was 2 p.m. in London and 3 p.m. in Europe when the planes struck. The German DAX index immediately fell more than 9 percent and ended the session around that level. London stocks suffered, but not as severely. There was a feeling that with the world's financial center, the United States, vulnerable to attack, some business might move to the United Kingdom. The British pound rallied, as did the euro against the dollar. Normally, it is the US dollar that gains in an international crisis. This time, with the attack centering on New York, foreign traders were unsure which direction to go.

When the NYSE reopened the following Monday, September 17, the Dow Industrials fell 685 points, or 7.13 percent, one of the largest percentage drops in its history. That fall was more than twice the 3.5 percent drop that occurred on the day following the attack on Pearl Harbor, and it was more than that of any other one-day decline when the United States was at war.

The Dow continued to fall during the week and closed Friday, September 21, at 8,236—down more than 14 percent from its September 10 close, and nearly 30 percent from its all-time high reached on January 14, 2000.

LARGEST MARKET MOVES

Table 20.1 lists the 54 largest single-day changes in the Dow Jones Industrials from 1885 through 2021.[1] During that whole period there have 157 days when the average has changed by 5 percent or more. Many of these occurred from 1929 through 1933, but recent history has not been exempted from volatility. Fifteen large moves took place from September 2008 through March 2009 when the world economy was in the grips of the financial crisis.

The volatility of the market during the Covid-19 pandemic was even more extreme. There were eight trading days between March 9 and March 18, when the severity of the coronavirus became apparent to world investors. On seven of those days, the Dow Industrials rose or fell by more than 5 percent (March 10 barely missed, with a change of 4.89 percent), an unprecedented concentration of large market movements.

TABLE 20.1

Largest changes in the Dow Industrial Average (negative changes are in bold)

Rank	Date	Change	Rank	Date	Change	Rank	Date	Change
1	**Oct 19, 1987**	**-22.61%**	19	Dec 18, 1931	9.35%	37*	Feb 1, 1917	**-7.24%**
2	Mar 15, 1933	15.34%	20	Feb 13, 1932	9.19%	38*	Oct 27, 1997	**-7.18%**
3*	Oct 6, 1931	14.87%	21*	May 6, 1932	9.08%	39	Oct 5, 1932	**-7.15%**
4*	**Mar 16, 2020**	**-12.93%**	22*	Apr 19, 1933	9.03%	40*	Sep 17, 2001	**-7.13%**
5	**Oct 28, 1929**	**-12.82%**	23	**Dec 18, 3799**	**-8.72%**	41	Jun 3, 1931	7.12%
6	Oct 30, 1929	12.34%	24	Oct 8, 1931	8.70%	42	Jan 6, 1932	7.12%
7	**Oct 29, 1929**	**-11.73%**	25	**Aug 12, 1932**	**-8.40%**	43	Sep 24, 1931	**-7.07%**
8*	Mar 24, 2020	11.37%	26	**Mar 14, 1907**	**-8.29%**	44	Jul 20, 1933	**-7.07%**
9	Sep 21, 1932	11.36%	27	**Oct 26, 1987**	**-8.04%**	45*	Sep 29, 2008	**-6.98%**
10*	Oct 13, 2008	11.08%	28	Jun 10, 1932	7.99%	46*	Oct 13, 1989	**-6.91%**
11	Oct 28, 2008	10.88%	29	**Oct 15, 2008**	**-7.87%**	47*	Jul 30, 1914	**-6.90%**
12	Oct 21, 1987	10.15%	30	**Jul 21, 1933**	**-7.84%**	48	Jun 11, 2020	**-6.90%**
13*	**Mar 12, 2020**	**-9.99%**	31*	**Mar 9, 2020**	**-7.79%**	49	Jan 8, 1988	**-6.85%**
14	**Nov 6, 1929**	**-9.92%**	32	Oct 18, 1937	**-7.75%**	50*	Mar 23, 2009	6.84%
15	Aug 3, 1932	9.52%	33*	Apr 6, 2020	7.73%	51	Oct 14, 1932	6.83%
16*	Feb 11, 1932	9.47%	34	**Dec 1, 2008**	**-7.70%**	52	Nov 11, 1929	**-6.82%**
17	Mar 13, 2020	9.36%	35	**Oct 9, 2008**	**-7.33%**	53*	May 14, 1940	**-6.80%**
18*	Nov 14, 1929	9.36%	36*	Sep 5, 1939	7.26%	54	Oct 5, 1931	**-6.78%**

*Changes associated with news item
Excludes 15.34% change from March 3 through 15, 1933 during US bank holiday when markets were closed.

There were six consecutive days during that time frame when the Dow changed by 5 percent or more, tying the record experienced during the Great Crash of October 1929.

On Thursday, March 12, 2020, the Dow fell by 9.99 percent and then rose on Friday, March 13, by 9.36 percent, the thirteenth and seventeenth largest moves in history.

Then came the weekend of March 14–15, 2020, when the world froze: almost all sporting events ceased, schools closed, and much of the world entered lockdown mode. On the following Monday, March 16, the market fell by 12.96 percent, a decline that exceeded October 28, 1929, which was heralded as the Great Crash. Chapter 24 provides a more detailed description of the reaction of the market and policy makers to the Covid-19 pandemic.

BIG MOVES AND NEWS EVENTS

It was clear why the markets fell after the terrorist attacks and during the pandemic. But it might surprise investors that in most cases, major market movements are *not* accompanied by any news of sufficient importance to explain the price change. Of all the 157 large changes, only 42, or one in four, can be identified with significant world political or economic events, such as wars, political changes, pandemics, or governmental policy shifts. Even during the financial crisis of 2008–2009, only 4 of the 15 large changes were associated with specific events.

Market changes greater than 5 percent that are associated with specific events are shown in Table 20.2.[2] Government policy changes are the biggest single driver of the largest market moves. Support by the government, or more importantly, the Federal Reserve, is often the cause of large rallies after the market has been in a steep decline. The top news-related change was the 14.87 percent gain on October 6, 1931, when President Herbert Hoover proposed a $500 million pool to help banks, and the second largest was an 11.37 percent gain on March 24, 2020, when hopes of a significant pandemic stimulus package from Washington rose dramatically.

TABLE 20.2

Largest news-related changes in the Dow Jones Industrial Average (negative changes are in bold)

Rank	Date	Change	News Headline
3	Oct 6, 1931	14.87%	Hoover Urges $500M Pool to Help Banks
4	**Mar 16, 2020**	**-12.93%**	**World Covid Lockdown**
8	Mar 24, 2020	11.37%	Hope for Bipartisan Relief Package
10	Oct 13, 2008	11.08%	Fed Gives "Unlimited Liquidity" to Foreign Central Banks
13	**Mar 12, 2020**	**-9.99%**	**Worsening Covid Pandemic**
16	Feb 11, 1932	9.47%	Liberalization of Fed Discount Policy
18	Nov 14, 1929	9.36%	Fed Lowers Discount Rate/Tax Cut Proposed
21	May 6, 1932	9.08%	U.S. Steel Negotiates 15% Wage Cut
22	Apr 19, 1933	9.03%	U.S. Drops Gold Standard
31	**Mar 9, 2020**	**-7.79%**	**Worsening Covid Pandemic**
33	Apr 6, 2020	7.73%	Slowing US Rate of Inflation
36	Sep 5, 1939	7.26%	World War II Begins in Europe
37	**Feb 1, 1917**	**-7.24%**	**Germany Announces Unrestricted Submarine Warfare**
38	**Oct 27, 1997**	**-7.18%**	**Attack on Hong Kong Dollar**
40	**Sep 17, 2001**	**-7.13%**	**World Trade Center Terrorist Attack**
45	**Sep 29, 2008**	**-6.98%**	**House voted down $700B bail out package**
46	**Oct 13, 1989**	**-6.91%**	**United Airline Buy-out Collapses**
47	**Jul 30, 1914**	**-6.90%**	**Outbreak of World War I**
50	Mar 23, 2009	6.84%	Treasury Announces $1T Public-Private Plan to Buy Bad Bank Debt
53	**May 14, 1940**	**-6.80%**	**Germans Invade Holland**
55	**May 21, 1940**	**-6.78%**	**Allied Reverses in France**
58	Jun 20, 1931	6.64%	Hoover Advocates Foreign Debt Moratorium
60	**Jul 26, 1934**	**-6.62%**	**Fighting in Austria; Italy Mobilizes**
63	**Sep 26, 1955**	**-6.54%**	**Eisenhower Suffers Heart Attack**
68	Jul 24, 2002	6.35%	J.P. Morgan Denies Involvement with Enron Scandel
71	**July, 26, 1893**	**-6.31%**	**Erie Railroad Bankrupt**
85	**Mar 11, 2020**	**-5.86%**	**Worsening Covid Pandemic**
87	Oct 31, 1929	5.82%	Fed Lowers Discount Rate
88	**Jun 16, 1930**	**-5.81%**	**Hoover to Sign Tariff Bill**
89	Apr 20, 1933	5.80%	Continued Rally on Dropping of Gold Standard
97	May 2, 1898	5.64%	Dewey Defeats Spanish
101	Mar 28, 1898	5.56%	Dispatches of Armistice with Spain
103	**Aug 8, 2011**	**-5.55%**	**Standard and Poor's Downgrades US Treasury Debt**
110	Dec 22, 1916	5.47%	Lansing Denies U.S. Near War
113	**Dec 18, 1896**	**-5.42%**	**Senate Votes for Free Cuba**
115	**Feb 25, 1933**	**-5.40%**	**Maryland Bank Holiday**
119	Oct 23, 1933	5.37%	Roosevelt Devalues Dollar
121	**Dec 21, 1916**	**-5.35%**	**Sec. of State Lansing implies U.S. Near War**
130	Apr 9, 1938	5.25%	Congress Passes Bill Taxing U.S. Government Bond Interest
151	**Nov 5, 2008**	**-5.05%**	**Democrats Sweep Congress, Presidency**
156	Oct 20, 1931	5.03%	ICC Raises Rail Rates
157	**Mar 31, 1932**	**-5.02%**	**House Proposes Stock Sales Tax**

The record 22.6 percent one-day fall in the stock market on October 19, 1987, is not associated with any one readily identifiable news event. From 1940 until the Great Financial Crisis in 2008, there have been only four days of big moves where the cause is identified: the 7.13 percent drop on September 17, 2001, when the markets reopened after the terrorist attacks; the 7.18 percent drop on October 27, 1997, when foreign exchange speculators attacked the Hong Kong dollar; the 6.91 percent fall on Friday, October 13, 1989, when the leveraged buyout of United Airlines collapsed; and the 6.54 percent drop on September 26, 1955, when President Eisenhower suffered a heart attack.[3]

What Causes the Market to Move?

Even when the day is filled with news events, there can be sharp disagreement over *what* news caused the market change. On November 15, 1991, when the Dow fell more than 120 points, or nearly 4 percent, *Investor's Business Daily* ran an article about the market entitled "Dow Plunges 120 in a Scary Stock Sell-Off: Biotechs, Programs, Expiration and Congress Get the Blame."[4] In contrast, the London-based *Financial Times* published a front-page article written by a New York writer entitled "Wall Street Drops 120 Points on Concern at Russian Moves." Interestingly, the news that the Russian government had suspended oil licenses and taken over the gold supplies was not mentioned even once in the *Investor's Business Daily* article! That one major newspaper highlights "reasons" that another news outlet does not even report illustrates the difficulty of finding fundamental explanations for the movements of markets.

UNCERTAINTY AND THE MARKET

The stock market hates uncertainty, which is why events that jar investors from their customary framework for analyzing the world can have devastating effects. September 11 serves as the perfect example: Americans were unsure what these terrorist attacks meant for the future. How severe would the drop in air travel—or any travel—be? How big a hit would the approximately $600 billion tourist industry take? The very same uncertainty enveloped the market during the early stages of the Covid-19 pandemic. Ambiguity generates anxiety and lower stock prices.

Instability surrounding the US presidency is another downer for stocks. The market almost always falls in reaction to sudden, unexpected changes related to the leader of the free world. As noted previously, President Eisenhower's heart attack on September 26, 1955, caused a 6.54 percent decline in the Dow Industrials. The assassination of President Kennedy on Friday, November 22, 1963, caused the Dow Industrials to drop 2.9 percent and persuaded the NYSE to close two hours early to prevent panic selling. Trading remained suspended the following Monday, November 25, for Kennedy's funeral. Yet the following Tuesday, by which time Lyndon Johnson had taken over the reins of government, the market soared 4.5 percent, representing one of the best days in the postwar period.

When William McKinley was shot on September 14, 1901, the market dropped by more than 4 percent, but stocks regained all their losses on the following trading day. The death of Warren Harding in 1923 caused a milder setback, which was soon erased. Sell-offs such as these often provide good opportunities for investors to buy stocks, since the market usually reverses itself quickly following the change in leadership. But there are politicians whom investors never forgive; stocks rallied over 4 percent in the week following the news of the death of Franklin Roosevelt, never a favorite on Wall Street.

DEMOCRATS AND REPUBLICANS

It is well known that investors generally prefer Republican leaders to Democrats. Most corporate executives and large stock investors are Republicans, and many Republican policies are perceived to be favorable to stocks and capital formation. Democrats are considered to be less amenable to favorable tax treatment of capital gains and dividends, and more in favor of regulation and income redistribution. Yet the stock market has historically done better under Democrats than Republicans.

Correlation Does Not Imply Causality

That is no reason to believe that there necessarily is a cause-and-effect explanation for this correlation. In fact, there is a completely plausible explanation where neither Democrats nor Republicans have any effect whatsoever over the stock market, yet stocks do better under the Democratic Party.

When the economy and stock market are rising, people become better off, and income and capital gains rise. This scenario is favorable to Republicans, who become favored to win the next election. When the economy turns down, not due to any policy or mistake attributed to the Republicans, the subsequent recession and bear market cause public disenchantment and voters throw the Republicans out of office. The Democrats take over at the bottom and rule during the early and middle stages of the bull markets until, once again, the tide turns.

Politics and Stock Returns

A graph of the performance of the Dow Jones Industrials during every administration since Grover Cleveland was elected in 1888 is shown in Figure 20.2.

The greatest bear market in history occurred during Herbert Hoover's Republican administration, while stocks did quite well under Franklin Roosevelt, even though he was frequently reviled in boardrooms and brokerage houses around the country.

FIGURE 20.2

The Dow Industrials and presidential administrations (shaded areas Democratic president)

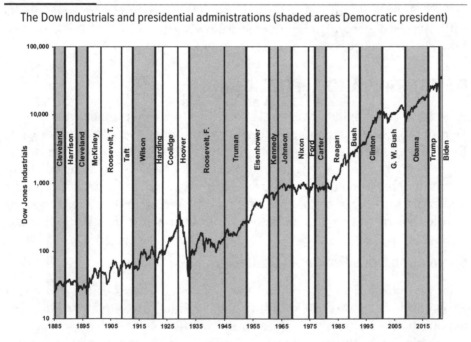

The immediate reaction of the market to presidential elections, measured from the day before to the day after, does indeed conform to the evidence that investors like Republicans better than Democrats. As Table 20.3 reveals, since 1888, the market fell an average of 0.3 percent on the day following a Democratic victory, but it rose by 0.7 percent on the day following a Republican victory. However, the market's reaction to the Republicans' success in presidential elections has been muted since World War II.

TABLE 20.3

Presidential administrations and stock returns: stock returns taken from election date or date of taking office, whichever is earlier (italics represent democratic administrations)

President's Name	Party	Election Date	From: 1 day before To: 1 day after	First Year of Term	Second Year of Term	Third Year of Term	Fourth Year of Term
Harrison	R	11/6/1888	0.4	11.8	-6.6	16.6	13.5
Cleveland	D	11/8/1892	*-0.5*	*-15.3*	*11.9*	*11.3*	*-4.5*
McKinley	R	11/3/1896	2.7	18.9	11.0	9.9	-1.3
McKinley	R	11/6/1900	3.3	35.3	0.3	-18.1	28.5
Roosevelt T.	R	11/8/1904	1.3	25.2	2.0	-32.5	39.0
Taft	R	11/3/1908	2.4	16.6	-0.6	0.5	11.7
Wilson	D	11/5/1912	*1.8*	*-13.0*	*-2.5*	*24.2*	*3.7*
Wilson	D	11/7/1916	*-0.4*	*-30.9*	*-5.8*	*13.5*	*-19.3*
Harding	R	11/2/1920	-0.6	4.0	53.4	-11.1	21.5
Coolidge	R	11/4/1924	1.2	33.3	15.8	36.0	36.5
Hoover	R	11/6/1928	1.2	33.2	-29.6	-32.3	-13.6
Roosevelt F.	D	11/8/1932	*-4.5*	*43.3*	*-4.1*	*37.2*	*43.6*
Roosevelt F.	D	11/3/1936	*2.3*	*-26.8*	*18.6*	*3.3*	*-11.8*
Roosevelt F.	D	11/5/1940	*-2.4*	*-10.2*	*-6.1*	*28.9*	*12.4*
Roosevelt F.	D	11/7/1944	*-0.3*	*30.6*	*-19.1*	*-0.5*	*4.3*
Truman	D	11/2/1948	*-3.8*	*7.9*	*28.8*	*18.2*	*8.1*
Eisenhower	R	11/4/1952	0.4	3.4	42.3	35.7	11.5
Eisenhower	R	11/6/1956	-0.9	-9.9	25.8	13.5	-3.8
Kennedy	D	11/8/1960	*0.8*	*29.6*	*-15.8*	*32.4*	*18.5*
Johnson	D	11/3/1964	*-0.2*	*8.8*	*-16.0*	*25.0*	*6.8*
Nixon	R	11/5/1968	0.3	-10.1	-13.1	14.7	12.1
Nixon	R	11/7/1972	-0.1	-4.3	-41.1	24.0	13.2
Carter	D	11/2/1976	*-1.0*	*-9.7*	*3.6*	*-2.4*	*16.2*
Reagan	R	11/4/1980	1.7	-12.2	11.6	28.4	-1.4
Reagan	R	11/6/1984	-0.9	14.2	30.1	16.3	-1.6
Bush	R	11/8/1988	-0.4	23.8	-13.9	26.5	6.5
Clinton	D	11/3/92	*-0.9*	*12.5*	*0.2*	*25.4*	*19.4*
Clinton	D	11/5/96	*2.6*	*35.2*	*8.6*	*24.3*	*4.6*
Bush, G.W.	R	11/7/2000*	-1.6	-23.1	-20.9	21.2	6.0
Bush, G.W.	R	11/2/04	1.1	4.0	14.9	11.0	-37.9
Obama	D	11/4/08	*-1.3*	*13.7*	*10.6*	*1.4*	*19.0*
Obama	D	11/6/12	*-1.5*	*20.9*	*12.9*	*6.4*	*6.4*
Trump	R	11/8/16	1.5	19.2	8.2	7.1	15.6
Biden	D	11/3/20	*4.0*	*24.6*			

*Outcome of race was officially undetermined until December 13, 2000

Average from 1888 to Dec. 2021	Democratic	-0.3	7.6	1.7	16.6	8.5
	Republican	0.7	10.2	5.0	9.3	8.7
	Overall	0.2	9.0	3.5	12.6	8.6
Average from 1948 to Dec. 2021	Democratic	-0.2	15.9	4.1	16.4	12.4
	Republican	0.1	0.5	4.4	19.8	2.0
	Overall	0.0	7.8	4.3	18.3	6.6

There have been occasions, like Clinton's second-term election victory, when the market soared because the Republicans kept control of Congress, not because Clinton was reelected. And the stock market jumped after Biden's victory in 2020, since it appeared that the Republicans unexpectedly took control of the US Senate.[5]

The returns in the first, second, third, and fourth years of a presidential term are also displayed in Table 20.4. The strong market returns in the first year of the Trump and Biden administrations has boosted the first-year average in the postwar period, but the returns in the third year of a presidential term are the best. It is striking that the third year is so good, since it includes the disastrous 43.3 percent drop that occurred in 1931, during the third year of Hoover's ill-fated administration and the worst single-year performance of any president in more than a century.

Why the third year of a presidential term stands out is not clear. One would think that the fourth year, when the administration might increase spending or put pressure on the Fed to stimulate the economy for the upcoming election, would be the best year for stocks. But the fourth year, although good, is clearly not the best. Perhaps the market anticipates favorable economic policies in the election year, causing stock prices to rise the year before.

The superior performance of the stock market under the Democrats in recent years is documented in Table 20.4. This table records the total real and nominal returns in the stock market and the rate of inflation under Democratic and Republican administrations. Since 1888, the market has fared better in nominal terms under Democrats than under Republicans, but since inflation has been lower when the Republicans have held office, real stock returns have been about the same under each party. But this has not been true since 1952, when the market performed far better under the Democrats whether inflation is considered or not.

STOCKS AND WAR

Since 1885, the US economy has been at war or on the sidelines of a world war about one-fifth of the time. The stock market does equally well in nominal returns whether there is war or peace. Inflation, however, has averaged nearly 6 percent during wartime and less than 2 percent during peacetime, so the real returns on stocks during peacetime greatly outstrip those during wars.

While returns are better during peacetime, the stock market has been more volatile during peacetime than during war, as measured by the monthly standard deviation of the Dow Industrials. The greatest

TABLE 20.4

Market returns during presidential administrations (italics represent Democratic administrations)

President's Name	Party	Date	Months in Office	Annualized Nominal Stock Return	Annualized Inflation	Annualized Real Return
Harrison	R	11/88 - 10/92	48	5.48	-2.73	8.43
Cleveland	*D*	*11/92 - 10/96*	*48*	*-2.88*	*-3.06*	*0.19*
McKinley	R	11/96 - 8/01	58	19.42	3.69	15.18
Roosevelt T.	R	9/01 - 10/08	86	5.02	1.95	3.01
Taft	R	11/08 - 10/12	48	9.56	2.59	6.80
Wilson	*D*	*11/12 - 10/20*	*96*	*3.55*	*9.26*	*-5.23*
Harding	R	11/20 - 7/23	33	7.43	-5.16	13.28
Coolidge	R	8/23 - 10/28	63	26.99	0.00	26.99
Hoover	R	11/28 - 10/32	48	-19.31	-6.23	-13.96
Roosevelt F.	*D*	*11/32 - 3/45*	*149*	*11.42*	*2.37*	*8.83*
Truman	*D*	*4/45 - 10/52*	*91*	*13.84*	*5.49*	*7.91*
Eisenhower	R	11/52 - 10/60	96	15.09	1.38	13.52
Kennedy	*D*	*11/60 - 10/63*	*36*	*14.31*	*1.11*	*13.06*
Johnson	*D*	*11/63 - 10/68*	*60*	*10.64*	*2.76*	*7.66*
Nixon	R	11/68 - 7/74	69	-1.39	6.02	-6.99
Ford	R	8/74 - 10/76	27	16.56	7.31	8.62
Carter	*D*	*11/76 - 10/80*	*48*	*11.66*	*10.01*	*1.50*
Reagan	R	11/80 - 10/88	96	14.64	4.46	9.75
Bush	R	11/88 - 10/92	48	14.05	4.22	9.44
Clinton	*D*	*11/92 - 10/00*	*96*	*18.74*	*2.59*	*15.74*
Bush, G.W.	R	11/00 - 10/08	96	-2.75	2.77	-5.38
Obama	*D*	*11/08 - 10/16*	*96*	*12.79*	*1.38*	*11.25*
Trump	*R*	*11/16 - 10/20*	*48*	*14.54*	*1.88*	*12.43*
Biden	*D*	*11/20-12/21*	*13*	*30.73*	*6.51*	*22.74*
Average from 1888 to Dec 2021	Democrat	733	11.33	3.75	7.41
	Republican	864	8.81	1.90	6.78
	Overall	100%	9.97	2.75	7.07
Average from 1952 to Dec 2021	Democrat	349	14.73	3.30	11.14
	Republican	480	8.99	3.61	5.24
	Overall	100%	11.40	3.48	7.73

volatility in US markets occurred in the late 1920s and early 1930s, well before the United States was engaged in World War II. Only during World War I and the short Gulf War did stocks have higher volatility than the historical average.

MARKETS DURING THE WORLD WARS

The market was far more volatile during World War I than during World War II. The market rose nearly 100 percent during the early stages of World War I, then fell 40 percent when the United States became involved in the hostilities, and finally rallied when the Great War ended. In contrast, during the six years of World War II, the market never deviated more than 32 percent from its prewar level.

The outbreak of World War I precipitated a panic, as European investors scrambled to get out of stocks and into gold and cash. After Austria-Hungary declared war on Serbia on July 28, 1914, all the major European stock exchanges closed. The European panic spread to New York, and the Dow Jones Industrials fell nearly 7 percent on Thursday, July 30, the most drastic decline since the 8.3 percent drop during the Panic of 1907. Minutes before the opening of the NYSE the next day, the exchange voted to close for an indefinite period.

The market did not reopen until December. Never before or since has the NYSE been closed for such a long period. Emergency trades were permitted, but only by approval of a special committee, and only at prices at or above the last trade before the exchange closed. However, the trading prohibition was observed in the breach, as illegal trades were made outside the exchange (on the curb) at prices that continued to decline through October. Unofficially, by autumn, prices were said to be 15 to 20 percent below the July closing.

It is ironic that the only extended period during which the NYSE was closed occurred when the United States was not yet at war nor in any degree of financial or economic distress. In fact, during that five-month period, traders realized that the United States would be a strong economic beneficiary of the European conflict. Once investors realized that America was going to make the munitions and provide raw materials to the belligerents, public interest in stocks soared.

By the time the exchange reopened on December 12, prices were rising rapidly. The Dow Industrials finished the historic Saturday session about 5 percent higher than the closing prices the previous July. The rally continued, and 1915 recorded the best single-year increase in the history of the Dow Industrials, as stocks rose a record 82 percent. Stocks continued to rise in 1916 and hit their peak in November, with prices more than twice the level they were when the war had started more than two years earlier. But then stocks settled back about 10 percent, when the United States formally entered the war on April 16, 1917, and fell another 10 percent through November 1918, when the Armistice was signed.

The message of the great boom of 1915 was not lost on traders a generation later. When World War II erupted, investors took their cue from what happened in World War I. When Great Britain declared war on Germany on September 3, 1939, the rise in stock prices was so explosive that the Tokyo Stock Exchange was forced to close early. When the market opened in New York, a buying panic erupted. The Dow Industrials gained over 7 percent, and even the European stock exchanges were firm when trading reopened.

The enthusiasm that followed the onset of World War II quickly faded. President Roosevelt was determined not to let corporations earn easy profits as they had in World War I. These profits had been a source of public criticism, as Americans felt that the war costs were not being borne equally as its young men died overseas while corporations earned record income at home. The excess profits tax enacted by Congress during World War II removed the wartime premium that investors had expected from the conflict.

The day before the Japanese attacked Pearl Harbor, the Dow was down 25 percent from its 1939 high and still less than one-third its 1929 peak. Stocks fell 3.5 percent on the day following the attack on Pearl Harbor and continued to fall until they hit a low on April 28, 1942, when the United States suffered losses in the early months of the war in the Pacific.

When the tide turned toward the Allies, the market began to climb. By the time Germany signed its unconditional surrender on May 7, 1945, the Dow Industrials were 20 percent above the prewar level. The detonation of the atomic bomb over Hiroshima, a pivotal event in the history of warfare, caused stocks to surge 1.7 percent as investors recognized that the end of the war was near. But World War II did not prove as profitable for investors as World War I, as the Dow was up only 30 percent during the six years from the German invasion of Poland to V-J Day.

POST-1945 CONFLICTS

Korea and Vietnam

The Korean War took investors by surprise. When North Korea invaded its southern neighbor on June 25, 1950, the Dow fell 4.65 percent, greater than the day following the attack on Pearl Harbor. The market reaction to the growing conflict was contained, and stocks never fell more than 12 percent below their prewar level.

The Vietnam War was one of the longest and least popular of all US wars. The starting point for US involvement in the conflict can be placed at August 2, 1964, when two American destroyers were reportedly attacked in the Gulf of Tonkin.

A year and a half after the Gulf of Tonkin incident, the Dow reached an all-time high of 995, more than 18 percent higher than before the Tonkin attack. It fell nearly 30 percent in the following months, after the Fed tightened credit to curb inflation. By the time American troop strength reached its peak in early 1968, the market had recovered. Two years later, when Nixon sent troops into Cambodia, interest rates were soaring and a recession was looming; the market fell again, down nearly 25 percent from its prewar point.

The peace pact between the North Vietnamese and the Americans was signed in Paris on January 27, 1973. The gains made by investors over the eight years of war were quite small, as the market was held back by rising inflation and interest rates as well as other problems not directly related to the Vietnam War.

The Gulf War I

If the war in Vietnam was the longest American war until Afghanistan, the 1991 Gulf War against Iraq was the shortest. The trigger occurred on August 2, 1990, when Iraq invaded Kuwait, sending oil prices skyward and sparking a US military buildup in Saudi Arabia. The rise in oil prices combined with an already slowing US economy to drive the United States deeper into a recession. The stock market fell precipitously, and on October 11, the Dow slumped over 18 percent from its prewar levels.

The United States began its offensive action on January 17, 1991. It was the first major war fought in a world where markets for oil, gold, and US government bonds were traded around the clock in Tokyo, Singapore, London, and New York.

The markets judged the victors in a matter of hours. Bonds sold off in Tokyo for a few minutes following the news of the US bombing of Baghdad, but the stunning reports of the United States and its allies' successes sent bonds and Japanese stocks straight upward in the next few minutes. Oil traded in the Far East collapsed in price, as Brent Crude fell from $29 a barrel before hostilities to $20.

On the following day, stock prices soared around the world. The Dow jumped 115 points, or 4.4 percent, and there were large gains throughout Europe and Asia. By the time the United States deployed ground troops to invade Kuwait, the market had known for two months that victory was at hand. The war ended on February 28, and by the first week in March, the Dow was more than 18 percent higher than when the war started.

Gulf War II and Afghanistan

Although Gulf War I pushed Iraq out of Kuwait, it left Saddam Hussein in power. The Bush administration determined that Hussein had weapons of mass destruction and began to threaten invasion in March 2003. Investors, fearing conflict, sent the Dow to an intraday low of 7,416 on March 12, 2003. But the anticipation of another fast victory like 1991 caused stocks to turn sharply higher as the invasion approached. The shock and awe attack on March 20 sent the Dow up almost 15 percent above where it was just eight days earlier.

The war against the Taliban in Afghanistan, launched soon after the 9/11 attack, was America's longest war and lasted from 2001 through 2021, yet it impacted markets little. Oil production was not involved, and fighting settled down to a long grinding engagement. Investors turned their focus away from international developments and turned inward.

CONCLUSION

When investigating the causes of major market movements, it is sobering to realize that only one in four can be linked to a news event of major political or economic import. This confirms the unpredictability of the market and the difficulty in forecasting market moves. Those who sold in panic at the outbreak of World War I missed out on 1915, the best year ever in the stock market. Those who bought at the onset of World War II, believing there would be a replay of the World War I gains, were sorely disappointed because of the government's determination to cap wartime profits. World events may shake the market in the short run, but they have proved unable to dent the superior long-term returns to equities.

Stocks, Bonds, and the Flow of Economic Data

The thing that most affects the stock market is everything.
                                        —James Palysted Wood, 1966

It's 8:28 a.m. eastern time, Friday, July 5, 1996. Normally a trading day wedged between a major US holiday and a weekend is slow, with little volume or price movement, but not today. Traders around the world are anxiously glued to their terminals, eyes riveted on the scrolling news that displays thousands of headlines daily. All week, stock, bond, and currency traders have anticipated this moment. It is just two minutes before the most important announcement each month—the US employment statistics. The Dow has been trading within a few points of its all-time high, reached at the end of May, but interest rates have been rising, giving traders cause for concern. The seconds tick down: at 8:30 a.m. sharp, the headlines scroll across the screen:

> PAYROLL UP 239,000, UNEMPLOYMENT AT SIX-YEAR LOW
> OF 5.3 PERCENT, WAGES UP 9 CENTS AN HOUR, BIGGEST
> INCREASE IN 30 YEARS.

President Clinton hailed the economic news, claiming, "We have the most solid American economy in a generation; wages for American workers are finally on the rise again."

But the financial markets were stunned; long-term bond prices immediately collapsed as traders expected the Fed to tighten, and interest rates rose by nearly a quarter point. Although the stock market would not open for an hour, the S&P 500 Index futures, which represent claims on this benchmark index and are described in detail in the next chapter, fell about 2 percent. European stock markets, which had been open for hours, sold off immediately. The benchmark DAX index in Germany, CAC in France, and FT-SE in Britain instantly fell almost 2 percent. Within seconds, world equity markets lost $200 billion, and world bond markets fell at least as much.

This episode demonstrates that what Main Street interprets as good news is often bad news on Wall Street. This is because it is more than mere profits that move stocks; interest rates, inflation, and the future direction of the Federal Reserve's monetary policy also have a major impact.

ECONOMIC DATA AND THE MARKET

News moves markets. The timing of much news is unpredictable—like war, political developments, and natural disasters. In contrast, news based on data about the economy comes at preannounced times that are set a year or more in advance. In the United States, there are hundreds of scheduled releases of economic data each year—mostly by government agencies, but increasingly by private firms. Virtually all these announcements deal with the economy, particularly economic growth and inflation, and all have the potential to move the market significantly.

Economic data not only frame the way traders view the economy but also impact traders' expectations of how the central bank will implement its monetary policy. Stronger economic growth or higher inflation increases the probability that the central bank will either tighten or stop easing monetary policy. All these data influence traders' expectations about the future course of interest rates, the economy, and ultimately stock prices.

PRINCIPLES OF MARKET REACTION

Markets do not respond only to what is announced; rather, they respond to the difference between what the traders *expect* to happen and what is *reported*. Whether the news is good or bad for the economy is of little importance. If the market expects that 400,000 jobs were lost last month, but the report shows that only 200,000 jobs were lost, this will be considered "stronger than expected" economic news by the financial markets—having about the same effect on markets as a gain of 400,000 jobs would when the market expected a gain of only 200,000.

The reason why markets react only to the difference between expectations and what is reported is that the prices of securities already incorporate all the information that is expected. If a firm is expected to report bad earnings, the market has already priced this gloomy information into the stock price. If the earnings report is not as bad as anticipated, the price will rise when earnings are released. The same principle applies to the reaction of bond and foreign exchange markets to economic data.

Therefore, to understand why the market moves the way it does, you must identify the *market expectation* for the data released. The market expectation, often referred to as the *consensus estimate*, is gathered by news and research organizations. They poll economists, professional forecasters, traders, and other market participants for their predictions for an upcoming government or private release. The results of their surveys are sent to the financial press and are widely reported online and in many other news outlets.[1]

INFORMATION CONTENT OF DATA RELEASES

The economic data are analyzed for their implications for future economic growth, inflation, and central bank policy. The following principle summarizes the reaction of the bond markets to the release of data relating to economic growth:

> Stronger-than-expected economic growth causes both long- and short-term interest rates to rise. Weaker-than-expected economic growth causes interest rates to fall.

Faster-than-expected economic growth raises interest rates for several reasons. First, stronger economic activity makes consumers feel more confident and more willing to borrow against future income, increasing loan demand. Faster economic growth also motivates firms to expand production. As a result, both firms and consumers will likely increase their demand for credit and push interest rates higher.

A second reason why interest rates rise in tandem with a stronger-than-expected economic report is that such growth might be inflationary, especially if it is near the end of an economic expansion. Economic growth associated with increases in productivity, which often occur in the early and middle stages of a business expansion, is rarely inflationary.

Going back to the example at the beginning of the chapter, inflationary fears were the principal reason why interest rates soared when the Labor Department released its report on July 5, 1996. Traders feared that the large increase in wages caused by the tight labor markets and falling unemployment would cause inflation, a nemesis to both the bond and the stock markets.

Reports on economic growth also have significant implications for the actions of central banks. The threat of inflation from an overly strong economy will make it likely that the central bank will tighten credit. If the aggregate demand is expanding too rapidly relative to the supply of goods and services, the monetary authority can raise interest rates to prevent the economy from overheating.

Of course, in the case of a weaker-than-expected employment report, the bond market will respond favorably as interest rates decline in response to weaker credit demand and lower inflationary pressures. Recall that the price of bonds moves in the opposite direction of interest rates.

An important principle is that the market reacts more strongly after several similar reports move in the same direction. For example, if an inflation report is higher than expected, then the following month the market will react even more strongly to another higher-than-expected reading. The reason for this is that there is a lot of noise in the individual data report, and a single month's observation may be reversed in subsequent data. If the subsequent data confirm the original data, then it is more likely that a new trend has been established, and the market will move accordingly.

ECONOMIC GROWTH AND STOCK PRICES

It surprises the public and even the financial press when a strong economic report sends the stock market lower. But stronger-than-expected economic growth has two important implications for the stock market, and each tugs in the opposite direction. A strong economy increases future corporate earnings, which is bullish for stocks. It also raises interest rates, which raises the discount rate at which these future profits are discounted. Similarly, a weak economic report may lower expected earnings, but if interest rates decline, stock prices could move up because of the decline in the rate at which these cash flows are discounted. It is a struggle, in asset pricing terms, between the *numerator*, which contains future cash flows, and the *denominator*, which discounts those cash flows.

Which effect is stronger—the change in the interest rate or the change in corporate profits—often depends on where the economy is in the business cycle. Recent analysis shows that in a recession, a stronger-than-expected economic report increases stock prices, since the implications for corporate profits are considered more important than the change in interest rates at this stage in the business cycle.[2] Inversely, a weaker-than-expected report depresses stock prices. During economic expansions, and particularly toward the end of an expansion, the interest rate effect is usually stronger since inflation is more of a threat.

Many stock traders look at the movements in the bond market to guide their trading. This is particularly true of portfolio managers, who actively apportion their portfolio between stocks and bonds on the basis of changes in interest rates and expected stock returns. When interest rates fall after a weak economic report, these investors are immediately ready to increase the proportion of stocks that they hold. On the other hand, investors who recognize that the weak employment report means lower future earnings may sell stocks. The stock market often gyrates throughout the day as different groups of investors digest the implications of the data for stock earnings and interest rates.

THE EMPLOYMENT REPORT

The *employment report*, compiled by the US Bureau of Labor Statistics (BLS), is the single most important data report released by the government each month. To measure employment, the BLS does two entirely different surveys, one that measures employment and another that measures unemployment. The *payroll survey* counts the total number of *jobs* that companies have on their payrolls, while the household survey counts the number of people who have and are looking for jobs. The *payroll survey*, sometimes called the *establishment survey*, collects payroll data from nearly 130,000 business establishments and government workers, representing 670,000 worksites. It is this survey that most forecasters use to judge the future course of the economy. Of the greatest importance to traders is the change in the *nonfarm payroll* (the number of farm workers is excluded, since it is very volatile and not associated with cyclical economic trends).

The *unemployment rate* is determined from an entirely different survey than the payroll survey. It is the unemployment rate, however, that often gets the top billing in the evening news. The unemployment rate is calculated from a "household survey" in which data from about 60,000 households are accumulated. It asks, among other questions, whether anyone in the household has "actively" sought work over the past four weeks. Those who answer yes are classified as unemployed. The resulting number of unemployed people is divided by the number of people in the total labor force, which yields the unemployment rate. The labor force in the United States, defined as those employed plus those unemployed, constitutes about two-thirds of the adult population. This ratio, called the labor force participation rate, had risen steadily in the 1980s and 1990s as more women successfully sought work, but it has fallen since then and took a big hit during the Covid-19 pandemic.

The BLS statistics can be very tricky to interpret. Because the payroll and household data are based on totally different surveys, it is not unusual for payroll employment to go up while the unemployment rate rises, and vice versa. One reason is because the payroll survey counts jobs, while the household survey counts people. So workers with two jobs are counted only once in the household survey, but twice in the payroll survey. Furthermore, self-employed individuals are not counted in the payroll survey, but are counted in the household survey. This has become more important as the self-employed, or gig, economy increases.

For these reasons, many economists and forecasters downplay the importance of the unemployment rate in forecasting the business cycle. This does not diminish the political impact of this number. The unemployment rate is an easily understood figure that represents the fraction of the workforce looking for, but not finding, work. Much of the public looks more to this statistic than any other to judge the health of the economy. For example, Fed Chairman Ben Bernanke made the unemployment rate a threshold for when the Federal Reserve would begin to raise interest rates following the financial crisis and Great Recession. However, the Federal Reserve under Chairman Jay Powell has downplayed the unemployment rate as a factor forecasting future inflationary trends.

Since 2005, the Automatic Data Processing (ADP) Corporation has released its own payroll data, called *The ADP National Employment Report*, two days before the BLS labor report. The ADP report is a measure of nonfarm private employment, based on nearly 500,000 US business clients and representing 26 million employees. Because ADP processes the paychecks for nearly one out of every six private-sector employees in the United States, every pay period across a broad range of industries, firm sizes, and geographies, ADP's numbers provide a clue for Friday's upcoming labor data.

THE CYCLE OF ANNOUNCEMENTS

The employment report is just one of several dozen economic announcements that come out every month. The usual release dates for the various data reports in a typical month are displayed in Figure 21.1. The number of asterisks represents the importance of the report to the financial market.

FIGURE 21.1

Monthly economic calendar

Monday	Tuesday	Wednesday	Thursday	Friday
1 10:00 Purchasing Mgrs. Index** (PMI)	**2** Vehicle Sales*	**3** 8:15 ADP Employment Est.** 10:00 Service PMI**	**4** 8:30 Jobless Claims**	**5** 8:30 Employment Report****
8	**9**	**10**	**11** 8:30 Jobless Claims**	**12** 8:30 CPI**** 9:55 U of Mich Cons Conf
15 8:30 NY Fed* Retail Sales***	**16** 8:30 PPI*** 9:15 Ind Prod* 10:00 NAHB Index**	**17** 8:30 Housing Starts*** Building Permits***	**18** 8:30 Jobless Claims** 10:00 Philly Fed*	**19**
22 10:00 Existing Home Sales**	**23** 8:30 Durable Goods Orders**	**24** 10:00 New Home Sales*	**25** 8:30 Jobless Claims** Durable Goods**	**26**
29	**30** 8:30 Quarterly GDP*** 10:00 Conf Board Cons Conf**	**31** 8:30 Empl Cost Index* Income, Spending, PCE Deflator*** 9:45 Chicago PMI*		

Stars Rank Importance to Market (** = most important)**

On the first business day of each month, a survey by the Institute for Supply Management (ISM, formerly the National Association of Purchasing Managers), called the *purchasing managers' index* (PMI), is released. The institute's report surveys 250 purchasing agents of manufacturing companies and inquires about whether orders, production, employment, or other indicators are rising or falling, forming an index from these data. A reading of 50 means that half the managers report rising activity and half report falling activity. A reading of 52 or 53 is the sign of a normally expanding economy. A reading of 60 represents a strong economy in which three-fifths of the managers report growth. A reading below 50 represents a contracting manufacturing sector, and a reading below 40 is almost always a sign of recession. Two days later, on the third business day of the month, the ISM publishes a similar index for the service sector of the economy.

There are other releases of timely data reports on manufacturing activity. The Chicago Purchasing Managers Index report comes out on the last business day of the month, the day before the national ISM report. The Chicago area is well diversified in manufacturing, so about two-thirds of the time the Chicago index will move in the same direction as the national index. Since 1968, the Philadelphia Fed Manufacturing Report has been published on the third Thursday of every month, which had made it the first regional manufacturing report to be published each month. In recent years, the New York Fed, not to be outdone by its southern neighbor, has published the NY Empire State Manufacturing Index on New York manufacturing a few days earlier. And since 2008, Markit Group Limited, a London-based financial information service corporation, has published Purchasing Managers' Indexes for many international countries (including the United States), which comes out before the ISM report.

Also of importance are the consumer sentiment indicators: one from the University of Michigan and another from the Conference Board, a business trade association. These surveys query consumers about their current financial situation and their expectations of the future. The Conference Board survey, released on the last Tuesday of the month, is considered a good early indicator of consumer confidence. For many years, the University of Michigan monthly index was not published until after the Conference Board release, but pressure for early data reports has persuaded the university to release a preliminary report before the Conference Board.

INFLATION REPORTS

Although the employment report forms the capstone of the news about economic growth, the market knows that the Federal Reserve is equally if not more interested in the inflation data. That's because inflation is the primary variable that the central bank can control in the long run. Some of the earliest signals of inflationary pressures arrive with the midmonth inflation statistics.

An important release is the *producer price index* (PPI), which was known before 1978 as the "wholesale price index." The PPI, first published in 1902, is one of the oldest continuous series of statistical data published by the government. In 2014, the PPI Index was revamped to include all prices paid by firms and government agencies for goods and services. Some economists consider the PPI report as a harbinger of future price trends. At the same time the PPI is announced, indexes for the prices of intermediate and crude goods are released, both of which track inflation at earlier stages of production.

A second monthly inflation announcement is the all-important *consumer price index* (CPI). Services, which include rent, housing, transportation, and medical services, now make up over half the weight of the CPI. The CPI is considered the benchmark measure of inflation. When price-level comparisons are made, on both a historical and an international basis, the CPI is almost always the chosen index. The CPI is also the price index to which so many private and public contracts, as well as social security and government tax brackets, are linked. The CPI index used to be released after the PPI index, but since the revision on the PPI, the CPI release often comes the day before.

The financial market gives more weight to the CPI than to the PPI because of the CPI's widespread use in indexing and political importance.

Core Inflation

Of significance to the market is not only the overall inflation rate, but inflation that excludes the volatile food and energy sectors. Since weather has a great influence on food prices, a rise or fall in the price of food over a month does not have much meaning for the overall inflationary trend. Similarly, the fluctuations of oil and natural gas prices are due to weather conditions, temporary supply disruptions, and speculative trading that frequently do not necessarily persist into future months. To obtain an index of inflation that measures the more persistent and long-term trends of inflation, the government also computes the *core* consumer and producer price indexes, which measure inflation excluding food and energy.

The core rate of inflation is more important to the central banks because it more reliably identifies the underlying trend of prices. Forecasters are usually able to predict the core rate of inflation better than the overall rate, since the latter is influenced by the volatile food and energy sectors. An error of 0.3 percentage points in the consensus forecast for the month-to-month rate of inflation might not be that serious, but such an error would be considered quite large for the core rate of inflation and would significantly affect the financial markets.

The index the Federal Reserve uses as its prime inflation indicator is the *personal consumption expenditure* (PCE) *deflator*, which is a price index calculated for the consumption component of the GDP accounts. The PCE deflator differs from the CPI in that the PCE deflator uses a more up-to-date weighting scheme and includes the cost of employee-paid medical insurance. The PCE deflator generally runs about 0.25 to 0.50 percentage points below the CPI. When the Federal Reserve forecasts inflation movements in its quarterly Open Market Committee meetings, it is the PCE deflator (both overall and core) that is projected, not the CPI.

Employment Costs

Other important releases that have a bearing on inflation relate to labor costs. The monthly employment report issued by the BLS contains data on the hourly wage rate and sheds light on cost pressures arising in the labor market. Since labor costs average nearly two-thirds of a firm's production costs, increases in the hourly wage not matched by increases in productivity may increase labor inflation. Every calendar quarter, the government also releases the employment cost index. This index includes benefit costs as well as wages, and it is considered the most comprehensive report of labor costs.

IMPACT ON FINANCIAL MARKETS

The following summarizes the impact of inflation on the financial markets:

> A lower-than-expected inflation report lowers interest rates and boosts bond and stock prices. Inflation worse than expected raises interest rates and depresses stock and bond prices.

That inflation is bad for bonds should come as no surprise. Bonds are fixed-income investments whose cash flows are not adjusted for inflation. Bondholders demand higher interest rates to protect their purchasing power when inflation increases.

Worse-than-expected inflation is also negative for the stock market. As I noted in Chapter 9, stocks have proved to be poor hedges against inflation in the short run. Stock investors know that worsening inflation increases the effective tax rate on both corporate earnings and capital gains and, more important, induces the central bank to tighten credit, raising real interest rates.

CENTRAL BANK POLICY

Central bank policy is of primary importance to financial markets. Martin Zweig, a noted money manager, described the relationship this way:

> In the stock market, as with horse racing, money makes the mare go. Monetary conditions exert an enormous influence on stock prices. Indeed, the monetary climate—primarily the trend in interest rates and Federal Reserve policy—is the dominant factor in determining the stock market's major direction.[3]

The last chapter showed that many of the largest moves in the market involved monetary policy. Reducing short-term interest rates and providing more credit to the banking system are actions that are almost always extremely welcome by stock investors. When the central bank eases credit, it lowers the rate at which stock future cash flows are discounted and stimulates demand, which increases future earnings.

The Federal Reserve holds eight scheduled meetings of the Federal Open Market Committee per year, and a statement is released after each one. The last meeting of each quarter, when the Fed releases its projections of key economic variables, including the Federal funds rate, is of particular importance. Fed testimony to Congress, particularly the semiannual testimony to the House and Senate in February and July, is also very significant. But any Fed official can drop hints about a change in the direction of policy at any time, so any speech has the capability of moving markets.

Although Chapter 18 indicated that, in the long run, Fed actions had a muted impact on stock prices, surprising central bank action—especially intermeeting moves—are as powerful as ever. The unexpected 0.50 percentage point cut in the funds rate from 6.5 to 6 percent that took place on January 3, 2001, sent the S&P 500 Index up 5 percent, and the tech-heavy Nasdaq up an all-time record 14.2 percent. When Fed Chairman Ben Bernanke announced that the Fed was planning to phase out its quantitative easing on June 19, 2013, the stock and bond markets suffered their largest loss in almost two years. Similarly, when Chairman Powell announced a pivot to more hawkish monetary policy in November 2021, stocks fell.

The only case in which stocks will react poorly to central bank easing is if the monetary authority eases excessively so that the market fears an increase in inflation. In such a case, an investor should still prefer stocks to bonds, because fixed-income assets are hurt more by unexpected inflation.

CONCLUSION

The reactions of financial markets to the release of economic data are not random, but instead can be predicted by economic analysis. Strong economic growth invariably raises interest rates, but it has an ambiguous effect on stock prices, especially in the late stages of an economic expansion, as higher interest rates offset stronger corporate profits. Higher inflation is negative for the stock market, but worse for the bond markets. Faster-than-expected central bank easing (or slower-than-expected tightening) is very positive for stocks and has historically sparked strong stock rallies.

This chapter emphasizes the *short-run* reaction of financial markets to economic data. Although it is fascinating to observe and understand the market's reaction, trying to beat the market by anticipating these data releases is a tricky game best left to speculators who can stomach the short-term volatility. Most investors will do well to watch from the sidelines and stick to a sound long-run investment strategy.

VI

MARKET CRISES AND
STOCK VOLATILITY

22

Market Volatility

The word crisis *in Chinese is composed of two characters: the first,*
the symbol of danger . . . the second, of opportunity.

—Said by John F. Kennedy in 1959. Some etymologists claim the
second symbol more correctly is interpreted as "changing point."

Does the past portend the future? The Dow Jones Industrial Average
from 1922 through 1932, and from 1980 through 1990, is shown in Figure 22.1A and B. There is an uncanny similarity between these two bull
markets. In October 1987, the editors of the *Wall Street Journal*, looking at
the stock chart up to that time, felt the similarity was so portentous that
they printed a similar graph in the *Journal* that hit the streets on Monday
morning, October 19, 1987. Little did they know that that day would wit-
ness the greatest one-day drop in US stock market history, far exceeding
the great crash of October 29, 1929. Ominously, the market continued to
trade very much like 1929 for the remainder of the year. Many forecasters, citing the similarities between the two periods, were certain that
disaster loomed and advised their clients to sell.

But the similarity between the 1929 and the 1987 episodes stopped
at year's end. The stock market recovered from its October 1987 crash,
and by August 1989, stocks hit new high ground. In contrast, two years
after the October 1929 crash, stocks were in the throes of the greatest
bear market in US history. The Dow had lost more than two-thirds of its
value and was about to lose two-thirds more.

What was different? Why did the eerie similarities between these
two events diverge so dramatically? The simple answer is that in 1987
the central bank had the power to control the ultimate source of liquidity in the economy—the supply of money. In contrast to 1929, it did not
hesitate to use it. Heeding the painful lessons of its mistakes in the
early 1930s, the Fed temporarily flooded the economy with money and

pledged to stand by all bank deposits to ensure that all aspects of the financial system would function properly.

The public was assured. There were no runs on banks, no contraction of the money supply, and no deflation in commodity and asset values. Indeed, the economy itself expanded despite the market collapse. The October 1987 stock market crash taught investors an important lesson—the world was indeed different from 1929, and a sharp sell-off can be an opportunity for profit, not a time to panic.

FIGURE 22.1

1929 and 1987 stock market crashes

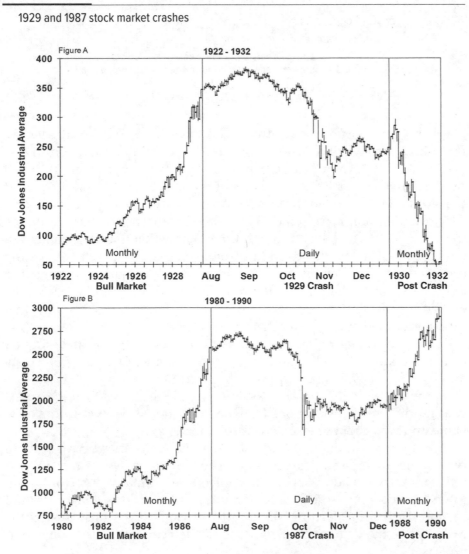

THE STOCK MARKET CRASH OF OCTOBER 1987

The stock crash of Monday, October 19, 1987, was one of the most dramatic financial events of the postwar era. The 508-point, or 22.6 percent, decline in the Dow Jones Industrials from 2,247 to 1,739 was by far the largest point drop up to that time and the largest one-day percentage drop in history. Volume on the NYSE soared to a record, exceeding 600 million shares on both Monday and Tuesday, and for that fateful week the number of shares traded exceeded the volume for all of 1966.

The crash on Wall Street reverberated around the world. Tokyo, which two years later was going to enter its own bear market, fell the least, but it still experienced a record one-day drop of 15.6 percent. Stocks in New Zealand fell nearly 40 percent, and the Hong Kong market closed because collapsing prices brought massive defaults in the stock index futures market. In the United States alone, stock values on that day dropped about $500 billion, and the total worldwide decline in stock values exceeded $1 trillion. A similar percentage decline in today's market would wipe out more than $20 trillion worldwide, a sum greater than the GDP of every country but the United States.[1]

The stock market decline began in earnest the week prior to "Black Monday," as October 19 came to be called. At 8:30 a.m. on the preceding Wednesday, the Department of Commerce reported that the United States suffered a $15.7 billion merchandise trade deficit, which at that time was one of the largest in US history and far in excess of market expectations. The reaction in the financial markets was immediate. Yields on long government bonds rose to over 10 percent for the first time since November 1985, and the dollar declined sharply. The Dow Industrials fell 95 points, or 4 percent, on Wednesday, a record point drop at that time.

The situation continued to worsen on Thursday and Friday as the Dow fell 166 points, or 7 percent, to 2,246. Late Friday afternoon, about 15 minutes prior to close, heavy selling hit the stock index futures markets in Chicago. The indexes had fallen below crucial support levels, which led to the barrage of selling in Chicago by those wanting to get out of stocks at almost any price.

The December S&P 500 futures contract fell to an unprecedented 3 percent below the spot index.[2] The development of such a wide discount meant that money managers were willing to sell large orders at a significant concession in order to sell quickly, rather than risk that their sell orders for individual stocks might sit in New York, unexecuted. At the close of trading on Friday, the stock market had experienced its worst week in nearly five decades.

Before New York opened the following Monday, there were ominous portents from the world markets. Overnight in Tokyo, the Nikkei average fell 2.5 percent, and there were sharp declines in Sydney and Hong Kong. In London, prices had fallen by 10 percent as many money managers were trying to sell US stocks, trading before the anticipated decline hit New York.

Trading on the NYSE on Black Monday was chaotic. No Dow Jones Industrial stock traded near the 9:30 a.m. opening bell, and only 7 Dow stocks traded before 9:45 a.m. By 10:30 that morning, 11 Dow stocks still had not opened. Portfolio insurers, described later in this chapter, heavily sold stock index futures, trying to insulate their clients' exposure to the plunging market. By late afternoon, the S&P 500 Index futures were selling at a 25-point, or 12 percent, discount to the spot market, a spread that was previously considered inconceivable. By the late afternoon, huge sell orders transmitted by program sellers cascaded onto the NYSE through the computerized system. The Dow Industrials collapsed almost 300 points in the final hour of trading, bringing the toll for the day to a record 508 points, or 22.6 percent.

Although October 19 is remembered in history as the day of the great stock crash, it was actually the next day—"Terrible Tuesday," as it has become known—that the market almost failed. After opening up over 10 percent from Monday's low, the market began to plunge by midmorning, and shortly after noon it fell below its Monday close. The S&P 500 Index futures market collapsed to 181—an incredible 40 points, or 22 percent, under the reported index value. If index arbitrage had been possible, the futures prices would have dictated a Dow at 1,450. Stock prices in the world's largest market, on this calculation, were off nearly 50 percent from their high of 2,722 set just seven weeks earlier.

It was at this time that near meltdown hit the market. The NYSE did not close, but trading was halted in almost 200 stocks. For the first time, trading was also halted in the S&P 500 Index futures in Chicago.

The only futures market of any size that remained open was the Major Market Index that traded on the Chicago Board of Trade and represented blue chip stocks like the Dow Industrials. These blue chips were selling at such deep discounts to the prices in New York that values proved irresistible to some investors. Since it was the only market that remained open, brave buyers stepped in and these futures shot up an equivalent of 120 Dow points, or almost 10 percent, in a matter of minutes. When traders and the exchange specialists saw the buying come back into the blue chips, prices rallied in New York, and the worst of the market panic passed. A subsequent investigative report by the *Wall*

Street Journal indicated that this futures market was a key to reversing the catastrophic market collapse.[3]

THE CAUSES OF THE OCTOBER 1987 CRASH

There was no single precipitating event—such as a declaration of war, a terrorist act, an assassination, or a bankruptcy—that caused Black Monday. However, worrying trends had threatened the rising stock market for some time: sharply higher long-term rates caused by a falling dollar, and the rapid development of a new strategy, called *portfolio insurance*, that was designed to insulate portfolios from a decline in the overall market. The latter was born from the explosive growth of stock index futures markets, which did not even exist six years earlier and are detailed in Chapter 26.

Exchange Rate Policies

The roots of the surge in interest rates that preceded the October 1987 stock market crash are found in the futile attempts by the United States and other G7 countries to prevent the dollar from falling in the international exchange markets. The dollar had bounded to unprecedented levels in the middle of the 1980s on the heels of huge Japanese and European purchases of dollar securities and a strong US economy. Foreign investors were attracted to high dollar interest rates, in part driven by a strengthening of the US economy and the capital-friendly presidency of Ronald Reagan. By February 1985, the dollar became massively overvalued, and US exports became very uncompetitive, severely worsening the US trade deficit. The dollar then reversed course and began a steep decline.

Central bankers initially cheered the fall of the overpriced dollar, but they grew concerned when the dollar continued to decline and the US trade deficit, instead of improving, worsened. Finance ministers met in February 1987 in Paris with the goal of supporting the dollar. They worried that if the dollar became too cheap, their own exports to the United States, which had grown substantially when the dollar was high, would suffer. The Federal Reserve reluctantly participated in the dollar stabilization program, whose success depended on either an improvement in the US trade position or, absent that, a commitment by the Federal Reserve to raise interest rates to support the dollar.

The trade deficit did not improve; in fact, it worsened after the initiation of the exchange stabilization policies. Traders, nervous about the deteriorating US trade balance, demanded ever higher interest rates to hold

US assets. Leo Melamed, chairman of the Chicago Mercantile Exchange, was blunt when asked about the origins of Black Monday: "What caused the crash was all that f— around with the currencies of the world."[4]

The stock market initially ignored rising interest rates. The US market, like most equity markets around the world, was booming. The Dow Jones Industrials, which started 1987 at 1,933, reached an all-time high of 2,725 on August 22—250 percent above the August 1982 low reached five years earlier. All world markets participated. Over the same five-year period, the British stock market was up 164 percent; the Swiss, 209 percent; German, 217 percent; Japanese, 288 percent; and Italian, 421 percent.

Rising bond rates, coupled with higher stock prices, spelled trouble for the equity markets. The long-term government bond rate, which began the year at 7 percent, topped 9 percent in September and continued to rise. As stocks rose, the dividend and earnings yield fell, and the gap between the real yield on bonds and the earnings and dividend yields on stocks reached a postwar high. By the morning of October 19, the long-term bond yield had reached 10.47 percent, despite the fact that inflation was well under control. The record gap between the yields on stocks and the real yields on bonds set the stage for the stock market crash.

The Futures Market

The S&P 500 futures market also clearly contributed to the market crash. Since the introduction of the stock index futures market, a new trading technique, called portfolio insurance, had been introduced into portfolio management.

Portfolio insurance was, in concept, not much different from an oft-used technique called a *stop-loss order*. If an investor buys a stock and wants to protect herself from a loss (or if it has gone up, protect her profit), it is possible to place a sell order below the current price that will be triggered when and if the price falls to or below this specified level.

Stop-loss orders are not guarantees that you can get out of the market. If the stock falls below your specified price, your stop-loss order becomes a *market order* to be executed at the *next best* price. If the stock *gaps*, or declines dramatically, your order could be executed far below your hoped-for price. This means a panic might develop if many investors place stop-loss orders around the same price. A price decline could trigger a flood of sell orders, overwhelming the market.

Portfolio insurers, who sold the stock index futures against large portfolios to protect them against market declines, felt they were immune to such problems. It seemed extremely unlikely that the S&P 500 Index futures would ever decline dramatically in price and that the whole US capital market, the world's largest, could fail to find buyers. This is one reason why the stock market continued to rise in the face of sharply higher long-term rates.

The entire market did gap on October 19, 1987. During the week of October 12, the market declined by 10 percent, and a large number of sell orders flooded the markets. So many traders and money managers using portfolio insurance strategies tried to sell index futures to protect their clients' profits that the futures market collapsed. There were absolutely no buyers, and liquidity vanished.

What stock traders once thought inconceivable became a reality. Since the prices of index futures were so far below the prices of the stocks selling in New York, investors halted their buying of shares in New York altogether. The world's largest market failed to attract any buyers.

Portfolio insurance withered rapidly after the crash. It was not an insurance scheme at all, because the continuity and liquidity of the market could not be ensured. There was, however, an alternative form of portfolio protection: index options. With the introduction of these options markets in the 1980s, investors could explicitly purchase insurance against market declines by buying puts on a market index. Options buyers never needed to worry about experiencing price gaps or being able to get out of their position since the price of the insurance was specified at the time of purchase.

Certainly, there were factors other than portfolio insurance contributing to Black Monday. But portfolio insurance and its ancestor, the stop-loss order, abetted the fall. All these schemes are rooted in the basic trading philosophy of letting profits ride and cutting losses short. Whether implemented with stop-loss orders, index futures, or just a mental note to get out of a stock once it declines by a certain amount, this philosophy can set the stage for dramatic market moves.

CIRCUIT BREAKERS

As a result of the crash, the Chicago Mercantile Exchange, where the S&P 500 Index futures traded, and the NYSE implemented rules that restricted or halted trading when certain price limits were triggered. To prevent destabilizing speculation when the Dow Jones Industrial Average changes by at least 2 percent, the NYSE Rule 80a placed "trading curbs" on index arbitrage between the futures market and the NYSE.

Of greater importance were measures that sharply restricted or stopped trading on both the futures market and the NYSE when market moves are very large. From 1988 through early 2013, new rules dictated that trading must be halted one hour, two hours, and the rest of the trading day if the Dow Industrials fell by 10 percent, 20 percent, and 30 percent, respectively. In April 2013, the SEC altered the circuit breaker rules to provide for a 15-minute break when the S&P 500 fell by 7 percent, and another when the market fell 13 percent. Trading would be halted for the entire day if the market fell by 20 percent, with these percentages recalculated to the level of the market each day. Futures trading must also cease trading when the NYSE is closed.[5] During the Covid-19 pandemic, trading was halted for 15 minutes on March 9, 12, 16, and 18 when the S&P 500 fell by more than 7 percent.

The rationale behind these circuit breakers is that halting trading gives investors time to reassess the situation and formulate their strategy based on rapidly changing prices. This time-out could bring buyers into the market and help market makers maintain a liquid market.

The argument against circuit breakers is that they increase volatility by discouraging short-term traders from buying when prices fall sharply, since they might be prevented from unwinding their position if trading is subsequently halted. This sometimes leads to an acceleration of price declines toward the price limits, thereby increasing short-term volatility, as occurred when prices fell to these limits on October 27, 1997.[6]

FLASH CRASH, MAY 6, 2010

Monday October 19, 1987, and the following Tuesday stand as the most volatile days in US stock market history. But investors were equally unnerved by the market collapse on May 6, 2010, an event that became known as the "flash crash." Figure 22.2 traces the market minute by minute through the day, a pattern of price volatility that eerily resembles the October 1987 stock market crash depicted in Figure 22.1A but taking place over a much shorter time period.

Shortly after 2:30 p.m. Eastern time, the Dow Industrials collapsed by more than 600 points, or more than 5 percent, and recovered just as quickly, as shown in Figure 22.2. There was no economic or financial news that could account for the decline. Furthermore, thousands of individual stocks traded at prices that were more than 60 percent below (and a few far above) the prices they sold at just a few minutes earlier; some shares in well-known stocks traded as low as a penny a share.

FIGURE 22.2

Flash crash, May 6, 2010

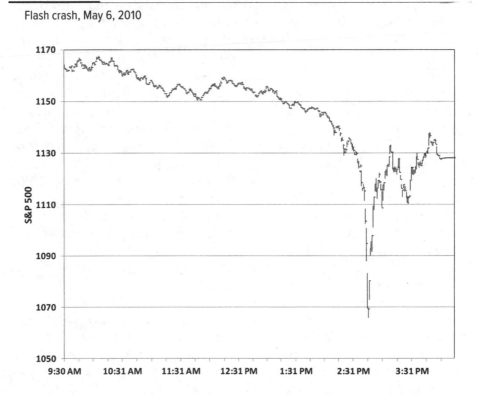

Stock prices had been under pressure all day because of the European debt crisis. At 2:42 p.m., with no significant news forthcoming and the Dow Industrials down by more than 300 points, stocks hit an "air pocket." The benchmark index hit a low at 2:47 p.m., 999 points, or nearly 10 percent, below the previous day's close. In five minutes, over $800 billion was erased from US equity values. In the next 30 minutes the market rallied by 700 points before closing the day at 10,520, down 348 points.

After almost five months of investigations, the US SEC and Commodity Futures Trading Commission (CFTC) issued a joint report[7] blaming an unusually large, $4 billion sale of S&P 500 futures by a large mutual fund that began at 2:41 p.m. and lasted three minutes, sending the market down quickly by another 3 percent.[8] Many of these sales were initially absorbed by *high-frequency traders* (HFTs), who are directed by computer programs to buy and sell securities rapidly to gauge market depth and predict future prices. But as the market continued to fall, many HFTs began to sell into a very thin and unstable market, precipitating further price declines.[9] At 2:45 p.m., trading on the E-mini was halted for five seconds when the Chicago Mercantile Exchange circuit breaker was triggered, and during that short pause buyers surfaced and prices recovered quickly.

The fall in the broad-based market averages was unnerving enough, but what caught the eye of many traders were the extraordinarily low prices that some blue chips fell to just after the S&P futures contracts hit their low. Procter & Gamble recorded a trade of $39.37, more than 50 percent below its opening price of $86, and the consulting group Accenture, also a member of the S&P 500, which had traded at $38 at 2:47 p.m., fell to *one penny* a share just two minutes later! Accenture was not alone. There were eight other stocks in the broad-based S&P 1500 Index that traded at one cent per share.[10] All told, there were 20,000 trades in 300 securities that were 60 percent or more away from the price they traded at just minutes earlier. After the close, the NYSE, in consultation with the Financial Industry Regulatory Authority (FINRA), "broke," or canceled, all trades that were 60 percent or more above or below their previous price.

It is very likely that these extreme prices would not have been realized if specialists, those exchange representatives who maintained markets in assigned stocks before the advent of computerized trading, still controlled the flow of buy and sell orders. These specialists would have stepped in to buy these stocks at prices well above the absurdly low price they traded at. But most modern computerized trading systems were programmed to react very differently than the specialists would have. When prices begin to fall steeply, the programs are instructed to withdraw from the market. This is because large moves in individual stocks are almost always associated with company-specific news that computerized traders do not have access to. These computers are programmed to profit from the normal ebb and flow of trading activity that clearly was absent that day.

When stock prices tumbled, a system of trading pauses that had been instituted by the NYSE, termed *liquidity replenishment points*, kicked in. Instead of providing liquidity, the pause sent some sell orders to other markets where dealers maintained *stub quotes*. Stub quotes are "placeholders," that is, quotes far from the market price (some at a penny bid, $100,000 asked) and are not meant to be traded against. With no other orders on the books, these stub quotes were executed for many stocks.

In response to the flash crash, the SEC staff worked with the exchanges and FINRA to promptly implement a circuit breaker pilot program for trading in individual securities that would apply across all markets. These new rules stop trading in a security for five minutes if that security has experienced a 10 percent price change over the preceding five minutes. On June 10, 2010, the SEC approved the application of the circuit breakers to stocks included in the S&P 500 Index, and on September 10, the SEC approved an expansion of the program to securities included in the Russell 1000 Index and certain ETFs. In April 2013, the SEC changed the 10 percent price change to a "limit-up and limit-down" rule that was tailored to the volatility of the individual security. For stocks trading over $3 a share (except leveraged ETFs), the limit remains at 10 percent, except for the first and last 15 minutes of trading, when the limit is expanded to 20 percent.[11]

The flash crash, coming just a year after the deepest bear market in 75 years, eroded the public's trust in a fair and orderly market for equities. Many cited the SEC indictment of high-frequency traders as evidence that the market is rigged against the small investor. But high-frequency trading declined after the flash crash, and several researchers questioned whether the trading played a significant role in that day's decline. New rules established by the SEC have virtually eliminated the kind of errant and extreme trades that took place during the flash crash.

From a broader perspective, individual investors should not fear short-term market volatility. Should you not want to shop in a store where every so often you hear "10 percent to 20 percent off the price of all items for the next 30 minutes!"? Short-run volatility has always been part of the stock market, and the flash crash had no lasting effect on the recovery from the 2007–2009 bear market.

THE NATURE OF MARKET VOLATILITY

Although most investors express a strong distaste for market fluctuations, volatility must be accepted to reap the superior returns offered by stocks. Accepting risk is required for above-average returns: investors cannot make any more than the risk-free rate unless there is some possibility that they can make less.

While the volatility of the stock market deters many investors, it fascinates others. The ability to monitor a position on a minute-by-minute basis fulfills the need of many to quickly validate their judgment. For many, the stock market is truly the world's largest casino.

Yet this ability to know exactly how much one is worth at any given moment can also provoke anxiety. Many investors do not like the instantaneous verdict of the financial market. Some retreat into investments such as real estate, for which daily quotations are not available. Others believe that not knowing the current price somehow makes an investment less risky. In Chapter 2, we cited John Maynard Keynes's warning that "The fact that you do not know how much its ready money quotation fluctuates does not, as is commonly supposed, make an investment a safe one."[12]

HISTORICAL TRENDS OF STOCK VOLATILITY

The annual variability of the US stock market from 1834 through 2021, measured by the standard deviation of the monthly returns, is plotted in Figure 22.3. It is striking that there is so little overall trend in the volatility of the market. The period of greatest volatility was during the Great Depression, and the year of highest volatility was 1932. The annualized volatility of 1932 was 63.7 percent, nearly 20 times higher than 1993, which is the least volatile year on record with a standard deviation of 3.36. The volatility of 2020 during the Covid-19 pandemic was the highest since the Great Depression, edging out 2008, the year of the financial crisis and 1987, the year of the October crash. Excluding the 1929–1939 period, volatility has averaged about 13 percent and , as noted,the trend has remained remarkably stable over the past 190 years.

FIGURE 22.3

Annual volatility of stock returns: annualized standard deviation of monthly nominal returns, 1834–2021

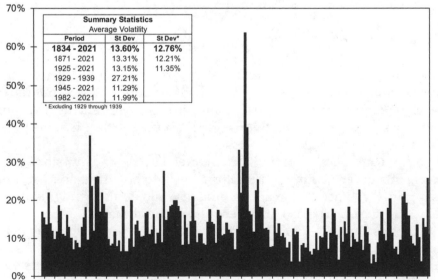

Summary Statistics		
Average Volatility		
Period	St Dev	St Dev*
1834 - 2021	**13.60%**	**12.76%**
1871 - 2021	13.31%	12.21%
1925 - 2021	13.15%	11.35%
1929 - 1939	27.21%	
1945 - 2021	11.29%	
1982 - 2021	11.99%	

* Excluding 1929 through 1939

Figure 22.4A displays the average daily percentage change in the Dow Jones Industrial Average for each year from 1896 through 2021. The average daily change over the past 125 years is 0.73 percent. Except for the 1930s, there was a downtrend in volatility from 1896 to 1960 and a subsequent uptrend. Some of the uptrend is due to the faster response of markets to economic developments; information that used to take hours if not days to be fully reflected in market averages is now processed in minutes, if not seconds. Some of the downward trend in the Dow volatility in the early twentieth century is due to the increase in the number of stocks in the Dow Industrials, from 12 to 20, and then to 30 in 1928. The daily volatility during the financial crisis in 2008, at 1.63 percent, was the highest since the Great Depression and edged out the daily volatility in the 2020 pandemic.

The percentage of trading days when the Dow Industrials changed by more than 1 percent is shown in Figure 22.4B. It has averaged 23 percent over the period, or about once per week. But it has ranged from as low as 1.2 percent in 1964, to a high of 67.6 percent in 1932, when the Dow changed by more than 1 percent in more than two out of every three trading days. The financial crisis of 2008 generated the highest daily volatility since the Great Depression of the 1930s.

Most of the periods of high volatility occur during bear markets. The standard deviation of daily returns is more than 25 percent higher in recessions than in expansions. There are two reasons why volatility increases in a recession. First, recessions, being the exception rather than the rule, are marked by greater economic uncertainty than expansions. The second is that if earnings fall, then the burden of fixed costs causes greater volatility of profits. This leads to increased volatility in stock prices.

If profits turn into losses, then the equity value of the firms is like an out-of-the-money call option that pays off only if the firm eventually earns enough profits to cover its costs. Otherwise, it is worthless. It is not a puzzle why stock volatility was the greatest during the Great Depression when, with aggregate profits negative, the equity market was trading like an out-of-the-money call.

THE VOLATILITY INDEX

Measuring *historical* volatility is a simple matter, but it is far more important to measure the volatility that investors *expect* in the market. This is because expected volatility is a signal of the level of anxiety in the market, and periods of high anxiety have often marked turning points for stocks.

FIGURE 22.4

Daily risk on the Dow Industrial Average

Figure A

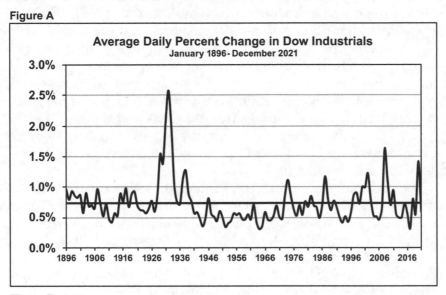

Figure B

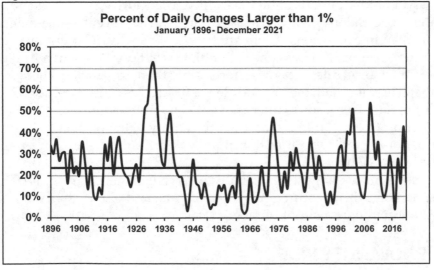

By examining the prices of put and call options on the major stock market indexes, one can determine the volatility that is built into the market, which is called the *implied volatility*.[13] In 1993, the Chicago Board Options Exchange introduced the *CBOE Volatility Index*, also called the *VIX Index* (VIX), based on actual index options prices on the S&P 500 Index, and it calculated this index back to the mid-1980s.[14] A weekly plot of the VIX Index from 1986 through 2021 appears in Figure 22.5.

FIGURE 22.5

The VIX Index 1986–2021

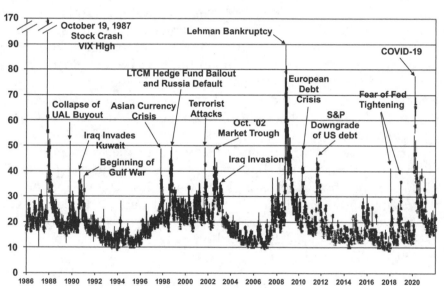

In the short run, there is a strong negative correlation between the VIX and the *level* of the market. When the market is falling, investors are willing to pay more for downside protection, and they purchase puts, pushing the option prices higher and causing the VIX to rise. When the market is rising, the VIX typically falls as investors gain confidence and have less incentive to insure their portfolio against a loss.

This correlation may seem puzzling since one might expect investors to seek more protection when the market is high, rather than low. One explanation of the behavior of the VIX Index is that historical volatility is higher in bear markets than bull markets, so falling markets cause the VIX to rise. But a more persuasive argument is that changes in investors' confidence change investors' willingness to hedge by buying puts. As put prices are driven up, arbitrageurs who write these puts then sell stocks to hedge their position. The reverse occurs when investors feel more confident of stock returns.

It is easy to see in Figure 22.5 that the peaks in the VIX corresponded to periods of extreme uncertainty and sharply lower stock prices. The VIX peaked at 172 on the Tuesday following the October 19, 1987, stock market crash, far eclipsing any other high.

In the early and mid-1990s, the VIX Index sank to between 10 and 20. With the onset of the Asian crises in 1997, the VIX moved up to a 20–30 range. Spikes between 50 and 60 in the VIX occurred on three occasions: in October 1987 when the Dow fell 550 points during the attack on the Hong Kong dollar, in August 1998 when Long-Term Capital Management was liquidated, and in the week following the terrorist attacks of September 11, 2001. Aside from the 1987 stock market crash, the highest VIX was reached shortly after Lehman Brothers went bankrupt in September 2008. The VIX peaked again during the European sovereign debt crises and during the Covid-19 pandemic. The all-time low value of the VIX occurred on November 24, 2017, when the volatility index fell to 8.56.

In recent years, buying when the VIX is high and selling when it is low has proved to be a profitable strategy for the short term. But so has buying during market dips and selling during market peaks. The real question is, how high is high, and how low is low. For instance, an investor might have been tempted to sell puts on Friday, October 16, 1987, when the VIX reached 40. Yet such a purchase would have proved disastrous, given the record one-day collapse that followed on Monday.

THE DISTRIBUTION OF LARGE DAILY CHANGES

Chapter 20 noted that there were 157 days from 1885 through 2021 when the Dow Jones Industrials changed by 5 percent or seventy-nine of these days, or more than one-half of the total, occurred from 1929 through 1933. The most volatile year by far, in terms of daily changes, was 1932, which contained 35 days when the Dow moved by at least 5 percent. The longest period between two successive changes of at least 5 percent was the 17-year period that preceded the October 19, 1987, stock crash.

The calendar properties of large daily changes are displayed in Figure 22.6. Most of the large changes have occurred on Monday, while Tuesday has experienced by far the least (excluding Saturday). Monday has the largest number of down days, and Wednesday has by far the highest number of up days.

FIGURE 22.6

Distribution of Dow Industrial changes over 5 percent, 1885–2021 (white rises, gray declines)

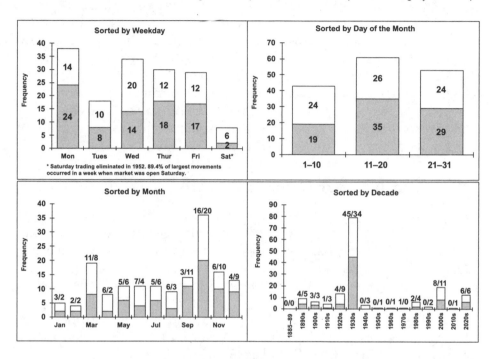

Thirty-six of the large changes occurred in October, which has witnessed more than twice the number of large moves as any other month. October's reputation as a volatile month is fully justified. Excluding the volatility during the Covid-19 pandemic, not only has October witnessed nearly one-quarter of all big moves, but it has also seen the two greatest stock crashes in history, in October 1929 and October 1987. Because of the volatility associated with the Covid-19 pandemic, March has become the second most volatile month. Excluding the Covid-19 pandemic, nearly two-thirds of the large declines have occurred in the last four months of the year. Chapter 17 presents other seasonal properties of stock returns.

One of the most surprising bits of information about large market moves relates to the period of the greatest stock market collapse. From September 3, 1929, through July 8, 1932, the Dow Jones Industrials collapsed nearly 89 percent. During that period, there were 37 episodes when the Dow changed by 5 percent or more. Surprisingly, 21 of those episodes were increases! Many of these sharp rallies were the result of short covering, which occurred as speculators who thought the market was on a one-way street rushed to sell stock they did not own and were then forced to buy it back, or "cover" their positions once the market rallied.

It is not uncommon for markets that appear to be trending in one direction to experience occasional sharp moves in the other direction. As noted earlier, in a bull market, the expression "up the staircase, down the elevator" is an apt description of market behavior. In a bear market it is "down the staircase, up the elevator." Ordinary investors must beware: it is not as easy to make money in trending markets as it looks, and investors who try to play these markets must be ready to bail out quickly when they see the market change direction.

THE ECONOMICS OF MARKET VOLATILITY

Many of the complaints about market volatility are grounded in the belief that the market reacts excessively to changes in news. How news should impact the market is so difficult to determine, that few can quantify the proper impact of an event on the price of a stock. As a result, traders often "follow the crowd" and try to predict how other traders will react when news happens.

Nearly a century ago, Keynes emphasized investors' difficulty in basing their strategy on fundamental financial variables such as dividends and earnings. In 1981, Robert Shiller of Yale University devised a method of determining whether stock investors tended to overreact to changes in dividends and interest rates, the fundamental building blocks of stock values.[15] From the examination of historical data, he calculated what the value of the S&P 500 Index should have been given the subsequent realization of dividends and interest rates.

What he found was that stock prices were far too variable to be explained merely by the subsequent behavior of dividends and interest rates. Stock prices appeared to overreact to changes in earnings and dividends. For example, investors priced stocks in a recession as if they expected dividends to go much lower, completely contrary to historical experience.

The word *cycle* in *business cycle* implies that ups in economic activity will be followed by downs, and vice versa. Since earnings and profits tend to follow the business cycle, they too should behave in a cyclical manner, returning to some average value over time. Under these circumstances, a temporary drop in dividends (or earnings) during a recession should have a very minor effect on the price of a stock, which discounts cash flows into the infinite future.

When stocks are collapsing, worst-case scenarios loom large in investors' minds. On May 6, 1932, after stocks had plummeted 85 percent from their 1929 high, Dean Witter issued the following memo to its clients:

> There are only two premises which are tenable as to the future. Either we are going to have chaos or else recovery. The former theory is foolish. If chaos ensues nothing will maintain value; neither bonds nor stocks nor bank deposits nor gold will remain valuable. Real estate will be a worthless asset because titles will be insecure. No policy can be based upon this impossible contingency. Policy must therefore be predicated upon the theory of recovery. The present is not the first depression; it may be the worst, but just as surely as conditions have righted themselves in the past and have gradually readjusted to normal, so this will again occur. The only uncertainty is when it will occur. . . . I wish to say emphatically that in a few years present prices will appear as ridiculously low as 1929 values appear fantastically high.[16]

Two months later the stock market hit its all-time low and rallied strongly. In retrospect, these words reflected great wisdom and sound judgment about the temporary dislocations of stock prices. Yet at the time they were uttered, investors were so disenchanted with stocks and so filled with doom and gloom that the message fell on deaf ears.

CONCLUSION

Despite the drama of the October 1987 market collapse, there was amazingly little lasting effect on the world economy or even the financial markets. Because the 1987 episode did not augur either a further collapse in stock prices or a decline in economic activity, it will never attain the notoriety of the crash of 1929. Yet its lesson is perhaps more important. Economic safeguards, such as prompt Federal Reserve action to provide liquidity to the economy and ensure the proper functioning of the financial markets, can prevent an economic debacle of the kind that beset our economy during the Great Depression.

This does not mean that the markets are exempt from violent fluctuations. Since the future will always be uncertain, psychology and sentiment often dominate economic fundamentals. As Keynes perceptively stated more than 80 years ago in *The General Theory*, "The outstanding fact is the extreme precariousness of the basis of knowledge on which our estimates of prospective yield have to be made."[17] Precarious estimates are subject to sudden change, so prices in free markets will be volatile. History has shown that investors who are willing to step into the market when others are running to the exits will reap large benefits.

23

The Great Financial Crisis of 2008–2009

Regarding the Great Depression. You're right, we did it. We're very sorry. But thanks to you, we won't do it again.

—Ben Bernanke, November 8, 2002, on the ninetieth birthday celebration for Milton Friedman

When the music stops, in terms of liquidity, things will get complicated. But as long as the music is playing, you've got to get up and dance. We're still dancing.

—Chuck Prince, CEO, Citigroup in July 2007, on the eve of the financial collapse.

THE WEEK THAT ROCKED WORLD MARKETS

It was only Wednesday, September 17, 2008, but I had already had an exhausting week trying to make sense of the upheaval in the financial markets. On Monday, stocks surprised investors by opening higher despite the Sunday night news of the bankruptcy of Lehman Brothers, the largest bankruptcy filing in US history. With no government aid forthcoming, Lehman Brothers, a 150-year-old investment firm that had survived the Great Depression, had no chance.

That hopeful opening was quickly countered by rumors that key firms would not clear trades for Lehman customers, throwing markets into a state of anxiety.[1] As Monday morning's gains turned into losses, fear enveloped the financial markets. Investors wondered: What assets were safe? Which firm would be the next to fail? Could this crisis be contained? Risk premiums soared as lenders backed away from all credit markets except US Treasury bonds.[2] By the end of the day, the Dow Industrials had fallen almost 5 percent.

The following day, speculators attacked AIG, the world's largest and most profitable insurance company. AIG's stock price, which had reached nearly $60 a share a year earlier, plunged below $3, down from its closing price of over $10 the previous Friday. AIG's collapse sent stocks sharply lower; but some traders speculated, correctly as it turned out, that the Fed could not risk letting another major financial firm go under, and the market stabilized later in the day. Indeed, after the close of trading, the Fed announced that it had loaned $85 billion to AIG, avoiding another market-shaking bankruptcy. The Fed's decision to bail out AIG was a dramatic turnaround, as Chairman Ben Bernanke rejected the giant insurer's request for a $40 billion loan just a week earlier.

But the crisis was far from over. After the markets closed on Tuesday, the $36 billion Reserve Primary Fund made a most ominous announcement. Because the Lehman securities that the money fund held were, by regulations, marked down to zero, Reserve was going to "break the buck" and pay investors only 97 cents on the dollar.[3]

Although other money funds reassured investors that they held no Lehman debt and that they were honoring all withdrawals at full value, I knew that these declarations would do little to calm investor anxiety. Bear Stearns had repeatedly reassured investors that everything was fine before the Fed forced the failing firm to merge into J.P. Morgan six months earlier. Similarly, Lehman CEO Richard Fuld told investors just a week before filing for bankruptcy that all was well and blamed short sellers for driving down the price of his stock.

COULD THE GREAT DEPRESSION HAPPEN AGAIN?

I returned to my office after lunch and looked at my Bloomberg screen. Yes, stocks were down again, and that didn't surprise me. But what caught my attention was the yield on US Treasury bills. A Treasury auction of three-month bills conducted that afternoon was so heavily oversubscribed that buyers sent the interest rate down to 0.06 of 1 percent.

I had monitored markets closely for almost 50 years, through the savings and loan collapse of the 1970s, the 1987 stock market crash, the Asian crisis, the Long-Term Capital Management crisis, the Russian default, the 9/11 terrorist attack, and many other crises. I had never seen investors rush to Treasuries like this. The last time Treasury bill yields fell toward zero was during the Great Depression, 75 years earlier. I recalled lecturing my MBA students back in the 1970s, when Treasury bill rates were 16 percent, that investors in the Depression were thrilled to get yields as high as 10 basis points. We all shook our heads and laughed about this curious piece of history that we believed would never happen again.

Never again? My eyes returned to the screen in front of me, and a chill went down my spine. Was this a replay of a dark period that economists had thought was dead and gone? Could this be the start of the second "Great Depression"? Can policy makers prevent a repeat of that financial and economic catastrophe, the worst in US history?

In the ensuing months, the answers to these questions emerged. The Federal Reserve, learning from the mistakes it made in the 1930s, implemented aggressive programs to prevent another depression. But the credit disruptions that followed the Lehman bankruptcy caused the world's deepest economic contraction and the steepest decline in equity prices since the Great Depression. The recovery from the financial crisis was one of the slowest in US history, causing many to question whether the future of the US economy could ever be as bright as it appeared when the Dow Industrials crossed 14,000, reaching record highs in October 2007.

RUMBLINGS OF FINANCIAL CRISIS

In contrast to the peak of the technology boom, when the S&P 500 was selling for 30 times earnings, there was no general overvaluation at the 2007 market peak; stocks were selling for a much more modest 16 times earnings. But cracks were beginning to show in the financial markets. The financial sector, which in the bull market had become the largest sector of the S&P 500 Index, peaked in May 2007, and the price of many large banks, such as Citi and BankAmerica, had been falling all year.

More ominous developments came from the real estate market. Real estate prices, after having nearly tripled in the previous decade, peaked in the summer of 2006 and were heading downward. Suddenly, subprime mortgages experienced large delinquencies. In April 2007, New Century Financial, a leading subprime lender, filed for bankruptcy, and in June, Bear Stearns informed investors that it was suspending redemptions from its High-Grade Structured Credit Strategies Enhanced Leverage Fund, a fund whose name is as complex as the securities that it held.

At first, the market ignored these developments, but on August 9, 2007, BNP Paribas, France's largest bank, halted redemptions in its mortgage funds, and world equity markets sold off sharply. Stocks recovered when the Fed lowered the Fed funds rate 50 basis points in an emergency meeting in August, and another 50 basis points at its regular September meeting. Investors believed the Fed could control the fallout and stocks continued to new highs.

Yet 2008 brought no relief from subprime troubles. Bear Stearns, which had to take an increasing volume of subprime mortgages back on its own balance sheets, began to experience funding problems, and the price of its shares plummeted. On March 17, 2008, the Federal Reserve, in an effort to shield Bear from imminent bankruptcy, arranged an emergency sale of all of Bear Stearns's assets to J.P. Morgan at a price of $2 (later raised to $10) a share, almost 99 percent below the high of $172.61 it reached in January of the prior year.

Bear Stearns was only the appetizer for this bear market, and the main dish was not far behind. Lehman Brothers, founded in the 1850s, had a storied history that included bringing public such great companies as Sears, Woolworth's, Macy's, and Studebaker. Its profitability soared after the firm itself went public in 1994, and in 2007 the firm reported its fourth consecutive year of record profitability as net revenues reached $19.2 billion and the number of employees neared 30,000.

Lehman Brothers, like Bear Stearns, was involved in the subprime market and other leveraged real estate investments. Its price had sunk from over $40 to $20 a share when Bear was merged into J.P. Morgan in March. Lehman was well known for financing large real estate deals, booking significant fees as investors sold and refinanced commercial real estate at ever higher prices. In July, Blackstone, another large investment house that went public in July 2007, had purchased Sam Zell's Equity Office Properties for $22.9 billion, earning high fees for selling almost all the properties before the market collapsed.

Lehman felt confident, despite the chaos enveloping the subprime market. Many analysts were convinced that commercial real estate did not suffer from the overbuilding that plagued the residential sector. In fact, commercial real estate prices continued to rise well after the general market peaked. Reacting favorably to lower interest rates, the Dow Jones REIT Index of all publicly traded REITs peaked in February 2008, four months after the general market and more than a year after the major commercial banks hit their highs.[4]

In May, just after commercial real estate prices reached their peak, Lehman financed a huge $22 billion stake in Archstone-Smith Trust, hoping to flip the properties to buyers, just as Blackstone did a few months earlier.[5] But as in the child's game of musical chairs, the music stopped in the summer of 2008. Blackstone got the very last chair in the real estate closing room, but Lehman was left standing. On September 15, 2008, as CEO Richard Fuld thrashed about to find a last-minute buyer, Lehman Brothers, an investment firm that had thrived for more than a century and a half, filed for bankruptcy. It was the largest in US history, and Lehman listed a record $613 billion in liabilities. Just as the Great Crash of 1929 launched the Great Depression of the 1930s, the fall of Lehman Brothers in 2008 precipitated the greatest financial crisis and deepest economic contraction that the world had seen in nearly a century.

THE GREAT MODERATION

The economic backdrop for the Great Financial Crisis (and its accompanying economic slump called the Great Recession) was the "Great Moderation," the name that economists gave to the remarkably long and stable economic period that preceded the downfall of Lehman Brothers. The volatility of key economic variables, such as the quarterly changes in real and nominal GDP, fell by about one-half during the 1983–2005 period compared with the average post levels.[6] Although part of this stability was ascribed to the increase in the size of the service sector and advances in inventory control that moderated the "inventory cycle," many attributed the reduction of economic volatility to the increasing effectiveness of monetary policy, primarily as practiced during the tenure of Alan Greenspan as Fed chairman from 1986 through 2006.

As one might expect, risk premiums on many financial instruments declined markedly during the Great Moderation as investors believed that prompt central bank action would counteract any severe shock to the economy. Indeed, the 2001 recession reinforced the market's opinion that the economy was more stable. That recession was very mild by historical standards, despite the popping of the huge tech bubble in 2000, and the consumer retrenchment that followed the 9/11 terrorist attacks.

The unusual economic stability that preceded the financial crisis was very similar to the moderation that prevailed during the 1920s, the decade that preceded the 1929 stock crash and the Great Depression. The standard deviation of changes in industrial production from 1920 to 1929 was also less than one-half of what it was in the preceding 20 years, like what occurred during the Great Moderation. During the 1920s, many economists, including the influential Irving Fisher of Yale University, attributed the increased stability to the Federal Reserve, as did economists before the Great Financial Crisis. And in the 1920s, investors also believed that the new central bank would "backstop" the economy in the case of a crisis, moderating any downturn.

Unfortunately, the increased appetite for risk assets during a stable economic environment can set the stage for a more severe crisis to follow. A slowdown in business activity, which under normal times would be well tolerated, can easily overwhelm highly leveraged borrowers who had too little cushion to insulate them from a market decline.

Some economists believe that the cycle of falling risk premiums and rising leverage is the major cause of economic fluctuations. Hyman Minsky, an economics professor from Washington University in St. Louis, formulated the *financial instability hypothesis*,[7] in which he believed long periods of economic stability and rising asset prices drew in not only speculators and momentum investors, but also swindlers who engage in Ponzi schemes that trap ordinary investors who wish to ride the market upward breaks. Minsky's theories never gained much currency with mainstream economists because he did not formulate them in a rigorous form. But Minsky had a strong impact on many, including the late Charles Kindleberger, an economics professor at MIT whose five editions of *Manias, Panics, and Crashes: A History of Financial Crises* attracted a large following.

SUBPRIME MORTGAGES

In contrast to 1929, where rampant lending against a soaring stock market contributed to the financial crisis, the primary cause of the 2008 financial crisis was the rapid growth of subprime mortgages and other real estate securities that found their way into the balance sheets of very large and highly leveraged financial institutions. When the real estate market reversed direction and the prices of these securities plunged, firms that had borrowed money were thrown into a crisis that sent some into bankruptcy, others into forced mergers with stronger firms, and still others to the government for capital to ensure their survival.

Many investors—and politicians—welcomed these higher-yielding mortgage securities, believing that the Great Moderation and a Federal Reserve "safety net" had significantly reduced their risks of default.[8] But the proliferation of these securities accelerated when the major rating agencies, such as Standard & Poor's and Moody's, gave these subprime mortgages their highest ratings. This allowed hundreds of billions of dollars of mortgage-based securities to be marketed worldwide to pension funds, municipalities, and other organizations that demanded only the highest-quality fixed-income investments. It also lured many Wall Street firms that were seeking higher yields, attracted by their AAA ratings.

Although some assume that the investment banks pressured the rating agencies to give these securities investment-grade ratings so that the banks could enlarge the pool of potential buyers, in fact these securities were rated by very similar statistical techniques used to evaluate other securities. Unfortunately, these techniques were ill suited to analyze default probabilities in a housing market where real estate prices soared far above fundamentals.

THE CRUCIAL RATING MISTAKE

Figure 23.1 is a yearly plot of housing prices from the end of World War II, measured both before and after inflation. The period from 1997 through 2006 was marked by an accelerating pace of real estate appreciation, in both real and nominal terms. Over these years, nominal home prices, as measured by the Case-Shiller index of 20 metropolitan communities, nearly tripled, and real home prices increased 130 percent, well exceeding the increase during the 1970s and topping the previous record-breaking increases that immediately followed World War II.

FIGURE 23.1

Nominal and real home prices, 1950–2011

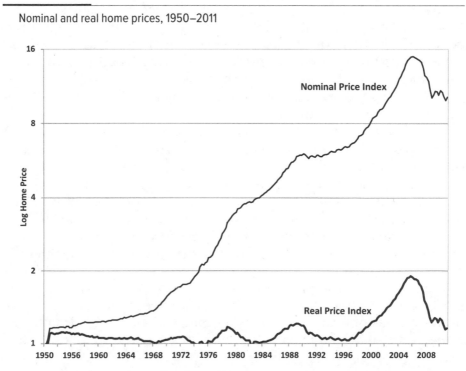

Before the housing price boom, conventional mortgages were based on an 80 percent loan-to-market ratio, and the creditworthiness of the borrower was important to the lender. This is because the price of an individual home, or even the average price of homes in specific geographic regions, could fall more than 20 percent and thus impair the value of the lender's collateral.

But what if mortgages from many diverse localities could be bundled together to form a security that would greatly reduce the risk of local real estate fluctuations? Then the price of the underlying assets backing the security should look more like the nominal home price series shown in Figure 23.1, which—until 2006—showed very little downside movement. In fact, prior to 1997 there were only three years when the nominal national home index had declined: two of these declines were less than 1.0 percent, and the third, from the second quarter of 1990 to the second quarter of 1991, was 2.8 percent. Therefore, based on postwar historical data, there would have been no period when the nationwide real estate price index even began to approach the 20 percent decline necessary to cut into the collateral of the standard mortgage.[9, 10]

Standard & Poor's, as well as Moody's and other rating agencies, analyzed these historical home price series and performed the standard statistical tests that measure the risk and return of these securities. Based on these studies, they reported that the probability that collateral behind a nationally diversified portfolio of home mortgages would be violated was virtually zero. The risk management departments of many investment banks agreed with this conclusion.

An equally important conclusion this analysis reached was that if the real estate behind the mortgage was virtually always going to be worth more than the mortgage, the creditworthiness of the borrower should not be important to the lender. If the borrower defaults, the lender can take over the property and sell it for more than the value of the loan. The rating agencies therefore stamped "AAA" on these securities, ignoring the creditworthiness of the home buyer. This assumption provided the impetus for the sale of hundreds of billions of dollars of subprime and other nonconventional mortgages backed by little or no credit documentation if the loan was collateralized by a pool of geographically diversified mortgages.

Some rating agencies knew that the high credit ratings for these mortgages depended on the continued appreciation and negligible downside risk of home prices. Even housing prices that leveled off presented a threat to their models.[11]

As home prices declined, the ratings of these top mortgage securities deteriorated rapidly. In April 2006, a few months before the peak of housing prices, Goldman Sachs sold investors 12 mortgage bonds, of which 10 were originally rated investment grade and 3 were rated AAA. By September 2007, 7 of the original 10 investment-grade tranches were downgraded to junk status, and 4 were totally wiped out.[12]

What should have alerted investors that the sustained increase in housing prices could not continue is by examining the ratio of housing prices to median family income. This ratio remained in a tight range between 2.5 and 3.1 from 1978 to 2002, but then moved sharply higher and eventually reached 4.1 in 2006, nearly 50 percent above previous levels.[13]

When the price of an asset rises relative to a fundamental variable such as the borrower's income, investors must ask whether there are structural changes that justify the price rise or whether this price rise might be temporary, to be followed by a decline back to historical levels. Certainly, if the price rise is likely caused by temporary factors, then the probability that house prices will subsequently decline is far greater than what would be found through the analysis of historical home prices conducted by the rating agencies.

This does not mean that it should have been obvious to all concerned that real estate was overvalued, or that home prices were in a bubble. There have been periods in history when prices have moved away from historical levels of valuation but were fully justified on the basis of ongoing economic factors.

One such episode that we described in Chapter 10 is the relationship between the dividend yield on stocks and the interest rate on long-term Treasury bonds. Between 1871 and 1956, the dividend yield was always above the bond yield, and this was thought to be necessary since stocks were seen as riskier than bonds. The strategy of selling stocks when the spread narrowed and buying them when the spread widened was profitable for many decades.

When the United States left the gold standard, chronic inflation began to be factored into the interest rate, and in 1957 rates rose above the dividend yield on stocks and remained that way for more than a half-century. Those who sold stocks and bought bonds in 1957 when this fundamental-based indicator flashed "Sell!" experienced poor returns, as stocks proved to be a much better hedge against inflation and provided far greater returns than fixed-income investments.

In a similar vein, there were plausible reasons why real estate prices rose above their historical relation to median family income in the early 2000s. First, there were significant declines in both nominal and real interest rates that made the cost of home financing extremely low. Second, there was the proliferation of new mortgage instruments, such as subprime and *full-funding* mortgages, which loaned up to—and in some cases more than—the purchase price of the home. These mortgages opened the door to borrowers who previously did not qualify for a loan and greatly expanded the demand for housing. The popularity of these full-funding mortgages was driven home by the National Association of Realtors (NAR) when in January 2006 the NAR announced that 43 percent of first-time home buyers purchased their homes with no-money-down loans, and that the median down payment was a mere 2 percent of a median-priced $150,000 home.[14]

There were well-known and highly respected economists, such as Charles Himmelberg, senior economist of the Federal Reserve Bank of New York; Chris Mayer, director of the Paul Milstein Center for Real Estate at Columbia University Business School; and Todd Sinai, an associate professor of real estate at the Wharton School, who argued that the lower interest rates justified the high level of real estate prices.[15] Some also pointed to the boom in second homes, a factor that many thought would persist for many years as the baby boomers entered retirement.[16]

But many others questioned the sustainability of the housing price increase. Professor Robert Shiller of Yale University and his colleague Karl Case, who developed the Case-Shiller residential housing indexes that have become the benchmark for the profession, first warned about the bubble of real estate in a 2003 *Brookings Papers* article entitled, "Is There a Housing Bubble?"[17] Dean Baker, codirector of the Center for Economic and Policy Research in Washington, also had written and lectured extensively about the dangers of the housing bubble in 2005 and early 2006.[18, 19] Nevertheless, the disagreement among experts about whether a real estate bubble actually existed does not justify the rating agencies rating these securities as if there were essentially no probability that they could default.[20]

REGULATORY FAILURE

Regulatory bodies in general, and the Federal Reserve in particular, did not believe the house price inflation posed a threat to the economy, and they did not question the high ratings given to the subprime mortgage securities. Furthermore, they did not monitor the buildup of risky mortgage-related securities in the balance sheet of key financial institutions.

It is especially tragic that Federal Reserve Chairman Alan Greenspan, by far the most influential public official in economic affairs, did not warn the public of the increasing risks posed by the unprecedented rise in housing prices. Greenspan should have been aware of the burgeoning subprime debt and the potential threat that it posed to the economy since one of his fellow governors at the Federal Reserve, Edward Gramlich, wrote extensively about these subprime instruments and published a book entitled *Subprime Mortgages: America's Latest Boom and Bust* in June 2007.[21]

Some have maintained that the Fed lacked oversight over nonbank financial institutions, and that the impact of higher real estate prices was outside its purview. Why then did Greenspan worry sufficiently about the rise in *stock prices* a decade earlier to fashion his famous "irrational exuberance" speech before the Economic Club in Washington, DC, in December 1996? All matters impacting the stability of the financial sector are the responsibility of the Federal Reserve, whether they originate in banks or not. Greenspan's lack of concern was revealed when he declared before congressional committees in October 2008 that he was in a state of "shocked disbelief" that the leading lending institutions did not take measures to protect shareholder's equity against a housing meltdown, nor had they neutralized their exposure to risk by using financial derivatives or credit default swaps.[22, 23]

Contrary to others,[24] I do not hold Greenspan responsible for creating the housing bubble. The Fed's policy of slowly raising interest rates was not the primary force driving real estate values upward. The forces propelling real estate prices were of far greater importance than the level of the short-term rates, particularly the fall in *long-term* interest rates of which the Fed has much less control, as well as the proliferation of subprime and full-funding mortgages. Furthermore, the forces pushing real estate prices upward asserted themselves on a worldwide basis and in currencies of nations with central banks following very different monetary policies. For example, housing prices soared in Spain and Greece, countries whose monetary policy was set by the European Central Bank. Fundamental forces operating on a worldwide basis (detailed in Chapter 8), such as the slowing of economic growth, the aging of investors which increased risk aversion, and the switch from equities to bonds in corporate pension funds were far more important factors pushing real and nominal interest rates downward than Greenspan's monetary policy.

OVERLEVERAGE BY FINANCIAL INSTITUTIONS IN RISKY ASSETS

It is unlikely that the rise and fall in real estate prices *by itself* would have caused either the financial crisis or a severe recession, had it not been for the buildup of risky assets in the balance sheets of key financial firms. The total value of subprime, alt-A (slightly higher-quality debt than subprime), and jumbo mortgages reached $2.8 trillion by the second quarter of 2007.[25] Even if the price of all these securities went to zero, the loss in value would be less than the decline in the value of technology stocks during the crash of the dot-com boom that occurred seven years earlier. That stock market collapse, even when followed by the economic disruptions that occurred after the devastating 9/11 terrorist attacks, caused only a mild recession.

The big difference between the two episodes is that at the peak of the tech boom, brokerage houses and investment banks did not hold large quantities of these stocks whose price was set to plummet. This is because investment firms had sold off virtually all their risky technology holdings to investors before the dot-com bubble burst.

In sharp contrast, at the peak of the real estate market, Wall Street was up to its ears in housing-related debt. In a declining interest rate environment, investors were hungry for yield, and these mortgage-based securities carried interest rates that were higher than comparably rated corporate and government debt. This tempted investment banks, such as Bear Stearns, to sell these bonds to investors, with the promise of higher yield with comparable safety.[26] Although many investment banks held these bonds for their own account, their holdings of subprime debt grew substantially when they were forced to take back the faltering subprime funds they had sold to investors, because of complaints that investors were not fully informed of their risks.[27]

Risks to the financial system were compounded when AIG, the world's largest insurance company, offered to insure hundreds of billions of dollars of these mortgages against default through an instrument called the *credit default swap*. When the prices of these mortgages fell, AIG had to come up with billions of dollars of reserves that it did not have. At the same time, the investment banks that had borrowed heavily to purchase these mortgages found that their funding had dried up when creditors called their loans that were pledged against these assets. The decline in the value of these real estate–related securities precipitated the financial crisis. It is probable that had investment banks held tech stocks on margin when prices collapsed in 2000, a similar liquidity crisis would have occurred.

THE ROLE OF THE FEDERAL RESERVE IN MITIGATING THE CRISIS

Lending is the lifeblood, the oil that lubricates the functioning of all large economies. In a financial crisis, institutions that were once believed as safe and trustworthy are suddenly viewed with suspicion. When Lehman failed, fears spread that many other financial institutions were also in difficulty. This prompted lenders to call their loans and cut their lines of credit at the same time investors sold risky assets and attempted to increase the liquidity—or proportion of "safe" assets—in their portfolios.

There is only one entity that can provide such liquidity in a time of crisis, and that is the central bank—an institution that Walter Bagehot, a nineteenth-century English journalist, dubbed "the Lender of Last Resort."[28] The central bank creates liquidity by crediting reserves to banks that either borrow from or sell securities to the central bank. Banks can, on demand, turn these reserves into central bank notes or *currency*, the ultimate liquid asset. In this way the central banks can respond to a run on a bank, or the desire of depositors to withdraw their deposits in the form of currency, by loaning such banks any quantity of reserves against their assets, whether or not the quality or price of these assets had declined.

THE LENDER OF LAST RESORT SPRINGS TO ACTION

After the Lehman bankruptcy, the Fed did provide the liquidity the market desired. On September 19, three days after the Reserve Primary Fund announced it would break below a dollar, the Treasury announced that it was insuring all participating money market funds to the full amount of the investor's balance. The Treasury indicated that it was using the money in its Exchange Stabilization Fund, normally used for foreign exchange transactions, to back its insurance plan. Since the Treasury had only $50 billion in its fund, less than 2 percent of the assets in money market funds, the Treasury would have had to rely on an unlimited line of credit to the Fed to make good on its pledge. The Fed itself created a credit facility to extend nonrecourse loans to banks buying commercial paper from mutual funds,[29] and a month later the Money Market Investor Funding Facility was established.

On September 29, 2008, the Federal Deposit Insurance Corporation (FDIC), announced that it entered into a loss-sharing arrangement with Citigroup on a $312 billion pool of loans, with Citigroup absorbing the first $42 billion of losses and the FDIC absorbing losses beyond that. The Fed provided a nonrecourse loan on the remaining $270 billion of the plan. This was followed in January by a similar agreement at about one-third the size with Bank of America. In return, Citigroup issued the FDIC $12 billion in preferred stock and warrants. On September 18, the Fed entered into a $180 billion swap arrangement with leading world central banks to improve liquidity within the global financial markets.

In addition to the money market mutual fund guarantees announced immediately following the Lehman bankruptcy, the FDIC announced on October 7 an increase in deposit insurance coverage to $250,000 per depositor, which was authorized by the Emergency Economic Stabilization Act of 2008 that Congress passed four days earlier. In addition, on October 14 the FDIC created a new Temporary Liquidity Guarantee Program to guarantee the senior debt of all FDIC-insured institutions and their holding companies, as well as deposits in non-interest-bearing deposit accounts.[30] In effect, the government's guarantee of senior debt effectively guaranteed all deposits, since deposits have prior claim in the bankruptcy code.

The only way the FDIC was able to guarantee the funds provided through these policy initiatives was with the full backing of the Federal Reserve. The FDIC does have a trust fund, but its size is a tiny fraction of the deposits it insures.[31] The credibility of the FDIC to make good on its promises, like that of the Exchange Stabilization Fund used to "insure" the money market accounts, depends on an unlimited line of credit that the agency has with the Federal Reserve.

Why did the Federal Reserve and Chairman Bernanke take all these bold actions to ensure sufficient liquidity to the private sector? Because of the lessons that he and other economists learned from what the central banks did *not* do during the Great Depression.

Every macroeconomist has studied the 1963 work *The Monetary History of the United States* written by the University of Chicago Nobel Prize–winning economist Milton Friedman. His research built a damning case against the Federal Reserve for failing to provide reserves to the banking system during the Great Depression. It was certain that Ben Bernanke, who received his PhD in economics with a specialty of monetary theory and policy at the Massachusetts Institute of Technology, was acutely aware of Friedman's research and was determined to avoid repeating the Fed's mistakes.[32] In a speech delivered at Milton Friedman's ninetieth birthday celebration in 2002, six years before the financial crisis, Bernanke, addressing Professor Friedman, said, "Regarding the Great Depression. You're right, we did it. We're very sorry. But thanks to you, we won't do it again."[33]

SHOULD LEHMAN BROTHERS HAVE BEEN SAVED?

Although the Federal Reserve sprang into action following the demise of Lehman Brothers, economists and policy analysts will debate for years whether the central bank should have bailed out the ailing investment bank in the first place. Despite denials by the Federal Reserve that it did not have full legal authority to rescue Lehman, the facts dictate otherwise. In 1932, Congress amended the original Federal Reserve Act of 1913 by adding Section 13(3), which stated:

> In unusual and exigent circumstances, the Board of Governors of the Federal Reserve System, by the affirmative vote of not less than five members, may authorize any Federal reserve bank, during such periods as the said board may determine . . . to discount for any individual, partnership, or corporation, notes, drafts, and bills of exchange when [they] are secured to the satisfaction of the Federal Reserve bank: *Provided*, That before discounting . . . the Federal Reserve bank shall obtain evidence that such individual, partnership, or corporation is unable to secure adequate credit accommodations from other banking institutions.[34]

The act makes it clear that on the weekend before Lehman Brothers declared bankruptcy, it qualified for Fed lending, as Lehman was clearly unable to secure adequate credit accommodations from other banking institutions. Lawrence Ball, chairman of the Economics Department at Johns Hopkins University and author of *The Fed and Lehman Brothers: Setting the Record Straight on a Financial Disaster*, comes to the same conclusions.

The reason that the Fed did not bail out Lehman was more about politics than legalities. Earlier government bailouts of Bear Stearns, Fannie Mae, and Freddie Mac garnered considerable criticism from the public and particularly Republicans. After the March bailout of Bear Stearns, the word went out from the Bush administration: "No More Bailouts." Secretary of Treasury Henry Paulson told Lehman Brothers shortly after the Bear bailout that it should get its house in order and that it should not expect help from the Fed. Just days before Lehman filed, the Fed had rejected a $40 billion loan request from the firm. Treasury Secretary Paulson hoped that with so much advance notice, a Lehman failure would be digested by the financial markets without significant disruption.[35]

But the truth of the matter was that in March, when the Treasury warned Lehman to clean up its balance sheet, it was already too late. Lehman not only had borrowed heavily to buy subprime mortgages, but had recently, with the Bank of America, lent $17 billion to Tishman Speyer to buy the Archstone-Smith Trust for $22.2 billion. Lehman was hoping to sell the debt to new buyers for hefty fees, much as Blackstone did when it sold Sam Zell's properties at the peak of the market. But Lehman was left with $5 billion in unsold real estate, in what some describe as the worst deal Lehman Brothers ever made.[36] Although CEO Richard Fuld continued to insist that Lehman was solvent, traders knew that because of the falling real estate market, Lehman had little chance to survive. The path to bankruptcy had been irrevocably set after Lehman plunged into mortgage-related securities and the overheated property market.

The Fed's decision to bail out AIG was necessitated by the financial chaos that followed the Lehman bankruptcy. The Fed and the Treasury, shocked by investors' rush to cash and the surging risk premiums in international money markets, believed that another bankruptcy that threw hundreds of billions of dollars of bonds and credit default swaps into question would likely bring down the global financial system. Even though AIG, as an insurance company, was arguably further from the Federal Reserve's sphere of responsibility than Lehman, the Fed saved the insurance giant.[37] I have little doubt that had AIG failed first, a similar financial panic would have forced the Fed to bail out Lehman the next day.

Despite its failure to bail out Lehman, the Federal Reserve did flood the financial system with credit following its bankruptcy, and this action stabilized both credit and the money supply. In the Great Depression, the money supply, measured as the sum of demand and savings deposits (M2), fell by 29 percent between August 1929 and March 1933.[38] In contrast, the money supply actually rose during the 2008 financial crisis as the Federal Reserve increased the total reserves by over $1 trillion. This action provided sufficient reserves, so that banks were not forced to call in loans as they were forced to in the 1930s. Although many questioned whether the later injections of reserves (called *quantitative easing*) aided the economy, there was little doubt that the initial provisions of liquidity were critical to stabilizing the financial markets and preventing the downturn from becoming substantially worse.

ECONOMIC AND FINANCIAL IMPACT OF GREAT FINANCIAL CRISIS

Impact on Real Output

The credit shock, sharply falling real estate prices, and plunging stock markets precipitated the deepest recession in the developed world economies since World War II. In the United States, real GDP declined 4.0 percent from the second quarter of 2008 through the second quarter of 2009, eclipsing the previous record of 3.1 percent during the 1973–1975 recession by a wide margin. The 18-month recession, which lasted from December 2007 to June 2009, was also the longest since the 43-month Great Depression of the early 1930s as unemployment reached 10.0 percent in October 2009. Although this was 0.8 percentage points below the record postwar level of 10.8 percent set in November 1982, the jobless rate remained above 8 percent for three years, more than twice as long as the 1981–1982 recession.

Although the crisis originated in the United States, the decline in US GDP was less than in most of the developed world: output declined 9.14 percent in Japan, 5.50 percent in the Eurozone, and 6.80 percent in Germany, Europe's largest economy. Canada, whose banks never became as overleveraged in real estate assets as in the United States, experienced the mildest downturn.

The emerging economies withstood the economic shock much better than the developed world; real GDP growth slowed but did not decline in fast-growing countries such as China and India. For emerging economies as a whole, GDP declined only 3 percent, and by the second quarter of 2009, their output had surpassed their previous high. In contrast, it was not until the end of 2011 that the United States regained the output lost. Japan reached its peak output at the end of 2013, and Europe not until 2015.

Despite the severity of the Great Recession, its depth in no way compares with the decline in economic activity that occurred during the Great Depression of the 1930s. Real GDP in the United States fell 26.3 percent between 1929 and 1933, more than five times the decline in the Great Recession, and unemployment soared to between 25 and 30 percent.[39, 40] One reason for the difference between the Great Depression of 1929–1933 and the Great Recession of 2007–2009 was the behavior of the price level. Consumer prices declined by 27 percent between September 1929 and March 1933, while the maximum decline of the CPI during the Great Recession was 3.5 percent.[41] By March 2010, the CPI surpassed its precrisis peak, while it took 14 years for consumer prices to recover to their 1929 level following the Great Depression.

Deflation worsens a business cycle, since a fall in wages and prices increases the burden of debt, which increases in real value as prices decline. Consumers were already burdened by record debt levels in 2007 before the financial crisis. Had wages and prices fallen as they did in the Great Depression, the burden of consumer and mortgage debt would have been more than one-third larger in real terms, greatly increasing the number of insolvencies.[42] This is the reason that stabilization of the price level was a priority for the Federal Reserve and is a major reason why consumer and business spending did not decline as much in the 2007–2009 recession compared with what happened in the 1930s.[43]

Financial Markets

Despite the actions taken by the Federal Reserve to moderate the economic contraction, the credit disruption that followed the Lehman bankruptcy had a devastating impact on the equity markets, which suffered their worst decline in 75 years. In the nine weeks following September 15, the S&P 500 Index fell 40 percent to an intraday low of 740 on November 21. Ultimately, this broad-based benchmark sank to a 12-year low of 676 on March 9, 2009, nearly 57 percent below its closing peak reached 1.5 years earlier. Although the decline in the benchmark index exceeded the previous postwar record of 48 percent that occurred between January 1973 and October 1974, it did not approach the decline that ushered in the Great Depression, when stocks fell by more than 87 percent.[44] From the market high of October 2007 through March 2009, US stock market wealth had declined $11 trillion, a sum of more than 70 percent of US GDP.

The volatility of stock prices increased sharply, as it always does in bear markets. The VIX volatility index, which measures the premium built into puts and calls on the stock market (in effect measuring the cost of insuring a stock portfolio), soared from under 10 in March 2007, before the crisis began, to nearly 90 immediately following the Lehman bankruptcy. This level exceeded any other in the postwar period, except that immediately following the October 19, 1987, stock market crash.[45]

Another measure of volatility, the number of days that the stock market rose or fell by 5 percent or more, increased sharply to levels not reached since the early 1930s. Between the Lehman bankruptcy on September 15 and December 1, there were nine days when the Dow

Industrials dropped by at least 5 percent, and six days when it rose by 5 percent or more. Except for the 1930s, when a record 78 days saw changes of 5 percent or more, these 15 days of changes of 5 percent or more exceeded the total for any other full decade since 1890.[46]

The plunge in the US equity markets was echoed abroad. Around the world, approximately $33 trillion of stock market wealth was lost, about half the world's annual GDP.[47] In local currency, the Morgan Stanley EAFE Index for non-US developed markets declined by nearly the same magnitude as in the United States, but because the dollar appreciated during the period, the total decline was 62 percent in dollar terms. The emerging market stocks fell 64 percent in dollar terms, although they fell less in their own currencies, as almost all emerging market currencies, except the Chinese yuan, depreciated against the dollar.[48]

The decline in the emerging stock markets was nearly identical to the decline suffered during the Asian financial crisis in 1997–1998, but the emerging market indexes at their 2009 lows remained well above the levels reached at the bottom of the 2002 bear market. This contrasted with the United States and most other developed markets, which fell below their 2002 bear market lows.

Certain equity sectors that held up well in the early stages of the market decline fell sharply as credit markets froze. REITs are a case in point: Buying them for their yield, investors at first flocked to these stocks as interest rates fell, and REITs actually rallied in the week after Lehman went under. But when investors feared that lenders would pull credit lines, REITs lost on average an astounding two-thirds of their value in the next 10 weeks and fell a total of 75 percent by the time the bear market ended in March 2009. Real estate trusts that were funded by short-term loans, or that took on extra leverage during the boom in an effort to boost yields to investors, were hit particularly hard.[49]

The financial sector of the S&P 500 declined 84 percent from its peak in May 2007 to its trough in March 2009, wiping out about $2.5 trillion of equity. The percentage decline exceeded the 82.2 percent decline in the S&P 500 technology sector that occurred from 2000 to 2002, but since the tech sector had valuations at the peak more than three times that of the financial sector, the equity values lost in the tech crash were a much higher $4 trillion.[50] Nevertheless, while the tech crash wiped out five years of total stock market gains, the financial crisis wiped out 17 years, sending equity prices down to 1992 levels.

Many financial firms declined much more than the 84 percent average for the sector. Peak to trough, Bank of America lost 94.5 percent of the market value of its equity, Citibank lost 98.3 percent, and AIG lost an astounding 99.5 percent.[51] The equity holders of Lehman Brothers, Washington Mutual, and a large number of smaller financial institutions, lost everything, while shareholders of Fannie Mae and Freddie Mac, the giant government-sponsored enterprises that went public in early 1980s, held on to a sliver of hope that they might recover some of their capital.[52] Many international banks fared just as poorly as US banks. From peak to trough, Barclays fell 93 percent, BNP Paribas 79 percent, HSBC 75 percent, and UBS 88 percent, and the Royal Bank of Scotland, which needed a loan from the Bank of England to survive, fell 99 percent.

Impact on Earnings

Because of mark-to-market accounting rules, the fall in the operating earnings of S&P 500 firms exactly matched the 58 percent fall in the index itself. S&P 500 operating earnings declined 58 percent, from a record $91.47 in the 12 months ending on June 30, 1997, to $39.61 in the 12 months ending September 30, 2009. But the decline in reported earnings was much greater: the 12-month reported earnings fell, from a high of $84.92 in 1997, to only $6.86 for the 12 months ending March 31, 2009. This 92 percent decline in earnings exceeded the 83 percent decline in earnings that took place in the Great Depression from 1929 through 1932.[53]

The huge write-downs by the financial firms were the main cause of the devastating earnings drop of the S&P 500 in 2008 and 2009. The $61 billion fourth-quarter 2008 loss of AIG, which had a weight of less than 0.2 percent in the index, more than wiped out the total profits of the 30 most profitable firms in the S&P 500, which comprised almost half the index value. In Chapter 10, we discussed that S&P's method of aggregating firms' earnings dollar for dollar vastly overstates the P/E ratio of the index during recessions. In fact, after-tax aggregate corporate profits taken from the national income and product accounts, which does not follow the mark-to-market approach, fell by less than 20 percent during the financial crisis.

The Short-Term Bond Market and LIBOR

One of the most watched spreads in the money market is that between the rate set by the Federal Reserve in the Fed funds market (a market to facilitate the lending of reserves between US banks) and the interbank lending rates outside the United States, called the London Interbank Offered Rate (LIBOR).

FIGURE 23.2

Stock prices, the LIBOR spread, and major events during the crisis

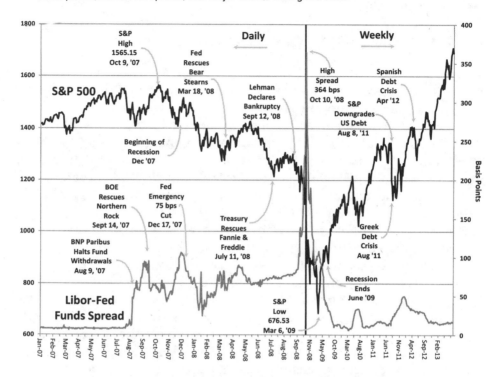

Figure 23.2 shows the S&P 500 and the LIBOR spread from 2007 through 2012. Before the crisis, the LIBOR stayed very close to the federal funds target, usually within 10 basis points. The first rumblings of trouble in the banking sector came in August 2007, when the LIBOR-Fed funds spread jumped above 50 basis points, in response to the BNP Paribas announcement of stopping fund redemptions and the problems at Northern Rock in the United Kingdom. Over the next 12 months, as the subprime crisis grew, the LIBOR-funds spread remained mostly between 50 and 100 basis points. But the LIBOR spread soared after the Lehman bankruptcy, and on October 10 the difference between the LIBOR and the Fed funds rate reached an unheard-of 364 basis points.

It was extraordinarily frustrating to policy makers that the interest rate upon which so many loans were based rose at the same time the Fed was aggressively lowering the Fed funds rate. After the Federal Reserve flooded the financial system with reserves, the LIBOR spread finally came down, but it did not fall decisively under 100 basis points until the stock market began to recover from its bear market low in March 2009, three months before the National Bureau of Economic Research called the recession over.[54]

CONCLUSION: REFLECTIONS ON THE CRISIS

The financial crisis that led to the severe 2008–2009 recession was caused by the overleveraging of real estate–related securities in the portfolios of key financial institutions. This overleveraging was motivated by several factors: the decline in risk that took place during the unusually long period of financial stability that preceded the financial crisis (the Great Moderation), the mis-rating of mortgage-related securities by the rating agencies, the approval by the political establishment of the expansion of homeownership, and the lack of oversight by critical regulatory organizations, particularly the Federal Reserve. But it is the executives of these financial firms who should be held the most accountable. They were unable to grasp the threats that would befall their firms once the housing boom ended, and they abdicated responsibility for assessing risks to technicians running faulty credit-rating programs.

On a macroeconomic level, the financial crisis punctured the myth that grew during Greenspan's tenure as Fed chairman that the Federal Reserve could fine-tune the economy and eliminate the business cycle. Nevertheless, despite having failed to see the crisis brewing, the Federal Reserve acted quickly to ensure liquidity and prevented the recession from becoming far more severe than it turned out to be.

The financial crisis of 2008 and the subsequent recession can be illustrated by the following analogy. There is no doubt that the improvements in engineering and safety factors have made the passenger car safer than it was 50 years ago, but that does not mean that the automobile is safe at any speed. A small bump on the road can flip the most advanced passenger car speeding 120 miles per hour today just as surely as an older model traveling 80 miles per hour. During the Great Moderation, risks were indeed lower, and financial firms understandably leveraged their balance sheets in response. But their leverage became too great, and all that was needed was an unexpected increase in the default rate on subprime mortgages—that "bump on the road"—to catapult the economy and financial markets into the biggest crisis in nearly a century.

24

Covid-19 Pandemic

March 2015: Early Warning

If anything kills over 10 million people over the next few decades it is most likely to be a highly infectious virus, not a war. Yet, we're not ready for the next epidemic.

—Bill Gates, Ted Talk, March 2015

January 21–24, 2020, World Economic Forum, Davos, Switzerland: Two Views

We have it totally under control. It's going to be just fine.

—Donald Trump, President of the United States

The virus may be a game changer. If you are long-term, you better not be leveraged.

—David Tepper, CEO of Appaloosa Money Management

On February 12, 2020, I flew to Scottsdale, Arizona, to address a group of high-level financial advisors on future stock and bond returns the following morning. As I arrived at the airport, stocks had just hit yet another all-time high. Investors were enjoying the second longest bull market in US history. Since the bottom of the Great Financial Crisis in March 2009, stocks had been on a tear and not fallen by 20 percent, the standard definition of a bear market, in nearly 12 years.[1] Many speculated what would or could bring this bull market to an end.

Certainly, there was ominous news of the spread of a novel virus in Wuhan, China. On January 31, the Department of Health and Human Services declared the coronavirus a public health emergency, and President Trump banned flights from China. Yet the stock market continued upward. We had virus scares before, the SARS-1 virus in 2003, the MERS virus in 2012, and extremely deadly Ebola outbreaks in Africa during the previous decade. Yet none of these impacted the United States, and in early February the emergence of SARS-Covid 2 appeared no different.

In my seminar, I posed the following question to the nearly 100 advisors assembled: What do you think will end this remarkable bull market? Listed were several choices: terrorist strikes, Mideast war, unexpected Fed tightening, political developments, and the one that I and nearly half the audience chose: "Momentum traders push the market too high and stocks self-correct." When the electronic vote was tallied, only one person chose my last choice: a pandemic.

As it turned out, we had reached the top of the bull market the day before my presentation. In short order, an explosive rise in Covid-19 cases turned investor complacency into outright panic. By March 12, stocks entered bear market territory and continued downward. Never had the market gone down so much in so few days. By the market bottom on March 29, the S&P 500 had declined by nearly 34 percent, and over $20 trillion had been wiped off the market value of stocks worldwide in less than seven weeks. Figure 24.1 show the rapidity of the market's decline, one of the most rapid in history.

FIGURE 24.1

S&P 500 during Covid-19, January–July 2020

PERCEPTION VERSUS REALITY

Investors' fears were real. But was the market reaction rational? Assume the disruptions caused by the pandemic wiped out the profits of each publicly traded company for one year, and by March 2021, with the development of vaccines and therapeutics, profits returned to normal.

If a stock is selling for 20 times earnings, (which was approximately the average P/E ratio of the US market before the pandemic hit), then eliminating one year's earnings should send the price down by only 5 percent, since one year of earnings represents 5 percent of the value of the company. Even if firms went profitless for two years, the drop in stock prices would be 10 percent. I often appeared on media saying the market should fall only between 5 and 10 percent, and the market plunge presented an excellent buying opportunity for long-term investors.

This history of pandemics also pointed to a market overreaction to the Covid-19 threat. The Spanish flu pandemic of 1918–1919, which was deadlier than Covid-19, especially for younger, healthy individuals, had a minor impact on the economy or the market. More recently, the influenza epidemics of 1957 (Asian flu) and 1968 (Hong Kong flu), although less deadly than Covid-19, had little economic or market consequence.

Yet those pandemics were in earlier times. With 24-7 news channels showing overtaxed hospitals and overflowing morgues, the public's anxiety about the pandemic soared. The market's reaction was not a surprise; I have always maintained that fear has a much stronger grip on investors' attitudes than the full weight of historical evidence.

The public's alarm brought many sectors of the economy to a complete stop, and layoffs soared. Weekly jobless claims in the United States, one of the most sensitive indicators to economic activity, jumped from just over 200,000 in the last week of February, to over 6.1 million by the first week of April, exceeding the previous high reached in 1982 by a factor of 9.

The economic swoon and market collapse prompted both the US government and the Federal Reserve to respond with support that far exceeded that of the Great Financial Crisis. The Fed lowered the target funds rate once again to near zero, flooded the banking system with reserves, and restarted many programs, such as the Primary Dealer Credit Facility and the Money Market Mutual Fund Liquidity Facility that had been initiated during the financial crisis 12 years earlier. But the Federal Reserve went much further than it had earlier, originating a main-street lending facility for businesses and nonprofit organizations and for the first time lent money to state and local governments.

The enormity of the fiscal response, and the money created by the Federal Reserve to facilitate the burst in federal spending, marked the biggest difference between the government's response to the financial crisis and to the Covid-19 pandemic. Twelve years earlier, federal fiscal support consisted of the American Recovery and Reinvestment Act (which included the Cash for Clunkers program) and totaled $830 billion. In contrast, the CARES Act enacted in March 2020 provided $2.2 trillion grants to individuals and businesses through the Payroll Protection Program (PPP), grants to state and local governments and businesses, significant tax cuts, and sharply enhanced unemployment compensation. Further December legislation added another $900 billion to the stimulus. The urgency of the crisis melted conservative opposition to spending, and both measures were almost unanimously passed by Congress and signed by President Trump.[2]

Almost all this spending was financed by the Federal Reserve. On March 15, 2020, the Fed said that it would buy at least $500 billion in Treasury securities and $200 billion in government-guaranteed mortgage-backed securities over "the coming months." Then on March 23, it announced the bond purchases to be "open-ended," indicating it would buy securities "in the amounts needed to support smooth market functioning and effective transmission of monetary policy to broader financial conditions."

This massive response by the government and Federal Reserve had an electrifying effect on the stock market. On March 24, the S&P 500 Index jumped 9.38 percent, the second highest one-day increase in history. On June 10, the Fed reinforced its accommodative policy by saying it would buy at least $80 billion a month in Treasuries and $40 billion in residential and commercial mortgage-backed securities until further notice. As a result of these purchases, between mid-March and early December 2020, the Fed's portfolio of securities grew from $3.9 trillion to $6.6 trillion through purchasing $2.7 trillion of newly issued government debt used to finance the fiscal spending. By March 2022, when the Fed stopped buying government securities, its balance sheet had ballooned to nearly $9 billion.

CENTRAL BANK MONETARY EXPANSION

The US Treasury is prohibited from buying bonds directly from the Federal Reserve,[3] requiring the US government to sell its bonds into the open market. But if investors know that the central bank is going to be a buyer of these securities in a matter of days, they are quite willing to purchase the bonds for a short period of time, especially if interest rates are low.

In that case, the Federal Reserve is in effect buying bonds directly from the Treasury and pays for them by crediting the Treasury's account at the Fed. The government then sends the money it receives from the Fed to individuals, businesses, and local governments who are eligible to receive the funds. In this manner, the monetary balances of the public, state, and local governments are enhanced by the fiscal stimulus.

Right after these programs were implemented, the money supply surged, defined either as M1 (currency plus checking accounts) or the broader based M2, which most economists believe is the more important definition of money.[4] The M2 money supply from March to April jumped over 3.5 percent, an annualized rate of 50 percent, one of the largest one-month increases in history. This increase far exceeded any increase in money that followed the Lehman bankruptcy 12 years earlier.

The sharp jump in the money supply prompted me to write an article on April 14, just five weeks after Covid-19 struck, which I circulated among my colleagues. It was entitled "Who Pays for the War on Covid 19?"[5] I wrote that the huge increase in the money supply will not come freely. History demonstrated that such an increase has inevitably sparked inflation, and I predicted that the current monetary surge would have "dramatic implications for both our economy and financial markets." I continued, "Rising inflation and interest rates will end the nearly forty-year bull market in bonds. There is no 'free lunch.' The 'War on Covid-19' will be paid for by those holding monetary assets whose value will be eroded by the upcoming inflation."

My article was greeted by much skepticism. Oil prices were plummeting, and the shift to work at home and online shopping sent commercial rental rates plummeting. Feeding skepticism was the fact that many economists had sent warnings about rapid inflation following the massive injections of liquidity that the Fed had implemented during and after the Great Financial Crisis. Yet no inflation came to pass. In fact, after the financial crisis, inflation ran significantly below the Federal Reserve's 2 percent target.

What was crucially different between the Fed response to the Great Financial Crisis and to the Covid-19 crisis was that in the former, most of the Fed's liquidity went to enhance the banks' excess reserves, and little was lent to the private sector. During the Covid-19 crisis, the government was crediting money directly in the bank accounts of individuals, businesses, and state and local governments, instead of just into the reserve accounts of the banking system. As Friedman showed in the

Monetary History, the Fed did in fact increase its open market purchases during the Great Depression, but not nearly enough to offset the sharp contraction in deposits. As a result, the money supply fell sharply, prices and incomes plunged, and unemployment subsequently soared to over 30 percent.

The historical behavior of the money supply before and during the Covid-19 pandemic is shown in Figure 24.2. The top panel covers the period from 2006 through 2021. After increasing moderately in the years preceding the pandemic, the M2 money supply increased 17.5 percent from March to July 2020. Furthermore, from May 2020 to the end of 2001, the annualized rate of growth exceeded 12.1 percent far more than double the prepandemic rate.

FIGURE 24.2

M2 money supply, 1970–2021

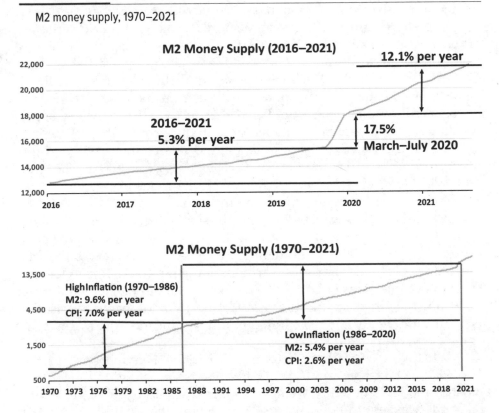

The contrast between the behavior of the money supply during Covid-19 and the financial crisis was stark. To be sure, the Fed expanded the money supply following the Lehman crisis, and M2 increased 5 percent in the following four months. But money growth flattened out in 2009 and then increased less than 4 percent per year.

The bottom panel gives a 50-year perspective on inflation and money supply growth. From 1970 through 1986, a high inflationary period, money supply growth averaged 9.6 percent per year, and the CPI increased at an annual rate of 7.0 percent per year, about 2.5 percentage points lower. This is very close to what monetary theory dictates: in the long run, the rate of inflation is equal to the rate of growth of money above the rate of growth of the economy, the latter approximated by real GDP growth, which averaged between 2 and 3 percent over that period.

After Paul Volcker, chairman of the Federal Reserve, squeezed the money supply and sent interest rates to record heights in the early 1980s to slow the rate of inflation, the United States entered a prolonged period of moderate inflation. From 1986 until the 2020 pandemic, a 34-year period, the money supply increased at 5.4 percent annualized rate and inflation averaged 2.6 percent per year. It should be noted that the close relation between money supply growth and inflation holds over a long period of time. In the short run, there can be substantial lags between monetary impulses and the rate of inflation.

Figure 24.3 presents the longest time series of inflation money growth. The nineteenth and early twentieth-century data are taken from Friedman's *Monetary History*. Inflation is lagged two years since this represents the average lag between the effect of money on inflation.

Money supply growth in 2020 was the highest single-year increase in US history, exceeding the years of rapid money growth in both World War I and World War II. From every perspective, it seemed very likely that the money explosion would have a significant impact on both inflation and the financial markets.

ALTERNATIVE FINANCING OF THE FISCAL STIMULUS

Had the Federal Reserve not accommodated the huge deficit of the federal government, the economy and the financial markets would have behaved very differently. The government would have had to borrow money from the public rather than from the central bank. This would have resulted in higher long-term interest rates and substantially offset the expansionary effect of the fiscal stimulus. The higher interest rates would have slowed the rise in stock prices, increased borrowing costs, and reduced liquidity growth. But inflation would be controlled.

FIGURE 24.3

Annual M2 money growth and inflation (lagged 2 years)

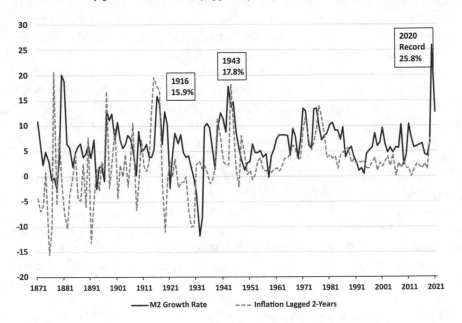

Raising taxes was another alternative to finance the fiscal expansion, reducing after-tax income to offset the increased benefits received by those most impacted by the Covid-19 pandemic. But there was no appetite for tax hikes in Congress, and that alternative was not pursued. Instead, the "war on Covid" was paid for by monetary expansion and higher inflation.

MISSED FORECASTS AND UNDERSTATED INFLATION

The Federal Reserve was clearly surprised by the inflation that broke out in 2021. In December 2020 the Fed forecast that the personal consumption expenditure (PCE), deflator, the Fed's preferred measure of measuring inflation, would rise by 1.8 percent in 2021 and rise only 0.10 of a percent further to 1.9 percent in 2022. Surprisingly, the highest estimate of 2021 inflation among all 19 members of the Federal Open Market Committee was only 2.3 percent. In fact, PCE inflation came in at nearly 5 percent, and inflation measured by the more popular CPI soared to 7.5 percent

The central bank was not alone in underestimating inflationary forces. Bloomberg published an article in December 2020 entitled, "Get Ready for the Great Inflation Mirage," which downplayed the fears that some had raised because of the magnitude of the fiscal and monetary response.[6] The median forecast of economists surveyed by Bloomberg calls for a subdued 1.1 percent year-over-year increase. Michael Feroli, chief US economist at JPMorgan Chase said, "We think inflation is going to be muted because unemployment will still be high."[7] That was the consensus: a surplus of labor would keep wages in check and prices low. The unprecedented expansion of the money supply was universally ignored. As inflation picked up in 2021, the Fed used the term *transitory* to describe rising prices, attributing the increases to unusual circumstances in specific sectors (such as used cars) and supply-chain disruptions that were determined temporary.

In fact, the supply chain problems that developed in 2021 were not due just to Covid-related disruptions, but mostly to the massive increase in the demand for goods caused by both the increase in fiscal stimulus and the shift to goods from services that accompanied the pandemic. As inflation worsened later in 2021, the "transitory" moniker became a much-mocked description of events, and Federal Reserve Chairman Jerome Powell announced late in November 2021 that he was "retiring" the term.

One of the reasons that so many underestimated the inflation rate in 2021 was that many overestimated the inflationary consequence of the quantitative easing that took place after the Great Financial Crisis. Many reasoned that if the massive provision of reserves combined with record deficits did not cause inflation in the 2010s, then why should there be any from the stimulus provided during Covid-19? As noted earlier, the key distinction between the two episodes was that the Fed expansion during the financial crisis expanded reserves but did little to increase the money supply.

Another reason for the underestimate of inflation is the methodology of the Bureau of Labor Statistics (BLS), the agency that gathers information on the consumer prices. Their procedure is extremely slow in recording price increases in the housing sector, which accounts for almost one-third of the weight in the CPI. That is because the cost of housing is determined by infrequently sampling of existing rental agreements and housing prices. The Bureau's computations ignored the fact that the Case-Shiller index of housing prices had increased by over 20 percent, and national rental cost indexes had increased by almost the same amount. Eventually these higher prices would be included in the computations, overstating inflation in the future while understating it in 2020 and 2021.

The Federal Reserve's mis-estimates of the nature of inflation and the impact of their monetary expansion eventually forced the central bank to step on the brakes in 2022. Chairman Jay Powell sharply raised interest rates which precipitated a bear market in stocks and slowed the upward movement of commodity and real estate prices. Had he raised interest rates much earlier, and speculative excesses in 2021 would have been contained and inflation would have been much lower.

EFFECT OF INFLATION ON STOCKS AND BONDS

In the media, I emphasized throughout the crisis that stocks were "real assets"; in other words, their value depended on the earnings power of capital such as plant, equipment, copyrights, trademarks, and intellectual property, whose value would rise with the price level. This contrasted with bonds and money, which are monetary assets that promise to pay returns in dollars that are not adjusted in any way by changes in the purchasing power of those dollars.[8]

In fact, firms that are "levered," that is, those who have large amounts of low-interest loans and bonds on their balance sheet, may gain significantly from inflation. In the early stages of the Covid-19 crisis, there was an emphasis on firms with low debt and high-quality balance sheets, since these firms were the most likely to survive an economic downturn. Indeed, the spreads between lower and higher quality debt soared in the early stages of the pandemic as fears mounted that firms tied to the travel and leisure industries, such as airlines, cruises, and hotels, may fail. Banks were also put on special watch and restricted (as during the financial crisis) to increasing dividends, since many of their loans were tied to commercial real estate, which might default. Instead, as the economy recovered and the government bestowed massive fiscal aid, there were very few bankruptcies.

Another form of leverage that benefits firms as inflation increases are fixed labor contracts. Many employees' wage rates and salaries are set once a year, based in part on the expectations of future inflation. If inflation increases more than expected, the real cost of labor will decline, raising firms' profit margins.

Of course, both of these effects do not last if inflation continues for a lengthy period. Labor will eventually demand compensation for the loss of purchasing power, and interest rates will rise to match higher inflationary expectations. In the interim, the unexpected increase in inflation caused by monetary and fiscal expansion will increase corporate profit margins.

STOCK VALUATIONS DURING AND AFTER THE PANDEMIC

When excess liquidity is created by the central bank, it will first flow into markets that are liquid. The stock market is certainly one of those markets. It should not be surprising that stocks increased 44 percent to record highs between February 2020 and December of 2021. From the bottom of the market in March 2020, the S&P 500 Index rose by over 100 percent.

Over this time, earnings on the S&P 500 increased from a forward-looking $180 in early 2020 to $220 per share in December 2021, a 22 percent increase. Since prices increased twice as fast as earnings, the P/E ratio of the market rose from approximately 18 to 21.

There were several reasons for the increase in the P/E ratio. One was the strong performance of tech stocks, which have a higher valuation than the overall market. But there were other forces at work; real interest rates continued their long slide from their peak of 4 percent in 2000, and the 10-year TIP fell below –1 percent. Furthermore, the real rate of return on nonindexed bonds fell ever more.

An acronym was used repeatedly to describe the continued upward trend of equity valuations in the years following the Great Financial Crisis: *TINA* for "There is no alternative." The meaning was that although stock prices were high relative to fundamentals on a historical basis, with interest rates so low, there was no alternative to stocks. Real assets, such as stocks, are attractive in a period of low rates and rising inflation.

COMMODITY PRICES

There are other assets to protect wealth during inflation: commodities and real estate. Both rose rapidly in 2020 and 2021, as the monetary fiscal stimulus increased incomes of individuals and liquidity in the market. The Commodity Research Bureau (CRB) index of 19 commodity prices, after falling sharply during the very early stages of the pandemic, rose by over 20 percent from prepandemic levels to the end of 2021.

Oil, the single most important commodity, was selling around $60 per barrel at the end of 2019, but began to fall soon after reports of the virus spread in China. Even as the US stock market reached its all-time high on February 12, oil had sunk to $50 a barrel. As the virus spread and travel shut down, oil prices experienced the greatest plunge in history. On March 19 it fell from $46 to $27 and continued downward. On April 20, a glut of oil at the Cushing, Oklahoma, pricing point in the United States, futures prices shockingly fell below zero and closed at −$40.32 a barrel. So much oil was delivered to the Cushing site that sellers had to pay for the oil to be carted away.[9]

The price of oil quickly recovered, but other commodities, such as lumber and steel, while sensitive to economic cycles, also responded to the building boom. Lumber prices increased fourfold from prepandemic level until the summer of 2021 before falling back, but by year-end 2021 they were still double the prepandemic level. Shipping rates also surged, and there were similar spurts in the price of other raw materials. The Baltic Dry Index, the major shipping rate of nonoil goods, rose fivefold from prepandemic levels, before falling back.

REAL ESTATE PRICES

Residential real estate prices rose more than 25 percent from March 2000 through December 2021. This increase was the fastest rate of increase recorded since at least 1986, when the Shiller-Case stock price indexes were first constructed. This pace exceeded the rate that occurred during the great housing bubble that preceded the 2008 financial crisis.

The causes of the increase in housing prices differed greatly from what happened 15 years earlier and were far more likely permanent. The housing bubble of 2005–2008 was caused by sharp easing of lending standards enabled by the proliferation of subprime mortgages that allowed buyers, previously unable to get a mortgage, to qualify. But the rise of prices in 2020–2021 was prompted by an increase in demand for housing caused by several factors: the decrease in interest rates, the desire for second vacation homes to escape the pandemic, and importantly, the desire for larger homes that could accommodate a home office as work-at-home opportunities expanded significantly.

The movements of the REIT index mirrored the stock market. The index fell by more than 43 percent from February 20 to March 23, 2020, slightly exceeding the fall in the S&P 500. Like the financial crisis, real estate was not an effective hedge against stock market downdrafts as it had been during the bursting of the tech bubble in 2000–2001. However, the REIT index rebounded sharply and by December 2021 was 18 percent above its prepandemic peak, although it was far less than the 42 percent increase in the S&P 500 Index.

The returns on the components of the REIT index differed widely. The price of commercial office space fell sharply and barely recovered to its prepandemic level by the end of 2021. However, the price of data centers rose steeply, and by the end of 2021 were almost 50 percent above their prepandemic level and the price of self-storage properties almost doubled over the same period.

PERMANENT CHANGES IN THE ECONOMY

The Covid-19 pandemic has killed more than 1 million Americans and perhaps more than 20 million people around the world.[10] It has sickened many more and left many of those who survived with long-term disabilities.

Crises cause individuals to change behavior. Some will be temporary, as the drop in attendance at live events, indoor dining, and tourism. But others will be permanent, both in the economic and financial spheres. The following are some of the changes I believe will be permanent and significant after the acute stage of the pandemic passes:

1. Longer Life Expectancy

The development and efficacy of the MRNA vaccines is breakthrough technology for controlling infectious diseases, enhancing the immune system, and fighting noninfectious diseases such as cancer. Longer life expectancy requires individuals to rethink their retirement planning and asset allocation.

This was a trend already in place before the pandemic, but this will likely accelerate because of the medical breakthroughs that have been achieved. Although the length of retirement is likely to increase, so is the number of years that individuals will work. Generally, there will be a boost of demand for goods and services desired during retirement such as retirement homes and health care, as well as travel and other leisure activities.

2. Increase in Work-at-Home Economy

The ability to connect virtually without gathering at a central office soared during the pandemic and was far more successful than most individuals and economists had expected. This shift will spur the following changes:

a. *Sharp decline in the demand for commercial office space.* This will lower the cost of office space and lower the business density of cities. The reduction of commuting time increases the time available for leisure activities (live events, sports, gaming, travel, etc.).

b. *Increase in online shopping and home entertainment.* The pandemic accelerated the trend to online shopping. It had a great effect on online entertainment, as most movie theaters closed during the pandemic, many permanently. Online entertainment systems will see increased demand.

c. *A fall in business-only travel.* Travel for business conferences will center on tourist destinations, where friends and family and other entertainment can provide motivation for the time and effort to travel to a destination.

d. *A rise in the gig economy.* More workers will engage in multiple activities to generate income, and there will be a marked increase in single-person and small firms. Although there will be a decrease in the importance of corporate culture, there is likely to be a rise in innovation, as individuals are freed from the groupthink that often infects large organizations.

e. *An increase in productivity,* but also a reduction in the number of hours worked. This will have an ambiguous effect on traditionally measured GDP. However, since GDP does not include the value of leisure time, economic welfare, which combines the value of consumption goods and leisure time, will be enhanced.

3. Financial Projections

a. *Flatter yield curves and frequently negative real rates.* Treasury bonds proved an excellent short-term hedge against the Covid-19 shock that sent risk assets plunging. Interest rates and consumer prices dropped in March and April 2020, making nominal Treasury bonds an even more effective hedge than TIPS against demand shocks. As a result, long-term bonds will not respond as strongly to tightening of the Federal Reserve as they had done in the past. This will lead to flatter yield curves and more instances of "inversion." But unlike the past, this yield-curve inversion, unless it is very strong, will not necessarily presage a recession.

b. *Resiliency of stocks and corporate profits.* Most corporations adapted to the crisis faster and more effectively than expected. This response emphasizes the importance of individuals not overreacting to short-term events and taking a long-term view.

Recognize that over 90 percent of the value of most assets relies on the earnings power *more than* one year into the future and that short-term disruptions do not justify sharp declines in asset prices.

c. *The importance of inflation hedges.* The long period of quiescent inflation lulled individuals into believing inflation would not become a problem, but under a fiat money economy, there is no natural limit to the creation of money. Real assets, such as real estate, commodities, and especially stocks, are a critical part of a portfolio. Real interest rates will stay deeply negative and will not be effective at protecting purchasing power. Stocks have positive real yields and inflation protection.

CONCLUSION

It is often said that individuals settle into a world of "local maxima." This means that we get comfortable in doing the things we have always done, perhaps making small changes to improve our conditions when they are easily implemented.

However, many individuals resist large changes, because the cost of these changes is high and a large change might make us worse off. This means there may be changes that make us better off—what we eat, where we live, whom we socialize with, and where we work—but most of us decide that the cost of making those changes is not worth the effort.

Events in the real world often force us to abandon our local maxima and push us into new behaviors. As a result, crisis often spurs innovation. World War II gave birth to atomic energy, the jet engine, and the widespread introduction of flu vaccines and penicillin. Similarly, the Covid-19 crisis, despite the tragic loss of life, accelerated MRNA technology, remote communications, and hopefully, the tools necessary to prevent the next pandemic.

VII

BUILDING WEALTH
THROUGH STOCKS

How Psychology Can Thwart Investment Goals

The rational man—like the Loch Ness monster—is sighted often, but photographed rarely.

—David Dreman, 1998[1]

The market is most dangerous when it looks best; it is most inviting when it looks worst.

—Frank J. Williams, 1930[2]

This book is filled with data, figures, and charts that support a diversified, long-term strategy for stock investors. Yet advice is much easier to take in theory than it is to put into practice. The finance profession is increasingly aware that psychological factors can thwart rational analysis and prevent investors from achieving the best results. The study of these psychological factors has burgeoned into the field of *behavioral finance*.

This chapter is written as a narrative conversation to make it easier to understand the basic research and issues of behavioral finance. Dave is an investor who falls into psychological traps that prevent him from being effective; you may notice similarities between his behavior and your own. If so, the advice in this chapter should help you become a more successful investor. Dave first talks to his wife, Jennifer, and then to an investment counselor who understands behavioral finance. The narrative begins in the fall of 1999, several months prior to the peak in the technology and dot-com bubble that dominated markets at the turn of the century.

THE TECHNOLOGY BUBBLE, 1999–2001

October 1999

Dave: Jen, I've made some important investment decisions. Our portfolio contains nothing but these "old fogy" stocks like Philip Morris, Procter & Gamble, and Exxon. These stocks just aren't doing anything right now. My friends Bob and Paul at work have been making a fortune in internet stocks. I talked with my broker, Allan, about the prospects of these stocks. He said the experts think the internet is the wave of the future. I'm selling some of our stocks that just aren't moving, and then I'm getting into the internet stocks like AOL, Yahoo!, and Inktomi.

Jennifer: I've heard that those stocks are very speculative. Are you sure you know what you're doing?

Dave: Allan says that we are entering a "new economy," spurred by a communications revolution that is going to completely change the way we do business. Those stocks that we owned are old economy stocks. They had their day, but we should be investing for the future. I know these internet stocks are volatile, and I'll watch them very carefully so we won't lose money. Trust me. I think we're finally on the right track.

March 2000

Dave: Jen, have you seen our latest financial statements? We're up 60 percent since October. The Nasdaq crossed 5,000, and no one believes it will stop there. The excitement about the market is spreading; it's become the topic of conversation around the office.

Jen: You seem to be trading in and out of stocks a lot more than you did before. I can't follow what we own!

Dave: Information is hitting the market faster and faster. I have to continually adjust my portfolio. Commissions are so cheap now that it pays to trade on any news affecting stocks. Trust me—look how well we're doing.

July 2000

Jen: Dave, I've looked at our broker's statement. We don't hold those internet stocks any more. Now we own (*she reads from the statement*)

Cisco, EMC, Oracle, Sun Microsystems, Nortel Networks, JDS Uniphase. I don't know what any of these companies do. Do you?

Dave: When the internet stocks crashed in April, I sold out right before we lost all our gains. Unfortunately, we didn't make much on those stocks, but we didn't lose either.

I know we're on the right track now. Those internet companies weren't making any money. All the new firms we now own form the backbone of the internet, and they're all profitable. Allan told me an important principle: Do you know who made the most money in the California gold rush of the 1850s? Not the gold miners. Some of the early diggers found gold, but most found nothing. The real winners from the gold rush were those who sold supplies to the miners—pickaxes, boots, pans, and hiking gear. The lesson is very clear; most of the internet companies are going to fail, but those supplying the backbone of the internet—those supplying the routers, software, and fiber-optic cables—will be the big winners.

Jen: But I think I heard some economist say those companies are way overpriced now; they're selling for hundreds of times earnings.

Dave: Yes, but look at their growth over the last five years—no one has ever seen this before. The economy is changing, and many of the traditional yardsticks of valuation don't apply. Trust me; I'll monitor these stocks. I got us out of those internet stocks in time, didn't I?

November 2000

Dave (*to himself*): What should I do? The last few months have been dreadful. I'm down about 20 percent. Just over two months ago, Nortel was over 80. Now it is around 40. EMC was 30, and now it is around 15. These prices are so cheap; I think I'll use some of my remaining cash to buy more shares at these lower prices. Then my stocks don't have to go up as much for me to get even.

August 2001

Jen: Dave, I've just looked at our brokerage statement. We've been devastated! Almost three-quarters of our retirement money is gone. I thought you were going to monitor our investments closely. Our portfolio shows nothing but huge losses.

Dave: I know; I feel terrible. All the experts said these stocks would rebound, but they kept going down.

Jen: This has happened before. I don't understand why you do so badly. For years you watch the market closely, study all these financial reports, and seem to be very well informed. Yet you still make the wrong decisions. You buy near the highs and sell near the lows. You hold on to losers while selling your winners. You . . .

Dave: I know, I know. My stock investments always go wrong. I think I'm giving up on stocks and sticking with bonds.

Jen: Listen, Dave. I have talked to a few other people about your investing troubles, and I want you to go see an investment counselor. Investment counselors use behavioral psychology to help investors understand why they do poorly. An investment counselor will help you correct this behavior. I made you an appointment already; please go see him.

BEHAVIORAL FINANCE

Dave was skeptical. He thought that understanding stocks required only knowledge of economics, accounting, and mathematics. Dave had never heard the word *psychology* used in any of those subjects. Yet he knew he needed help, and it couldn't hurt to check it out.

Investment Counselor (IC): I have read your profile and talked to your wife, and I believe you are typical of the investor that we counsel here. I adhere to a branch of economics called *behavioral finance*. Many of the ideas my profession explores are based on psychological concepts that have rarely been applied to the stock market and portfolio management.

Let me give you some background: Until recently, finance was dominated by theories that assumed investors maximized their expected utility, or well-being, and always acted rationally. This was an extension of the rational theory of consumer choice under certainty applied to uncertain outcomes.

In the 1970s two psychologists, Amos Tversky and Daniel Kahneman, noted that many individuals did not behave as this theory predicted. Tversky and Kahneman developed a new model—called *prospect theory*—of how individuals actually behave and make decisions when faced with uncertainty.[3] Their model established them as the pioneers of behavioral finance, and their research has been making much headway in the finance profession.

Fads, Social Dynamics, and Stock Bubbles

IC: Let us first discuss your decision to get into the internet stocks. Think back to October 1999. Do you remember why you decided to buy those stocks?

Dave: Yes—my stocks were simply not going anywhere. My friends at work were investing in the internet and making a lot of money. There was so much excitement about these stocks; everyone claimed that the internet was a communications revolution that would change business forever.

IC: When everyone is excited about the market, you should be extremely cautious. Stock prices are not based just on economic values, but on psychological factors that influence the market. Yale economist Robert Shiller, one of the leaders of the behavioral finance movement, has emphasized that fads and social dynamics play a large role in the determination of asset prices.[4] Shiller showed that stock prices have been far too volatile to be explained by fluctuations in economic factors, such as dividends or earnings.[5] He has hypothesized that much of the extra volatility can be explained by fads and fashions that have a large impact on investor decisions.

Dave: I did have my doubts about these internet stocks, but everyone else seemed so sure they were winners.

IC: Note how others influenced your decision against your better judgment. Psychologists have long known how hard it is to remain separate from a crowd. This was confirmed by a social psychologist named Solomon Asch: He conducted a famous experiment where subjects were presented with four lines and asked to pick the two that were the same length. The right answer was obvious, but when confederates of Dr. Asch presented conflicting views and incorrect answers, the subjects often gave the incorrect answer instead.[6]

Follow-up experiments confirmed that it was not social pressure that led the subjects to act against their own best judgment, but their disbelief that a large group of people could be wrong.[7]

Dave: That's exactly it. So many people were hyping these stocks that I felt there had to be something there. If I didn't buy the internet stocks, I thought that I was missing out.

IC: I know. The internet and technology bubble is a perfect example of social pressures influencing stock prices. The conversations around the office, the newspaper headlines, and the analysts' predictions—they all fed the craze to invest in these stocks. Psychologists call this penchant to follow the crowd the *herding instinct*—the tendency of individuals to adapt their thinking to the prevailing opinion.

The internet bubble has many precedents. In 1852, Charles Mackay wrote the classic *Extraordinary Delusions and the Madness of Crowds*, which chronicled a number of financial bubbles during which speculators were driven into a frenzy by the upward movement of prices: the South Sea bubble in England and the Mississippi bubble in France around 1720 and the tulip mania in Holland a century earlier.[8] Let me read you my favorite passage from the book. Maybe you can relate to this:

> We find that whole communities suddenly fix their minds upon one subject, and go mad in its pursuit; that millions of people become simultaneously impressed with one delusion and run after it. . . . Sober nations have all at once become desperate gamblers, and risked most of their existence upon the turn of a piece of paper. . . . Men, it has been well said, think in herds. . . . They go mad in herds, while they only recover their senses slowly and one by one.

Dave (*shaking his head*): This happens again and again through history. Even though others were pointing to those very same excesses last year, I was convinced that "this time is different."

IC: As were many others. The tendency of investors to follow the crowd is a permanent fixture of financial history. There are times when the "crowd" is right,[9] but often following the crowd can lead you astray.

Dave, have you ever been in a new town and found yourself choosing between two restaurants? One perfectly rational way of deciding, if they are close in distance, is to see which restaurant is busier, since there's a good chance that at least some of those patrons have tried both restaurants and have chosen to eat at the better one. But when you eat at the busier restaurant, you are increasing the chance that the next diner, using the same reasoning, will also eat there, and so on. Eventually, everybody will be eating at that one restaurant, even though the other one could be much better.

Economists call this decision-making process an *information cascade*, and they believe that it happens often in financial markets.[10] For example, when one company bids for another, often other suitors will join in. When an IPO gets a strong following, other investors join in. Individuals have a feeling that "someone knows something" and that they shouldn't miss out. Sometimes that's right, but very often that is wrong.

Excessive Trading, Overconfidence, and the Representative Bias

IC: Dave, let me shift the subject. From examining your trading records, I see that you were an extremely active trader.

Dave: I had to be. Information was constantly bombarding the market; I felt I had to reposition my portfolio constantly to reflect the new information.

IC: Let me tell you something. Trading does nothing but cause extra anxiety and lower returns. A couple of economists published an article in 2000 called "Trading Is Hazardous to Your Wealth." And, I may add, to your health also. Examining the records of tens of thousands of traders, they showed that the returns of the heaviest traders were 7.1 percent below the returns of those who traded infrequently.[11]

Dave: You're right. I think trading has hurt my returns. I thought that I was one step ahead of the other guy, but I guess I wasn't.

IC: It is extraordinarily difficult to be a successful trader. Even bright people who devote their entire energies to trading stocks rarely make superior returns. The problem is that most people are simply *overconfident* in their own abilities. To put it another way, the average individual— whether a student, a trader, a driver, or anything else—believes he or she is better than average, which of course is statistically impossible.[12]

Dave: What causes this overconfidence?

IC: Overconfidence comes from several sources. First, there is what we call a *self-attribution bias*, which causes someone to take credit for a favorable turn of events when credit is not due.[13] Do you remember bragging to your wife in March 2000 about how smart you were to have bought those internet stocks?

Dave: Yes. And was I wrong!

IC: Your early success fed your overconfidence.[14] You and your friends attributed your stock gains to skillful investing, even though those outcomes were frequently the result of chance.

Another source of overconfidence comes from the tendency to see too many parallels between events that seem the same.[15] This is called the *representative bias*. This bias actually arises because of the human learning process. When we see something that looks familiar, we form a representative heuristic to help us learn. But the parallels we see are often not valid, and our conclusions are misguided.

Dave: The investment newsletters I get say that every time such-and-such event has occurred in the past, the market has moved in a certain direction, implying that it is bound to do so again. But when I try to use that advice, it never works.

IC: Conventional finance economists have been warning for years about finding patterns in the data when, in fact, there are none. Searching past data for patterns is called data mining, and with computing power becoming so cheap it is easier than ever to do.[16] Throw in a load of variables to explain stock price movements, and you are sure to find some spectacular fits—like over the past 100 years stocks have risen on every third Thursday of the month when the moon is full!

The representative bias has been responsible for some spectacularly wrong moves in the stock market, even when the situations seem remarkably similar. When World War I broke out in July 1914, officials at the New York Stock Exchange thought it was such a calamity that the exchange closed down for five months. Wrong! The United States became the arms merchant for Europe, business boomed, and 1915 was one of the single best years in stock market history.

When Germany invaded Poland in September 1939, investors looked at the behavior of the market when World War I broke out. Noting the fantastic returns, they bought stocks like mad and sent the market up by more than 7 percent on the next day's trading! But this was wrong again; FDR was determined not to let the corporations prosper from World War II as they had from World War I. After a few more up days, the stock market headed into a severe bear market, and it wasn't until nearly six years later that the market returned to its September 1939 level. Clearly, the two events weren't as similar as people thought, and the representative bias was the culprit for this error.

Psychologically, human beings are not designed to accept all the randomness that is out there.[17] It is very discomforting to learn that most movements in the market are random and do not have any identifiable cause or reason. Individuals possess a deep psychological need to know why something happens. That is where the reporters and "experts" come in. They are more than happy to fill the holes in our knowledge with explanations that are wrong more often than not.

Dave: I can relate personally to this. I remember that before I bought the technology stocks in July 2000, my broker compared these companies to the suppliers providing the gear for the gold rushers of the 1850s. It seemed like an insightful comparison at the time, but in fact the situations were very different. It is interesting that my broker, who is supposed to be the expert, is subject to the same representative bias and overconfidence that I am.

IC: There is actually evidence that experts are even more subject to overconfidence than nonexperts. These experts have been trained to analyze the world in a particular way, and they sell their advice based on finding supporting—not contradictory—evidence.[18]

Recall the failure of analysts in 2000 to change their earnings forecasts for the technology sector, despite the news that suggested that something was seriously wrong with their view of the whole industry. After being fed an upbeat outlook by corporations for many years, analysts had no idea how to interpret the downbeat news, so most just ignored it.

The propensity to shut out bad news was even more pronounced among analysts in the internet sector. Many were so convinced that these stocks were the wave of the future that despite the flood of ghastly news, many downgraded these stocks only *after* they had fallen 80 or 90 percent!

The tendency to disregard news that does not align with one's worldview is called *cognitive dissonance*. Cognitive dissonance is the discomfort we encounter when we confront evidence that conflicts with our view or suggests that our abilities or actions are not as good as we thought. We all display a natural tendency to minimize this discomfort, which makes it difficult for us to recognize our overconfidence.

Prospect Theory, Loss Aversion, and the Decision to Hold on to Losing Trades

Dave: I see. Can we talk about individual stocks? Why do I end up holding so many losers in my portfolio?

IC: Remember I said before that Kahneman and Tversky had kicked off behavioral finance with prospect theory? A key concept in their theory was that individuals form a reference point from which they judge their performance. Kahneman and Tversky found that from that reference point, individuals are much more upset about losing a given amount of money than about gaining the same amount. The researchers called this behavior *loss aversion*, and they suggested that the decision to hold or sell an investment will be dramatically influenced by whether your stock has gone up or down—in other words, whether you have had a gain or loss.

Dave: One step at a time. What is this "reference point" you talk about?

IC: Let me ask you a question. When you buy a stock, how do you track its performance?

Dave: I calculate how much the stock has gone up or down since I bought it.

IC: Exactly. Often the reference point is the purchase price that investors pay for the stock. Investors become fixated on this reference point to the exclusion of any other information. Richard Thaler from the University of Chicago, who has done seminal work in investor behavior, refers to this as *mental accounting*, or *narrow framing*.[19]

When you buy a stock, you open a mental account, with the purchase price as the reference point. Similarly, when you buy a group of stocks together, either you will think of the stocks individually, or you may aggregate the accounts together.[20] Whether your stocks are showing a gain or loss will influence your decision to hold or sell the stock. Moreover, in accounts with multiple losses, you are likely to aggregate individual losses together, because thinking about one big loss is an easier pill for you to swallow than thinking of many smaller losses. Avoiding the realization of losses becomes the primary goal of many investors.

Dave: You're right. The thought of realizing those losses on my technology stocks petrified me.

IC: That is a completely natural reaction. Your pride is one of the main reasons why you avoided selling at a loss. Every investment involves an emotional as well as financial commitment that makes it hard to evaluate objectively. You felt good that you sold out of your internet stocks with a small gain, but the networking stocks you subsequently bought never showed a gain. Even as prospects dimmed, you not only hung on to those stocks, but you bought more, hoping that they would recover.

Prospect theory predicts that many investors will do just as you did—increase your position, and consequently your risk, in an attempt to get even.[21] Interestingly, researchers have found that individuals do sell mutual funds that have lost money, and chase those that record gains. But behavioral finance has a good explanation for that: with funds, investors can always blame the fund manager for picking bad stocks, which you can't do if you make your own decisions about which stock to buy.[22]

Dave: I never bought any mutual funds, so I only had myself to blame for my losses. I thought that buying more shares when the price sank would increase my chances of recouping my losses when the price went back up.

IC: You and millions of other investors, too. In 1982, Leroy Gross wrote a manual for stockbrokers in which he called this phenomenon the "get-even-itis disease."[23] He claimed get-even-itis has probably caused more destruction to portfolios than any other mistake.

It is hard for us to admit we've made a bad investment, and it is even harder for us to admit that mistake to others. But to be a successful investor, you have no choice but to admit when you're wrong. Decisions on your portfolio must be made on a *forward-looking basis*. What has happened in the past cannot be changed. It is a "sunk cost," as economists say. When prospects don't look good, sell the stock whether or not you have a loss.

Dave: I thought the stocks were cheap when I bought more shares. Many were down 50 percent or more from their highs.

IC: Cheap, relative to what? Cheap relative to their past price or their future prospects? You thought that a price of $40 for a stock that had been $80 made the stock cheap; what you never considered is the possibility that $40 was still too high a price for that stock. This demonstrates another one of Kahneman and Tversky's behavioral findings: *anchoring*, or the tendency of people facing complex decisions to use an "anchor" or a suggested number to form their judgment.[24] Figuring out the "correct" stock price is such a complex task that it is natural to use the recently remembered stock price as an anchor, and then judge the current price a bargain.

Dave: If I follow your advice and sell my losers whenever prospects are dim, I'm going to register a lot more losses on my trades.

IC: Good! Most investors do exactly the opposite, to their detriment. Research has shown that investors sell stocks for a gain of 50 percent more frequently than they sell stocks for a loss.[25] This means that stocks that are above their purchase price are 50 percent more likely to be sold than stocks that show a loss. Traders do this, even though it is a bad strategy from a trading standpoint and a tax standpoint.

Let me tell you of one short-term trader I successfully counseled. He showed me that 80 percent of his trades made money, but he was down overall, since he had lost so much money on his losing trades that they drowned out his winners.

After I counseled him, he became a successful trader. Now he says that only one-third of his trades make money, but overall he's way ahead. When things don't work out as he planned, he gets rid of losing trades quickly while holding on to his winners. There is an old adage on Wall Street that sums up successful trading: "Cut your losers short and let your winners ride."

Rules for Avoiding Behavioral Traps

Dave: I don't feel secure enough to trade again soon. I just want to learn the right long-term strategy. How can I get over these behavioral traps and be a successful long-term investor?

IC: Dave, I'm glad you are not trading, since trading is right for only a very small fraction of my clients.

To be a successful long-term investor, you must set up rules and incentives to keep your investments on track—this is called *precommit-ment*.[26] Set an asset allocation rule and then stick to it. If you have enough knowledge, you can do this yourself, or you can do it with an investment advisor. Don't try to second-guess your rule. Remember that the basic factors generating returns change far less than we think as we watch the day-to-day ups and downs of the market. A disciplined investment strategy is almost always a winning strategy.

If you wish, you don't have to eliminate your trading altogether. If you do buy stocks for a short-term trade, establish an absolute selling point to minimize your losses. You don't want to let your losses mount, rationalizing that the stock will eventually come back. Also, don't tell your friends about your trades. Living up to their expectations will make you even more reluctant to take a loss and admit that you were wrong.

Dave: I must admit that I often enjoyed trading.

IC: If you really enjoy trading, set up a small trading account that is completely separate from the rest of your portfolio. All brokerage costs and all taxes must be paid from this account. Consider that the money you put into this trading account may be completely lost, because it very well may be, and you should never consider exceeding the rigid limit you place on how much money you put into that account.

If that doesn't work, or if you feel nervous about the market or have a compulsion to trade, call me—I can help.

Myopic Loss Aversion, Portfolio Monitoring, and the Equity Risk Premium

Dave: Because of how badly I was doing in the market, I even considered giving up on stocks and sticking with bonds, although I know that in the long run that is a very bad idea. How often do you suggest that I monitor my stock portfolio?

IC: This is an important question. If you buy stocks, it is very likely that the value will drop below the price you paid, if but for a short time after your purchase. We have already spoken about how loss aversion makes this decline very disturbing. However, since the long-term trend in stocks is upward, if you wait a period of time before checking your portfolio, the probability that you will see a loss decreases.

Two economists, Shlomo Benartzi and Richard Thaler, tested whether the monitoring interval affected an investor's choice between stocks and bonds.[27] They conducted a learning experiment in which they allowed individuals to see the returns on two unidentified asset classes. One group was shown the yearly returns on stocks and bonds, and other groups were shown the same returns, but instead of annually, the returns were aggregated over periods of 5, 10, and 20 years. The groups were then asked to pick an allocation between stocks and bonds.

The group that saw yearly returns invested a much smaller fraction in stocks than the groups that saw returns aggregated into longer intervals. This was because the short-term volatility of stocks dissuaded people from choosing that asset class, even though over longer periods it was clearly a better choice.

This tendency to base decisions on the short-term fluctuations in the market has been referred to as *myopic loss aversion*. Since over longer periods, the probability of stocks showing a loss is much smaller, investors influenced by loss aversion would be more likely to hold stocks if they monitored their performance less frequently.

Dave: That's so true. When I look at stocks in the very short run, they seem so risky that I wonder why anyone holds them. But over the long run, the superior performance of equities is so overwhelming, I wonder why anyone doesn't hold stocks!

IC: Benartzi and Thaler claim that myopic loss aversion is the key to solving the *equity premium puzzle*.[28] For years, economists have been trying to figure out why stocks have returned so much more than fixed-income investments. Studies show that over periods of 20 years or more, a diversified portfolio of equities not only offers higher after-inflation returns, but is actually safer than government bonds. Because investors concentrate on an investment horizon that is too short, stocks seem very risky, and investors must be enticed to hold stocks with a fat premium. If investors evaluated their portfolio less frequently, the equity premium might fall dramatically.

Benartzi and Thaler have shown that the high equity premium is consistent with myopic loss aversion and yearly monitoring of returns. But they also showed that if investors had evaluated their portfolio allocation only once every 10 years, the equity premium needed to be only 2 percent to entice investors into stocks. With an evaluation period of 20 years, the premium fell to only 1.4 percent, and it would have been close to 1 percent if the evaluation period were 30 years. Stock prices would have had to rise dramatically to reduce the premium to these low levels.

Dave: Are you saying that perhaps I should not look at my stocks too frequently?

IC: You can look at them all you want, but don't alter your long-term strategy. Remember to set up rules and incentives. Commit to a long-run portfolio allocation, and do not alter it unless there is significant evidence that a certain sector is becoming greatly overpriced relative to its fundamentals, as the technology stocks did at the top of the bubble.

Contrarian Investing and Investor Sentiment: Strategies to Enhance Portfolio Returns

Dave: Is there a way for an investor to take advantage of others' behavioral weaknesses and earn superior returns from them?

IC: Standing apart from the crowd might be quite profitable. An investor who takes a different view is said to be a *contrarian*, one who dissents from the prevailing opinion. Contrarian strategy was first put forth by Humphrey B. Neill in a pamphlet called "It Pays to Be Contrary," first circulated in 1951 and later turned into a book entitled *The Art of Contrary Thinking*. In it Neill declared: "When everyone thinks alike, everyone is likely to be wrong."[29]

Some contrarian approaches are based on psychologically driven indicators such as investor "sentiment." The underlying idea is that most investors are unduly optimistic when stock prices are high and unduly pessimistic when they are low.

This is not a new concept. The great investor Benjamin Graham stated almost 80 years ago, "[T]he psychology of the speculator militates strongly against his success. For by relation of cause and effect, he is most optimistic when prices are high and most despondent when they are at bottom."[30]

Dave: But how do I know when the market is too pessimistic and too optimistic? Is that not subjective?

IC: Not entirely. Investors Intelligence, a firm based in New Rochelle, New York, publishes one of the longstanding indicators of investor sentiment. Over the past 40 years, the company has evaluated scores of market newsletters, determining whether each letter is bullish, bearish, or neutral about the future direction of stocks. When bullish sentiment is very high, be very wary, but when bearish sentiment spikes, it is often a good time to buy.

Similarly the VIX Index, the measure of implied market volatility computed from options prices, spikes upward at virtually the same time investor sentiment plunges.[31] Anxiety in the market, which can be measured from the premiums on put options, is almost a perfect reflection of investor sentiment.

Dave: Can you use contrarian strategy to pick individual stocks?

IC: Yes, you can. Contrarians believe that the swings of optimism and pessimism infect individual stocks as well as the overall markets. Therefore, buying out-of-favor stocks can be a winning strategy.

Werner De Bondt and Richard Thaler examined portfolios of both past stock winners and losers to see if investors became overly optimistic or pessimistic about future returns from studying the returns of the recent past.[32] Portfolios of winning and losing stocks were analyzed over five-year intervals. Portfolios that had been winners in the past five years subsequently lagged the market by 10 percent, while the subsequent returns on the loser portfolio beat the market by 30 percent.

One of the explanations for why this strategy works relates to the representativeness heuristic we talked about before. People extrapolate recent trends in stock prices too far in the future. Although there is some evidence that short-term momentum is positive in stock returns, over the longer term many stocks that have done poorly outperform, and stocks that have done well underperform. Another strategy based on out-of-favor stocks is called the Dogs of the Dow, or the Dow 10 strategy.[33]

Dave: There has been so much for me to absorb from today's session. It seems like I fell into almost all of these behavioral traps. The comforting news is that I'm not alone and that your counseling has helped other investors.

IC: Not only have they been helped, but they have also prospered. For many people, success in investing requires a much deeper knowledge of themselves than does success in their jobs or even in their personal relationships. There is much truth to an old Wall Street adage, "The stock market is a very expensive place to find out who you are."

26

Exchange-Traded Funds, Stock Index Futures, and Options

*When I was a kid—a runner for Merrill Lynch at 25 dollars a week—
I'd heard an old timer say, "The greatest thing to trade would be
stock futures—but you can't do that, it's gambling."*

—Leo Melamed, 1988[1]

*Warren Buffett thinks that stock futures and options ought to be
outlawed, and I agree with him.*

—Peter Lynch, 1989[2]

If someone were to ask what security traded on a stock exchange had the largest dollar volume in the United States in 2021, what would you guess? Apple, Google, Tesla? The surprising answer is a security that was not in existence before 1993 and does not even represent a company. The security with the highest dollar volume is *spiders*, the nickname given to the S&P 500 Depository Receipts (SPDRs), an exchange-traded fund (symbol SPY) that represents the value of the S&P 500 Index. In 2021, over 18.6 billion shares, worth over $7 trillion were traded.

EXCHANGE-TRADED FUNDS

Exchange-traded funds (ETFs) are the most innovative and successful new financial instruments since stock index futures contracts debuted two decades prior. ETFs are shares issued by an investment company that represent an underlying portfolio. They are traded throughout the day on an exchange where the prices are determined by supply and demand. Most ETFs issued in the 1990s tracked only well-known stock indexes, but more recently they track new customized indexes and even actively managed portfolios.

FIGURE 26.1

Mutual fund and ETF assets

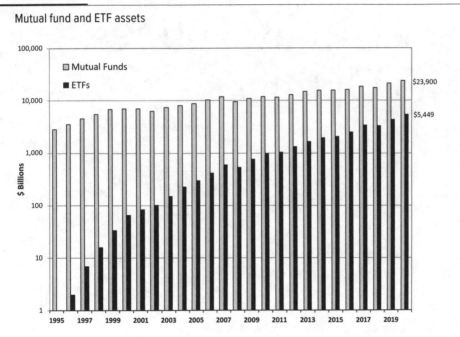

Figure 26.1 shows the growth of mutual fund assets and ETFs from 1995 through 2020.[3] At the end of 2012, ETF assets totaled only 10 percent of the assets in mutual funds; by 2020 that percentage has approached 30 percent and the growth of ETFs is much faster than mutual funds.

Spiders were the first and most successful ETF, launched in 1993. But spiders were soon joined by others, with nicknames like *cubes,* a corruption of the QQQ ticker symbol given to the Nasdaq-100 Index, and *diamonds,* with the ticker symbol DIA, which represents the Dow Jones Industrial Average.

These ETFs track their respective indexes extremely closely. That's because designated institutions, market makers, and large investors, called *authorized participants,* can buy the underlying shares of the stocks in the index and deliver them to the issuer in exchange for units of ETFs, and deliver units of ETFs in exchange for the underlying shares. The minimum size for such an exchange, called a *creation unit*, is usually 50,000 shares. For example, an authorized participant who delivers 50,000 shares of spiders to State Street Bank & Trust will receive a pro-rated number of shares of each member of the S&P 500 Index. These authorized participants keep the prices of the ETFs extremely close to the value of the index. For the active ETFs, such as spiders and cubes, the bid-ask spread is as low as 1 cent.

There are several advantages of ETFs over mutual funds. ETFs, unlike mutual funds, can be bought or sold at any time during the day. Second, an investor can sell ETFs short, hoping to make a profit by buying them back at a lower price. This proves to be a very convenient way of hedging portfolio gains if an investor fears the market may fall. Finally, ETFs are extremely tax efficient since, unlike mutual funds, they generate almost no capital gains, either from the sales of other investors or from portfolio changes to the index. This is because swaps between the ETFs and underlying shares are considered *exchanges in kind* and are not taxable events. Later in this chapter we will list the advantages and disadvantages of ETFs compared with alternative forms of index investing.

STOCK INDEX FUTURES

ETFs are really the outgrowth of another important trading innovation—the development of stock index futures in the early 1980s. Despite the enormous popularity of ETFs, the total dollar volume in ETFs is still dwarfed by the dollar volume represented by trading in index futures, most of which began trading in Chicago but are now traded on electronic exchanges. Shifts in overall market sentiment often impact the index futures market first and then are transmitted to stocks traded in New York.

EARLY DOMINANCE OF FUTURES MARKETS

To understand how important index futures became for stock prices in the 1980s and 1990s, one need only look at what happened on April 13, 1992. It began as an ordinary trading day, but at about 11:45 in the morning, the two big Chicago futures exchanges, the Board of Trade and the Mercantile Exchange, were closed when a massive leak from the Chicago River coursed through the tunnels under the financial district and

triggered extensive power outages. The intraday movement of the Dow
Industrials and the S&P futures is shown in Figure 26.2. As soon as the
Chicago futures trading was halted, the volatility of the stock market
declined significantly.

FIGURE 26.2

Stock and futures market on April 13, 1992

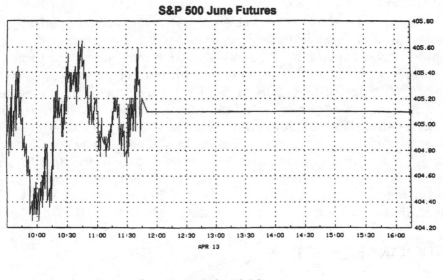

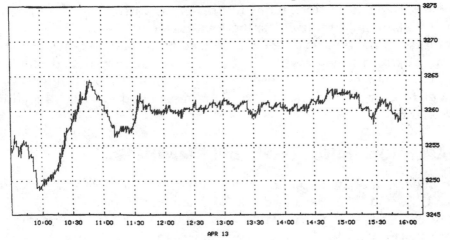

It almost appears as if the NYSE went "brain-dead" when there was no lead from Chicago. The volume in New York dropped by more than 25 percent on the day the Chicago futures market was closed, and some dealers claimed that if the futures market remained inoperative, it would cause liquidity problems and difficulty in executing some trades in New York.[4] Michael Metz, a market strategist at Oppenheimer & Co., declared: "It's been absolutely delightful; it seems so sedate. It reminds me of the halcyon days on Wall Street before the program traders took hold."[5]

Who are these *program traders* that investors hear so much about, and what do they do? The floor of the NYSE has always been alive with a constant din of people scurrying about delivering orders and making deals. In the mid-1980s, just a few years after index futures were introduced, the background noise was punctuated every so often by the rat-tat-tat of dozens of automated machines printing hundreds of buy or sell tickets. These orders were almost always from stock index futures *arbitrageurs*—that is, program traders who rely on differences between the prices of stock index futures traded in Chicago and the prices of the component stocks traded in New York.

The noise signaled that the futures market was moving quickly in Chicago and that stock prices would soon change accordingly in New York. It was an eerie warning, something akin to the buzz of locusts in biblical times, portending decimated crops and famine. And famine it might be; during the 1980s and early 1990s, some of the most vicious declines in stock prices had been preceded by computers tapping out orders emanating from the futures markets.

In those days, most of the changes in the overall level of stocks did not originate on Wall Street but on Wacker Drive at the Chicago Mercantile Exchange. *Specialists* on the NYSE, those dealers assigned to make and supervise markets in specific stocks, kept their eyes glued on the futures markets to find out where stocks would be heading. These dealers learned from experience not to stand in the way of index futures when they are moving quickly. If they did, they might get caught in an avalanche of trading, such as the one that buried several specialists on October 19, 1987, that fateful day when the Dow crashed nearly 23 percent.

High-Frequency Traders

Today many of these traders have morphed into high-frequency traders (HFTs) who use ultra-fast computers to execute thousands of orders to capitalize on new information as it hits the market. These traders were demonized in Michael Lewis's bestselling 2005 book, *Flash Boys*. He documented the wasteful "arms race," where HFTs spend millions of dollars on high-speed computers just to gain a few microseconds advantage over other HFTs. Lewis implied HFTs hurt ordinary traders who cannot begin to match the speed by which HFTs make their transactions.

Although there is much truth in Lewis's book, there has been much controversy about the degree HFTs harm the market. Those who are critical claim that HFTs discourage other traders from entering "limit orders," buy or sell orders at a given price, which are the key to providing liquidity in the market. This is because such liquidity providers fear they will be picked off by HFTs who can act on information before they can pull their own quotes. Some claim that the 2010 Flash Crash, described in Chapter 22, was exacerbated by computers executing millions of sell orders because they were automatically programmed to sell when prices fell by a given amount.

However, others maintain that HFTs themselves provide liquidity and that bid-asked spreads are much smaller than they used to be. The specialists who controlled the pricing of individual stocks until the 1990s posted much larger bid-ask spreads than exist now, making even large profits (per trade) at the expense of the smaller traders.

One study estimates that better design of capital markets could save all traders $5 billion annually in transaction costs, some of which is now taken by HFTs.[6] Changes might include "speed bumps" that eliminate the advantages of superfast computers or "batch auctions," where every few seconds, all bids and offers for a particular stock are aggregated to determine the equilibrium price, much like the procedure that is used to open trading on many stock exchanges.[7]

The bottom line is that HFTs may make the spread between bids and asks very slightly wider, which may be a concern those who make millions of trades, but this is of virtually no consequence to individual, long-term investors.

BASICS OF THE FUTURES MARKETS

Many investors regard index futures and ETFs as off-beat securities that have little to do with the stock market, and many investors do very well trading stocks without any knowledge of these new instruments. No one can comprehend the short-run market movements without an understanding of stock index futures and ETFs.

Futures trading goes back hundreds of years. The term *futures* was derived from the promise to buy or deliver a commodity at some future date at some specified price. Futures trading first flourished in agricultural crops, where farmers wanted to have a guaranteed price for the crops they would harvest at a later date. Markets developed where buyers and sellers who wanted to avoid uncertainty could come to an agreement on the price for future delivery. The commitments to honor these agreements, called *futures contracts*, were freely transferable, and markets developed where they were actively traded.

Stock index futures were launched in February 1982 by the Kansas City Board of Trade using the Value Line Index of about 1,700 stocks. Two months later, at the Mercantile Exchange in Chicago, the world's most successful stock index future, based on the S&P 500 Index, was introduced. By 1984, the value of the contracts traded on this index future surpassed the dollar volume on the NYSE for all stocks. Today, the value of stocks represented by S&P 500 futures trading exceeds $300 billion *per day*.

All stock index futures are constructed similarly. In the case of the seller, the S&P Index future is a promise to deliver a fixed multiple of the value of the S&P 500 Index at some date in the future, called a *settlement date*. In the case of the buyer, the S&P Index future is a promise to receive a fixed multiple of the S&P 500 Index's value. Originally, each contract was worth 250 times the index, but in 1998, a "mini" version of the contract (called an *E-mini*), was introduced with a multiple of 50 times the index and now far exceeds trading in the larger-sized contracts.

There are four evenly spaced settlement dates each year. They fall on the third Friday of March, June, September, and December. Each settlement date corresponds to a contract. If you buy a futures contract, you are entitled to receive (if *positive*) or obligated to pay (if *negative*) 50 times the difference between the value of the S&P 500 Index on the settlement date and the price at which you purchased the contract.

For example, if you buy one September S&P futures contract at 4,400, and on that third Friday of September the S&P 500 Index is at 4,410, you have made 10 points, which translates into a $500 profit ($50 times 10 points). Of course, if the index has fallen to 4,390 on the settlement date, you will lose $500. For every point the S&P 500 Index goes up or down, you make or lose $50 per contract. Of course, the returns to the seller of an S&P 500 futures contract are the mirror image of the returns to the buyer.

An immediate source of the popularity of stock index futures was their unique settlement procedure. With a standard futures contract, if you bought it, you would be obligated at settlement to receive, or if you sold it, you would be obligated to deliver, a specified quantity of the good for which you have contracted. Many apocryphal stories abound about how traders, forgetting to close out their contract, find bushels of wheat, corn, or frozen pork bellies dumped on their lawn on settlement day.

If commodity delivery rules applied to the S&P 500 Index futures contracts, delivery would require a specified number of shares for each of the 500 firms in the index. Surely this would be extraordinarily cumbersome and costly. To avoid this problem, the designers of the stock index futures contract specified that settlement be made in cash, computed simply by taking the difference between the contract price at the time of the trade and the value of the index on the settlement date. No delivery of stock takes place. If a trader does not close a contract before settlement, his or her account would just be debited or credited depending on the value of the index on the settlement date.

The creation of cash-settled futures contracts was no easy matter. In most states, particularly Illinois where the large futures exchanges were located, settling a futures contract in cash was considered a wager—and wagering, except in some special circumstances, was illegal. In 1974, however, the Commodity Futures Trading Commission, a federal agency, was established by Congress to regulate all futures trading. Since futures trading was now governed by this new federal agency, and since there was no federal prohibition against wagering, the prohibitory state laws were superseded.

INDEX ARBITRAGE

The prices of commodities (or financial assets) in the futures market do not stand apart from the prices of the underlying commodity. If the value of a futures contract rises sufficiently above the price of the commodity that can be purchased for immediate delivery in the open market, often called the *cash* or *spot market*, traders can buy the commodity, store it, and then deliver it at a profit against the higher-priced futures contract on the settlement date. If the price of a futures contract falls too far below its current spot price, owners of the commodity can sell it today, buy the futures contract, and take delivery of the commodity later at a lower price—in essence, earning a return on goods that would be in storage anyway.

Such a process of buying and selling commodities against their futures contracts is one type of arbitrage. Another involves traders, called arbitrageurs, who take advantage of temporary discrepancies in the prices of identical or nearly identical goods or assets. Arbitrage is very common in both the stock index futures market and the ETF market. If the price of futures contracts sufficiently exceeds that of the underlying S&P 500 Index, it pays for arbitrageurs to buy the underlying stocks and sell the futures contracts. If the futures price falls sufficiently below that of the index, arbitrageurs will sell the underlying stocks and buy the futures. On the settlement date, the futures price must equal the underlying index by the terms of the contract, so the difference between the futures price and the index—called a *premium* if it is positive and a *discount* if it is negative—is an opportunity for profit.

Index arbitrage has become a finely tuned art. The prices of stock index futures and ETFs usually stay within very narrow bands of the index value based on the price of the underlying shares. When the buying or selling of stock index futures or ETFs drives the price outside this band, arbitrageurs step in, and a flood of orders to buy or sell are immediately transmitted to the exchanges that trade the underlying stocks in the index. These simultaneously placed orders are called *programmed trading*, and they consist of either *buy programs* or *sell programs*. When market commentators talked about "sell programs hitting the market," they mean that index arbitrageurs are selling stock and buying futures or that ETFs that have fallen to a discount to their component stocks.

PREDICTING THE NEW YORK OPEN WITH FUTURES TRADING

Index futures trade day and night, except for a one-hour pause between 5 p.m. and 6 p.m. eastern time. They are closed from Friday 6 p.m. until Sunday night at 6 p.m., when they begin trading for the new week. Trading is very active in the early morning, when the European exchanges are open, and again around 8:30 a.m., when many of the government economic data, such as the employment report and the CPI, are announced.

Market watchers can use the futures in the S&P, the Nasdaq, and the Dow to predict how the market will open in New York. The *fair market value* of these index futures is calculated based on the arbitrage conditions between the future and current prices of stocks.

The fair market value for the futures contract is determined on the basis of the current index value when markets are open and on the previous closing level when markets are closed. Because of the continuous stream of news, the futures price overnight will usually be either above or below the fair market value computed at the close. If, for instance, the European markets are up or US firms have reported good quarterly earnings, then the US stock futures prices will often trade above fair market value based on the previous closing prices. The amount by which the futures contract trades above or below its fair market value will be the best estimate of where stocks will trade when the exchanges open in New York. Many financial news channels post the likely openings of the major indexes based on the futures prices.

The formula to calculate the fair market value of the futures contracts depends on two variables: the dividend yield on stocks and the interest rate. If an investor puts a sum of money today in risk-free bonds, that sum will earn interest at the ongoing interest rate. If, instead, the investor buys a portfolio of stocks and simultaneously sells a one-year futures contract that guarantees the price of those stocks one year from now, the investor will earn the dividend yield on stocks and be guaranteed a return on his stocks that is the difference between the futures price and the current price.

Since both these investments deliver a guaranteed, riskless sum, they must earn the same rate of return. Whether the futures price trades above or below the current (or spot) value of the index depends on the difference between the short-term interest rate and the dividend yield on the index. Before the financial crisis, when interest rates almost always exceeded the dividend yield, the futures price of stocks was above the spot (or current) level of the index. Since the financial crisis, as short-term rates have hovered near zero, the futures price of stock indexes are below the current spot price.

DOUBLE AND TRIPLE WITCHING

Index futures play some strange games with stock prices on the days when futures contracts expire. Recall that index arbitrage works through the simultaneous buying or selling of stocks against futures contracts. On the day that contracts expire, arbitrageurs unwind their stock positions at precisely the same time that the futures contracts expire.

As noted earlier, index futures contracts expire on the third Friday of the last month of each quarter: in March, June, September, and December. Index options and options on individual stocks, which are described later in the chapter, settle on the third Friday of every month. Four times a year, all three types of contracts expire at once. This expiration has, in the past, often produced violent price movements in the market, and it has consequently been termed a *triple witching hour*. The third Friday of a month when there are no futures contract settlements is called a *double witching*, and it displays less volatility than triple witching.

There is no mystery why the market is volatile during double or triple witching dates. On these days, the specialists on the NYSE and the market makers on the Nasdaq are instructed to buy or sell large blocks of stock on the close, whatever the price, because institutional investors are closing out their arbitrage positions. If there is a huge imbalance of buy orders, prices will soar; if sell orders predominate, prices will plunge. These swings, however, do not matter to arbitrageurs since the profit on the future position will offset losses on the stock position and vice versa.

In 1988, the NYSE urged the Chicago Mercantile Exchange to change its procedures and stop futures trading at the close of Thursday's trading, settling the contracts at Friday opening prices rather than at Friday closing prices. This change gave specialists more time to seek out balancing bids and offers, and it has greatly moderated the movements in stock prices on triple witching dates.

MARGIN AND LEVERAGE

One of the reasons for the popularity of futures contracts is that the cash needed to enter the trade is a very small part of the value of the contract. Unlike stocks, there is no money that transfers between the buyer and seller when a futures contract is bought or sold. A small amount of good-faith collateral, or *margin*, is required by the broker from both the buyer and seller to ensure that both parties will honor the contract at settlement. For the S&P 500 Index, the current initial margin is about 5 percent of the value of the contract. This margin can be kept in Treasury bills with interest accruing to the investor, so trading a futures contract involves neither a transfer of cash nor a loss of interest income.

The *leverage*, or the amount of stock that you control relative to the amount of margin you must put down with a futures contract, is very large. For every dollar of cash (or Treasury bills) that you put in margin against an S&P futures contract, you command almost $20 of stock value. For *day trading*, when you close your positions by the end of the day, the margin requirements are significantly less. These low margins contrast with the 50 percent margin requirement for the purchase of individual stocks or ETFs that has prevailed since 1974.

This ability to control so much more of stock with so little cash is reminiscent of the rampant speculation that existed in the 1920s before the establishment of minimum stock margin requirements. In the 1920s, individual stocks were frequently purchased with a 10 percent margin.

It was popular to speculate with such borrowed money, because if the market was rising, few investors lost money. But if the market dropped precipitously, margin buyers often found that not only did they lose their equity, but they were also indebted to the brokerage firm. Buying futures contracts with low margins can result in similar repercussions today.

TAX ADVANTAGES OF ETFS AND FUTURES

The use of ETFs or index futures greatly increases an investor's flexibility to manage portfolios. Suppose an investor has built up gains in individual stocks, but is now getting nervous about the market. Selling one's individual stocks may trigger a large tax liability. By using ETFs (or futures), a good solution is available. The investor sells enough ETFs to cover the value of the portfolio that she seeks to hedge and continues to hold her individual stocks. If the market declines, the investor profits on her ETF position, offsetting the losses of the stock portfolio. If the market instead goes up, contrary to expectation, the loss on ETFs will be offset by the gains on the individual stock holdings. This is called *hedging stock market risk*. Since the investor never sells her individual stocks, she triggers no tax liability from these positions.

Another advantage of ETFs is that they can yield a profit from a decline in the market, even if one does not own any stock. Selling ETFs substitutes for *shorting stock*, or selling stock you do not own, in anticipation that the price will fall and you can buy it back at a lower price. Using ETFs to bet on a falling market is much more convenient than shorting a portfolio of stocks, since regulations prohibit individual stocks from being shorted if their price has declined by more than 10 percent.[8]

COMPARISON OF ETFS, FUTURES, AND INDEXED MUTUAL FUNDS

With the development of index futures and ETFs, investors have three major choices to match the performance of one of many stock indexes: ETFs, index futures, and index mutual funds. The important characteristics of each type of investment are given in Table 26.1.

As far as trading flexibility, ETFs and index futures far outshine mutual funds. ETFs and index futures can be bought or sold virtually anytime during the trading day. In contrast, mutual funds can be transacted at the market close, and the investor's order must often be in several hours earlier. ETFs and index futures can also be shorted to hedge one's portfolio or speculate on a market decline, while mutual funds cannot. ETFs can be margined like any stock (with current Fed regulations at 50 percent), while index futures possess the highest degree of leverage, as investors can control stocks worth almost 20 times the margin deposit.

TABLE 26.1

Characteristics of ETFs, index futures, and indexed mutual funds

	ETFs	Index Futures	Indexed Mutual Funds
Continuous Trading	Yes	Yes	No
Can Be Sold Short	Yes	Yes	No
Leverage	Yes	Can Borrow Up to 90%	None
Expense Ratio	Extremely Low	None	Very Low
Trading Costs	Stock Commission	Futures Commission	None
Dividend Reinvestment	Yes	No	Yes
Tax Efficiency	Extremely Good	Poor	Very Good

The trading flexibility of ETFs or futures can be either a bane or a boon to investors. It is easy to overreact to the continuous stream of optimistic and pessimistic news, causing an investor to sell near the low or buy near the high. Furthermore, the ability to short stocks (except for hedging) or to leverage might tempt investors to play their short-term hunches on the market. This is a very dangerous game. For most investors, restricting the frequency of trades and reducing leverage is beneficial.

On the cost side, all these vehicles are very efficient. Index mutual funds are available at an annual cost of 10 basis points or less a year, and most ETFs are even cheaper. Both ETFs and futures must be bought through a brokerage account, and this may involve paying a commission and a bid-ask spread, although these are quite low for actively traded ETFs. On the other hand, most index funds are *no-load funds*, meaning there is no commission when the fund is bought or sold. Furthermore, although index futures involve no annual costs, these contracts must be rolled over into new contracts at least once a year, entailing additional commissions.

It is on the tax side that ETFs really shine. Because of the structure of ETFs, these funds generate very few if any capital gains. Index mutual funds are also very tax efficient, but they often throw off capital gains. This means funds must sell individual shares from their portfolio if investors redeem their shares or if stocks are removed from the index. Although capital gains have been small for most index mutual funds, they are larger than ETFs.[9] Futures are not tax efficient, since any gains or losses must be realized at the end of the year whether the contracts are sold or not.

Of course, these tax differences between ETFs and index mutual funds do not matter if an investor holds these funds in a tax-sheltered account, such as an individual retirement account (IRA). However, if these funds are held in taxable accounts, the after-tax return on ETFs is apt to be higher than it would be for even the most efficient index fund.

Leveraged ETFs

In June 2006, ProShares introduced indexed ETFs that were designed to double your daily return on the popular Nasdaq 100 Index. Soon to follow were ETFs that were constructed to double or triple your daily return on Nasdaq and the S&P 500 Index. In 2009, an ETF firm called Direxion constructed ETFs designed to go up when the market went down, called "bear" ETFs, and this was followed up by "2× and 3× Bear Indices" that doubled and tripled the *negative* daily change on the index. These products used leverage in the futures and options markets to achieve their objectives and became very popular among the trading public.

But leveraged ETFs are often poorly understood; they are constructed so that they must constantly be rebalanced and this introduces a *downward* bias to their price movement. This means that during the day, a trader will realize a return that is very close to double and triple that on the index, but over longer periods, returns will lag and an investor will not gain two or three times the index. The downward drift is particularly severe for the bear ETFs that are constructed to go up when the index goes down.

Table 26.2 shows the annual return from December 31, 2015, through December 31, 2021, and during the Covid-19 pandemic for the S&P 500 and Nasdaq 100 ETFs, and their leveraged counterparts. Although the S&P 500 Index and Nasdaq 100 Index gave an annual return of 17.3 percent and 24.5 percent, respectively, during this six-year period, the 2× and 3× ETFs fell well short of doubling and tripling the index return. The 3× bear index lost almost 50 percent per year; a $100,000 investment in the triple bear SPXS on December 31, 2015, was worth $2,000 six years later.

TABLE 26.2

Returns to leveraged ETFs, from 2016–2022 and during pandemic bear market

	S&P 500				Nasdaq		
	1x	2x	3x	-3x	1x	2x	3x
Tickers	SPY	SSO	UPRO	SPXS	QQQ	QLD	TQQQ
Expense Ratio	0.095%	0.75%	0.75%	1.01%	0.20%	0.75%	0.75%
Returns							
12/31/2015-12/31/2021 Annualized Return	17.3%	29.8%	39.6%	-49.9%	24.5%	44.5%	61.1%
2/12/20-3/23/20	-33.5%	-58.6%	-76.2%	134.9%	-26.4%	-49.4%	-67.9%

The triple bear ETF did shine during the pandemic bear market, rising almost 135 percent from February 12 through March 23, 2020, when the market fell by more than one-third. But Figure 26.3 shows that by the time the market fully recovered from the bear plunge, none of the other levered ETFs recovered, with the double bull ETF down 10 percent, the triple bull down 28 percent, and the triple bear down 50 percent

FIGURE 26.3

Price of S&P 500 leverage products during the Covid-19 pandemic

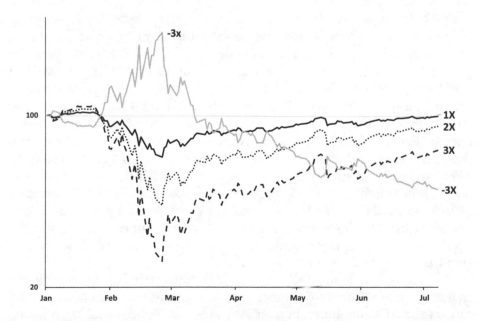

INDEX OPTIONS

Although ETFs and index futures are very important to investment professionals and institutions, the options market has caught the fancy of many investors. This is not surprising. The beauty of an option is embedded in its very name: you have the option, but not the obligation, to buy or sell stocks or indexes at a given price by a given time. For the option buyer, this option, in contrast to the futures market, automatically limits your maximum liability to the amount you invested.

There are two major types of options: puts and calls. *Calls* give you the right to buy a stock (or stocks) at a fixed price within a given period of time. *Puts* give you the right to sell a stock. Puts and calls have existed on individual stocks for decades, but they were not bought and sold through an organized trading system until the establishment of the CBOE in 1974.

The limited liability feature of options is extremely attractive. If the market moves against options buyers, they can forfeit the purchase price, forgoing the option to buy or sell. This contrasts sharply with futures contracts with which, if the market goes against buyers, losses can mount quickly and the investor can receive a "margin call" requiring him to put up further funds. In a volatile market, futures can be extremely risky, and it could be impossible for investors to exit a contract without substantial losses.

An index allows investors to buy the stock index at a set price within a given period of time. Assume that the S&P 500 Index is 4,600, but you believe that the market is going to rise. Let us assume you can purchase a six-month call option at 4,700 for 80 points, or $8,000. The purchase price of the option is called the *premium*, and the price at which the option has value when it expires—in this case 4,700—is called the *strike price*. At any time within the next three months you can, if you choose, exercise your option and receive $100 for every point that the S&P 500 Index is above 4,700. You will break even if the market rises to 4,780, to cover the price of the premium, and profit if it moves above that level. If the market rises to 4,880, you will make a profit of 100 points or $10,000, more than 100 percent return on your original investment. You need not exercise your option to make a profit. There is an extremely active market for options, and you can always sell them before expiration to other investors.

An index put works the same way as a call, but in this case the buyer makes money if the market goes down. Assume you buy a six-month put on the S&P 500 Index at a strike price of 4,500, paying 80 points or

$8,000. Every point the S&P 500 Index is below 4,500 will recoup $100 of your initial premium. If the index falls to 4,400, you will break even and if the market goes below 4,320, you will profit.

The price for options is determined by the market and depends on many factors, including interest rates and dividend yields. The most important factor is the expected volatility of the market, and this volatility is measured by the VIX Index discussed in Chapter 22. Clearly, the more volatile the market, the more expensive it is to buy either puts or calls.

Options pricing was given a big boost in the 1970s when two academic economists, Fischer Black and Myron Scholes, developed the first mathematical formula to price options. The *Black-Scholes formula* was an instant success. It gave traders a benchmark for valuation where as previously they used only their intuition. The formula was programmed on traders' handheld calculators and PCs around the world. Although there are conditions when the formula must be modified, empirical research has shown that the Black-Scholes formula closely approximates the price of traded options. Myron Scholes won the Nobel Prize in Economics in 1997 for his discovery.[10]

BUYING INDEX OPTIONS

Options are more flexible than futures or ETFs. You can replicate any future or ETF with options, but the reverse is not true. Options offer the investor far more strategies than futures. Such strategies can range from the very speculative to the extremely conservative.

Suppose you want to be protected against a decline in the market. You can buy an index put, which increases in value as the market declines. Of course, you have to pay a premium for this option, very much like an insurance premium. If the market does not decline, you have forfeited your premium. If it does decline, the increase in the value of your put has cushioned, if not completely offset, the decline in your stock portfolio.

Another advantage of puts is that you can buy just the amount of protection that you like. If you want to protect yourself against only a total collapse in the market, you can buy a put that is far *out-of-the-money*, in other words, a put whose strike price is far below that of the current level of the index. This option pays off only if the market declines precipitously. In addition, you can also buy puts with a strike price above the current market so the option retains some value even if the market does not decline. Of course, these *in-the-money* puts are far more expensive.

There are many recorded examples of fantastic gains in puts and calls. But for every option that gains so spectacularly in value, there are thousands of options that expire worthless. Some market professionals estimate that 85 percent of individual investors who play the options market lose money. Not only do options buyers have to be right about the direction of the market, but also their timing must be nearly perfect, and their selection of the strike price must be appropriate.

SELLING INDEX OPTIONS

Of course, for anyone who buys an option, someone must sell—or "write"—an options contract. The writers of call options believe that the market will not rise sufficiently to make a profit for options buyers. Sellers of call options usually make money when they sell options, since the vast majority of options expire worthless. Should the market move sharply against the options sellers, their losses could be enormous.

For that reason, many sellers of call options are investors who already own stocks. This strategy, called *buy and write*, is popular with many investors since it is viewed by some as a win-win proposition. If the stock goes down, they collect a premium from buyers of the call, and so the investors are better off than if they had not written the option. If the stock does nothing, they also collect the premium on the call, and they are still better off. If the stock goes up moderately in price, call writers gain more on the stock than they lose on the call they wrote, so they are still ahead. However, if stocks go up strongly, they lose, since they have promised to deliver stock at a price below the market. In that case, call writers certainly would have been better off if they had not sold the call.

The buyers of put options are insuring their stock against price declines. Who are the sellers of these options? They are primarily those who are willing to buy the stock, but only if the price declines. A seller of a put collects a premium, but receives the stock only if it falls sufficiently to go below the strike price.

CONCLUSION: THE IMPORTANCE OF INDEXED PRODUCTS

The development of stock index futures and options in the 1980s was important for investors and money managers. Heavily capitalized firms, such as those represented in the Dow Jones Industrial Average, have always attracted investment dollars because of their outstanding liquidity. With stock index futures, investors were able to buy all the stocks in the index at once.

Twenty years later, ETFs gave investors still another way to diversify across all markets at low cost. These ETFs had the familiarity of stocks with higher liquidity and superior tax efficiency. Today when investors want to take a position in the market, it is most easily done with stock index futures or ETFs. Index options give investors the ability to insure the value of their portfolio and save on transaction costs and taxes.

Despite the initial opposition of such notable investors as Warren Buffett and Peter Lynch, there is no hard evidence that these index products have increased volatility or harmed investors. In fact, it is my belief that these index products have increased the liquidity of the world's stock markets and enabled better diversification, which leads to higher stock prices than would have prevailed without them.

Fund Performance, Indexing, and Investor Returns

I have little confidence even in the ability of analysts, let alone untrained investors, to select common stocks that will give better than average results. Consequently, I feel that the standard portfolio should be to duplicate, more or less, the DJIA.

—Benjamin Graham[1]

How can institutional investors hope to outperform the market . . . when, in effect, they are the market?

—Charles D. Ellis, 1975[2]

There is an old story on Wall Street: Two managers of large equity funds go camping in a national park. After setting up camp, the first manager mentions to the other that he overheard the park ranger warning that black bears had been seen around this campsite. The second manager smiles and says, "I'm not worried; I'm a pretty fast runner." The first manager shakes his head and says, "You can't outrun black bears; they've been known to sprint over 25 miles an hour to capture their prey!" The second manager responds, "Of course I know that I can't outrun the bear. The only thing that matters is that I can outrun you!"

In the competitive world of money management, performance is measured not by absolute returns, but returns relative to some benchmark. For stocks, these are the S&P 500 Index, the Russell 3000 Index, and their growth or value counterparts, among others.

There is a crucial difference between investing skill compared with virtually any other competitive activity. Most of us have no chance of being nearly as good as those who practice for years to hone their skills; we're not likely to beat Roger Federer in a match. But anyone can be as good as the *average* investor in the stock market with no effort at all.

The reason for this surprising statement is based on a very simple fact: since the sum of each investor's stocks must be equal to the market, then the performance of the market must be equal to the *average* dollar-weighted performance of each investor. Therefore, for each investor's dollar that outperforms the market, there must be another investor's dollar that underperforms the market. By just *matching* the performance of the overall market, you are guaranteed to do no worse than the average investor, whether they study the market or not.

How do you match the performance of the whole market? Who can hold shares in each of the thousands of firms listed on world exchanges? Until 1975, this goal would have been virtually impossible for all but the most affluent investors.

However, since that time, the development of index mutual funds and ETFs have enabled small investors to closely match the performance of these broad stock indexes. These index funds have revolutionized investing and empowered small investors to match, if not exceed, the returns realized by active investors with much larger portfolios.

THE PERFORMANCE OF EQUITY MUTUAL FUNDS

Many assert that striving for the average market performance is not a good strategy. They maintain that if there are enough poorly informed traders who consistently underperform the market, then it should not be too difficult for informed investors to outperform the market.

Unfortunately, the historical record does not support this contention. S&P Dow Jones Indices puts out a biannual review of the performance of actively managed mutual and exchange traded funds. The performance is shown in Table 27.1 for midyear 2021, and it is not encouraging for those investing in actively managed funds.[3] For all domestic funds, more than three-quarters have underperformed their respective index over the 3-year period ending June 30, 2021, and more than 90 percent have underperformed over 10- and 20-year periods.[4]

TABLE 27.1

Percentage of US equity funds underperforming benchmarks (risk adjusted)

Fund Category	Comparison Index	3-Year %	5-Year %	10-Year %	20-Year %
All Domestic Funds	S&P Composite 1500	75.79	78.26	92.42	93.80
All Large Cap Funds	S&P 500	68.38	74.92	89.49	94.05
All Mid Cap Funds	S&P MidCap 400	46.73	56.75	72.30	88.70
All Small Cap Funds	S&P SmallCap 600	53.01	62.77	83.16	92.25
All Multi Cap Funds	S&P Composite 1500	73.72	74.69	93.21	93.91
Large Cap Growth Funds	S&P 500 Growth	66.95	62.30	98.48	99.71
Large Cap Core Funds	S&P 500	74.80	85.20	96.14	95.67
Large Cap Value Funds	S&P 500 Value	68.90	70.96	82.78	75.12
Mid Cap Growth Funds	S&P MidCap 400 Growth	22.66	34.72	61.14	90.81
Mid Cap Core Funds	S&P MidCap 400 ·	61.29	70.97	86.92	90.91
Mid Cap Value Funds	S&P MidCap 400 Value	59.26	72.41	78.38	79.38
Small Cap Growth Funds	S&P SmallCap 600 Growth	18.68	30.57	79.61	98.76
Small Cap Core Funds	S&P SmallCap 600	65.44	76.89	93.33	89.52
Small Cap Value Funds	S&P SmallCap 600 Value	76.29	80.70	90.48	82.26
Multi Cap Growth Funds	S&P Composite 1500 Growth	75.72	80.77	98.52	96.49
Multi Cap Core Funds	S&P Composite 1500	85.17	89.43	97.02	91.95
Multi Cap Value Funds	S&P Composite 1500 Value	88.33	83.33	88.33	83.91
Real Estate Funds	S&P United States REIT	38.27	44.19	59.09	81.67

Source: S&P Dow Jones Indices LLC ©2021

Figure 27.1 shows the percentage, each year, of equity funds that outperformed the market, defined as the CRSP capitalization-weighted returns of all US stocks. The results are equally dismal. In only 11 years of the last half-century have more than half the funds outperformed the market, and those were usually years when small stocks outperformed large stocks. Furthermore, the trend is getting worse: from 2008 through 2021, there has not been a single year where more than half the funds have outperformed the market.

Figure 27.2 shows the distribution of returns of the 132 funds that have *survived* over the entire 50-year period, 1972–2021. Only one fund (AMF Large Cap Equity) beat the S&P 500 by more than 2 percentage points per year, and 83, almost two-thirds, underperformed the market index.

Also plotted in Figure 27.2 is the theoretical distributions of fund returns, assuming that managers made random picks of stocks in their portfolio. Pure randomness would have predicted that 21 funds would have outperformed the market by 3 percent or more per year, but as you can see, only one did.

FIGURE 27.1

Percentage of equity funds that outperform the market, 1972–2021

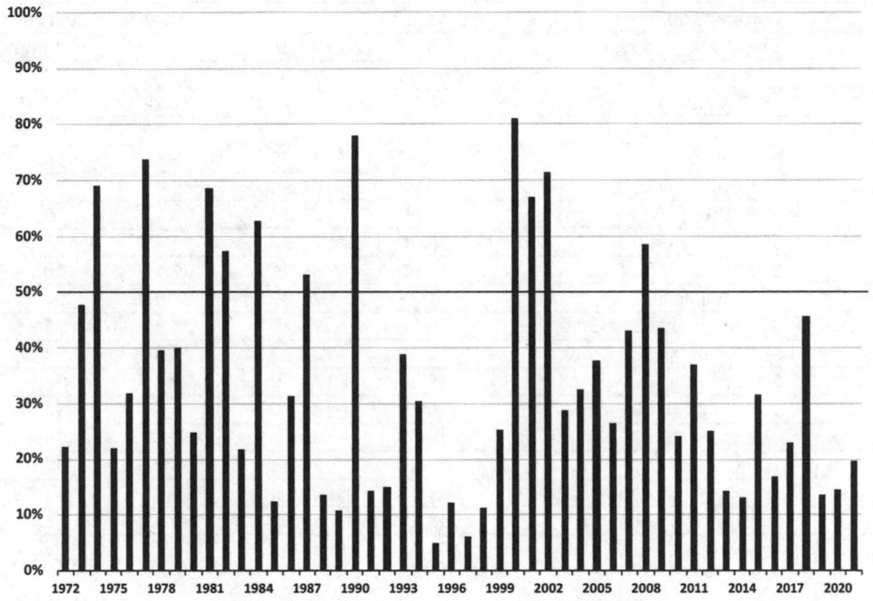

The historical performance of managed funds is actually significantly worse than these figures indicate. These studies only include funds that have survived for all 50 years and excludes poorly performing funds that are often terminated. This bias, called *survivorship bias*, means that the actual performance of all actively managed mutual funds would be lower than those shown in Table 27.2. Furthermore, the returns that were calculated exclude sales and redemption fees, quite common in the earlier years, that would have further reduced their net returns to investors.

FIGURE 27.2

Distribution of theoretical and actual surviving mutual funds returns relative to market (1972–2021)

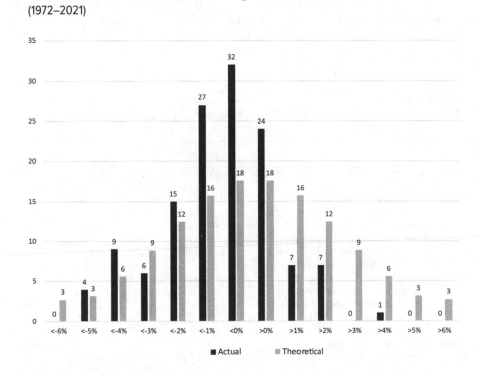

Best-Performing Funds

Many investors believe that the funds that will outperform in the future will be those that have outperformed over long periods in the past. Table 27.2 shows the best-performing survivor funds from 1972 onward, listing their performance over the first 40 years and the last 10 years.

The case for continued outperformance is not encouraging. On average, the 15 top-performing funds in the first 40 years, which beat the S&P 500 by nearly 3 percentage points per, underperformed by nearly the same margin in the next 10 years! The four best-performing funds from 1972 through 2012, which beat the S&P 500 by from 3.5 percentage points to more than 6 percentage points per year, all underperformed the S&P 500 in the following decade, some dramatically. Fidelity's Magellan Fund, ranked fifth, was the highest-ranking fund to outperform in the first 40 years *and* the next 10 years. Fidelity's Magellan Fund, run from 1977 to 1990 by the famed money manager Peter Lynch, realized astounding returns of over 29 percent per year, more than double that of the S&P 500 Index. Magellan took somewhat greater risks in achieving this return, but the probability that Magellan would outperform the market by this margin over that 14-year period by luck alone is only 1 in 500,000! After Lynch's tenure, the Magellan Fund continued to outperform, albeit by a much smaller margin.

TABLE 27.2

Best-performing funds from 1972–2012 and subsequent 10-year performance

Ticker	Name	Total Return		Relative to S&P	
		1972–2012	2012–2022	1972–2012	2012–2022
IICAX	Asset Management Fund Large Cap Equity Fund	16.19%	13.76%	6.26%	-2.87%
SEQUX	Sequoia Fund	14.11%	10.51%	4.18%	-6.11%
MUTHX	Franklin Mutual Shares Fund Class Z	13.43%	9.24%	3.50%	-7.38%
ACRNX	Columbia Acorn Fund Institutional Class	13.42%	12.35%	3.49%	-4.27%
FMAGX	Fidelity® Magellan® Fund	13.03%	17.67%	3.10%	1.05%
TWCGX	American Century Growth Fund Investor Class	12.95%	18.22%	3.01%	1.60%
OTCFX	T. Rowe Price Small-Cap Stock Fund	12.89%	14.68%	2.96%	-1.95%
TEPLX	Templeton Growth Fund, Inc. Class A	12.60%	7.36%	2.66%	-9.26%
FCNTX	Fidelity® Contrafund® Fund	12.41%	17.95%	2.47%	1.33%
ACSTX	Invesco Comstock Fund Class A	12.12%	12.79%	2.19%	-3.83%
TWCIX	American Century Select Fund Investor Class	11.97%	18.21%	2.04%	1.59%
FDESX	Fidelity Advisor® Diversified Stock Fund Class O	11.89%	16.70%	1.95%	0.08%
NYVTX	Davis New York Venture Fund Class A	11.84%	12.27%	1.90%	-4.35%
SGENX	First Eagle Global Fund Class A	11.68%	8.31%	1.75%	-8.31%
SPECX	Alger Spectra Fund Class A	11.44%	18.37%	1.51%	1.75%
	Average	12.80%	13.89%	2.87%	-2.73%
	Berkshire Hathaway	17.88%	14.66%	7.95%	-1.96%
	S&P 500	9.93%	16.62%		

Included is Warren Buffett's famed Berkshire Hathaway, which beat all other mutual funds from 1972 through 2012 and returned 17.88 percent per year, almost 8 percentage points above the S&P 500 during that period. The probability that randomness alone could cause this outperformance is about 1 in 100. Nevertheless, Buffett's Berkshire underperformed the S&P 500 in the next 10 years.

History of Fund Underperformance

The underperformance of mutual funds did not begin in the 1970s. In 1970, Becker Securities Corporation startled Wall Street by compiling the track record of managers of corporate pension funds. Becker showed that the median performance of these managers lagged behind the S&P

500 by 1 percentage point and that only one-quarter of them were able to outperform the market.[5] This study followed on the heels of academic articles, particularly those by William Sharpe and Michael Jensen, and the famed 1962 mutual fund study of Irwin Friend[6] that also confirmed the underperformance of equity mutual funds.

Although the results reported in Table 27.2 do not support the continued long-term outperformance of top-performing mutual funds, there is some evidence that funds that outperform in *one* year are more likely to outperform the next.[7] This short-run persistence is probably because managers follow a particular *style* of investing, and styles often stay in favor over several years.

Edward Elton, Martin Gruber, and Christopher Blake claim that outperformance persists over three-year periods,[8] but Burton Malkiel, Jack Bogle, and others disagree.[9] Over longer periods, star performers often falter. Perhaps Fidelity's Magellan Fund's mediocre performance in the immediate years following Peter Lynch's departure did not surprise investors. Even if the lead manager of a successful fund remains at the helm, results can change dramatically. Bill Miller's hot hand with Legg Mason's Value Trust, which recorded a record 15 consecutive years of beating the S&P 500 Index from 1991 through 2005, suddenly turned very cold from 2006 to 2008.

FINDING SKILLED MONEY MANAGERS

It would be hard to deny that Warren Buffett's and Peter Lynch's performances were due to their skill in picking stocks. For more mortal portfolio managers, it is extremely difficult to determine with any degree of confidence whether the superior returns of money managers are due to skill or luck. Table 27.3 computes the probability that managers with better-than-average stock-picking ability will outperform the market.[10]

The results are surprising. Even if money managers choose stocks that have an *expected* return of 1 percent per year better than the market, there is only a 62.7 percent probability that they will exceed the average market return after 10 years, and only a 71.2 percent probability that they will exceed the market after 30 years given the volatility of the market. If managers pick stocks that will outperform the market by 2 percent per year, there is still only a 74.0 percent chance that they will outperform the market after 10 years. This means there is a one-in-four chance that they will still fall short of the market. The length of time needed to be reasonably certain that superior managers will outperform the market will most surely outlive their trial period for determining their real worth.

TABLE 27.3

Probability of outperforming the market

Expected Excess Return	Holding Period (years)						
	1	**2**	**3**	**5**	**10**	**20**	**30**
1%	54.1%	55.7%	57.0%	59.0%	62.7%	67.6%	71.2%
2%	58.1%	61.3%	63.8%	67.5%	74.0%	81.9%	86.7%
3%	61.9%	66.6%	70.1%	75.2%	83.2%	91.3%	95.2%
4%	65.7%	71.6%	75.8%	81.7%	89.9%	96.4%	98.6%
5%	69.2%	76.1%	80.8%	86.9%	94.4%	98.8%	99.7%

Detecting a bad manager is an equally difficult task. In fact, a money manager would have to underperform the market by 4 percent a year for almost 15 years before you could be statistically certain (defined to mean being less than 1 chance in 20 of being wrong) that the manager is actually poor and not just having bad luck. By that time, your assets would have fallen to half of what you would have had if you indexed to the market.

Even extreme cases are hard to identify. Surely you would think that a manager who picks stocks that are expected to outperform the market by an average of 5 percent per year, a feat achieved by no sur-viving mutual fund since 1970, would quickly stand out. But that is not necessarily so; after one year there is only a 7-in-10 chance that such a manager will outperform the market. The probability rises to only 76.8 percent that the manager will outperform the market after two years.

Assume you gave a young, undiscovered Peter Lynch—someone who over the long run will outperform the market with a 5 percent per year edge—an ultimatum: that he will be fired if he does not at least match the market after two years. Table 27.3 shows that the probability he will beat the market over two years is only 76.1 percent. This means there is almost a one-in-four chance that he will still underperform the market and you will fire Lynch, judging him incapable of picking winning stocks!

REASONS FOR UNDERPERFORMANCE OF MANAGED MONEY

The generally poor performance of funds relative to the market is not because the fund managers are systematically picking losing stocks. Their performance lags the benchmarks largely because funds impose fees and trading costs that are often as high as 2 percent or more per year. First, in seeking superior returns, a manager buys and sells stocks, which involves paying brokerage commissions and also paying the bid-ask spread, or the difference between the buying and the selling price of shares. Second, investors pay management fees (and possibly sales fees, or *load*) to the organizations and individuals that sell these funds. Finally, managers are often competing with other managers with equal or superior skills at choosing stocks. It is a mathematical impossibility for everyone to do better than the market—for every dollar that outperforms the average, some other investor's dollar must underperform the average.

A LITTLE LEARNING IS A DANGEROUS THING

It is important to note that an investor who has some knowledge of the principles of equity valuations often performs worse than someone with no knowledge who decides to index his portfolio to the market. For example, take the novice—an investor who is just learning about stock valuation. This is the investor to whom most of the books entitled *How to Beat the Market* are sold. A novice might see that a stock has just reported very good earnings, but its price is not rising as much as he believes is justified by this good news, and so he buys the stock.

Yet highly informed investors know that special circumstances caused the earnings to increase and that these circumstances will not likely be repeated in the future. Informed investors are more than happy to sell the stock to novices, realizing that the rise in the price of the stock is not justified. Informed investors make a return on their special knowledge, from novices who believe they have found a bargain. Uninformed indexed investors, who do not even know what the earnings of the company are, often do better than the investor who is just beginning to learn about equities.

The saying "a little learning is a dangerous thing" proves itself to be apt in financial markets. Many seeming anomalies or discrepancies in the prices of stocks (or most other financial assets, for that matter) are due to the trading of informed investors with special information that is not easily processed by others. When a stock looks too cheap or too dear, the easy explanation—that emotional or ignorant traders have incorrectly priced the stock—is usually wrong. Often (but not always) there are good reasons why stocks are priced as they are. This is why beginners who buy individual stocks on the basis of their own research often do quite badly.

PROFITING FROM INFORMED TRADING

As novices become more informed, they will no doubt find some stocks that are genuinely undervalued or overvalued. Trading these stocks will begin to offset their transaction costs and their other poorly informed, losing trades. At some point, a trader might become well enough informed to overcome the transaction costs and match, or perhaps exceed, the market return. The key word here is *might*, because the number of investors who have consistently been able to outperform the market is small indeed. For individuals who do not devote much time to analyzing stocks, the possibility of consistently outperforming the averages is remote.

Yet the apparent simplicity of picking winners and avoiding losers lures many investors into active trading. We learned in Chapter 25 that there is an inherent tendency of individuals to view themselves and their performance as above average. The investment game draws some of the best minds in the world. Many investors are convinced that they are smarter than the next guy who is playing the same investing game. But even being just as smart as the next investor is not good enough. Being average at the game of finding market winners will result in underperforming the market, since transaction costs will cause such an investor to fall behind the indexes.

In 1975, Charles D. Ellis, a managing partner at Greenwood Associates, wrote an influential article called "The Loser's Game." In it he showed that, with transaction costs considered, average money managers must outperform the market by margins that are not possible, given that they themselves are the major market players. Ellis concludes: "Contrary to their oft articulated goal of outperforming the market averages, investment managers are not beating the market; the market is beating them."[11]

HOW COSTS AFFECT RETURNS

Trading and advisory costs of 2 or 3 percent a year might seem small to investors who are gunning for 20 or 30 percent annual returns, but such costs are extremely detrimental to long-term wealth accumulation. Investing $1,000 at a compound return of 11 percent per year will accumulate to $23,000 over 30 years. A 1 percent annual fee will reduce the final accumulation by almost a third. With a 3 percent annual fee, the accumulation amounts to just over $10,000, less than half the market return. Another way of understanding the importance of transactions fees: every extra percentage point of annual costs requires investors aged 25 to retire two years later to accumulate the same nest egg.

THE INCREASED POPULARITY OF PASSIVE INVESTING

An increasing number of investors have realized that the poor performance of actively managed funds relative to benchmark indexes strongly implies that they would do very well to just *equal* the market return of one of the broad-based indexes. Since 1990, there has been an enormous increase in *passive investing*, the placement of funds whose sole purpose was to match the performance of an index.

The oldest, and for many years the most popular, of the index funds was the Vanguard 500 Index Fund.[12] The fund, started by visionary John Bogle, raised only $11.4 million when it debuted in 1976, and few thought the concept would survive. But slowly and surely, indexing gathered momentum, and the fund's assets reached $17 billion at the end of 1995.

In the 1990s bull market, the popularity of indexing soared. By March 2000, when the S&P 500 Index reached its all-time high, the fund claimed the title of the world's largest equity fund, with assets over $100 billion. By end of 2021, the fund reached $800 billion and the Total Stock Market Fund, which holds all US stocks, has attracted more than $1.3 trillion in assets.

One of the attractions of index funds is their extremely low cost. The total annual cost in the Vanguard 500 Index Fund is only 4 basis points (0.04 of 1 percent) per year, and this is exactly the amount it has trailed the S&P 500 total return index (with reinvested dividends) from 2012 through 2021.

DOWNSIDES OF THE S&P 500 INDEX

Despite the past success of index funds, their popularity, especially those funds linked to the S&P 500 Index, may cause investors to underperform the whole market. The reason is simple: if a firm's mere entry into the S&P 500 causes the price of its stock to rise due to the anticipated buying by index funds, these funds will hold overpriced stocks that will depress future returns.

An example of overpricing occurred when Yahoo! was added to the S&P 500 Index in December 1999. Standard & Poor's announced after the close of trading on November 30 that Yahoo! would be added on December 8. In just five trading days between the announcement and its formal membership, the stock surged 64 percent.

A similar surge occurred when Tesla was added to the S&P 500 Index on December 21, 2020. Immediately after the announcement that the electric vehicle manufacturer was going to be added to this prestigious index, its price jumped by 7 percent and continued to rise over 56 percent in price until December 21, when it entered the index. On that day, over 200 million shares of traded with a market value of over $150 billion.

This story is repeated with most stocks added to the index, although the average size of the gain is considerably less than Yahoo!'s or Tesla's. Standard & Poor's published a study in September 2000 that determined how adding a stock to an S&P index influenced the price. This study noted that from the announcement date to the effective date of admission in the S&P 500 Index, shares rose by an average of 8.49 percent.[13] During the next 10 days following their entrance, these stocks fell by an average of 3.23 percent, or about one-third of the pre-entry gain. Yet one year after the announcement, these post-entry losses were wiped out, and the average gain of new entrants was 8.98 percent. All these percentages were corrected for movements in the overall market. A later study has shown that although the pre-entry gain has fallen in recent years, the price of stocks admitted to the S&P 500 still has jumped over 4 percent in response to the announcement.[14]

These jumps in price when a stock is added to the S&P 500 Index is one of the advantages of holding a *total stock market index*, which includes all traded stocks and is not subject to this overpricing. However, despite these pricing headwinds, the S&P 500 has outperformed almost all more-inclusive index funds through 2021.

FUNDAMENTALLY WEIGHTED VERSUS CAPITALIZATION-WEIGHTED INDEXATION

Virtually all indexes that have a significant investment following, such as those created by Standard & Poor's, Russell Investments, and others, are *capitalization weighted*. That means that each firm in the index is weighted by the *market value*, or the current price times the number of shares outstanding.[15]

Capitalization-weighted indexes have some very good properties. First, as noted earlier in the chapter, these indexes represent the *average* dollar-weighted performance of all investors; so for anyone who does better than the index, someone else must do worse. Furthermore, these portfolios, under the assumptions of an efficient market, give investors the "best" trade-off between risk and return. This means that for any given risk level, these capitalization-weighted portfolios give the highest returns, and for any given return, these portfolios give the lowest risk. This property is called *mean-variance efficiency*.

But the assumptions under which these desirable properties prevail are very stringent. Capitalization-weighted portfolios are optimal only if the market is *efficient*, in the sense that the price of each stock is at all points in time an unbiased estimate of the true underlying value of the enterprise. This does not mean that the price of each stock is always right, but it does mean that there is no easily obtainable information that allows investors to make a better estimate of its true value. Under efficient markets, if a stock goes from $20 to $25 a share, the best estimate of the change in the underlying value of the enterprise is also 25 percent, and there are *no* factors unrelated to fundamentals that would change the stock price.

As we learned in Chapter 13, there are many reasons why stock prices change that do not reflect changes in the underlying value of the firm. Transactions made for liquidity, fiduciary, or tax reasons can impact stock prices, as well as speculators acting on unfounded or exaggerated information. When stock price movements can be caused by factors unrelated to fundamental changes in firm value, market prices are noisy and are no longer always unbiased estimates of true value. As noted in that chapter, I call this way of conceptualizing the market the *noisy market hypothesis*.

If the noisy market hypothesis is a better representation of how markets work, the capitalization-weighted indexes are no longer the best portfolios for investors. A better index is a *fundamentally weighted* index, in which each stock is weighted by some measure of a firm's fundamental financial data, such as dividends, earnings, cash flows, and book value, instead of the market capitalization of its stock.[16]

In a capitalization-weighted index, stocks are never sold, no matter what price they reach. This is because if markets are efficient, the price represents the fundamental value of the firm, and no purchase or sale is warranted.

However, in a fundamentally weighted index, if a stock price rises but the fundamentals, such as earnings, do not, then shares are sold until the value of the stock in the index is brought down to the level justified by the fundamentals. The opposite happens when a stock falls for reasons not related to fundamentals—in this case, shares are purchased at the lower price to bring the stock's value back to the original levels. Making these sales or purchases is called *rebalancing* the fundamentally weighted portfolio.[17]

One of the advantages of fundamentally weighted portfolios is that they mitigate the impact of bubbles, those meteoric increases in the prices of stocks that are not accompanied by increases in dividends, earnings, or other objective metrics of firm values. This was certainly the case in 1999 and early 2000, when the technology and internet stocks jumped to extraordinary valuations based on the hope that their profits would eventually justify their price. Any fundamentally weighted portfolio would have sold these stocks as their prices rose, while capitalization-weighted indexes continued to hold them, because the efficient market hypothesis assumes that all price increases are justified.

Note that fundamental indexation does not identify which stocks are overvalued or undervalued. It is a "passive" index, and the purchases and sales of individual stocks are made according to a predetermined formula. Certainly, some overpriced stocks will be bought and some underpriced stocks sold. It can be shown that if prices are determined by the noisy market hypothesis, then on average a portfolio that buys stocks that falls relative to fundamentals and sells stocks that rise relative to fundamentals will likely outperform capitalization-weighted indexes over the long run.[18]

THE HISTORY OF FUNDAMENTALLY WEIGHTED INDEXATION

The motivation for fundamentally weighted indexation began in the international markets. In the 1980s, when Japan's stock market was in a bubble, many investors with internationally diversified portfolios were seeking a consistent way to reduce the weight of Japanese stocks. At that time, Morgan Stanley Capital International (MSCI) formulated an international index that weighted each country by GDP rather than market capitalization and fortunately reduced the allocation to Japanese stocks.[19]

In 1987, Robert Jones of Goldman Sachs's quantitative asset management group developed and managed a US stock index in which the weights of each firm in the index were corporate profits. Jones referred to his strategy as "economic investing," because the proportion of each firm in the index was related to its economic importance rather than its market capitalization.[20] Later David Morris, founder and CEO of Global Wealth Allocation, devised a strategy that combined several fundamental factors into one *wealth* variable.

In 2003, Paul Wood and Richard Evans published research on a fundamentally based approach that evaluated a profit-weighted index of the 100 largest companies.[21] In early 2005, Robert D. Arnott of Research Affiliates, along with Jason Hsu and Philip Moore, published a paper in the *Financial Analysts Journal* entitled "Fundamental Indexation" that exposed the flaws of capitalization-weighted indexes and laid the case for fundamentally based strategies.[22] In December 2005, the first fundamentally weighted ETF was launched by PowerShares (FTSE RAFI US 1000) to track an index constructed by Research Affiliates based on sales, cash flows, book values, and dividends. Six months later, WisdomTree Investments launched 20 ETFs based on dividends.

Table 27.4 shows the performance, since their inception in 2007, of the PowerShares (now Invesco) fund and the two fundamentally weighted WisdomTree funds, EPS, based on earnings weighting, and DTD, based on dividends. To be sure, the returns on these funds fell short of the S&P 500, but they performed better than either the S&P 500 value or the Russell 1000 Value funds.

TABLE 27.4

Performance of selected fundamentally weighted funds and their benchmarks

Average Annual Returns (2/23/07-3/4/22)		
Ticker	Name	Return
PRF	Invesco FTSE RAFI US 1000 ETF	9.15%
EPS	WisdomTree U.S. LargeCap Fund	9.19%
DTD	WisdomTree U.S. Total Dividend Fund	8.22%
SPY	SPDR S&P 500 ETF Trust	9.66%
IVE	iShares S&P 500 Value ETF	7.00%
IWD	iShares Russell 1000 Value ETF	6.89%

Of course, I must give the warning that past performance is no guarantee for the future. But if investors want to tilt their portfolio toward value investing, fundamentally weighted indexes are generally better diversified than most value funds.

CONCLUSION

The past performance of *actively* managed equity funds is not encouraging. The fees that most funds charge do not compensate investors with superior returns and therefore can be a significant drag on wealth accumulation. Furthermore, a good money manager is extremely difficult to identify, for luck plays a role in all successful investment outcomes.

When costs are considered, an overwhelming percentage of actively managed equity funds significantly lag behind the benchmark indexes, and most investors may be better off in capitalization-weighted or fundamentally weighted index funds.

Structuring a Portfolio for Long-Term Growth

[The] long run is a misleading guide to current affairs. In the long run we are all dead. Economists set themselves too easy, too useless a task if in tempestuous seasons they can only tell us when the storm is long past, the ocean will be flat.

—John Maynard Keynes, 1924[1]

My favorite holding period is forever.

—Warren Buffett, 1994[2]

No one can argue with Keynes's statement that in the long run we are all dead. But a vision of the long run must serve as a guide for action today. Those who keep their focus and perspective during trying times are far more likely to emerge as successful investors. Knowing that the sea will be flat after the storm passes is not useless, as Keynes asserted, but enormously comforting.

PRACTICAL ASPECTS OF INVESTING

To be a successful long-term investor is easy in principle but difficult in practice. It is easy in principle because the strategy of buying and holding a diversified portfolio of stocks, forgoing any forecasting ability, is available to all investors, no matter their intelligence, judgment, or financial status. Yet it is difficult in practice, because we are all vulnerable to emotional forces that can lead us astray. Tales of those who have quickly achieved great wealth in the market tempt us to play a game very different from what we had intended.

Selective memory also pushes us in the wrong direction. Those who follow the market closely often exclaim: "I knew that stock [or the market] was going up! If I had only acted on my judgment, I would have made a mint!" But hindsight plays tricks on our minds. We forget the doubts we had when we made the decision not to buy. Hindsight can distort our past experiences and affect our judgment, encouraging us to play hunches and try to outsmart other investors, who in turn are playing the same game.

For most investors, going down this path leads to disastrous results. We take far too many risks, our transaction costs are high, and we find ourselves giving into the emotions of the moment—pessimism when the market is down and optimism when the market is high. This leads to frustration as our misguided actions result in substantially lower returns than we could have achieved by just staying in the market.

GUIDES TO SUCCESSFUL INVESTING

Achieving good returns in stocks requires keeping a long-term focus and a disciplined investment strategy. The following principles come from the research described in this book and enable both new and seasoned investors to better achieve their investing goals:

1. **Historically stocks have returned between 6 and 7 percent after inflation over the last two centuries and have sold at an average P/E ratio of about 15. But there are circumstances indicating that future real returns are apt to be lower, in the range of 5 percent per year after inflation.**

   Lower transaction costs and the ability to diversify one's portfolio at an extremely low cost implies a higher valuation for equities. It is not unreasonable to expect that P/E ratios on stock will fluctuate around 20 instead of the 15 that prevailed in the nineteenth to the middle of the twentieth century. A P/E ratio of 20 is consistent with a 5 percent after inflation return on stocks.

2. **Stocks are real assets and as such serve as excellent long-term hedges against inflation.**

   Stocks are claims on real capital: plant, equipment, copyrights, trademarks, and other intellectual capital. Virtually all the inflation that the United States has experienced has occurred since the end of World War II, but that has had no negative impact on the real return on stocks. However, in the short run, as central banks tighten credit to rein in inflation, stocks tend to have below-average returns.

3. **The variability of average stock returns declines as time lengthens, while the variability of bond returns increases. This means that investors with longer investment horizons should hold a higher percentage of stocks compared to those with shorter horizons.**

Stock returns display *mean reversion*, in other words, shocks in one direction are often offset by shocks in the opposite direction that keep long-term returns stable. Bonds are subject to much inflation uncertainty in the long run. This means that investors with longer time horizons should hold a greater proportion of their portfolio in equities and a lower proportion in bonds.

4. **Invest the largest percentage of your stock portfolio in low-cost stock index funds that span a global portfolio.**

Chapter 27 showed that the broad-based indexes have outperformed the vast majority of actively managed funds over the past half-century. By matching the market year after year, an indexed investor is likely to be near the top of the pack when the long-term returns are tallied.

5. **Invest at least one-third of your equity portfolio in international stocks, defined as those not headquartered in the United States. Stocks in high-growth countries often become overpriced and yield poor returns for investors.**

Today, the United States has about one-half of the world's equity capital. Although US stocks have outperformed the rest of the world over the past decade, in 2022 the United States is the highest priced major market in the world. In the long run, the lower equity valuation ratios are apt to result in superior returns.

6. **Historically, value stocks—those with lower prices relative to their fundamentals, such as earnings and dividends—have superior returns and lower risk than growth stocks. Tilt your portfolio toward value by buying passive indexed portfolios of value stocks or, more recently, fundamentally weighted index funds.**

From 2006 through 2021, value stocks have experienced their worst performance relative to growth stocks in almost a hundred years. Historically, growth stocks have become overpriced every 25 or so years: the Nifty-Fifty mania of the mid-1970s, the dot-com bubble of 2000, and the huge surge of big-capitalization growth stocks in 2020 to 2021. The latest outperformance of stocks, dominated by large-cap tech stocks, is far better grounded than their previous runs—the valuations of large-cap tech stocks are not as high and their earnings growth is more strongly supported than in 2000.

Nevertheless, the long history of the stock market dictates that any group of stocks, sectors, or countries that have been out of favor for a long time often provide better future returns. Value investing is based on the principle that individual stocks are subject to noise traders that deflect their price from fundamentals, and stocks that are priced low relative to fundamentals will likely offer investors better future returns. Investors can take advantage of this mispricing by buying low-cost, passively managed portfolios of value stocks or index funds that are weighted by a stock's fundamentals rather than market capitalization.

7. **Finally, establish firm rules to keep your portfolio on track, especially if you find yourself giving in to the emotion of the moment. If you are particularly anxious about the market, sit down and reread the first two chapters of this book. Or for a quick fix, look at the 220-year graph of real assets returns (Figure 1.1) that motivated me to write this book.**

Swings in investor emotion often send stock prices above and below their fundamental values. The temptations to buy when everyone is bullish and sell when everyone is bearish are hard to resist. Since it is so difficult to stand apart from this market sentiment, most investors who trade have poor returns. This book provides lessons on how to keep long-term focus by understanding the basic forces driving long-term returns in stocks.

IMPLEMENTING THE PLAN AND THE ROLE OF AN INVESTMENT ADVISOR

I wrote *Stocks for the Long Run* to spell out what returns could be expected on stocks and bonds, and to analyze the major factors influencing those returns. Many investors will consider this book a "do-it-yourself guide" to choosing stocks and structuring a portfolio. But knowing the right strategy and implementing the right strategy are not one and the same. As Peter Bernstein so aptly indicated in the Foreword, there are many pitfalls on the path to successful investing that prevent investors from achieving their intended goals.

The first pitfall is trading frequently in an attempt to beat the market. Many investors are not satisfied earning the robust historical return on equity when they know there are always stocks that will double or triple in price over the next 12 months. Finding such gems is extremely gratifying, and many dream of buying the next corporate giant on the ground floor. But the evidence is overwhelming that such investors will suffer poor returns, as transaction costs and bad timing sink returns.

Investors who have been burned by picking individual stocks often turn to mutual funds in their search for higher returns, but choosing a mutual fund poses similar obstacles. Hot managers with superior past performance replace hot stocks as the new strategy to beat the market. As a result, many investors end up playing the same game as they had with individual stocks and also suffer below-average returns.

Those who abandon trying to pick the best funds are tempted to pursue an even more difficult strategy: they attempt to beat the market by timing market cycles. Surprisingly, it is often the best-informed investors who fall into this trap. With the abundance of financial news, information, and commentary at our beck and call, it is extraordinarily difficult to stay aloof from market opinion. As a result, one's impulse is to capitulate to fear when the market is plunging or to greed when stocks are soaring.

Many try to resist this impulse. The intellect may say, "Stay the course!" but this is not easy to do when one hears so many others—including well-respected experts—advising investors to beat a hasty retreat. It is easier to follow what everyone else is doing rather than act independently. As John Maynard Keynes aptly stated in *The General Theory*, "Worldly wisdom teaches that it is better for reputation to fail conventionally than to succeed unconventionally."[3] Failing by following the advice of experts is far easier than failing by rejecting the investment consensus and standing apart from the crowd.

What does all this mean to the reader of this book? Proper investment strategy is as much of a psychological as an intellectual challenge. As with other challenges in life, it may be best to seek professional help to structure and maintain a well-diversified portfolio. If you should decide to seek help, be sure to select a professional investment advisor who agrees with the basic principles of diversification and long-term investing that I have espoused in *Stocks for the Long Run*. It is within the grasp of all to avoid investing pitfalls and reap the generous rewards that are available in equities.

CONCLUSION

The stock market is exciting. Its daily movements dominate the financial press and mark the flows of trillions of dollars of investment capital. Stock markets are far more than the quintessential symbol of capitalism. Stock markets are now found in virtually every country in the world, and they are the driving forces behind the allocation of the world's capital and the fundamental engines of economic growth. The main thesis of this book, that stocks represent the best way to accumulate wealth in the long run, remains as true today as it was when I published the first edition of *Stocks for the Long Run* in 1994.

Notes

CHAPTER 1

1. Benjamin Graham and David Dodd, *Security Analysis*, New York: McGraw-Hill, 1934, 11.
2. Roger Lowenstein, "A Common Market: The Public's Zeal to Invest," *Wall Street Journal*, September 9, 1996, A11.
3. Irving Fisher, *The Stock Market Crash and After*, New York: Macmillan, 1930, xi.
4. "The Crazy Things People Say to Rationalize Stock Prices," *Forbes* (April 27, 1992), 150.
5. Raskob succumbed to those investors in the 1920s who wanted to get rich quickly by devising an alternative scheme by which investors borrowed $300, adding $200 of personal capital, to invest $500 in stocks. Although in 1929 this was certainly not as good as putting money gradually in the market, even this plan beat investment in Treasury bills after 20 years.
6. Irving Fisher, *How to Invest When Prices Are Rising*, Scranton, PA: G. Lynn Sumner & Co., 1912.
7. Edgar L. Smith, *Common Stocks as Long-Term Investments*, New York: Macmillan, 1925, v.
8. Edgar L. Smith, *Common Stocks as Long-Term Investments*, 81.
9. "Ordinary Shares as Investments," *Economist* (June 6, 1925), 1141.
10. John Maynard Keynes, "An American Study of Shares versus Bonds as Permanent Investments," *The Nation & the Athenaeum* (May 2, 1925), 157.
11. Edgar Lawrence Smith, "Market Value of Industrial Equities," *Review of Economic Statistics* 9 (January 1927), 37–40, and "Tests Applied to an Index of the Price Level for Industrial Stocks," *Journal of the American Statistical Association*, Supplement (March 1931), 127–135.
12. Siegfried Stern, *Fourteen Years of European Investments*, 1914–1928, London: Bankers' Publishing Co., 1929.
13. Chelcie C. Bosland, *The Common Stock Theory of Investment, Its Development and Significance*, New York: Ronald Press, 1937.
14. From the Foreword by Irving Fisher in Kenneth S. Van Strum, *Investing in Purchasing Power*, New York: Barron's, 1925, vii. Van Strum was a writer for *Barron's* weekly and confirmed Smith's research.
15. Robert Loring Allen, *Irving Fisher: A Biography*, Cambridge: Blackwell, 1993, 206.

16. *Commercial and Financial Chronicle* (September 7, 1929).

17. "Fisher Sees Stocks Permanently High," *New York Times* (October 16, 1929), 2.

18. Lawrence Chamberlain and William W. Hay, *Investment and Speculations*, New York: Henry Holt & Co., 1931, 55 (emphasis his).

19. Benjamin Graham and David Dodd, *Security Analysis*, 2nd ed., New York: McGraw-Hill, 1940, 357.

20. He estimated the undervaluation at approximately 25 percent of intrinsic value. Alfred Cowles III and associates, *Common Stock Indexes 1871–1937*, Bloomington, IN: Pricipia Press, 1938, 50.

21. Wilford J. Eiteman and Frank P. Smith, *Common Stock Values and Yields*, Ann Arbor: University of Michigan Press, 1962, 40.

22. Lawrence Fisher and James H. Lorie, "Rates of Return on Investment in Common Stocks," *Journal of Business* 37 (January 1964), 1–21.

23. Lawrence Fisher and James H. Lorie, "Rates of Return on Investment in Common Stocks," 20.

24. Roger Ibbotson and Rex Sinquefield, "Stocks, Bonds, Bills, and Inflation: Year-by-Year Historical Returns (1926–74)," *Journal of Business* 49 (January 1976), 11–43.

25. Roger Ibbotson and Rex Sinquefield, *Stocks, Bonds, Bills, and Inflation Yearbooks, 1983–1997*, Chicago: Ibbotson and Associates.

26. Three months later, in December 1995, Shulman capitulated to the bullish side, claiming his longtime emphasis on dividend yields was incorrect.

27. Roger Lowenstein, "A Common Market: The Public's Zeal to Invest," *Wall Street Journal*, September 9, 1996, p. A1.

28. Floyd Norris, "In the Market We Trust," *New York Times*, January 12, 1997.

29. Henry Kaufman, "Today's Financial Euphoria Can't Last," *Wall Street Journal*, November 25, 1996, p. A18.

30. Robert Shiller and John Campbell, "Valuation Ratios and the Long-Run Stock Market Outlook," *Journal of Portfolio Management* 24 (Winter 1997).

31. *Newsweek* (April 27, 1998). Cover stories about the stock market in major newsweeklies have often been poorly timed. *BusinessWeek*'s cover article "The Death of Equities" on August 13, 1979, occurred 14 years after the market had peaked and 3 years before the beginning of the greatest bull market in stocks.

32. I immediately rebutted their arguments in the *Wall Street Journal* (see Jonathan Clements's interview of me in "Throwing Cold Water on Dow 36,000 View" in *Wall Street Journal*, September 21, 1999) stating that their analysis was faulty and that stocks must have real returns exceeding those on US Treasury inflation-protected bonds, whose yield had reached 4 percent at that time.

33. Jeremy Siegel, "Big Cap Tech Stocks Are a Sucker's Bet," *Wall Street Journal*, March 14, 2000, A8.

34. William Gross, "Dow 5,000," PIMCO Investment Outlook, September 1, 2002.

35. Paul Sloan, "The Craze Collapses," *US News and World Report Online*, November 30, 2000.

36. "In Defense of the Shiller P/E," *Economist* (May 18, 2011). After receiving criticism, the *Economist* followed up with another article, "Defending Shiller (again)," *Economist* (September 13, 2011). The 10-year real returns on the US stock market since these articles appeared to have been in excess of 12 percent per year, almost double the historical average.

37. "Pay the Premium," *Economist* (February 6, 2013).

38. Cliff Asness, "An Old Friend: The Stock Market's Shiller P/E," (November 1, 2012), https://www.aqr.com/Insights/Research/White-Papers/An-Old -Friend-The-Stock-Markets-Shiller-PE.

39. Robert D. Arnott, Denis B. Chaves, and Tzee-man Chow, "King of the Mountain: The Shiller P/E and Macroeconomic Conditions," *Journal of Portfolio Management* (Fall 2017) 44 (1), 55–68.

40. Ben Carlson, "Expected Returns & the 7 Year Itch," A Wealth of Common Sense (August 21, 2018), https://awealthofcommonsense.com/2018/08 /expected-returns-the-7-year-itch/.

41. "Jeremy Grantham Predicted Two Previous Bubbles, and Now?" *Wall Street Journal*, November 5, 2017, and *Institutional Investor*, "Why Is No One Listening to Jeremy Grantham?" (February 28 , 2018).

CHAPTER 2

1. Speech at the Virginia Convention, March 23, 1775.

2. Robert Shiller, *Market Volatility*, Cambridge: MIT Press, 1989.

3. Roger G. Ibbotson, *Stocks, Bonds, Bills, and Inflation* (SBBI) Classic Yearbook, published annually by Morningstar, Chicago.

4. G. William Schwert, "Indexes of United States Stock Prices from 1802 to 1897," *Journal of Business* 63 (July 1990), 399–426.

5. See Walter Werner and Steven Smith, *Wall Street*, New York: Columbia University Press, 1991, for a description of some early dividend yields. See also the earlier work by William Goetzmann and Phillipe Jorion, "A Longer Look at Dividend Yields," *Journal of Business* 68, no. 4 (1995), 483–508, and William Goetzmann, "Patterns in Three Centuries of Stock Market Prices," *Journal of Business* 66, no. 2 (1993), 249–270.

6. William Goetzmann and Roger G. Ibbotson, "A New Historical Database for NYSE 1815–1923: Performance and Predictability," reprinted in *The Equity Risk Premium*, New York: Oxford University Press, 2006, 73–106.

7. Goetzmann and Ibbotson formed two stock return series, one assuming that those stocks for which they could not find dividends had zero dividends (their "low dividend yield" estimate), and another that assumes those stocks for which they could not find dividends had the same average dividend yield as those for which they did have dividends (their "high

dividend yield estimate"). The midpoint of their high and low estimate is 6.52 percent, slightly higher than the 6.4 percent that I had originally assumed.

8. See Edward McQuarrie, "Stock for the Long Run? Sometimes Yes, Sometimes, No," Edblogger, July 1, 2021. And "The First 50 Years of the U.S. Stock Market: New Evidence on Investor Total Return Including Dividends: 1793–43," *SSRN Electronic Journal* (January 2018).

9. Edward McQuarrie, "The First 50 Years," 84–85.

10. Samuel Blodget, an early nineteenth-century economist, estimated the wealth of the United States at that time to be nearly $2.5 billion so that $1 million would be only about one-half of 1 percent of the total wealth: S. Blodget, Jr., *Economica, A Statistical Manual for the United States of America*, 1806 edition, 68.

11. See Jeremy Siegel, "The Real Rate of Interest from 1800–1990: A Study of the U.S. and the U.K.," *Journal of Monetary Economics* 29 (1992), 227–252, for a detailed description of the process by which a historical yield series was constructed.

12. Ironically, despite the inflationary bias of a paper money system, well-preserved paper money from the early nineteenth century is worth many times its face value on the collectors' market, far surpassing gold bullion as a long-term investment. An old mattress found containing nineteenth-century paper money is a better find for an antiquarian than an equivalent sum hoarded in gold bars!

13. The 6 to 7 percent long-run real return on the US market was dubbed "Siegel's constant" by Andrew Smithers and Stephen Wright, *Valuing Wall Street: Protecting Wealth in Turbulent Markets*, New York: McGraw-Hill, 2000.

14. Bill Gross, "The Death of the Cult of Equities," PIMCO newsletter (August 2012).

15. GDP growth is consistent with investors consuming about one-half of the annual 6.8 percent long-term real return from stocks.

16. For a review of the equity premium, see Jeremy Siegel and Richard Thaler, "The Equity Premium Puzzle," *Journal of Economic Perspectives* 11, no. 1 (Winter 1997), 191–200. A rigorous and complete analysis is given in John Y. Campbell, *Financial Decision and Markets*, Chapter 6, "Consumption Based Asset Pricing."

17. Robert Shiller, "Do Stock Prices Move Too Much to Be Justified by Subsequent Changes in Dividends?" *American Economic Review* 71 (1981), 421–435.

18. See Stephen J. Brown, William N. Goetzmann, and Stephen A. Ross, "Survival," *Journal of Finance* 50 (1995), 853–873.

19. Elroy Dimson, Paul Marsh, and Michael Staunton, *Triumph of the Optimists: 101 Years of Global Investment Returns*, Princeton, NJ: Princeton University Press, 2002.

20. Elroy Dimson, Paul Marsh, and Michael Staunton, *Triumph of the Optimists: 101 Years of Global Investment Returns, op. cit.* The researchers added three countries to their list since publication.

21. In fact, *Triumph of the Optimists* may have actually *understated* long-term international stock returns. The US stocks markets and other world markets for which we have data did very well in the 30 years prior to 1900, when their study begins. US stock returns measured from 1871 significantly outperform those returns taken from 1900. Data from the United Kingdom show a very similar pattern.

22. See Òscar Jordà, Katharina Knoll, Dmitry Kuvshinov, Moritz Schularick, and Alan Taylor, "The Rate of Return on Everything, 1870–2015," *Quarterly Journal of Economics* 134, 2019, 1225–1298.

23. See http://www.econ.yale.edu/~shiller/data.htm.

24. Jordà, "The Rate of Return on Everything."

25. Jack Francis and Roger Ibbotson, "Real Estate Returns," *Journal of Alternative Investments* (Fall 2020).

26. David Chambers, Christophe Spaenjers, and Eva Steiner, "The Rate of Return on Real Estate, Long-Run Micro-Level Evidence," working paper (January 2021).

27. REITs were first permitted in 1960 after President Dwight D. Eisenhower signed Public Law 86-779.

28. Early work on the returns on the REIT Index can be found in Joseph Gyourko and Jeremy Siegel, "Long-Term Characteristics of Income Producing Real Estate," *Real Estate Finance* (Spring 1994), 14–22. The REIT Equity Index is primarily comprised of commercial, retail, and industrial real estate and only more recently added other real estate categories, such as self-storage, infrastructure, data centers, and others. Single-family homes were added in 2015. REIT returns can be found at https://www.reit.com /data-research/reit-indexes/annual-index-values-returns.

29. Charles D. Ellis, ed., "Memo for the Estates Committee, King's College, Cambridge, May 8, 1938," *Classics*, Homewood, IL: Dow Jones-Irwin, 1989, 79.

30. In fact, in 2018, REITs were removed from the financial sector of the S&P 500 and given their own sector status, raising the number of industries represented in the S&P 500 to 11. This was the first and only sector addition since the index was established in 1958.

CHAPTER 3

1. Irving Fisher, Edwin Kemmerer, and Harry Brown, *How to Invest When Prices Are Rising*, Scranton, PA: G. Lynn Sumner & Co., 1912, 6.

2. Chapter 25 shows why investors' aversion to taking losses, no matter how small, impacts portfolio performance.

3. Robert Arnott, "Bonds, Why Bother?" *Journal of Indexes* (May/June 2009).

4. Paul A. Samuelson, "Proof That Properly Anticipated Prices Fluctuate Randomly," *Industrial Management Review* 6 (1965a), 41–49.

5. James C. Van Horne and George G. C. Parker, "The Random-Walk Theory: An Empirical Test," *Financial Analysts Journal* 23, no. 6 (1967), 87–92, http://www.jstor.org/stable/4470248. Benoit Mandelbrot, "Some Aspects of the Random Walk Model of Stock Market Prices: Comment," *International Economic Review* 9, no. 2 (1968), 258–59, https://doi.org/10.2307/2525479.

6. Paul A. Samuelson, "Risk and Uncertainty: A Fallacy of Large Numbers," *Scientia* 57, no. 98 (1963), 108.

7. Professor Zvi Bodie of Boston University often mentioned my book *Stocks for the Long Run* as providing the basis for this incorrect belief. When I confronted Zvi and said that I never claimed that in my book, he agreed and replied, "I know you don't, Jeremy, but everyone thinks you do!" Zvi Bodie, "On the Risks of Stocks in the Long Run," *Financial Analysts Journal* 51, no. 3 (1995), 18–21.

8. James Poterba and Lawrence Summers, "Mean Reversion in Stock Returns: Evidence and Implications," *Journal of Financial Economics* 22 (1988), 27–59. Eugene F. Fama and Kenneth R. French, "Permanent and Temporary Components of Stock Prices," *Journal of Political Economy* 96e, no. 2 (1988), 264–273.

9. Paul Samuelson, "At Last, a Rational Case for Long-Horizon Risk Tolerance and for Asset-Allocation Timing," in *Active Asset Allocation, State of the Art Polio Policies, Strategies and Tactics*, eds. R. Arnold and F. Fabozzi, Chicago: Probus, 1992, 415–416.

10. Paul Samuelson, "The Long-Term Case for Equities," *Journal of Portfolio Management* (Fall 1994), 17.

11. In early 1996, Zvi Bodie of Boston University, who shared Samuelson's skepticism about mean reversion, invited me to a debate about the long-term risks and returns of stocks and bonds. At the end of my presentation, Samuelson asked for a show of hands from the audience: "How many believed in mean reversion of equity returns?" The audience was split, about fifty-fifty.

12. John Cochrane, "New Fact in Finance, Economic Perspectives," Federal Reserve Bank of Chicago 23, no. 3 (1999).

13. Email received April 12, 2018.

14. Ľuboš Pástor and Robert F. Stambaugh, "Are Stocks Really Less Volatile in the Long Run," *Journal of Finance* 67, no. 2 (April, 2012), 431–477.

15. This would mean that bond *yields* and stock prices move in the same direction.

16. The existence of TIPS gives investors the ability to avoid much (but not all) inflation risk. However, in 2021 their real returns were negative.

17. Paul Samuelson has shown that mean reversion will increase equity proportions for investors with longer holding periods if investors have a risk aversion coefficient greater than unity, which most researchers find is the case. J. J. Siegel, "Climbing Mount Everest: Paul Samuelson on Financial

Theory and Practice," eds. Robert Cord, Richard, Anderson and Willian Barnett. Paul Samuelson, *Remaking Economics: Eminent Post-War Economists*, London: Palgrave Macmillan, https://doi.org/10.1057/978-1-137-56812-0_13.

18. William Bengen, "Determining Withdrawal Rates Using Historical Data," *Journal of Financial Planning* (October 1994), 171–180.

19. Steven Dolvin, William Templeton, and William Rieber, "Asset Allocation for Retirement: Simple Heuristics and Target-Date Funds," *Journal of Financial Planning* (March 2010), 60–71.

20. Javier Estrada, "The Retirement Glidepath: An International Perspective," IESE Business School, Department of Finance, Barcelona, Spain, 13.

21. Paul Samuelson, "Prudent Investment, II" in *Samuelson Sampler* (September 1967), 132–134.

22. For the new Monte Carlo simulations, I lowered each year's historical stock return by 2.66 percentage points and each year's bond return by 3.08 percentage points and ran thousands of simulations.

CHAPTER 4

1. From a transcript of an address delivered to the Annual Conference of the Financial Analysts Federation, May 2, 1984.

2. Eric D. Nelson, "Should You Still Own International Stocks," Servo Wealth Management (March 26, 2021).

3. Martin Mayer, *Markets*, New York: Norton, 1988, 60.

4. James O'Neill, Global Economics, paper, no. 66 (November 30, 2001).

5. Dominic Wilson and Roopa Purushothaman, 1st October 2003, Global Economics, paper no. 99.

6. Dominic Wilson and Roopa Purushothaman, Executive Summary, 2. Investments firms are always required to put disclaimer words such as "could" and "may" into their forecasts that are sent to publication no matter what their degree of enthusiasm.

7. EM countries include Brazil, Chile, China, Colombia, Czech Republic, Egypt, Greece, Hungary, India, Indonesia, Korea, Kuwait, Malaysia, Mexico, Peru, Philippines, Poland, Qatar, Russia, Saudi Arabia, South Africa, Taiwan, Thailand, Turkey, and United Arab Emirates.

8. FTSE puts South Korea in the developed world index.

9. Russia comprises 3 percent of the index.

10. Frontier markets countries include Bahrain, Bangladesh, Burkina Faso, Benin, Croatia, Estonia, Guinea-Bissau, Iceland, Ivory Coast, Jordan, Kenya, Lithuania, Kazakhstan, Mauritius, Mali, Morocco, Niger, Nigeria, Oman, Pakistan, Romania, Serbia, Senegal, Slovenia, Sri Lanka, Togo, Tunisia, and Vietnam.

11. The other five were the Canadian companies Nortel Networks, Alcan, Barrick Gold, Placer Dome, and Inco.

12. Jose Menchero and Andrei Morozov, "Decomposing Global Equity Cross-Sectional Volatility," *Financial Analysts Journal 67*, no. 5 (2011), 58–68.

13. Evidence supplied by WisdomTree Investments, Inc.

CHAPTER 5

1. The index is maintained by S&P Dow Jones Indices, a joint venture majority-owned by S&P Global.

2. General Electric, booted out in 2018 after 122 years, was the last to exit. Chicago Gas Company became Peoples Energy, Inc., and was a member of the Dow Utilities Average until May 1997.

3. A price-weighted index has the property that when a component stock splits, the split stock has a reduced impact on the average, and all the other stocks have a slightly increased impact. Before 1914, the divisor was left unchanged when a stock split, and the stock price was multiplied by the split ratio when computing the index. This led to rising stocks having greater weight in the average, something akin to value-weighted stock indexes today.

4. For a related situation in which a longstanding benchmark was broken because of inflation, see the first section in Chapter 10, "An 'Evil Omen' Returns."

5. In 2004 Standard & Poor's went to a "float adjusted" weighting of shares, which excluded shares held by insiders, other corporations, and governments. This reduced the weights of such large corporations as Wal-Mart in the S&P 500 Index, where many shares are owned by the Walton family.

6. The 2021 criteria for admission includes a market capitalization of (1) at least $13.1 billion, (2) meets liquidity requirements, (3) most recent and last four consecutive quarters of positive as-reported (GAAP earnings), and (4) US based. Since 2017, companies that issue dual shares have been excluded.

7. However, in 2021, Nasdaq added a controversial diversity requirement for the boards of directors of newly listed firms.

8. There is admittedly some double counting of volume in the Nasdaq dealer system since a dealer buys the stock rather than acting as an auctioneer. See Anne M. Anderson and Edward A. Dyl, "Trading Volume: NASDAQ and the NYSE," *Financial Analysts Journal 63*, no. 3 (May/June 2007), 79.

9. Closely related to the CRSP indexes is the Dow Jones Wilshire 5000 Index, which was founded in 1974.

10. Hendrik Bessembinder, "Do Stock Outperform Treasury Bills?," *Journal of Financial Economics* (May 28, 2018), SSRN: https://ssrn.com/abstract=2900447 or http://dx.doi.org/10.2139/ssrn.2900447

11. Hendrik Bessembinder, "Do Stocks Outperform T-bills?" August 2017, 21.

12. J.P. Morgan, "The Agony and the Ecstasy," *Eye on the Markets, Special Edition*, March 2021.

CHAPTER 6

1. Criteria for listing and other information are found on Standard & Poor's website.
2. In 1997 the SIC codes were expanded to include firms in Canada and Mexico, and the revised listing was renamed the North American Industry Classification System (NAICS).
3. There has been much consolidation in the oil industry since 1957. Gulf Oil, Standard Oil of California, and Texaco are now all part of Chevron. Socony Mobil and Standard Oil of NJ are part of ExxonMobil. Royal Dutch and Shell merged and are no longer in the S&P 500 since the index purged all foreign firms in 2008. Phillips is now part of ConocoPhillips, and St. Oil of Indiana merged into British Petroleum and is therefore not in the index.
4. Jeremy J. Siegel and Jeremy D. Schwartz, "Long-Term Returns on the Original S&P 500 Companies," *Financial Analysts Journal* 62, no. 1 (2006), 11–12, http://www.jstor.org/stable/4480755.
5. The firm retained its ticker symbol MO, or "Big Mo," as traders affectionately call Philip Morris.
6. For those non-sports-fans, reaching the cover of this magazine has often spelled the downfall of the athlete or team featured.

CHAPTER 7

1. Robert Arnott, "Dividends and the Three Dwarfs," *Financial Analysts Journal* 59, no. 2 (March/April 2003), 4.
2. This contrasts to the situation when a dividend is paid, where the dividend will reduce the share price by the cash distributed.
3. William Lazonick, Mustafa Erdem Sakinc, and Matt Hopkins, "Why Stock Buybacks Are Dangerous for the Economy," *Harvard Business Review* (January 7, 2020).
4. Myron J. Gordon, *The Investment, Financing, and Valuation of the Corporation*, Homewood, IL: Irwin, 1962.
5. This also assumes that there is no differential tax on capital gains and dividends. See Chapter 9 for more discussion of this issue.
6. The sum of dividend yield and capital gains falls short of the total real return because of the use of averages.
7. John Burr Williams, *The Theory of Investment Value*, Cambridge, MA: Harvard University Press, 1938, 30.
8. Warren Buffett maintained that investor taxes are one reason why Berkshire Hathaway does not pay dividends.
9. Although earnings filed with the IRS may differ from these.
10. These standards are no long called SFAS. All rules are now organized in one *accounting standard codification* (ASC), and FASB now issues an accounting standard update (ASU).
11. Dan Givoly and Carla Hayn, "Rising Conservatism: Implications for Financial Analysis," *Financial Analysts Journal* 58, no.1 (Jan.-Feb. 2002), 56–74.

12. International Financial Reporting Standards (IFRS) allow the write-ups of asset values in some situations.

13. Berkshire Hathaway, 2017 *Annual Report.*

14. These differences in the two series prompted the BEA to put out a brief entitled "Comparing NIPA Profits with the S&P 500 Profits" in "2011 Comparing NIPA Profits with AS&P 500 Profits," by Andrew W. Hodge, *Survey of Current Business* 91 (March 2011). The BEA defines "corporate profits" as the income earned from the current production by US corporations based on "adjusting, supplementing, and integrating financial-based and tax-based source data." Hodges indicates that the Table 1.12, line 45 is the most comparable data to the S&P 500 earnings.

15. Wall Street analysts forecast the operating earnings knowing which items those firms have traditionally included or excluded from their reports. GAAP earnings are rarely forecast, since it is difficult to predict when firms will take special charges for restructuring or report one-time items such capital gains.

16. If there are tax differentials between dividends and capital gains, then the current price will be influenced by dividend policy.

CHAPTER 8

1. See Irving Fisher, *The Rate of Interest*, New York: Macmillan, 1920, in *The Works of Irving Fisher*, 3rd ed., William J. Barber, London: Pickering and Chatto, 1997; Eugen von Böhm-Bawerk, *Capital and Interest: A Critical History of Economical Theory*, London: MacMillan, 1890; Knut Wicksell, *The Rate of Interest*, 1898, in *Interest and Prices*, translated by R. F. Kahn, London: Macmillan, 1936; reprinted New York: Augustus M. Kelley, 1965.

2. On January 17, the National Bureau of Statistics of China said the birth rate fell so sharply in 2021 that it is barely higher than the death rate.

3. "India's Population: The Patter of Few Tiny Feet," *Economist* (December 4, 2021), 39–40.

4. Austria, Australia, Belgium, Canada, Chile, Colombia, Costa Rica, Czech Republic, Denmark, Estonia, Finland, France, Germany, Greece, Hungary, Iceland, Ireland, Israel, Italy, Japan, Korea, Latvia, Lithuania, Luxembourg, Mexico, the Netherlands, New Zealand, Norway, Poland, Portugal, Slovak Republic, Slovenia, Spain, Sweden, Switzerland, Turkey, United Kingdom, and United States.

5. United States, Canada, United Kingdom, France, Germany, Italy, and Japan.

6. Austria, Belgium, Cyprus, Estonia, Finland, France, Germany, Greece, Ireland, Italy, Latvia, Lithuania, Luxembourg, Malta, the Netherlands, Portugal, Slovakia, Slovenia, and Spain.

7. John Y. Campbell, Adi Sunderam, and Luis M. Viceira, "Inflation Bets or Deflation Hedges? The Changing Risks of Nominal Bonds," *Critical Finance Review* 6 (September, 2017), 265, 263–30.

8. Richard Clarida, "Monetary Policy, Price Stability, and Equilibrium Bond Yields: Success and Consequences, delivered in Zurich Switzerland at the High-level Conference on Global Risk, Uncertainty, and Volatility" (November 12, 2019), p. 9.

CHAPTER 9

1. On a monthly basis, the year-over-year inflation declined to –2.1 percent in July 2008 on the heels of the collapse in oil prices, but for the full calendar year there was no deflation during the recession that followed the financial crisis.
2. See Irving Fisher, *The Rate of Interest*, New York: Macmillan, 1907.
3. Gallup poll taken August 2–5, 1974.
4. Figure 9.2 assumes a total real return of 7 percent (real appreciation of 5 percent, a dividend yield of 2 percent) and tax rates of 23.8 percent on capital gains and dividend income. If inflation is 3 percent, the total before-tax return on stocks will be 10 percent in nominal terms.
5. In 1986, the US Treasury proposed the indexation of capital gains, but this provision was never enacted into law. In 1997, the House of Representatives included capital gains indexation in its tax law, but it was removed by House-Senate conferees under threat of a presidential veto.
6. Michael Darby has indicated that if all lenders and borrowers are taxed at the same rate, the interest rate will rise by more than the rate of inflation to compensate for taxes, eliminating the interest distortion. Darby, M. R. "The Financial and Tax Effects of Monetary Policy on Interest Rates *Economic Inquiry*, 13 (June 1975), 266–76

CHAPTER 10

1. Benjamin Graham and David Dodd, "The Theory of Common-Stock Investment," *Security Analysis*, 2nd ed., New York: McGraw-Hill, 1940, 343.
2. *BusinessWeek*, August 9, 1958, 81.
3. "In the Markets," *BusinessWeek*, September 13, 1958, 91.
4. Nicholas Molodovsky, "The Many Aspects of Yields," *Financial Analysts Journal* 18, no. 2 (March–April 1962), 49–62.
5. See Jeremy J. Siegel, "The S&P Gets Its Earnings Wrong," *Wall Street Journal*, February 25, 2009, A13.
6. John Y. Campbell and R. J. Shiller, "Valuation Ratios and the Long-Run Stock Market Outlook," *Journal of Portfolio Management* (Winter 1998), 11–26. Their earlier paper was "Stock Prices, Earnings and Expected Dividends," *Journal of Finance* 43, no. 3 (July 1988), 661–76. Robert Shiller posted a paper, "Price Earnings Ratios as Forecasters of Returns: The Stock Market Outlook in 1996" on his website on July 21, 1996, which served as the basis for his presentation to the Federal Reserve.
7. In that July paper, Shiller forecast the real S&P 500 would decline by 38.07 percent over the next 10 years. Although the S&P 500 appreciated by 41

percent after inflation over that period and real stock returns were 5.6 percent, the CAPE ratios warnings became more accurate as time progressed. In fact since March 1999, the real S&P 500 Index fell by more than 50 percent, vindicating Shiller's bearishness.

8. In 2019 Shiller noted on his website the creation of *total return CAPE ratio*, which corrects for the dividend payout ratio.

9. Jeremy Siegel, "The CAPE Ratio: A New Look" *Financial Analysts Journal* 72, no. 3 (May/June 2016), 1–10.

10. Robert Shiller, Laurence Black, and Farouk Jivraj, "Making Sense of Sky-High Stock Prices," Project Syndicate, November 30, 2020.

11. Jason Zweig, "The Market Doesn't Care About History," *Wall Street Journal*, February 12, 2022, B6.

12. Joel Lander, Athanasios Orphanides, and Martha Douvogiannis, "Earnings Forecasts and the Predictability of Stock Returns: Evidence from Trading the S&P," Federal Reserve, January 1997. Reprinted in the *Journal of Portfolio Management* 23 (Summer 1997), 24–35. It refers to an earlier version that was presented in October 1996.

13. Warren Buffett and Carol Loomis, "Warren Buffett on the Stock Market," *Fortune Magazine*, December 10, 2001.

14. James Tobin, "A General Equilibrium Approach to Monetary Theory," *Journal of Money, Credit, and Banking* 1 (February 1969), 15–29.

15. In 2000 Andrew Smithers and Stephen Wright of the United Kingdom published *Valuing Wall Street: Protecting Wealth in Turbulent Markets*, New York: McGraw-Hill, 2000, which maintained that Tobin's Q was the best measure of value.

16. "Science and Stocks," *The Samuelson Sampler*, Thomas Horton and Company, September 1966, 110–112.

17. Charles M. Jones, "A Century of Stock Market Liquidity and Trading Costs," May 23, 2002.

18. Rajnish Mehra and Edward C. Prescott, "The Equity Premium: A Puzzle," *Journal of Monetary Economics* 15 (March 1985), 145–162.

19. Mehra and Prescott used the Cowles Foundation data going back to 1872. In their research they did not even mention the mean reversion characteristics of stock returns that would have shrunk the equity premium even more.

20. See Jeremy Siegel, "Perspectives on the Equity Risk Premium," *Financial Analysts Journal* 61, no. 1 (November/December 2005), 61–73. Reprinted in Rodney N. Sullivan, ed., *Bold Thinking on Investment Management, The FAJ 60th Anniversary Anthology*, Charlottesville, VA: CFA Institute, 2005, 202–217.

21. Chelcie C. Bosland, *The Common Stock Theory of Investment*, New York: Ronald Press, 1937, 132.

CHAPTER 11

1. Attributed to Mark Twain.
2. Benjamin Graham, *The Intelligent Investor: A Book of Practical Counsel*, Prabhat Prakashan, 1965, 23.
3. Jay R. Ritter, "Economic Growth and Equity Returns," *Pacific-Basin Finance Journal* 13 (2005), 489–503. Elroy Dimson, Paul Marsh, and Mike Staunton, *Triumph of the Optimists: 101 Years of Global Investment Returns*, Princeton NJ: Princeton University Press, 2002.
4. Anthony Bianco, "Homespun Wisdom from the 'Oracle of Omaha'" *Businessweek*, July 5, 1999.
5. Elroy Dimson, Terry Marsh, and Michael Staunton, "Industries: Their Rise and Fall, *Credit Suisse Global Investment Returns Yearbook*, 2015, 7.

CHAPTER 12

1. Rey Mashayekhi, "Why Warren Buffett's 'Bible of Investing' Still Matters More Than 70 Years Later," *Fortune Magazine*, April 17, 2021.
2. Warren Buffett, "The Superinvestors of Graham-and-Doddsville," *Columbia Business School Magazine*, 1984.
3. Prior to the 1980s, value stocks were more often called *cyclical stocks* because low-P/E stocks were often found in those industries whose profits were closely tied to the business cycle. With the growth of style investing, many equity managers that specialized in these stocks were uncomfortable with the "cyclical" moniker and preferred the term *value*.
4. Graham and Dodd, *Security Analysis,* 1st ed., 453. Emphasis theirs.
5. Graham and Dodd, *Security Analysis,* 2d ed., 533.
6. S. F. Nicholson, "Price-Earnings Ratios," *Financial Analysts Journal*, July/August 1960, 43–50, and Sanjoy Basu, "Investment Performance of Common Stocks in Relation to Their Price-Earnings Ratio: A Test of the Efficient Market Hypothesis," *Journal of Finance* 32 (June 1977), 663–682.
7. Earnings based on the last 12 months. Returns were calculated from February 1 to February 1 so that investors could use actual instead of projected earnings for the fourth quarter. Firms with zero or negative earnings were put into the high P/E ratio quintile.
8. Graham and Dodd, *Security Analysis,* 2nd ed., 381.
9. See Robert Litzenberger and Krishna Ramaswamy, "The Effects of Personal Taxes and Dividends on Capital Asset Prices: Theory and Empirical Evidence," *Journal of Financial Economics* (1979), 163–195.
10. James P. O'Shaughnessy, *What Works on Wall Street,* 3rd ed., New York: McGraw-Hill, 2003.
11. Repurchase data not available before 1963; chart substitutes market return until that time.
12. See Jamie Catherwood, "Shareholder Yield," O'Shaugnessy Asset Management, November 2019.

13. John R. Dorfman, "Study of Industrial Average Finds Stocks with High Dividends Are Big Winners," *Wall Street Journal*, August 11, 1988, C2.

14. Eugene Fama and Ken French, "The Cross Section of Expected Stock Returns," *Journal of Finance* 47 (1992), 427–466. Some of the foundational work for the study by Fama and French was performed by Dennis Stattman in his 1980 unpublished MBA honors paper, "Book Values and Expected Stock Returns."

15. Fama and French, "Cross Section of Expected Stock Returns."

16. Graham and Dodd, *Security Analysis*, 1st ed., 493–494.

17. Cate M. Elsten and Nick Hill, "Intangible Asset Market Value Study," *les Nouvelles: Journal of the Licensing Executives Society*, LII, no. 4 (September 2017), 245, https://ssrn.com/abstract=3009783.

18. Robert D. Arnott, Campbell R. Harvey, Vitali Kalesnik, and Juhani T. Linnainmaa, "Reports of Value's Death May Be Greatly Exaggerated," *Financial Analysts Journal* 77 no. 1, 44–67.

19. Jeremy Siegel, "The Nifty Fifty Revisited: Do Growth Stocks Ultimately Justify their Price," *Journal of Portfolio Management* 2, no. 4 (Summer 1995).

20. See Siegel, "Big Cap Tech Stocks Are a Sucker's Bet." *Wall Street Journal*, March 12, 2000.

21. The top 30 percent book to price (H) minus the bottom 30 percent book to price (HML) averaged between large-cap stocks and small-cap stocks

22. Despite the 2007–2020 drawdown, the total accumulation of the value investor's portfolio is still 4.3 times that of a growth investor's portfolio over the 57-year period from July 1963 through June 2020. Using the intellectual-enhanced definition of book value, the drawdown is a less severe 43 percent and started in December 2016 after being relatively flat for the previous 10 years. Robert D. Arnott, Campbell R. Harvey, Vitali Kalesnik, and Juhani T. Linnainmaa, "Reports of Value's Death May Be Greatly Exaggerated," *Financial Analysts Journal* 77, no. 1, 44–67.

23. Ľuboš Pástor, Robert Stambaugh, and Lucian Taylor, "Dissecting Green Returns," working paper, September 7, 2011.

24. When Jim Cramer, host of CNBC's *Mad Money*, gave these stocks the acronym, he also praised these companies for being "totally dominant in their markets." Originally, the acronym FANG was used, with Apple added in 2017.

CHAPTER 13

1. Benjamin Graham and David Dodd, "Price Earnings Ratios for Common Stocks," *Security Analysis*, 2nd ed., New York: McGraw-Hill, 1940, 530.

2. Harry Roberts, "Statistical Versus Clinical Prediction of the Stock Market," Unpublished manuscript, 1967. Eugene Fama, "Efficient Capital Markets: A Review of Theory and Empirical Work," *Journal of Finance* 25, no. 2 (1970), 383–417. An excellent history is also provided by Martin Sewell, "History of the Efficient Market Hypothesis," UCL Research Note, January 20, 2011.

3. Harry Markowitz, "Portfolio Selection," *Journal of Finance* 7, no. 1 (1952), 77–91; Harry Markowitz, *Portfolio Selection*. New York: John Wiley & Sons, Inc., 1959.

4. See Andre Perold, "The Capital Asset Pricing Model," *Journal of Economic Perspectives* 18, no 3 (Summer 2004), 3–24, for an excellent summary of the development of CAPM.

5. As we have noted most of the popular stock indexes, excluding the Dow, are capitalization-weighted portfolios.

6. The foundation of this result was derived by Professor James Tobin of Yale University in his path-breaking article, "Liquidity Preference as Behavior Towards Risk," *Review of Economic Studies* 25, no. 1 (1958), 65–86.

7. Jack L. Treynor, "How to Rate the Performance of Mutual Funds," *Harvard Business Review* 43 (January/February 1965), 43, 63–75, and Michael C. Jensen, "The Performance of Mutual Funds in the Period 1945–64." *Journal of Finance* 23 (May 1968), 389–416. Also see Irwin Friend's influential 1962 *Study on Mutual Funds*.

8. Fischer Black, Michael C. Jensen, and Myron Scholes, "The Capital Asset Pricing Model: Some Empirical Tests," *Studies in the Theory of Capital Markets*, Michael C. Jensen, ed., New York: Praeger, 1972, 79–121; Eugene Fama and James D. MacBeth, "Risk, Return, and Equilibrium: Empirical Tests," *Journal of Political Economy* (May/June 1973), 753–55.

9. Eugene Fama and Ken French, "The Cross Section of Expected Stock Returns," *Journal of Finance* 47 (1992), 427–466.

10. Eugene Fama and Ken French, "The CAPM Is Wanted, Dead or Alive," *Journal of Finance* 51, no. 5 (December 1996), 1947–1958.

11. Sanford J. Grossman and Joseph E. Stiglitz, "On the Impossibility of Informationally Efficient Markets," *American Economic Review* 70 (June 1980), 393–408.

12. See Eugene F. Fama, "The Behavior of Stock Market Prices," *Journal of Business* 38 (January 1965), 34–105; Fischer Black, "Noise," *Journal of Finance* 41, no. 3 (July 1986), 529–543.

13. Jeremy Siegel, "The Noisy Market Hypothesis," *Wall Street Journal*, June 6, 2006.

14. Fundamentally weighted indexing products were jointly developed by WisdomTree Investments and Research Affiliates. See Robert Arnott, Jason Hu, and Philip Moore, "Fundamental Indexation," *Financial Analyst Journal* 63, no. 2 (March/April 2004). Consulting group Willis Towers Watson minted the term *smart beta* in the early 2000s.

15. Milton Friedman, "The Case for Flexible Exchange Rates," *Essays in Positive Economics*, Chicago: University of Chicago Press, 1953.

16. While noise traders may earn higher returns, they do take on more risk. See James Bradford De Long, Andrei Shleifer, Lawrence Summers, and Robert Waldmann, "Noise Trader Risk in Financial Markets," *Journal of Political Economy* 98, no. 4 (1990) 703–738.

17. Fischer Black, "Noise," *Journal of Finance* 41, no. 3 (July 1986), 528–543. Rarely, if ever, has an academic been so explicit!

18. John Maynard Keynes, *General Theory*, London: Macmillan, 1936, 157.

19. This phrase has been attributed to Keynes, but has never been confirmed. The first time this phrase has been noted is by A. Gary Shilling, a financial analyst in the 1980s.

20. Andrei Shleifer and Robert Vishny, "The Limits of Arbitrage," *Journal of Finance* 52, (1997), 35–55.

21. Robert F. Stambaugh, Jian Feng Yu, and Yu Yuan, "The Short of It: Investor Sentiment and Anomalies," *Journal of Financial Economics* 104 (2012), 288–302. These anomalies included momentum, probability of failure, distress, net and composite stock issuance, accruals, operating assets, gross profitability, asset growth, return on assets, and capital investment. In their study, the long-short portfolio involves going long in the top 10 percent of the best-performing stocks (for each strategy) and selling short the worst-performing stocks.

22. Malcolm Baker and Jeffrey Wurgler, "Investor Sentiment and the Cross-Section of Stock Returns," *Journal of Finance* 61, no. 4 (2006).

23. Richard Roll, "A Critique of the Asset Pricing Theory's Tests," *Journal of Financial Economics* 4 (1977), 129–76. Also see D. Mayers, "Nonmarketable Assets and Capital Market Equilibrium Under Uncertainty," in M. Jensen, ed., *Studies in the Theory of Capital Markets*, New York, NY: Praeger (1972).

24. Leonid Kogan, Dimitris Papanikolaou, and Noah Stoffman, "Left Behind: Creative Destruction, Inequality, and the Stock Market," *Journal of Political Economy* 128, no. 3 (2020).

25. Robert C. Merton, "An Intertemporal Capital Asset Pricing Model," *Econometrica* 41, no. 5 (September 1973), 867–887.

26. John Y. Campbell and Tuomo Vuolteenaho, "Bad Beta, Good Beta," *American Economic Review* 94, no. 5 (December 2004), 1249–1275.

27. Daniel Kahneman and Amos Tversky, "Prospect Theory: An Analysis of Decision Under Risk," *Econometrica* 47, (1979), 263–291.

CHAPTER 14
This chapter has benefited enormously from discussion with my colleague Robert Stambaugh from the Wharton School.

1. Campbell R. Harvey and Yan Liu, "A Census of the Factor Zoo" (February 25, 2019), 1–2, available at SSRN: https://ssrn.com/abstract=3341728 or http://dx.doi.org/10.2139/ssrn.3341728.

2. Eugene F. Fama and Kenneth R. French, "Dissecting Anomalies with a Five-Factor Model," *The Review of Financial Studies* 29, no. 1 (2016), 69–103. http://www.jstor.org/stable/43866012.

3. John H. Cochrane, "Presidential Address: Discount Rates," *Journal of Finance* 66, no. 4 (August 2011), 1047–1108.

4. For valuation and momentum factors, the portfolio is an equally weighted average of the return on stocks with higher-than-median capitalizations and those with lower-than-median capitalization.

5. Rolf Banz, "The Relationship Between Return and Market Value of Common Stock," *Journal of Financial Economics* 9 (1981), 3–18.

6. For a good review of the theories of the small firm effect, see Bruce I. Jacobs and Kenneth N. Levy, "Forecasting the Size Effect," *Financial Analysts Journal* 45, no. 3 (May–June 1989), 38–54.

7. The small-cap stock index is the bottom quintile (20 percent) size of the NYSE stocks until 1981, then it is the performance of Dimensional Fund Advisors (DFA) Small Company fund from 1982 through 2000, and then it is the Russell 2000 Index from 2001 onward.

8. Cliff Asness in an email, dated May 10, 2021.

9. Clifford Asness, Andrea Frazzini, Ronen Israel, Tobias J. Moskowitz, and Lasse H. Pedersen, "Size Matters, If You Control Your Junk," *Journal of Financial Economics* 129 (2018), 479–509.

10. For a good summary of arguments, see Robert Stambaugh and Yu Yuan, "Mispricing Factors," *Review of Financial Studies* 30, no. 4 (2017), and 1270–1315; Ron Alquist, Ronen Israel, and Tobias Moskowitz, "Fact, Fiction, and the Size Effect," *Journal of Portfolio Management* 45, no. 1 (Fall 2018), 3–30.

11. Werner F. M. De Bondt and Richard Thaler, "Does the Stock Market Overreact? *Journal of Finance* 40, no. 3 (July 1985) papers and proceedings of the Forty-Third Annual Meeting, American Finance Association, Dallas, Texas, December 28–30, 1984 793–805.

12. Werner F. M. De Bondt and Richard H. Thaler, "Further Evidence on Investor Overreaction and Stock Market Seasonality," *The Journal of Finance* 42, no. 3 (July 1987) and papers and proceedings of the Forty-Fifth Annual Meeting, American Finance Association, New Orleans, Louisiana, December 28–30, 1986 (July 1987), 557–581

13. Werner F. M. De Bondt and Richard H. Thaler, 579. One of the puzzles that De Bondt and Thaler could not explain was that most of the gains of the "losers'" portfolio occurred in the month of January.

14. Narasimhan Jegadeesh, "Evidence of Predictable Behavior of Security Returns," *Journal of Finance* 45, no. 3, papers and proceedings, Forty-Ninth Annual Meeting, American Finance Association, Atlanta, Georgia, December 28–30, 1989 (July 1990), 881–898.

15. See Geert K. Rouwenhorst, "International Momentum Strategies," *Journal of Finance* 53 (1998), 267–284.

16. David Blitz, Joop Huij, and Martin Martens, "Residual Momentum," *Journal of Empirical Finance* 18, no. 3 (June 2011), 506–521.

17. "Buffett Takes Stock," *New York Times Magazine*, Section 6 (April 1, 1990), 16.

18. Eugene Fama and Robert Litterman, "An Experienced View on Markets and Investing," *Financial Analysts Journal* 68, no. 6, CFA Institute, 2012, 15–19, http://www.jstor.org/stable/41714292.

19. Nicholas Barberis, Andrei Shleifer, and Robert Vishny, "A model of investor sentiment," *Journal of Financial Economics* 49 (1998), 307–343.

20. Kent Daniel, David Hirshleifer, and Avanidhar Subrahmanyam, "Investor Psychology and Security Market Under- and Overreactions," *Journal of Finance* 53 (1998), 1839–1886.

21. Cliff Asness, Andrea Frazzini, Ronen Israel, and Tobias Moskowitz, "Fact, Fiction, and Momentum Investing," *Journal of Portfolio Management*, 40th Anniversary Issue, Fama-Miller working paper (May 9, 2014), SSRN: https://ssrn.com/abstract=2435323 or http://dx.doi.org/10.2139/ssrn.2435323 .

22. Eugene Fama and Kenneth R. French, "A Five-Factor Asset Pricing Model," *Journal of Financial Economics* 116, no. 1 (April 2015), 1–22.

23. Sheridan Titman, K. C. John Wei, and Feixue Xie, "Capital Investment and Stock Returns," *Journal of Financial and Quantitative Analysis* 39 (2004), 677–700.

24. Jim Collins, *Good to Great*, New York, NY: HarperCollins Publishers Inc., 2001.

25. Jay Ritter, "The Long-Run Performance of Initial Public Offerings," *Journal of Finance* 46 no. 3 (1991), 3–27.

26. They first identified this factor in 2006, in Eugene Fama and Kenneth French, "Profitability, Investment and Average Returns," *Journal of Financial Economics* 82, no. 3 (December 2006), 491–518.

27. Robert Novy-Marx, "The Other Side of Value: The Gross Profitability Premium," *Journal of Financial Economics* 108, no. 1 (2013), 1–28.

28. Sunil Wahal, "The Profitability and Investment Premium: Pre-1963 Evidence," *Journal of Financial Economics*, 2018.

29. Fama and French suggest that these factors can be derived from the dividend discount model discussed in Chapter 12, but in my opinion, they do not do so convincingly.

30. Richard G. Sloan, "Do Stock Prices Fully Reflect Information in Accruals and Cash Flows About Future Earnings?" *Accounting Review* 71 (1996), 289–315.

31. Cliff Asness, Andrea Frazzini, and Lasse Pedersen, "Quality Minus Junk," *Review of Accounting Studies* 24 (2019), 34–112.

32. Robert Stambaugh and Yu Yuan, "Mispricing Factors," *Review of Financial Studies* 30, no. 4 (2017).

33. Andrew Ang, Robert J. Hodrick, Yuhang Xing, and Xiaoyan Zhang, "The Cross-Section of Volatility and Expected Returns," *Journal of Finance* 61, no. 1 (2006), 259–299; Roger Clarke, Harindra de Silva, and Steven Thorley, "Minimum-Variance Portfolios in the US Equity Market," *Journal of Portfolio Management* 33, no. 1 (Fall 2006), 10–24; David Blitz and Pim van Vliet, "The Volatility Effect: Lower Risk Without Lower Return," *Journal of Portfolio Management* 34, no. 1 (2007), 102–113.

34. See David Swedroe, "Deconstructing the Low Volatility/Low Beta Anomaly," *Research Insights* (July 12, 2018).

35. Yakov Amihud and Haim Mendelson, "Asset Pricing and the Bid-Ask Spread," *Journal of Financial Economics* 17, no. 2 (December 1986), 223–249.

36. Roger G. Ibbotson, Zhiwu Chen, Daniel Y.-J. Kim, and Wendy Y. Hu, "Liquidity as an Investment Style," *Financial Analysts Journal* 69, no. 3 (May/June 2013), 30–44.

37. Ľuboš Pástor and Robert F. Stambaugh, "Liquidity Risk and Expected Stock Returns," *Journal of Political Economy* 111, no. 3 (June 2003), 642–685.

38. Xiaomeng Lu, Robert F. Stambaugh, and Yu Yuan, "Anomalies Abroad: Beyond Data Mining," working paper (January 9, 2018).

39. Professor Robert Stambaugh has indicated to me in an email on March 17, 2022, that momentum also does not work in China.

40. Cliff Asness finds that momentum is significant in Japan if combined with a value factor. See Cliff Asness, "Momentum in Japan: The Exception That Proves the Rule," *Journal of Portfolio Management* 37 no. 4 (2011).

41. The quality returns are taken from Cliff Asness's "Quality Minus Junk," cited previously. The liquidity returns are on average Robert Stambaugh's, Robert Ibbotson's, and Yakov Amihud's returns.

CHAPTER 15

1. Milton Friedman, "The Social Responsibility of Business Is to Increase Its Profits," *New York Times Magazine*, September 13, 1970.

2. "Greed Is Good. Except When It's Bad," DealBook/*New York Times Magazine*, September 13, 2020.

3. https://www.businessroundtable.org/business-roundtable-redefines -the-purpose-of-a-corporation-to-promote-an-economy-that-serves-all -americans.

4. "Greed Is Good. Except When It's Bad," DealBook/*New York Times Magazine*, September 13, 2020.

5. Friedman did accept that corporations that made charitable contributions that improved the political or regulatory climate in which they worked were appropriate and served their shareholders. See Edward Nelson, *Milton Friedman & Economic Debate in the United States, 1932–72*, vol. 2, Chicago: University of Chicago Press, 2020, 185–188.

6. The discussion in this chapter has benefited enormously from the academic research embodied in the article by Ľuboš Pástor, Robert Stambaugh, and Lucian Taylor, "Sustainable Investing in Equilibrium," *Journal of Financial Economics*, February 21, 2021. I would also like to thank Erica A. DiCarlo for providing me excellent background data for ESG investing.

7. More specifically, these three categories comprise:
Environment: Stewardship of the Planet, such as emission control, renewables, water conservation, recycling, pollution, and others;
Social: Welfare of Stakeholders, comprising human rights, Employee health and safety and well-being, child labor and antibribery laws, fairtrade policy, diversity, community development, equal opportunity;
Governance: Corporate Good Practices, Executive Compensation, Voting Classes, Transparency, Independent Board of Directors, and so on.

8. US SIF Foundation, "Report on US Sustainable and Impact Investment Trends," 2020. See also, "Advancing Environmental, Social, and Governance Investing," *Deloitte Insights*, 2021, https://www2.deloitte.com /us/en/insights/industry/financial-services/esg-investing-performance .html.

9. Note that as ESG becomes more popular and investors purchase high-ranked ESG firms, there may be some temporary pricing pressure that may also send their prices higher. But these higher prices will dissipate after the purchases are completed, sending prices back down. Similar one-time jumps in prices have been observed when firms are added to such popular indexes such as the S&P 500, see Chapter 27.

10. In this view ESG investing is like buying art, where the enjoyment of viewing it offsets its resale value.

11. John Authers, "ESG: Everything Sounds Good: But Is It?" *Bloomberg Opinion*, April 26, 2021.

12. Ibid.

13. Ľuboš Pástor, et al., "Dissecting Green Returns."

14. Casey Clark and Harshad Lalit, "ESG Improvers, an Alpha Enhancing Factor," Rockefeller Asset Management, 2020.

15. Elroy Dimson, Paul Marsh, and Mike Staunton, "Industries: Their Rise and Fall," *Credit Suisse Global Investment Returns Yearbook*, 2015.

16. In economist language, an individual has a utility function that includes the state of the environment in addition to his level of wealth.

17. It should be noted that this hedge demand for green stocks is *not* generated by pure "regulatory risk" that changes not due to unanticipated shifts in the climate outlook. Regulatory risk arises from unexpected changes in regulations that impose costs of firms. Certain green firms may outperform the market if a political party putting a higher weight on climate risk takes office. But these risks are subsumed under the normal market risks and do not require the formation of a hedge portfolio.

CHAPTER 16

1. Benjamin Graham and David Dodd, *Security Analysis*, New York: McGraw-Hill, 1934, 618.

2. Burton Malkiel, *A Random Walk Down Wall Street*, New York: Norton, 1990, 133. In an email sent to me on February 23, 2022, he indicates that he holds the same opinion today.

3. See William Brock, Josef Lakonishok, and Blake LeBaron, "Simple Technical Trading Rules and the Stochastic Properties of Stock Returns," *Journal of Finance* 47, no. 5 (December 1992), 1731–1764, and Andrew Lo, Harry Mamaysky, and Jiang Wang, "Foundations of Technical Analysis: Computational Algorithms, Statistical Inference, and Empirical Implementation," *Journal of Finance* 55 (2000), 1705–1765.

4. Martin Pring, *Technical Analysis Explained*, 3rd ed., New York: McGraw-Hill, 1991, 31. Also see David Glickstein and Rolf Wubbels, "Dow Theory Is Alive and Well!" *Journal of Portfolio Management* (April 1983) 28–32.

5. *Journal of the American Statistical Association* 20 (June 1925), 248. Comments made at the Aldine Club in New York on April 17, 1925.

6. Paul Samuelson, "Proof That Properly Anticipated Prices Fluctuate Randomly," *Industrial Management Review* 6 (1965), 49.

7. More generally, the sum of the product of each possible price change times the probability of its occurrence is zero. This is called a *martingale*, of which a random walk (50 percent probability up, 50 percent probability down) is a special case.

8. Figure 16-1B covers February 15 to July 1, 1991; Figure 16-1E covers January 15 to June 1, 1992; and Figure 16-1H covers June 15 to November 1, 1990.

9. Martin Zweig, *Winning on Wall Street*, New York: Warner Books, 1990, 121.

10. See William Brock, Josef Lakonishok, and Blake LeBaron, "Simple Technical Trading Rules and the Stochastic Properties of Stock Returns," *Journal of Finance* 47, no. 5 (December 1992), 1731–1764. The first definitive analysis of moving averages comes from a book by H. M. Gartley, *Profits in the Stock Market*, New York: H. M. Gartley, 1930.

11. William Gordon, *The Stock Market Indicators*, Palisades, NJ: Investors Press, 1968.

12. Robert W. Colby and Thomas A. Meyers, *The Encyclopedia of Technical Market Indicators*, Homewood, IL: Dow Jones-Irwin, 1988.

13. In fact, if stock prices are random walks, the number of buy and sell orders is inversely proportional to the size of the band.

14. Historically, the daily high and low levels of stock averages were based on the highest or lowest price of each stock reached at any time during the day. This is called the *theoretical high* or *low*. The *actual high* is the highest level reached at any given time by the stocks in the average.

15. Benjamin Graham and David Dodd, *Security Analysis*, 2nd ed., New York: McGraw-Hill, 1940, 715–716.

CHAPTER 17

1. Donald Keim, "Size-Related Anomalies and Stock Return Seasonality: Further Empirical Evidence," *Journal of Financial Economics* 12 (1983), 13–32.

2. See Gabriel Hawawini and Donald Keim, "On the Predictability of Common Stock Returns: World-Wide Evidence," in Robert A. Yarrow, Vojislav Macsimovic, and William T. Ziemba, eds., *Handbooks in Operations Research and Management Science*, 9, North Holland: Elsevier Science BV, (1995), 497–544.

3. For an excellent summary of the early international evidence, see Gabriel Hawawini and Donald Keim, "The Cross Section of Common Stock Returns: A Review of the Evidence and Some New Findings," in Donald B. Keim and William T. Ziemba, eds., *Security Market Imperfections in World-wide Equity Markets*, Cambridge: Cambridge University Press, 2000.

4. Edward M. Saunders, Jr., "Stock Prices and Wall Street Weather," *American Economic Review* 83 (December 1993), 1337–1345.

5. Of course, many investors in the Australian and New Zealand market live north of the equator.

6. Robert A. Ariel, "A Monthly Effect in Stock Returns," *Journal of Financial Economics* 18 (1987), 161–174.

7. Historically, about two-thirds of the Dow Industrial stocks pay dividends in the first half of the month.

CHAPTER 18

1. Martin Zweig, *Winning on Wall Street*, updated ed., New York: Warner Books, 1990, 43.

2. Linda Grant, "Striking Out at Wall Street," *U.S. News & World Report* (June 30, 1994), 59.

3. "World Crisis Seen by Vienna Bankers," *New York Times*, September 21, 1931, 2.

4. "British Stocks Rise, Pound Goes Lower," *New York Times*, September 24, 1931, 2.

5. When the government issued non-gold-backed money during the Civil War, the notes were called "greenbacks" because the only "backing" was the green ink printed on the notes. Yet just 20 years afterward, the government redeemed every one of those notes in gold, completely reversing the inflation of the Civil War period.

6. "We Start," *BusinessWeek* (April 26, 1933), 32.

7. *Economic Report of the President*, Washington, DC: Government Printing Office, 1965, 7.

8. *Economic Report of the President*, Washington, DC: Government Printing Office, 1969, 16.

9. In 2000, Congress allowed the Humphrey-Hawkins Act to lapse, but legislation still required the Federal Reserve chairman to report biannually to Congress.

10. This used to include the London Interbank Offered Rate (LIBOR), which is now being phased out in favor of other short-term market indicators, such as SOFR (Secured Overnight Funding Rate).

11. The averages computed at the bottom of the table are with and without the December 1986 hike. That set of increases, which was smallest since 1976, occurred during a strong bull market and which finally culminated in the October 1997 stock market crash.

12. M2 is the name that Professor Milton Friedman gave to the sum of all deposits and circulating bank currency (excluding reserves) in his *Monetary History of the United States*.

13. Written on every US Federal Reserve Note is "This note is legal tender for all debts, public and private."

CHAPTER 19

1. Paul Samuelson, "Science and Stocks," *Newsweek* (September 19, 1966), 92.
2. Peter Lynch, *One Up on Wall Street*, New York: Penguin Books, 1989, 14.
3. Wesley C. Mitchell and Arthur Burns, "Measuring Business Cycles," *NBER Reporter*, 1946, 3.
4. The data from 1802 through 1854 are taken from Wesley C. Mitchell, *Business Cycles: The Problem and Its Setting*, Studies in Business Cycles No. 1, Cambridge, MA: National Bureau of Economic Research, 1927, 444. The data on US recessions are taken from the NBER's website (http://www.nber.org), which lists business cycles from 1854 onward.
5. Robert Hall, "Economic Fluctuations," *NBER Reporter*, Summer 1991, 1.
6. Chapter 22 will discuss the 1987 stock crash and explain why it did not lead to an economic downturn.
7. There are two ways to treat the 2000–2002 bear market. The first interpretation is that there was one bear market that peaked on a total return basis on September 1, 2000, and bottomed on October 9, 2002, for a loss of 47.4 percent. The second is that there were two bear markets: one bear market with a drop of 35.7 percent from September 1, 2000, through September 21, 2001, just 10 days after the 9/11 terrorist attacks, then a subsequent rally of 22.1 percent to March 19, 2002; and another bear market of 33.0 percent, ending in October.
8. See "Does It Pay Stock Investors to Forecast the Business Cycle?" *Journal of Portfolio Management* 18 (Fall 1991), 27–34.
9. Stephen K. McNees, "How Large Are Economic Forecast Errors?" *New England Economic Review* (July/August 1992), 33.
10. "New Wave Economist," *Los Angeles Times*, March 18, 1990, Business Section, 22.
11. Leonard Silk, "Is There Really a Business Cycle?," *New York Times*, May 22, 1992, D2.
12. See Steven Weber, "The End of the Business Cycle?" *Foreign Affairs* (July/August 1997).
13. *Blue Chip Economic Indicators*, September 10, 2001, 14.
14. *Blue Chip Economic Indicators*, February 10, 2002, 16.
15. Transcript of Federal Open Market Committee meeting on December 11, 2007, 35.

CHAPTER 20

1. Table 20.1 excludes the 15.34 percent change from March 3 to March 15, 1933, to account for the US bank holiday.
2. This expands the research originally published in David M. Cutler, James M. Poterba, and Lawrence H. Summers, "What Moves Stock Prices," *Journal of Portfolio Management* (Spring 1989), 4–12.
3. The decline in October 1989, although sometimes attributed to the collapse of the leveraged buyout, can be questioned since the market was already

down substantially on very little news before the buyout talks were terminated.

4. Virginia Munger Kahn, *Investor's Business Daily* (November 16, 1991), 1.

5. Two runoff senatorial elections in January 2021 in Georgia, however, went to the Democrats who took control of the Senate and all branches of government.

CHAPTER 21

1. Usually both the median and range of estimates are reported. The consensus estimate does vary a bit from service to service, but the estimates are usually quite close.

2. John H. Boyd, Jian Hu, and Ravi Jagannathan, "The Stock Market's Reaction to Unemployment News: 'Why Bad News Is Usually Good for Stocks,'" EFA 2003 Annual Conference, December 2002, Paper No. 699.

3. Martin Zweig, *Winning on Wall Street*, New York: Warner Books, 1986, 43.

CHAPTER 22

1. This is based on a $55 trillion worldwide total stock value at the end of 2012.

2. Futures markets are discussed in Chapter 26.

3. James Stewart and Daniel Hertzberg, "How the Stock Market Almost Disintegrated a Day After the Crash," *Wall Street Journal*, November 20, 1987, 1.

4. Martin Mayer, *Markets*, New York: Norton, 1988, p. 62.

5. Before 1998, the NYSE suspended trading for one-half hour when the Dow fell by 350 points and closed the exchange when the Dow fell by 550 points. Both of these halts were triggered on October 27, 1997, when the Dow Industrials fell by 554 points in response to the Asian currency crisis. Because of intense criticism of these closings, the NYSE sharply widened the limits to keep trading open.

6. When the markets reopened after the 350-point limit was reached, traders were so anxious to exit that the 550-point limit was reached in a matter of minutes. See also note 4.

7. SEC and CFTC, *Findings Regarding the Market Events of May 6, 2010*, September 30, 2010.

8. These were sold through the E-mini market, valued at about $50,000 per contract.

9. These explanations were immediately challenged by the Chicago Monetary Exchange, which claimed that the large sell order represented less than 5 percent of the total volume in the S&P futures market during the three and a half minutes that preceded the market bottom at 1:45:28. The CME response can be found on its website at http://cmegroup.mediaroom .com/index.php?s=43&item=3068.

10. Tom Lauricella and Peter McKay, "Dow Takes a Harrowing 1010.14 Point Trip," *Wall Street Journal*, May 7, 2010.

11. For leveraged securities or securities trading under $3, the limits are higher.

12. Charles D. Ellis, ed., "Memo for the Estates Committee, King's College, Cambridge, May 8, 1938," *Classics*, Homewood, IL: Dow Jones-Irwin, 1989, 79.

13. This is done by solving for the volatility using the Black-Scholes options pricing formula. See Chapter 26.

14. Until 2003, the VIX Index was based on the S&P 100 (the largest 100 stocks in the S&P 500 Index).

15. Robert Shiller, *Market Volatility*, Cambridge, MA: MIT Press, 1989. The seminal article that spawned the excess volatility literature was "Do Stock Prices Move Too Much to Be Justified by Subsequent Changes in Dividends?," *American Economic Review* 71 (1981), 421–435. Shiller was awarded the 2013 Nobel Prize in Economics in part for this research on market volatility.

16. Memorandum from Dean Witter, May 6, 1932.

17. John Maynard Keynes, *The General Theory of Employment Interest, and Money*, London: Macmillan, 1936, 149.

CHAPTER 23

1. As early as June, Natixis, a French investment bank, had cut off all activity with Lehman, and in early September, it was reported by *The Financial Crisis Inquiry Report* that J.P. Morgan, Citigroup, and Bank of America all demanded more collateral from Lehman with the threat that they might "cut Lehman off if they don't receive it."

2. Risk spreads, such as the TED spread (Treasuries over Eurodollars), the LIBOR-OIS spread (LIBOR over Fed funds), and commercial paper over Treasuries, and others jumped dramatically. By Wednesday the Bloomberg Financial Conditions Index of risk had deteriorated to four to five standard deviations below normal levels based on the past 16 years of data. (See Michael G. Rosenberg, "Financial Conditions Watch," *Bloomberg*, September 18, 2008.)

3. On Monday, September 15, the Reserve Primary Fund valued Lehman's commercial paper at 80 cents on the dollar. On Tuesday it posted on its website, "The value of the debt securities issued by Lehman Brothers Holdings, Inc (face value $785 million) and held by the Primary fund has been valued at zero effective as of 4:00 p.m. New York time today. As a result, the NAV of the Primary Fund, effective as of 4:00 p.m. is $0.97 per share."

4. In fact, just days before the Lehman bankruptcy, the REIT Index was only 25 percent below its record level that it reached in July 2007. In contrast, homebuilder stocks peaked in July 2005 and were already down more than 60 percent by the time the Lehman crisis broke.

5. See Alex Frangos, "At Lehman, How a Real-Estate Start's Reversal of Fortune Contributed to Collapse," *Wall Street Journal*, October 1, 2008.

6. The standard deviation of quarterly changes in nominal GDP fell from 5.73 percent from 1947 to 1983 to 2.91 percent from 1983 to 2009.

7. The Jerome Levy Economics Institute of Bard College, Working Paper No. 74, May 1992; see also Robert Pollin, "The Relevance of Hyman Minsky," *Challenge*, March/April 1997.

8. Politicians wanted to give millions of Americans their first chance to realize the American Dream of home ownership and encouraged the government-sponsored lenders Fannie Mae and Freddie Mac to issue these loans to those who would not ordinarily qualify for conventional mortgages.

9. Since mortgages are denominated in dollars, it is the nominal, not the real, index that is of interest to bond buyers.

10. It is true that there were substantial declines in nominal house prices during the Great Depression and that the real estate price index declined 25.9 percent between 1928 and 1932. But that was entirely due to a deflation in the general price index, as the CPI fell almost exactly the same percentage. Since the Federal Reserve had committed to avoid deflation and could do so through the power of money creation, it would be quite reasonable to assume that researchers would ignore those data.

11. "Absence of Fear," CFA Society of Chicago Speech, June 28, 2007, reported by Robert Rodriguez, CEO of First Pacific, http://www.fpafunds.com/docs/special-commentaries/absence_of_fear.pdf?sfvrsn=2.

12. Deutsche Bank Trustee Reports, October 15, 2007.

13. Data from the Census Bureau and the Case-Shiller Home National Home Price Series.

14. Noelle Knox, "43% of First-Time Home Buyers Put No Money Down," *USA Today*, January 18, 2006, 1A.

15. Charles Himmelberg, Chris Mayer, and Todd Sinai, "Assessing High House Prices, Bubbles, Fundamentals and Misperceptions," *Journal of Economic Perspectives* 19, no. 4 (Fall 2005), 67–92. They also wrote an article, "Bubble Trouble? Not Likely," which appeared on the editorial page of the *Wall Street Journal* (September 19, 2005) at the peak of housing prices.

16. According to Home Mortgage Disclosure Act data, the national share of purchase loans for second homes—defined as "other than owner-occupied as a principal dwelling"—increased from 8.6 to 14.2 percent from 2000 to 2004. That represents an annual average growth rate of 16 percent during that time period. The actual number of purchase loans doubled, increasing from 405,000 to 881,200. See Kenneth R. Harney and Washington Post Writers Group, "Boomer Homeowners Going Back for Seconds," *Chicago Tribune*, April 2, 2006, https://www.chicagotribune.com/news/ct-xpm-2006-04-02-0604020254-story.html. Keunwon Chung is a statistical economist at the NAR.

17. Robert Shiller, *Irrational Exuberance*, 2nd ed., Princeton, NJ: Princeton University Press, 2005, Chapter 2. Also see *Forbes* columnist Gary Shilling, "End of the Bubble Bailouts," *Forbes* (August 29, 2006).

18. Dean Baker, "The Menace of an Unchecked Housing Bubble," *Economists' Voice* 3, no. 4 (2006), article 1; Dean Baker, "The Run-Up in Home Prices: Is

It Real or Is It Another Bubble?" *CEPR,* August 2002; and Dean Baker, "The Housing Bubble and the Financial Crisis," *Real-World Economics Review* 46 (March 20, 2008).

19. Others who warned about the economic crisis were Gary Shilling ("End of the Bubble Bailouts," *Forbes,* August 29, 2006), an economic consultant and *Forbes* columnist, and George Magnus ("What This Minsky Moment Means," *Financial Times,* August 22, 2007), senior economic advisor to UBS.

20. Many who questioned the sustainability of the price rise noted that when increases in demand bring about a rise in the price of real estate, the consequent increase in supply dampens and reverses price increases. Only factors that are fixed in supply, such as scarce land, will experience a sustained increase in prices if demand permanently rises. Since land costs for residential real estate are only about 20 percent of the total price of a home, land prices would have to rise fivefold in order for the price of a home to double in value.

21. This was just published three months shy of Gramlich's untimely death at age 68.

22. Testimony of Dr. Alan Greenspan before the Committee of Government Oversight and Reform, October 23, 2008, 2.

23. Some blame Greenspan's naïve belief in the market and the efficient market hypothesis (EMH) for his silence. But if Greenspan always thought market prices were right, he would have never made his "irrational exuberance" speech in December 1996. Furthermore EMH does not say that prices are "always right"; in fact, they are most always wrong based on all future information that becomes available. The EMH does imply, because of the interaction of informed traders, that market prices are not "obviously" wrong in a way that makes it easy for the average investor to profit. As noted previously, there was widespread disagreement, even among experts, about whether there was a paradigm shift in the housing market that justified higher prices.

24. John G. Taylor, professor at Stanford and author of *Getting off Track: How Government Actions and Invention Caused, Prolonged, and Worsened the Financial Crisis,* blamed Greenspan's Fed for keeping interest rates too low too long. Other who blamed the Fed for causing the housing crisis included Gerald O'Driscoll, Jr., of the Cato Institute; David Malpass, president of Encima Global; and Representative Ron Paul of Texas, a steadfast critic of the Fed.

25. BBC news sourcing Federal Reserve, Bank of England, and SIFMA, news .bbc.co.uk/2/hi/business/7073131.stm.

26. These funds carried fancy names such as High-Grade Structured Credit Strategies Enhanced Leverage Fund.

27. Bear Stearns and Citibank tried to insulate themselves by issuing funds and special investment vehicles that were off-balance sheet items. As defaults mounted, investors complained that they were not fully apprised

of the risks of these securities, and the firms' legal counsel recommended that they take back many of these mortgages onto their own balance sheets.

28. When federal governments are not explicitly backed by the central bank, government debt is no longer assumed "riskless," as was illustrated in the Eurozone crisis of 2011–2012.

29. The new facility was called the Asset-Backed Commercial Paper Money Market Mutual Fund Liquidity Facility.

30. Non-interest-bearing accounts (demand deposits) were used by business to process wage and other payments. Their security was deemed of paramount importance to the Fed in order to keep the payments systems functioning.

31. In 1996 the ratio of the FDIC's trust fund to deposits, called the designated deposit ratio, was set at 1.25 percent, but by September 2008 it fell below 1.0 percent.

32. Bernanke earned his doctorate eight years after I received mine in the same specialty from the Department of Economics. Although MIT was known as a "Keynesian" school, monetarist thought and, in particular, monetary history were well covered.

33. Reported on November 8, 2002. Chapter 18 gives a more extensive description of monetary policy.

34. 12 USC 343. As added by act of July 21, 1932 (47 Stat. 715), and amended by acts of August 23, 1935 (49 Stat. 714), and December 19, 1991 (105 Stat. 2386).

35. See Chapter 8 in Henry M. Paulson, Jr., *On the Brink*, New York: Hachette Book Group, 2010.

36. See Peter Chapman, *The Last of the Imperious Rich: Lehman Brothers 1844–2008*, New York: Penguin Group, 2010, 262–263.

37. Bernanke, a Republican, did not relish bailing out these financial firms. At a town hall meeting in Kansas City in July 2009, he stated, "I was not going to be the Federal Reserve Chairman who presided over the second Great Depression. I had to hold my nose . . . I'm as disgusted as you are [when I had to bail out these financial companies]." Reported by the Associated Press, Monday, July 27, 2009, "Bernanke Had to 'Hold My Nose' over Bailouts."

38. From Table A-1, in Milton Friedman and Anna Schwartz, *A Monetary History of the United States, 1867–1960*, Princeton, NJ: Princeton University Press, 1963.

39. The decline would be greater if quarterly data were available. Quarterly GDP was not available until 1946.

40. Joseph Swanson and Samuel Williamson, "Estimates of National Product and Income for the United States Economy, 1919–1941," *Explorations in Economic History* 10, no. 1 (1972), and Enrique Martínez-García and Janet Koech, "A Historical Look at the Labor Market During Recessions," Federal Reserve Bank of Dallas, *Economic Letter* 5, no. 1 (January 2010).

41. That decline occurred between July 2008 and December 2008 as oil prices plummeted.
42. This is calculated from the 27 percent price-level decline (1/0.73) noted previously.
43. There were other factors moderating the fall in GDP during the Great Recession that were absent during the Great Depression: the existence of FDIC deposit insurance; generous unemployment compensation; the automatic reduction of tax revenues as income and asset prices fell, which cushioned the decline in disposable income; and the expansion of federal government spending.
44. In real terms, the 1974 and 2008 stock market declines were almost identical due to the far greater inflation that occurred in the 1973–1974 episode.
45. On the morning of October 20, the VIX (computed using slightly different index options) hit almost 170. Since then, the VIX reached 50 in 1997 during the Asian monetary crisis, in 1998 when Long-Term Capital Management collapsed, in 2001 immediately following the 9/11 terrorist strikes, and at the bottom of the previous bear market in 2002. See Chapter 19 for more details.
46. See Chapters 16 and 19 for a more detailed analysis of market volatility and the events that caused it.
47. In dollar terms, all markets fell by at least 50 percent. Italy, Finland, Belgium, Russia, Greece, and Austria fell by at least 70 percent, and Ireland fell by more than 80 percent. After rallying from their March 2009 lows, a number of European markets fell to new lows during the euro crisis, including Italy, Portugal, Spain, and Greece. The Athens Stock Exchange Index fell 92.7 percent from its high in September 1999 to June 2012.
48. The JPMorgan Index of emerging market currencies fell about 19 percent relative to the dollar from October 2007 through March 2009. On average, in local currencies, emerging markets fell about 53 percent, approximately the same as developed markets.
49. General Growth Properties, containing some of the highest-quality malls in the United States, fell from over $20 a share when Lehman went under to less than 20 cents as creditors demanded repayment of loans extended.
50. The more speculative Morgan Stanley Internet Index fell 96 percent from January 2000 through March 2002.
51. By September 2012, two and a half years after the bear market bottom, these stocks were still down 89 percent, 95 percent, and 98 percent, respectively, from their highs.
52. Banks that largely avoided the financial crisis, such as Wells Fargo, which had lost up to 80 percent of its equity value at the bottom of the bear market, and J.P. Morgan, which has lost over 70 percent, both rebounded to new highs in 2013.

53. Because of the decline in the price level in the Great Depression, the decline in *real* earnings was even less severe in the 1930s. See Chapter 10 for more discussion.

54. Because of scandals and mispricing of LIBOR that took place during the crisis, in the early 2020s, LIBOR was being replaced by other short-term indicators. In the United States, the Secured Overnight Funding Rate (SOFR) has emerged in 2022 as the leading substitute.

CHAPTER 24

1. The longest bull market, measured by the S&P 500, lasted over 13 years between December 4, 1987, and March 24, 2000, and withstood a 19.92 percent decline in 1990.

2. In the following year, as the economy recovered, conservative opposition to further spending resuscitated, although the Democrats, narrowly taking both branches of Congress and the presidency passed a $1.9 American Rescue Act in March 2021. A $700 bipartisan infrastructure bill was passed in November, with future spending plans, as of this writing, deadlocked in Congress.

3. Federal Reserve Bank of New York Staff Reports "Direct Purchases of U.S. Treasury Securities by Federal Reserve Banks," Kenneth D. Garbade, Staff Report No. 684, August 2014.

4. M2 includes M1 plus savings accounts, certificates of deposits, money market mutual funds, and several other readily available liquid assets. Money creation by the Fed is described in Chapter 18.

5. It can be found on the website of the global Interdependence Center: https://www.interdependence.org/blog/who-is-paying-for-war-on-covid19/. An updated version of the article was printed in *The Financial Times*, January 19, 2021, https://on.ft.com/38UjWPp.

6. Reade Pickert and Vince Golle, "Get Ready for the Great U.S. Inflation Mirage of 2021" Bloombergquint.com (December 7, 2020), https://www.bloombergquint.com/global-economics/get-ready-for-the-great-u-s-inflation-mirage-of-2021.

7. Ibid.

8. Of course, TIPS do adjust for inflation but offer far lower (and of this writing) negative real yields.

9. Erik P. Gilje, Robert Ready, Nick Roussanov, and Jérôme P. Taillard, "When Benchmarks Fail: The Day That WTI Died," working paper, November 30, 2021.

10. These are year-end 2021 projected estimates from the *Economist Magazine*.

CHAPTER 25

1. David Dreman, *Contrarian Investment Strategies: The Next Generation*, New York: Simon & Schuster, 1998.

2. Frank J. Williams, *If You Must Speculate, Learn the Rules*, Burlington, VT: Freiser Press, 1930.
3. Daniel Kahneman and Amos Tversky, "Prospect Theory: An Analysis of Decision Under Risk," *Econometrica* 47, no. 2 (March 1979).
4. Robert Shiller, "Stock Prices and Social Dynamics," *Brookings Papers on Economic Activity*, Washington, DC: Brookings Institution, 1984.
5. Robert Shiller, "Do Stock Prices Move Too Much to Be Justified by Subsequent Movements in Dividends?" *American Economic Review* 71, no. 3 (1981), 421–436. See Chapter 22 for further discussion.
6. Solomon Asch, *Social Psychology*, Englewood Cliffs, NJ: Prentice Hall, 1952.
7. Morton Deutsch and Harold B. Gerard, "A Study of Normative and Informational Social Influences upon Individual Judgment," *Journal of Abnormal and Social Psychology* 51 (1955), 629–636.
8. Charles Mackay, *Memoirs of Extraordinary Popular Delusions and the Madness of Crowd*, London: Bentley, 1841.
9. See James Surowiecki, *The Wisdom of Crowds*, New York: Anchor Books, 2005.
10. Robert Shiller, "Conversation, Information, and Herd Behavior," *American Economic Review* 85, no. 2 (1995), 181–185; S. D. Bikhchandani, David Hirshleifer, and Ivo Welch, "A Theory of Fashion, Social Custom and Cultural Change," *Journal of Political Economy* 81 (1992), 637–654; and Abhijit V. Banerjee, "A Simple Model of Herd Behavior," *Quarterly Journal of Economics* 107, no. 3 (1992), 797–817.
11. Brad Barber and Terrance Odean, "Trading Is Hazardous to Your Wealth: The Common Stock Investment Performance of Individual Investors," *Journal of Finance* 55 (2000), 773–806.
12. B. Fischhoff, P. Slovic, and S. Lichtenstein, "Knowing with Uncertainty: The Appropriateness of Extreme Confidence," *Journal of Experimental Psychology: Human Perception and Performance* 3 (1977), 552–564.
13. A. H. Hastorf, D. J. Schneider, and J. Polefka, *Person Perception*, Reading, MA: Addison-Wesley, 1970. This is also called the *Fundamental Attribution Error*.
14. For reference to a model that incorporates success as a source of overconfidence, see Simon Gervais and Terrance Odean, "Learning to Be Overconfident," *Review of Financial Studies* 14, no. 1 (2001), 1–27.
15. For references to models that incorporate the representative heuristic as a source of overconfidence, see either N. Barberis, A. Shleifer, and R. Vishny, "A Model of Investor Sentiment," National Bureau of Economic Research (NBER) Working Paper No. 5926, NBER, Cambridge, MA, 1997, or Kent Daniel, David Hirshleifer, and Avanidhar Subrahmanyam, "Investor Psychology and Security Market Under- and Overreactions," *Journal of Finance* 53, no. 6 (1998), 1839–1886.
16. For a reference to data mining, see Andrew Lo and Craig MacKinlay, "Data-Snooping Biases in Tests of Financial Asset Pricing Models," *Review of Financial Studies* 3, no. 3 (Fall 1999), 431–467.

17. See Nassim Taleb, *Fooled by Randomness: The Hidden Role of Chance in Life and the Markets*, 2005.
18. David Dreman, *Contrarian Investment Strategies*, New York: Free Press, 1998.
19. Richard Thaler, "Mental Accounting and Consumer Choice," *Marketing Science* 4, no. 3 (Summer 1985), 199–214; and Nicholas Barberis, Ming Huang, and Richard H. Thaler, "Individual Preferences, Monetary Gambles, and Stock Market Participation: A Case for Narrow Framing," *American Economic Review* 96, no. 4 (September 2006), 1069–1090.
20. Richard H. Thaler, "Mental Accounting Matters," *Journal of Behavioral Decision Making* 12 (1999), 183–206.
21. Hersh Shefrin and Meir Statman, "The Disposition to Sell Winners Too Early and Ride Losers Too Long: Theory and Evidence," *Journal of Finance* 40, no. 3 (1985), 777–792.
22. See Tom Chang, David Solomon, and Mark Westerfield, "Looking for Someone to Blame: Delegation, Cognitive Dissonance, and the Disposition Effect," May 2013.
23. Leroy Gross, *The Art of Selling Intangibles*, New York: New York Institute of Finance, 1982.
24. Amos Tversky and Daniel Kahneman, "Judgment Under Uncertainty: Heuristics and Biases," *Science* 185 (1974), 1124–1131.
25. Terrance Odean, "Are Investors Reluctant to Realize Their Losses?" *Journal of Finance* 53, no. 5 (October 1998), 1786.
26. Hersh Shefrin and Richard Thaler, "An Economic Theory of Self-Control," *Journal of Political Economy* 89, no. 21 (1981), 392–406.
27. Shlomo Benartzi and Richard Thaler, "Myopic Loss Aversion and the Equity Premium Puzzle," *Quarterly Journal of Economics* 110, no. 1 (1995), 73–91.
28. See Chapter 10 for a further description of the equity premium puzzle.
29. Humphrey B. Neill, *The Art of Contrary Thinking*, Caldwell, ID: Caxton Printers, 1954, 1.
30. Benjamin Graham and David Dodd, *Security Analysis*, New York: McGraw-Hill, 1934, 12.
31. A discussion of the VIX Index is found in Chapter 22.
32. Werner F. M. De Bondt and Richard H. Thaler, "Does the Stock Market Overreact?" *Journal of Finance* 49, no. 3 (1985), 793–805.
33. This strategy is discussed in Chapter 12.

CHAPTER 26

1. Leo Melamed is the founder of the International Money Market, the home of the world's most successful stock index futures market. Quoted in Martin Mayer, *Markets*, New York: Norton, 1988, 111.
2. Peter Lynch, *One up on Wall Street*, New York: Penguin, 1989, 280.
3. *2013 Investment Company Fact Book*, Investment Company Institute, 9.
4. Robert Steiner, "Industrials Gain 14.53 in Trading Muted by Futures Halt in Chicago," *Wall Street Journal*, April 14, 1992, C2.

5. "Flood in Chicago Waters Down Trading on Wall Street," *Wall Street Journal*, April 14, 1992, C1. Today the proliferation of electronic trading has made it impossible for an incident such as the one that crippled the Chicago exchange 20 years ago to happen again.

6. Matteo Aquilina, Eric Budish, and Peter O'Neill, "Quantifying the High-Frequency Trading 'Arms Race'" Becker-Friedman Institute Working Papers, July 13, 2021.

7. Also see Eric Budish, Peter Cramton, and John Shim, "The High-Frequency Trading Arms Race: Frequent Batch Auctions as a Market Design Response," *Quarterly Journal of Economics 130*, no. 4 (2015), 1547–1621.

8. The SEC eliminated the *uptick rule* (shorting prohibited unless the last change was an uptick) in 2007, but in February 2010 the SEC reinstated the rule to apply when the price declines by 10 percent or more.

9. From 1997 through 2012, there was no capital gain distribution from spiders (S&P 500 ETFs), while the Vanguard 500 Index Fund has had several (although none since 2000).

10. The original article was published in 1973: Fischer Black and Myron Scholes, "The Pricing of Options and Corporate Liabilities," *Journal of Political Economy* 81, no. 3 (1973), 637–654. Fischer Black was deceased when the Nobel Prize was awarded in 1997. Myron Scholes shared the Nobel Prize with William Sharpe and Bob Merton, the latter contributing to the discovery of the formula.

CHAPTER 27

1. Benjamin Graham and Seymour Chatman, ed., *Benjamin Graham: The Memoirs of the Dean of Wall Street*, New York: McGraw-Hill, 1996, 273.

2. Charles D. Ellis, "The Loser's Game," *Financial Analysts Journal* 31, no. 4 (July/August 1975).

3. SPIVA mid-year 2021.

4. Since most actively traded funds take on more risk than index funds, these returns are "risk adjusted."

5. Burton G. Malkiel, *A Random Walk Down Wall Street: The Time-Tested Strategy for Successful Investing*, 5th ed., New York: Norton, 1990, 362.

6. Irwin Friend, F. E. Brown, Edward S. Herman, and Douglas Vickers, *A Study of Mutual Funds*, prepared for the SEC by the Securities Research Unit at the Wharton School, 1962.

7. Darryll Hendricks, Jayendu Patel, and Richard Zeckhauser, "Hot Hands in Mutual Funds: Short-Run Persistence of Relative Performance, 1974–1988," *Journal of Finance* 48, no. 1 (March 1993), 93–130.

8. Edwin J. Elton, Martin J. Gruber, and Christopher R. Blake, "The Persistence of Risk-Adjusted Mutual Fund Performance," *Journal of Business* 69, no. 2 (April 1996), 133–157.

9. Burton G. Malkiel, *A Random Walk Down Wall Street*, 8th ed., New York: Norton, 2003, 372–274, and John C. Bogle, *The Little Book of Common Sense Investing*, Hoboken, NJ: Wiley, 2007, Chapter 9.

10. For this table, money managers are assumed to expose their clients to the same risk as would the market, and the money managers have a correlation coefficient of 0.88 with market returns, which has been typical of equity mutual funds since 1971.

11. Ellis, "The Loser's Game," 19.

12. Five years before the Vanguard 500 Index Fund, Wells Fargo created an equally weighted index fund called Samsonite, but its assets remained relatively small.

13. Roger J. Bos, *Event Study: Quantifying the Effect of Being Added to an S&P Index*, New York: McGraw-Hill, Standard & Poor's, September 2000.

14. See David Blitzer and Srikant Dash, "Index Effect Revisited," *Standard & Poor's*, September 20, 2004, and Hanis Preston and Aye Soa, "What Happened to the Index Effect? A Look at Three Decades of S&P 500 Adds and Drops," S&P Global Research, September 2021.

15. Most of these indexes adjust the quantity of shares by excluding *insider holdings*, which consist of large positions held by insiders and governments from the total shares outstanding. Government holdings can be especially large in the emerging economies. The number of shares after this adjustment is called *float-adjusted shares*, where *float* refers to the number of shares that are readily available to buy.

16. As a matter of full disclosure, I am a senior investment strategy advisor at WisdomTree Investment, Inc., a company that issues fundamentally weighted ETFs.

17. Fundamentally weighted indexes are constructed as follows. Assume earnings are chosen as the measure of firm value. If E represents the total dollar earnings of the stocks chosen for the index, and E_j is the earnings from a particular firm j, then the weight given to firm j in the fundamental index is E_j/E, its share of total earnings rather than its share of the market value as is done in capitalization-weighted indexes.

18. Robert D. Arnott, Jason C. Hsu, and Philip Moore, "Fundamental Indexation," *Financial Analysts Journal* 61, no. 2 (March/April 2005).

19. Henry Fernandez, "Straight Talk," *Journal of Indexes* (July/August 2007).

20. Robert Jones, "Earnings Basis for Weighting Stock Portfolios," *Pensions and Investments*, August 6, 1990.

21. Paul C. Wood and Richard E. Evans, "Fundamental Profit-Based Equity Indexation," *Journal of Indexes*, second (2003).

22. Robert D. Arnott, Jason C. Hsu, and Philip Moore, "Fundamental Indexation." *Financial Analysts Journal* 61, no. 2 (2005).

CHAPTER 28

1. John Maynard Keynes, *A Tract on Monetary Reform*, London: Macmillan, 1924, 80.

2. Quoted in Linda Grant, "Striking out at Wall Street," *U.S. News & World Report* (June 20, 1994), 58.

3. John Maynard Keynes, *The General Theory of Employment, Interest, and Money*, New York: Harcourt, Brace & World, 1965, First Harbinger Edition, 158. (The book was originally published in 1936 by Macmillan & Co.)

Index

About the Author

Jeremy Siegel is the Russell E. Palmer Professor Emeritus of Finance at The Wharton School of the University of Pennsylvania, having recently retired after 45 years of active service. He received his BA in economics and mathematics from Columbia University in 1967 and his PhD in economics from the Massachusetts Institute of Technology in 1971. His thesis *Stability of a Monetary Economics with Inflationary Expectations* was written under the guidance of Paul Samuelson, Robert Solow, and Franco Modigliani. Professor Siegel spent one year as a National Science Foundation postdoctoral fellow at Harvard University before joining the faculty of the Graduate School of Business at the University of Chicago in 1972. Over the next four years he gained great insights on macroeconomic and monetary theory from his colleague, Professor Milton Friedman.

Professor Siegel has written and lectured extensively about the economy and financial markets and has appeared frequently on CNBC, Bloomberg, CNN, and other major networks. He was a regular columnist for *Kiplinger's* for more than 10 years and has written many op-ed pieces for the *Wall Street Journal, Barron's,* and the *Financial Times.*

He is the author of numerous professional articles and two books. His bestselling book, *Stocks for the Long Run*, was named by the *Washington Post* and *BusinessWeek* as one of the 10 best investment books of all time. His other book, *The Future for Investors*, was named one of the best business books published in 2005 by *BusinessWeek*, the *Financial Times,* and *Barron's.*

Professor Siegel has received many awards and citations for his research and excellence in teaching. In November 2003 he was presented the Distinguished Leadership Award by the Securities Industry Association and in May 2005 he was presented the prestigious Nicholas Molodovsky Award by the Chartered Financial Analysts Institute. Other awards include the Graham and Dodd Award for the best article published in the *Financial Analysts Journal* and the Peter Bernstein and Frank Fabozzi Award for the best article published in the *Journal of Portfolio Management.*

In 1994 Professor Siegel received the highest teaching rating in a worldwide ranking of business school professors conducted by *BusinessWeek* and in 2001 when Wharton attained a number one ranking for best business school for a record eight consecutive years.

In addition, Professor Siegel is the academic director of the Securities Industry Institute and the senior investment strategy advisor of WisdomTree Investments, Inc.

On a personal note, he lives in Philadelphia and has a beach home on the South Jersey shore. He is married with two married sons and one granddaughter and loves traveling with all of them. He also enjoys bridge, being a few master points away from Gold Life Master status, and relishes stimulating political conversations with his friends and colleagues from around the world.

Jeremy Schwartz serves as WisdomTree's Global Chief Investment Officer and leads investment strategy across equities, fixed income, model portfolios, and alternatives. Jeremy has worked for WisdomTree since 2005 and with Professor Siegel since 2001, when he began conducting research for the 3rd edition of *Stocks for the Long Run*. Jeremy and Professor Siegel co-host the Wharton Business Radio program *Behind the Markets* on SiriusXM 132. Jeremy lives in Wynnewood, Pennsylvania, with his wife, Bonnie, and daughters, Emma and Jolie.